Language shift and cultural reproduction is a f[...] study of language and cultural change among [...] the Sepik region of Papua New Guinea. Despi[...] to their own language as a source of identity a[...] [...] [...] [...] [...], people are abandoning their vernacular in favour of Tok Pisin, the most widely spoken language in Papua New Guinea. By examining village language socialization practices and drawing on Marshall Sahlins's ideas about structure and event, Don Kulick reveals how daily interactions, attitudes towards language, children, change, and personhood, all contribute to a shift in language and culture that is beyond the villagers' understanding and control.

This is the first detailed documentation of the process of language shift. It places linguistic change within an interpretive framework, and treats language as a symbolic system that affects, and is affected by, the thoughts and actions of everyday life.

'An excellent guide to the cultural logic and socio-political contradictions of language loss', *Language*

'... an extraordinary study ... Kulick displays formidable talents as both ethnographer and linguistic investigator ... This is one of those rare works, which, while highly sophisticated and nuanced, never fails to be accessible and lively', *Anthropological Linguistics*

Studies in the Social and
Cultural Foundations of Language No. 14

Language shift and cultural reproduction

Studies in the Social and Cultural Foundations of Language

The aim of this series is to develop theoretical perspectives on the essential social and cultural character of language by methodological and empirical emphasis on the occurrence of language in its communicative and interactional settings, on the socioculturally grounded "meanings" and "functions" of linguistic forms, and on the social scientific study of language use across cultures. It will thus explicate the essentially ethnographic nature of linguistic data, whether spontaneously occurring or experimentally induced, whether normative or variational, whether synchronic or diachronic. Works appearing in the series will make substantive and theoretical contributions to the debate over the sociocultural–functional and structural–formal nature of language, and will represent the concerns of scholars in the sociology and anthropology of language, anthropological linguistics, sociolinguistics, and socioculturally informed psycholinguistics.

1. Charles L. Briggs: *Learning how to ask: a sociolinguistic appraisal of the role of the interview in social science research*
2. Tamar Katriel: *Talking straight: Dugri speech in Israeli Sabra culture*
3. Bambi B. Schieffelin and Elinor Ochs (eds.): *Language socialization across cultures*
4. Susan U. Philips, Susan Steele, and Christine Tanz (eds.): *Language, gender, and sex in a comparative perspective*
5. Jeff Siegel: *Language contact in a plantation environment: a sociolinguistic history of Fiji*
6. Elinor Ochs: *Culture and language development: language acquisition and language socialization in a Samoan village*
7. Nancy C. Dorian (ed.): *Investigating obsolescence: studies in language contraction and death*
8. Richard Bauman and Joel Sherzer (eds.): *Explorations in the ethnography of speaking*
9. Bambi B. Schieffelin: *The give and take of everyday life: language socialization of Kaluli children*
10. Francesca Merlan and Alan Rumsey: *Ku Waru: language and segmentary politics in the Western Nebilyer Valley, Papua New Guinea*
11. Allesandro Duranti and Charles Goodwin: *Rethinking context: language as an interactive phenomenon*
12. John A. Lucy: *Language diversity and thought: a reformulation of the linguistic relativity hypothesis*
13. John A. Lucy: *Grammatical categories and cognition: a case study of the linguistic relativity hypothesis*
14. Don Kulick: *Language shift and cultural reproduction: socialization, self, and syncretism in a Papua New Guinean village*
15. Jane Hill and Judith Irvine (eds.): *Responsibility and evidence in oral discourse*
16. Niko Besnier: *Literacy, emotion and authority: reading and writing on a Polynesian atoll*

Language shift
and cultural reproduction

Socialization, self, and syncretism in a
Papua New Guinean village

DON KULICK
Stockholm University

CAMBRIDGE
UNIVERSITY PRESS

PUBLISHED BY THE PRESS SYNDICATE OF THE UNIVERSITY OF CAMBRIDGE
The Pitt Building, Trumpington Street, Cambridge, United Kingdom

CAMBRIDGE UNIVERSITY PRESS
The Edinburgh Building, Cambridge CB2 2RU, UK   http://www.cup.cam.ac.uk
40 West 20th Street, New York, NY 10011–4211, USA   http://www.cup.org
10 Stamford Road, Oakleigh, Melbourne 3166, Australia
Ruiz de Alarcón 13, 28014 Madrid, Spain

First published 1992
Reprinted 1995
First paperback edition published 1997
Reprinted 1998, 2000

Printed in the United Kingdom at the University Press, Cambridge

Library of Congress Cataloging-in-Publication Data is available

A catalogue record for this book is available from the British Library

ISBN 0 521 41484 9 hardback
ISBN 0 521 59926 1 paperback

Maps by Theo Baumann

For Veronica Kulick
and
for Kruni Aiarpa and Raia Aiarpa

Kem, a 45-year-old big man in Gapun, is talking directly to his ancestral spirits in the men's house:

> You all know, a new time has come up now. Plenty of new ways have come up and we can't look after you too much. I think we're the last generation who will care for you. Our children won't care for you. And you'll vanish. Now all us fathers we care for you so you're still here with us. In the future, no. Your time is ending. You'll soon be gone forever.

Nangam, an 8-year-old Gapun girl, is sitting in a canoe with her mother, Tambong:

Nangam:	*Mama, ol Wongan save kolim "pukpuk" olsem wanem?*	N:	Mamma, how do the people in Wongan say *"pukpuk"* [i.e., "crocodiles" in Tok Pisin]?
Tambong:	*"ɔrɛɔ."*	T:	*"ɔrɛɔ."*
Nangam:	*Na long tok ples Gapun ol i save kolim "pukpuk" olsem wanem?*	N:	And in Gapun's language how do they say *"pukpuk"*?
Tambong:	*Ol i save tok "ɔrɛm."*	T:	They say *"ɔrɛm."*
Nangam:	*Na mipela save tok "pukpuk."*	N:	And we say *"pukpuk."*
Tambong:	[laughs] *Em nau. Long tok ples bilong yupela yupela save kolim "pukpuk."*	T:	[laughs] That's right. In your [generation's] language, you all call them *"pukpuk."*

Contents

List of tables and illustrations   *page* viii
Preface   ix
Note on transcriptions   xiv

Introduction: Papua New Guinea and the study of
language shift   1

1   The villagers and their village   27

2   Language and talk in the village   61

3   Having *hed*   92

4   Showing *save*   118

5   Preparing to change   157

6   Becoming monolingual   190

7   Contextualizing the self   223

Conclusion: The process of language shift   248

Appendix: On being a ghost   268

Notes   276
References   303
Index   315

Tables and illustrations

Tables

1.1 Villagers' incomes in 1986 *page* 46
2.1 Languages known by villagers living in Gapun in 1987 70
6.1 Baby-talk lexicon in Taiap 197

Maps

1 Lower Sepik and Ramu regions 25
2 Gapun village 26
3 Language distribution in the lower Sepik and
   Ramu regions 62

Figures

4.1 Letter to the author from Allan Kasia and Sake Martin 137
5.1 "The death of a sinner" 171
5.2 "The death of a believer" 172

Photographs appear on pages 150–6.

Preface

About a month after my arrival in Gapun, I was solemnly informed that I was a ghost. The villagers had been watching me, I was told, observing me closely as I copied down genealogies, politely tried to force down foul-tasting pink globs of sago jelly during meals with them, attempted to mouth phrases in their vernacular language. They were unsure when I first came into the village; initially they were confounded. But now, after a month, the villagers were convinced. I was a ghost.

The moment that had been chosen to impart this disclosure could not have been better timed to heighten my own anxiety. It was night, the rickety house in which we were seated on the floor seemed on the verge of being flattened by the fat drops of tropical rain that splattered down unceasingly, and the only source of light was the orange glow of cigarette tips, floating eerily around in the blackness like disembodied eyes. I wasn't sure who, or even how many people, were in the house with me. It kept thundering hard, of course, and the sudden flashes of lightning that periodically froze everything into sinister, bluish tableaux conjured forth a lifetime of cinematic horror scenes: piercing screams in the shadows, full moons and foggy graveyards, supernatural secrets too monstrous even to be whispered. In all of this, I found myself being told knowingly that I was a ghost. I didn't know what to say.

The explanation that I had given the villagers for my presence in Gapun – that I wanted to write a book about their language – had been brushed impatiently aside. Why, they wondered among themselves, had a white-skinned man chosen to live among *them* and not some other village? What was my *real* reason for coming to Gapun? Who was I *really?*

What I did not understand at the time was that these questions and the way the villagers answered them were grounded in a context in which skin color had acquired a fundamental metaphysical significance. As I came to know the people of Gapun during the fifteen months I spent in the village in 1986–7, I slowly discovered that much of their thought was given over to trying to make sense of the white presence in their world and of their own place in the world of white people. The importance of this project escaped me at first. I had come to Gapun to study language shift, and I was prepared to analyze the decline of the vernacular and the expansion of Tok Pisin, the most widely used of Papua New Guinea's three national languages, in the usual ways, applying concepts like ethnicity, social prestige, and the desire for socioeconomic mobility. It took me some time to appreciate that these concepts had little relevance for what was happening in Gapun. Instead, it gradually became apparent that what was most central in understanding why the villagers were abandoning their vernacular was precisely those ideas that led them to identify me as a ghost.

The perspective developed in this book is the result of that insight. Had I been more courageous, the book's title might have been "The Power of Culture," because that is, in essence, what it is about: the impact that the conceptions and understandings held by a group of people – about personhood, language, children, interpersonal relations, and change – can come to have on their language.

While being written, this book has traveled the globe. Parts of it have been written, ventilated, revised, or discarded in Ukarumpa, Canberra, Palo Alto, Linköping, and Stockholm. The original draft of Chapters 1 and 2 was even stolen in Kuala Lumpur. Because of this geographic spread, I have a large number of people to thank (in every place except Kuala Lumpur). I take great pleasure in finally being able to do so here.

First, I gratefully acknowledge funding from the Swedish Agency for Research Cooperation with Developing Countries (SAREC) and the Swedish Council for Research in the Humanities and Social Sciences (HSFR). Modest grants from the *Svenska Sällskapet för Antropologi och Geografi,* and from the Department of Social Anthropology, Stockholm University, enabled me to conduct a three-month reconnaissance trip to Papua New Guinea in 1985, which included a one-month stay in Gapun.

Before entering the field, I benefited from a visit to Oxford University, where Peter Mühlhäusler kindly took the time to listen to my research plans and explain to me the sorts of things one should know before attempting to carry out linguistically oriented fieldwork in Papua New Guinea. During my stay in Papua New Guinea, I came to owe debts of gratitude to many people. In Port Moresby, Dicks Thomas took it upon himself to teach me the rudiments of Tok Pisin. In the East Sepik provincial capital of Wewak, Tony Power and John Alman were extremely kind in helping me to arrange transport to and from Gapun the first few times I traveled there. Steve Thomas and Christine Howes graciously opened their home to me during several of my stays in Wewak, and the Christian Mission in Many Lands in Wewak kindly allowed me to stay in its beautiful flats whenever one was available. Ralph Stuttgen always made me feel welcome in his guest house in Wewak, and was always willing to share with me some of his thorough knowledge of Sepik societies. Janice Blackwell and I had many enlightening conversations about schooling, and she kindly put me up in her Angoram bungalow a few times. At the Marienberg mission station, Fr. Piotr Zarzecki shared with me his insights about the Catholic church in Papua New Guinea, his knowledge of Sepik mythology, and his sherry. Also at Marienberg was Marianne Peer: no-nonsense nurse, crocodile breeder, connoisseur of Bavarian yodeling, and *personnage extraordinaire*. "Sista Mariana," as she is affectionately known, has been providing medical services virtually single-handedly to the entire lower Sepik area for more than three decades. Her hospitality and generosity always made it a great pleasure to travel to Marienberg.

In late June 1987, I left Gapun and spent two weeks doing linguistic research at the Summer Institute of Linguistics' Papua New Guinea headquarters in Ukarumpa, Eastern Highlands Province. I thank Mary Stringer for orchestrating that visit, and for being a delightful and gracious host.

Immediately upon leaving Papua New Guinea in August 1987, I spent three months at the Australian National University, where I was received as a visiting scholar at the Department of Linguistics, Research School of Pacific Studies. For their help, hospitality, and willingness to share their immense knowledge about Papua New Guinea, I thank Lois Carrington, Tom Dutton, Malcom Ross, and Darrell Tryon. In addition, I wish to acknowledge a special, very deep debt of gratitude to the late Don Laycock. It was Don Laycock who suggested that I go to Gapun – almost nothing was known about the village or the language spoken there, but, he reasoned when I told him I was interested in language shift, "it's such a small language, something must be happening to it." Throughout my stay in Canberra, Don and I were engaged in a running conversation about the linguistics and sociolinguistics of Gapun and other Sepik societies, and much of what I know about Papuan languages I learned from him.

The bulk of this work was completed at the Department of Social Anthropology at Stockholm University, Sweden. I am particularly grateful to Tomas Gerholm, Lenore Arnberg, and Kenneth Hyltenstam for their comments on individual chapters, and to Per Linell and Karin Aronsson at the University of Linköping for inviting me to present parts of this work to their departments. In addition, I have benefited from brief but intensive lunchtime conversations with Bruce Kapferer, Henrietta Moore, and Marilyn Strathern as they passed through Stockholm.

Others I would like to thank are Nancy Dorian and Suzanne Romaine, for kindly reading through and commenting on the manuscript, and Michael Prenter and Karen Teel, for their fun and inspiring teaching, still fondly remembered. Shirley Brice Heath deserves special thanks as an important source of inspiration throughout the writing process. Her thorough comments on an earlier draft of the manuscript have been very influential in shaping the final form the book has taken. I also want to thank Bambi Schieffelin, whose encouragement, wisdom, and advice have been and continue to be important in inestimable ways.

I wish to give special recognition to Christopher Stroud, who has been deeply involved with this work from the outset. It was with Christopher's encouragement that I first decided to go to Papua New Guinea, and the vast bulk of the interpretations in this volume were originally developed in conversations with him. Some of these interpretations have already been presented in a number of published works coauthored with him, and I am thankful to him for allowing me to use parts of that material in this book. Christopher worked with me in Gapun for a three-month spell in early 1987, and that visit not only permitted a period of intensive work on the grammar of the Taiap language; it also saved me from an existential distress of almost Malinowskian proportions. Without Christopher's help, insights, bibliographic knowledge, and critical sting, this book could never have been written.

And now, the villagers. Short of metamorphosing into a deity and delivering to them myself the cargo they all anxiously await, I will never be able to repay the debt of gratitude that I owe the people of Gapun. As an outsider and intruder into other people's lives, an anthropologist has no right to expect anything from the people that he or she wishes to study. So expecting nothing, but hoping, of course, for quite a lot, I suddenly turned up in Gapun one day and asked, through my guides there, to be allowed to stay. The kindness and generosity with which the villagers responded to that request still overwhelm me. If I must single out any individual villagers for special thanks, then those would be Kruni Aiarpa and his stern brother Raia, who befriended me and taught me and opened their lives to me, to the point that they even shared what they sometimes considered to be painful and embarrassing memories of the "ways of the ancestors." I also remember with great fondness Kem Masambe and his wife, Wandi Ekwapi, always gracious and generous, and concerned that I was eating properly; Mukar Raia, Raia's adolescent son, who was an absolute wiz at explaining vernacular speech and helping me to transcribe it; Ambuli Waiki, who also initially helped me with Taiap; and those women and men with whom I worked most intensively gathering and transcribing caregiver–child language data: Sopak Waiki and her husband, Mone Banang; Paso Yuki and her husband, Ariba Amani; and Tambong Umba and her husband, Marame Kruni. I am especially grateful to my adoptive *mama na papa* in the village, Sake Kruni and Allan Kasia. Without their care, concern, and daily meals of sago jelly or rice, I don't know how I would have managed.

In the village of Wongan, Joe Sumur and his wife, Tundu Kwanga, put me up for two weeks and fed me wonderful meals of fish and flying fox while I studied what went on in the school there. Tundu's old father, Kwanga Ondeng, was a master storyteller and an invaluable source of information about traditional lifestyles and beliefs in Wongan and Gapun. I also thank the headmaster and two teachers at Wongan Community School, partly for allowing me to sit in on classes and observe, and partly for picking up my mail and buying a few occasional supplies for me during their biweekly trips to Angoram to pick up their pay. My visits to the village of Sanae were always made pleasurable by the hospitality of Mapis Demoi and his wife, Rondi; Philip Yakas and his wife, Mbgat Ekwapi; and John Awopia and his wife.

A great, warm hug of thanks must go to my mother, Veronica Kulick, for her indefatigable supplies to the field of unnecessary necessities like chocolate, cookies, and small packets of corn nuts; and for her ability to always make me laugh by expressing horror and incomprehension whenever I mention Papua New Guinea. And finally, I thank Jonas Schild Tillberg, for *divertissements*.

Note on transcriptions

In transcribing the vernacular language of the people of Gapun, I have used the phonetically based orthography that is presented in Kulick and Stroud (in press b). Only a few of these symbols may be unfamiliar to some readers. These are:

ŋ	velar nasal; like *ng* in *sing*
ɔ	rounded back vowel; like *o* in the Italian *cosa*
ɨ	unrounded central vowel; like *u* in *put*
ə	schwa; like *a* in *about*
ε	unrounded front vowel; like *e* in *pen* and *get*

To facilitate easy and comfortable reading, I have not used this orthography in the main text to transcribe the names of people and places.

In a few of the texts appearing in this book, morpheme-by-morpheme glosses of Taiap speech appear immediately underneath the Taiap. The following abbreviations are used throughout to specify grammatical information about Taiap utterances:

A	actor, subject of transitive verb
ALL	allative
CONJ	conjunction
CONSEC	consecutive
DL	dual
ERG	ergative
fem	feminine
FUT	future
HAB	habitual
IMPER	imperative
INTENT	intentional mood
IRR	irreal status
LOC	locative
masc	masculine

NEG   negation
PL   plural
POSS   possessive
S   subject of intransitive verb
S1   first element of discontinuous subject marker
S2   second element of discontinuous subject marker
SG   singular
U   undergoer, object of transitive verb
v   vowel

Speech in Tok Pisin is transcribed in the standard way according to the conventions outlined in F. Mihalic's (1971) *Jacaranda Dictionary and Grammar of Melanesian Pidgin*. Where the spelling of words differs from the spellings more commonly used in Papua New Guinea, the difference reflects the pronunciation of the villagers of Gapun.

Because one of the most characteristic features of speech in Gapun is the villagers' tendency to switch between languages, it has been necessary to devise transcription conventions that make very clear which language is being used when villagers speak. This is done in the transcribed texts through italicization and underlining. Words in italics are words in Tok Pisin. Taiap speech is signaled through italicization *and* underlining. In the translations, which are not italicized, talk that occurred in Taiap is underlined; Tok Pisin speech is not. In addition, the texts in this book contain several examples of switches to vernaculars other than Taiap. Words in vernacular languages other than Taiap are marked through italicization and double underlining.

The villagers' speech has been translated into a colloquial form of American English. The formal, stilted literal translations that characterize so much of ethnographic writing and that generally work to create an impression that non-Western peoples speak in an abstruse and archaic manner have been avoided. Instead, my goal in translating has been to convey the sense and tone of the villagers' speech. I have also been concerned with accurately reproducing the structure of village talk, which is heavily repetitive and influenced by a syntactic convention known as "tail-head linkage," in which the final verb phrase of an utterance is repeated as the initial verb phrase of the following utterance (Haiman 1979, Reesink 1990). In order to highlight the rhetorical structure of village speech, I have represented some examples in a nonblock form, basing the structure of these representations on considerations derived from the field of ethnopoetics (e.g., the articles in Sherzer and Woodbury 1987).

All transcribed texts and some lengthier passages of quotation are numbered in order of their appearance in the book to facilitate cross-reference. Notes on situational context and nonverbal actions are given in square brackets in the body of the texts/quotations. In addition, the following transcription conventions are used for passages of texts:

=   Contiguous utterances (used when there is no break between adjacent utterances, the second latched onto, but not overlapping, the first)

[Overlapping utterances

/   Interruption (between utterances, used when speaker is interrupted by following speaker; within an utterance this indicates self-interruption or false start)

*   Ungrammatical utterance

Introduction: Papua New Guinea and the study of language shift

Papua New Guinea has the provocative distinction of being the most linguistically diverse country on earth. Packed into an area roughly the size of Sweden, or the American state of California, are approximately 760 different languages. Spread throughout a population of three million people, these languages represent about one fifth of the total number of languages spoken in the world today.

The languages of Papua New Guinea are not distributed evenly among its three million citizens. A handful of languages have 30,000 or more speakers (the largest, Enga, has about 150,000), but the majority are spoken by less than 1,000 people. Indeed, according to Sankoff's 1977 calculations, a full 35 percent of the languages spoken in the country have fewer than 500 speakers.[1]

Why so many tiny languages? The most popular guess used to be that they arose out of isolation. A common assumption for quite some time was that the New Guinean landscape, with its endless rainforests, boggy swamps, and craggy mountain ranges, simply inhibited intervillage contact. Isolated and cut off from their neighbors, communities had no possibility of converging linguistically. Instead, for thousands of years, they had been diverging.[2]

Once the identification and classification of these languages got under way in the 1950s, however, it soon became clear that the cause of the diversity found in Papua New Guinea was not isolation. Laycock (1982: 33) points out that:

we find, typically, the largest languages (that is, the least diversity) in the most isolated areas (such as the Highlands . . .) and the greatest divergence in areas of easy terrain and extensive trading contacts (as in north coast Papua New Guinea and Island Melanesia).

This discovery, and the understanding that patterns of trade, marriage, migration, and warfare have linked linguistically distinct peoples for centuries (Allen 1982; Hughes 1977; Swadling 1984; Wurm 1975),

1

has led researchers working with New Guinea languages to turn their attention to the social and cultural correlates of the linguistic diversity.

What has been realized is that the development and maintenance of 760 languages has been made possible in very large part due to particular, widespread attitudes toward language. It is now generally agreed that New Guinea communities have purposely fostered linguistic diversity because they have seen language as a highly salient marker of group identity (Foley 1986: 9, 27; Laycock 1979, 1982; Sankoff 1976, 1977). In other words, New Guinea villagers have traditionally seized upon the boundary-marking dimension of language, and they have cultivated linguistic differences as a way of "exaggerating" themselves (Boon 1982) in relation to their neighbors and trading partners.[3]

Linguists have found a great deal of evidence to support this view. Foley (1986: 27) reports that the people of Wombun, one of the three Chambri-speaking villages located along the shores of Lake Chambri in the East Sepik Province, speak a dialect of the language that diverges phonologically, lexically, and morphosyntactically from the dialect of Chambri that is spoken in the other two neighboring villages. "In spite of the small size of the Chambri language groups (about 1,000 speakers) and the close proximity of the villages," writes Foley, "the Wombun people have preserved a dialect different from that of other villages. . . . This is correlated with a feeling of the Wombun people of their uniqueness within the larger Chambri-speaking group."

Laycock (1982: 36) encountered a similar divergence in the small Usai dialect (1,500 speakers) of the Buin language (17,000 speakers) of Bougainville island. In this dialect, all anaphoric gender agreements are reversed, so that all that is masculine in the other Buin dialects is feminine in Usai, and all that is feminine in Buin is masculine in Usai. Laycock explains that "there is no accepted mechanism for linguistic change which can cause a flip-flop of this kind and this magnitude." He therefore proposes that "at some stage in the past, some influential speaker of the Usai dialect announced that from now on his people were not to speak like the rest of the Buins. Once the change was adopted, it would become the natural speech of the community within one or two generations."

The linguist K. McElhanon actually witnessed an instance of this kind of linguistic innovation during his research in the Huon valley. In 1978, McElhanon (personal communication) observed that the people living in the Selepet-speaking village of Indu had gathered together for a meeting. During this meeting, a decision was reached to "be different" from other Selepet speakers. It was agreed that the villagers of Indu would immediately stop using their usual word for "no," *bia*, which was shared by all their fellow speakers of Selepet. Instead, they would begin saying *buŋe,* which they did and have continued doing since that time.

Clearly, this kind of conscious manipulation of language could, over time, lead to significant divergence. Such a stress on divergence has been feasible in practical terms, because even as they have fostered a "difference" through language, many Papua New Guinean communities simultaneously have placed a high value on multilingualism. The public display of knowledge of foreign speech varieties has been one important means of gaining prestige in traditional society (Salisbury 1972; Sankoff 1977; Taylor 1968). The situation throughout most of the country has been one in which "each group was ethnocentric about its own variety, but since such groups were all very small, since people knew that other people thought their own was the best, and since within a region there was no consensus that a particular variety was the best, the situation was certainly an egalitarian one" (Sankoff 1976: 10). So language used as a boundary-marking device, coupled with "egalitarian" bi- or multilingualism, has for centuries worked to sustain a momentum that has generated and perpetuated linguistic diversity.

This momentum came to be interrupted in the latter half of the nineteenth century. In 1884, Great Britain, prompted by Australian colonists who worried over Germany's interest in New Guinea, claimed the southeastern portion of the island (later known as Papua) as a British protectorate. Soon afterward, German marines raised the Imperial flag on the island of Matupit in east New Britain, thus proclaiming their dominance over New Britain (which they called Neu Pommern), New Ireland (Neu Mecklenburg), and the other islands of what to this day is called the Bismarck Archipelago and, over the northeastern mainland, New Guinea (Kaiser Wilhelmsland). (The entire western half of the island had been claimed, and subsequently ignored, by the Dutch in 1848.)

At the time, these puffs of European hegemony had no consequences for the vast majority of people living in New Guinea and Papua. Most of these people were to have no contact whatsoever with Europeans until the 1920s or later. But for those villagers living on the islands or near the coasts, encounters with European missionaries, police, and labor recruiters now became intensified, and the consequences of such encounters were far-reaching. Villagers who attempted to defend their land from European confiscation were imprisoned or shot, and entire villages were routinely burned to the ground at the whim of a visiting Patrol Officer.[4] The European presence dramatically altered traditional balances of power between different villages and clans. In their discussion of early consequences of colonialism in Papua New Guinea, Griffin et al. (1979: 15) have observed that:

The death of five or more adult men could permanently damage the power of a clan; it would be less able to defend itself, form alliances or acquire wealth through work, marriage and trade. By using local communities in alliance with the police MacGregor [the first Lieutenant-Governor of British New Guinea (later Papua) 1888–1898] increased the prestige of one group, while humiliating another. MacGregor's patrols did not merely kill a few people in a total population of perhaps two or three thousand; they transformed relationships between groups which normally lived and acted separately.

Although Griffin et al. here exemplify their argument with colonialism in British Papua, their remarks apply even more emphatically to the Germans in their territory of New Guinea, who "used more force than the British or Australians in Papua, and they killed more people" (ibid: 42).

But although killings and the destruction of villages had a great impact on villagers in areas under European influence, the single most significant disruption was the massive programs of labor recruitment carried out by the colonial governments. Even before the colonial flags had been hoisted, several thousand men from New Ireland, northern New Britain, and southeastern Papua had been taken away to Queensland, Fiji, and Samoa to work as laborers on plantations (Griffin et al. 1979: 7; Siegel 1986). After 1884, the recruitment of plantation laborers intensified, particularly in German New Guinea, where large copra and tobacco plantations had been established. The German governor of the territory, Albert Hahl, estimated that 100,000 New Guineans had been recruited as contract laborers up to 1913. After Australia assumed control of the German territory in 1914, the number of New Guineans under indenture continued to grow – from 17,500 in 1914 to over 41,000 in 1939 (Griffin et al. 1979: 54).

New Guinean men were cajoled, threatened, and sometimes even forced to "sign on" as laborers. They were then taken from their villages and most often transported to faraway plantations, where they would work for at least three years. At the end of that time, they could return to their villages. Arriving back home, these men brought with them steel tools, cloth, fabulous stories, and a new language – a language that has come to be called Tok Pisin.

Tok Pisin is known variously in the earlier anthropological and linguistic literature as Pidgin English, neo-Melanesian, and New Guinea Pidgin. It is called Tok Pisin by the people who speak it, and since 1981 Tok Pisin has been the language's official name in Papua New Guinea. Tok Pisin arose as a pidgin language in the mid- to late 1800s on the plantations that had been established by the colonial powers, where the men transported there from scores of different language groups had to live together and find a common basis for communication. The language's primary lexifier language has been English, but other languages, in particular the Austronesian language Tolai, spoken on the island of New Britain, have contributed up to 30 percent of Tok Pisin's lexicon. Although there is still vigorous debate about the precise genesis of Tok Pisin and about the relative contributions to its grammar of the superstrate and substrate languages (i.e., English and the various Papuan and Austronesian vernaculars of the first generations of plantation laborers),[5] it is clear that the formal structure of Tok Pisin is very different from Papuan languages, in that Tok Pisin is rigidly verb medial and largely isolating in its verbal morphology (Mühlhäusler 1985a, b).

Despite official and nonofficial colonial attitudes that branded it as gibberish and baby talk and discouraged its usage,[6] Tok Pisin spread rapidly in the territory of New Guinea as a contact language and as a lingua franca among indigenous populations. In Papua, this role was fulfilled largely by a pidginized version of the Austronesian vernacular Motu, called Hiri Motu (Dutton 1985). The English language began to be seriously promoted in Papua New Guinea only after World War II. Today English is the language of education in all schools, but it remains more of an elite language than a lingua franca.

The spread of Tok Pisin, Hiri Motu, and English in Papua New Guinea has had a number of positive consequences, not least of which has been the facilitation of communication between speakers from geographically distant parts of the country. But the expansion of these lingua francas has also had at least one very poorly documented and, in the view of many, less positive consequence, namely language shift. Since the spread of the colonial lingua francas from the beginning of the 1900s, and especially since World War II, it seems as though the momentum for linguistic diversity and egalitarian bilingualism referred to above has halted and even reversed. A qualitative change in language use and attitudes may be currently under way in a large number of Papua New Guinean communities. Throughout the country, there are a growing number of reports that indigenous vernaculars are entering phases of obsolescence.[7]

One of the first researchers to draw attention to language shift in Papua New Guinea was the linguist Otto Nekitel, who in 1984 published a short paper asking, "What is happening to our vernaculars?" Later, in his dissertation at the Australian National University, Nekitel sketched the language shift occurring in his own community, a village of about 320 people called Womsis, located in the West Sepik Province. Children are no longer learning the village vernacular, Abu', he writes. And even among adults, Tok Pisin is increasingly replacing the vernacular in everyday interaction:

Tok Pisin is predominantly used in most speech situations by Abu' speakers.
... Thus although it is sad to have to recognize this it is a fact that even though
Abu' is the vernacular of the community, it is no longer the primary language
of the Abu' [people]. (1985: 251–2)

Nekitel notes as well that a similar situation exists in a number of other
nearby villages (ibid: 247).

The same phenomenon is reported in Bradshaw's brief 1978 article
on language death among the Numbami. The Numbami, a group of 300
speakers living near the coast in Morobe Province, are now shifting from
their vernacular. The language most widely known in the small community is not Numbami – it is Tok Pisin. There are in fact no remaining
monolingual speakers of Numbami. When it is spoken, Numbami remains confined to topics concerning village life. But even in these domains, the language is becoming increasingly relexified due to heavy
borrowing from Tok Pisin and Yabem, an Austronesian language
adopted as a missionary and church language by the Lutheran mission.
Bradshaw reports that "there is a definite feeling among Numbami
speakers that their language is an endangered species" (ibid: 31), and
that "many children of Numbami-speaking parents speak only Tok
Pisin" (ibid: 28). Given the small size of this group and these current
trends, it seems likely that Numbami will disappear completely within
the next several generations.

A number of other articles and short descriptions point to similar
processes occurring elsewhere in the country. Dutton has recently reported that the Koiari language (spoken in the 1960s by 1,800 people
living in villages inland from Papua New Guinea's capital, Port Moresby)
seems to be "losing its vitality and dying" (Dutton and Mühlhäusler
1989: 10), being replaced by Hiri Motu. Erima Nambis, formerly the
language of 410 people living in three villages in the Madang Province,
was in the late 1970s no longer spoken actively by children under 10.
Indeed, "for most people under twenty, New Guinea Pidgin [Tok Pisin]
is the language of everyday communication (Mühlhäusler 1979: 176; cf.
Colburn 1985, a more detailed report on this language). And Hooley
observes that while the Buang language of the Morobe Province (4,600
speakers) cannot be said to be dying out, it is under "external pressures"
from processes of modernization and urbanization. He writes that "unless some change of attitude occurs among the Buangs themselves, or
some other factor emerges, the language will eventually disappear"
(1987: 283).

Judging from the scattered reports such as these that have emerged
so far, the process of language shift seems to have progressed furthest
among coastal and island peoples (Colburn 1985; Dutton and Mühl-

häusler 1989; Hollyman 1962; Hooley 1987; Lithgow 1973; Mühlhäusler 1979: 176–8, 1989; Sankoff 1980: 24–7; Smith in press; Wurm 1986). But shift may be taking place elsewhere as well, and there are brief mentions of it for the middle Sepik region (Foley 1986: 28) and even for the Highlands, where, the linguist John Haiman (1979: 40) remarks, "some Hua [3,000 speakers, Eastern Highlands Province] people predict that their grandchildren will grow up speaking only Pidgin [Tok Pisin]. If mass emigration to Goroka and other urban centers should weaken the structure of village-based social life, their predictions may come true."

This book is about one such community where language shift is under way. The community is called Gapun. Gapun is a small village with a population that in 1986–7 fluctuated between 90 and 110 people. The village is located about ten kilometers from the northern coast of Papua New Guinea, roughly midway between the lower Sepik and Ramu rivers. It is an isolated village, surrounded on all sides by rainforest and sago swamps, connected to other villages (the nearest of which is about a two-hour journey away) and to the outside world only by narrow, choked waterways and slim bush paths subject to flooding.

The villagers in Gapun speak a language they call *Taiap mɛr* (Taiap language). The language exists only in Gapun and is spoken actively and fluently by exactly eighty-nine people.[8] Even by the somewhat extreme standards of Papua New Guinea this is a small language. Since the late 1970s, however, the number of people who speak Taiap has been getting even smaller, despite the fact that the village population is the largest within memory. As of 1987, no village child under 10 actively used this village vernacular in verbal interactions. These children either speak or, in the case of the 1- to 3-year-olds, are clearly on their way to acquiring Tok Pisin. Many children under 8, especially boys, appear not even to understand much Taiap.

The adult villagers are at a loss to understand why their children are suddenly no longer learning the vernacular. Knowledge of Taiap is seen as a self-evident attribute of all villagers. Taiap is the language of the ancestors, and it has strong associations with the "ground." It is what most strikingly sets one apart from one's neighbors. Several villagers described it as "sweet." Taiap, others explained, has a foundation, a deep-rootedness (*i gat as bilong em*), and the capacity for nuance and subtlety (*i gat ol liklik liklik mining*) that Tok Pisin lacks. Every villager wants his or her child to learn the vernacular. There has been no conscious effort on anyone's behalf not to teach their children Taiap.

So to what do villagers attribute the shift? Before elaborating an answer to that question, it will be useful first to contextualize it by considering how scholars from a number of academic disciplines have attempted to explain the phenomenon of language shift in speech communities throughout the world.

Approaches to language shift

Since the mid-1960s, linguists, sociologists, and sociolinguists have become increasingly interested in the process of language shift for a variety of reasons. Linguists have generally been concerned with understanding the internal dynamics of obsolescent linguistic systems, and they have wondered whether structural attrition in dying languages can in any way be considered the reverse of processes like creolization or first-language acquisition.[9] Sociologists have viewed the question of language shift in relation to processes of migration, assimilation, national identity, and ethnic revival. In these studies, the tenacity of minority languages has been regarded as an indicator of ethnic group viability and boundary maintenance.[10] Sociolinguists, finally, have tended to concentrate on how social structure affects a group's language attitudes, and on how these attitudes, in turn, cumulatively affect language choice in such a way that one of the group's languages eventually becomes abandoned.

Despite these somewhat different approaches, students of language shift have identified a number of factors that seem to be significant in accounting for why people's attitudes change and why shift occurs. These include migration, industrialization, urbanization, proletarianization, and government policies concerning which languages can and cannot be used in schools and other institutions. But although there is general agreement that these factors somehow are important in explaining language shift, there has been, as Fasold (1984: 217) points out in his summary of research, "very little success in using any combination of [these factors] to predict when language shift will occur." There is, "in fact, . . . considerable consensus that we do not know how to predict shift."

In addition to their lack of predictive power, macrosociological factors such as those listed above have also been criticized for their limited explanatory power. "What is of interest to know," writes Gal in the preface to her monograph on Hungarian–German language shift in Austria, "is not whether industrialization, for instance, is correlated with language shift, but rather: By what intervening processes does industrialization, or any other social change, affect changes in the uses to which speakers put their languages in everyday interactions?" (1979: 3; see also Dressler 1988: 190–1; Sankoff 1980: xxii).

Considerations such as these led Gal to conduct an "ethnographic description" (1979: 1) of the process of shift among farmers and workers in one community on the Austro-Hungarian border. Gal's study was a harbinger of a greater ethnographic orientation in studies of language shift. From having been based on census data, questionnaires, or surveys covering large populations, studies of shift since the end of the 1970s have increasingly come to concentrate on the intensive analysis of a limited community or area. The most widely read monographs on language shift all make heavy use of participant observation as a means of gathering and evaluating data on shift in such communities (Dorian 1981; Gal 1979; Hill and Hill 1986; Schmidt 1985).

These monographs represent a growing tendency to eschew mechanical theories of shift and to turn away from earlier attempts to find universal patterns of causality. Increasingly, investigators are realizing that shift in language is caused, ultimately, by shifts in personal and group values and goals. Social changes such as urbanization or industrialization certainly may lead people to revise their perceptions of themselves and their world. And these revisions may eventually be responsible for a group's giving up its vernacular language. But this is not necessary or predictable. And, as Gal makes clear, to say that urbanization or other social change "causes" shift is to leave out the crucial step of understanding how that change has come to be interpreted by the people it is supposed to be influencing. Most significantly for the perspective to be developed in this book: To evoke macrosociological changes as a "cause" of shift is to leave out the step of explaining how such change has come to be interpreted in a way that dramatically affects everyday language use in a community. If the investigation of language shift is modified to include such steps, the question that then must be answered is: Why and how do people come to interpret their lives in such a way that they abandon one of their languages? Viewed in this way, the study of language shift becomes the study of a people's conceptions of themselves in relation to one another and to their changing social world, and of how those conceptions are encoded by and mediated through language.

The analytical tool most commonly used in elucidating these types of relations is the concept of ethnicity. From this perspective, the process of language shift is one in which a vernacular language becomes closely linked to a stigmatized ethnic identity. Once this link becomes salient, the possibility opens for members of the stigmatized group to signal their abandonment of their ethnic identity by giving up their minority language in favor of that spoken by the dominant groups. This option appears to become especially viable and successful during periods in which a certain amount of social mobility becomes possible.

The work of linguist Nancy Dorian on language death in Scotland illustrates this process clearly. In the early nineteenth century, Gaelic-speaking farmers in the Scottish Highlands were forcibly "cleared" from their small holdings by large landowners, who wanted the farmers' land for sheep herding. Those tenants living on the lands of the Earl of East Sutherland were moved to the coast and told to take up fishing to support themselves. These people, who previously had been farmers and who knew nothing whatsoever of the sea or of fishing, had no choice but to learn to become fishermen. With great hardship, the farmers and their descendants eventually learned to earn their living from the sea. But these fisher communities became socially ostracized from the surrounding population, and even came to live in a special part of town called "Fishertown." Because the surrounding population was predominantly English-speaking, the Gaelic of the fisherfolk was seized upon as a symbol for that segregation and ostracism.

This situation began to change following World War II, when a steep decline in the East Sutherland fishing industry forced the fisherfolk to move into other jobs. This slight social mobility combined with a certain amount of in-migration from other areas of Scotland gave rise to a higher number of exogamous marriages. All of these factors contributed to a local shift away from the stigmatized "fisher" status. And that shift involved and was evidenced by a shift from Gaelic to English:

Since Gaelic had become one of the behaviors which allowed the labelling of individuals as fishers, there was a tendency to abandon the Gaelic along with other "fisher" behaviors. As [one] woman said: "I think, myself, as the children from Lower Brora got older they . . . were ashamed to speak the Gaelic, in case they would be classed as – a fisher." (Dorian 1981: 76)

The concept of ethnicity has proven to be very important in understanding language shift because it throws a conceptual bridge between macrosociological factors seen to bring about social change and the ways in which those factors come to influence people's perceptions and strategies. Ethnicity is not, however, always relevant. Certainly it is possible for a group to shift languages without substantially shifting its ethnicity, as the Irish have demonstrated. And although the situation seems to be changing rapidly (Mühlhäusler 1989), it would probably be misleading at present to describe language shift in any rural Papua New Guinean community in terms of ethnicity. Unlike the East Sutherland case described by Dorian, socioeconomic differentiation between groups in contact throughout this area has not yet become so significant that it invites the ranking of those groups in relation to one another. The only distinction of hierarchical salience at present among rural villagers is not expressed in terms of ethnicity. Rather, the crucial difference seems to be between people who are regarded as capable of participating in the modernization process and those who are seen as unable to participate because they lack Tok Pisin. The boundary is thus drawn between "civilized" villagers (who speak Tok Pisin, who are Christian, and who largely, *because of these attributes,* are portrayed as having succeeded in "pulling" cash-generating schemes, such as coffee plants, cocoa trees, or trade stores into their villages) and "backward" villagers (*ol bus kanaka*), who have not yet acquired Tok Pisin and the Word of God, and who consequently still live in villages without cash crops, outboard motors, or corrugated-iron water tanks. The important point is that *bus kanaka* villagers are not considered backward and stupid because of their ethnic-group affiliation or because they speak a vernacular language. They are derided, rather, because they don't speak Tok Pisin *in addition to* their vernacular. So, unlike the situations described by scholars like Dorian, shedding a stigmatized status in rural Papua New Guinea does not at present appear necessarily to involve shedding one's native language. Divesting oneself of such a status merely involves adding another language to one's communicative repertoire (cf. Sankoff 1980: 25–6).

In addition to being irrelevant in some cases, analytic stress on ethnicity may lead researchers to downplay or miss important steps in the language shift process. East Sutherland speakers of Gaelic, for example, are not just "fisherfolk" who interact with nonfishers. They are also mothers, uncles, husbands, daughters, lovers, friends, workmates, and neighbors. Even if we accept the fact that members of a group wish to alter their ethnic identification in relation to out-group members, we still need to explain the processes though which this desire comes to transform their interactions with one another.[11] Because the focus of the concept of ethnicity is on the boundary between two or more groups, it is less useful in helping us to understand the dynamics of intragroup interaction.

Intimately bound up with the problem of intragroup interaction is the issue of transmission. To date, the overwhelming majority of studies on language shift have concentrated on the speech of adults.[12] This has been done largely in order to establish that the different languages used within a community have different connotations of solidarity and prestige. In language shift situations it is thus common, for example, for speakers to switch consistently from their vernacular to Spanish or English or some other national language in order to lend more weight to their arguments (Gal 1979: 117; Hill and Hill 1986: 104) and/or as a way to appeal to prestigious values or lifestyles (Blom and Gumperz 1972; Sankoff 1971; Scotton 1979).

Although close attention to the speech of adults does indeed allow researchers to establish the kinds of associations that are linked to each language used in a community, it leaves uninvestigated the question of exactly how those value-language complexes become transmitted to children in such a way that the latter do not acquire the vernacular of their parents. This issue of transmission is at the very heart of language shift, since languages cannot be said to be shifting until it can be established that children are no longer learning them. By the time the first generation of nonvernacular-speaking children has been raised, the boundary between language shift and incipient language death has in most cases quite intractably been traversed.

In spite of the importance of understanding exactly how and why the transmission of a vernacular language simply ceases within a community, no study has yet concentrated on the socialization of the first generation of nonvernacular-speaking children. Work on language shift has concentrated heavily on examining the end result of shift. The process has been documented most extensively in its advanced stages, and much of the research on language shift, especially by linguists, focuses on languages in their final death throes (e.g., Cooley 1979; Elmendorf 1981). For nonlinguists not concentrating on structural decay in dying languages, this emphasis on the terminal stages of shift is sometimes unintentional; while recognizing the value of observing earlier phases, most investigators simply "arrived too late" (Dorian 1981: 53) to document them.

Another reason for the lack of detailed attention to the process of language transmission, however, has been that researchers have not seemed to think it necessary. Throughout the literature, parents are either portrayed as having consciously and explicitly decided not to teach their children their own vernacular or, phrased more passively, reported to decide not to encourage their children to learn the vernacular, even if they continue to use it among themselves. Usually the reasons underlying such a decision are said to have to do precisely with their opinions about the relative prestige of the vernacular in relation to a language of wider currency; i.e., parents consider that their children "don't need" to learn the vernacular to get by in society or they are concerned that the child's school language might suffer if he or she speaks the vernacular, etc. (e.g., Denison 1977: 21; Gal 1979: 164, Giles 1977; Hill and Hill 1986: 112–13; articles in Schach 1980; Schmidt 1985: 24). This widely held view that parents consciously decide not to pass on their vernacular to their children and that this is the "direct cause" (Denison 1977: 22) of shift has led some researchers to wonder whether language shift in most cases should not perhaps be more accurately referred to as "language suicide" (Denison 1977; Dutton 1978; Edwards 1985: 51–3).

A major difficulty with such terminology and the assumptions that underlie it is that it is not in fact always clear to what extent a parental decision not to pass on their vernacular is a "direct cause" of shift, and to what extent this decision is a consequence and recognition of shift already under way. It is also important to keep in mind that a child's language acquisition is influenced by many factors other than parental decisions and wishes. Dorian, for example, has pointed out that the role older siblings play in the language socialization of their younger brothers and sisters has great significance for whether these children become bilingual, semi-speakers (i.e., markedly imperfect speakers of the vernacular), or monolingual in the majority language (Dorian 1981: 107, 1980; Hill and Hill 1977: 60, 1986: 112–13; also Schmidt 1985: 25–6). Other scholars have documented the influence that peers have on a child's language (Goodwin and Goodwin 1987; Heath 1983; Watson-Gegeo and Gegeo 1989). And studies of children in bilingual households have highlighted a wide variety of factors – including type of input and parental reactions to their children's responses – that influence what language(s) these children acquire (Arnberg 1981; Döpke 1986; Fantini 1985; Lanza 1988). In general, recent studies on child language acquisition have been increasingly moving away from a view of socialization that sees it as "something done to novices by members" (Wentworth 1980: 64) to a framework stressing the interactional nature of language socialization. Ochs, for example, makes the point that "even infants and small children have a hand in socializing other members of their family into such roles as caregiver, parent, and sibling" (1986a: 2; see also Bourdieu 1977; Giddens 1979; Halliday 1975; Schieffelin 1990; Scollon and Scollon 1981: 139–65).

What emerges very clearly from the literature in these fields is that parental decisions and wishes regarding their children's language are only one factor of many that influence which language a child learns. Once this is fully appreciated, the issue of why a particular generation of children in a bilingual community suddenly grows up not speaking the vernacular becomes more complicated than parental wishes and more problematic than the lack of attention accorded the process in the literature would seem to indicate.

The nonobvious nature of this process is underscored starkly in the community this book is about. In Gapun, parents explicitly see themselves not as acting, but as *re*-acting to language shift. As mentioned earlier, no adult in the village devalues the vernacular. Without exception, everyone agrees that Taiap is a good language and desirable to know. No conscious decision has been made by anyone to stop transmitting the vernacular to their children, and some villagers, especially old men, occasionally express great annoyance at the fact that children only speak to them in Tok Pisin. So what, then, is causing the shift? The children, say the adults. "It's them, these little kids," explained one woman, echoing the conclusion of others and indicating her suckling 14-month-old baby with a sharp jab of her chin, "They're all *bikhed*

(big-headed, strong-willed). They don't want to know our village language. They just want to speak Tok Pisin all the time."

So, in contrast to those cases described in the literature, language
shift in Gapun is not occurring with the encouragement or consent of
parents. On the contrary, this shift is occurring *against* the expressed
desires and wills of village parents. In this context, the question "How
do a group's perceptions of themselves and language become transmitted
to their children in such a way that the latter do not learn the vernacular?" becomes perplexing and problematically insistent.

Approaches to language socialization

One way of approaching the question of the (non-) transmission of
particular languages in a community is to pay close attention to the
precise ways in which language is used as part of the child socialization
process. The conceptual framework with which to undertake such an
investigation has been under development for a number of years now,
by scholars working with what have come to be known as "language
socialization" studies. Language socialization is a relatively new area of
inquiry that attempts to synthesize the study of child language acquisition
and the study of socialization. This synthesis highlights a new area of
research that takes as its focus the documentation of "both socialization
through the use of language and socialization to use language" (Schieffelin and Ochs 1986b: 163). The goal of such a focus is to understand
the ways in which "children and other novices in society acquire tacit
knowledge of principles of social order and systems of beliefs (ethno-
theories) through exposure to and participation in language-mediated
interactions" (Ochs 1986a: 2).

Although it is a truism that children learn to be competent members
of their society in large measure through language, the processes through
which this occurs are not well known because the relationship between
the transmission and acquisition of language and the transmission and
acquisition of sociocultural knowledge has not been thoroughly inves-
tigated. Socialization studies, for example, have paid little attention to
the structure and organization of language used in speaking to and by
children (Ochs and Schieffelin 1984).

Similarly, studies of first-language acquisition have traditionally shown
little regard for cultural context. Even though these studies, since Chom-
sky, have largely been concerned with determining the extent to which
biological and social processes interact or are independent of one another in language development, the overwhelming focus has been on
the biological dimensions of the acquisition process. Questions regarding
the sociocultural organization of language acquisition have been slow
to emerge, in large part because the children studied have tended to

come from the same types of white, middle-class North American or European homes as did most researchers studying acquisition. Combined with a lack of comparative studies from other groups, this fact has meant that many of the features specific to Euro-American middle-class caregiver–child interactions have not been recognized as such. Instead, many of these features, such as the particular characteristics of what is usually called the "baby talk" register, have been assumed to be natural, universal, and, according to some, even necessary for normal language acquisition (articles in Snow and Ferguson 1977).

Recently, language socialization studies have begun to highlight the unconsciously ethnocentric bias of this traditional work on language acquisition by providing detailed data from groups who interact with children in ways that systematically differ from the interactional patterns described in the language acquisition literature. For example, studies of black working-class Americans, Papua New Guinean swidden agriculturalists, and Samoan villagers have recently shown that baby-talk registers are not universal (Heath 1983; Ochs 1988; Schieffelin 1990). This kind of information has led to a reevaluation of the role that modified speech plays in a child's acquisition of language. In general, it is increasingly being appreciated that only when language socialization data from a wide variety of other groups are analyzed and evaluated will scholars be in a position to begin adequately assessing the complex relationship between nature and nurture (Ochs and Schieffelin 1984).

In practice, the study of language socialization patterns is done by carefully analyzing caregiver–child interactions, showing how the structure and content of these interactions is organized by and expressive of wider cultural patterns of thought and interaction. In her recent essay on the acquisition of what she calls communicative style ("the way in which language is used and understood in a particular culture") in Japanese, for instance, Clancy (1986) attempts to account for the ways in which some of the most important elements of Japanese culture, such as the value placed on consensus and on indirection, are embedded in and constitutive of verbal interactions between Japanese children and their mothers. Clancy does this by paying close attention to the specific interactional characteristics between mother and child that facilitate the acquisition of particular culturally desirable behaviors. One way children learn the meaning and social significance of indirection, for example, is through the pairing, by mothers, of indirect with direct utterances having the same communicative intent. This juxtaposition appears to teach children "how to interpret the indirect, polite speech of others as expressing the same strong feelings and wishes as more direct utterances" (ibid: 229). Clancy also demonstrates how conformity to social expectations is engendered in children in large part through mothers' regular appeals "to the imagined reactions of *hito* – other people – who are watching and evaluating the child's behavior" (ibid: 236). In expressing their disapproval of certain types of behavior, Japanese mothers tell their children that their actions are "strange" or "scary" and that "no one does X." Mothers rarely direct a child's attention to their own feelings (saying something like "I don't want you to do that"); they choose instead to emphasize how *hito* would react to the child. This communicative strategy "locates the source of disapproval and constraint outside the mother, in society at large" (ibid: 236), thereby laying the groundwork for the well-known Japanese apprehension of group disapproval.

Other studies of language socialization similarly link local ideas about language, society, behavior, and personhood to the ways in which caregiver–child interactions are structured and to what children learn. Thus, the prompts used by American white working-class caregivers to coach their children to tell stories are shown to be determined by local ideas surrounding the nature of truth (Heath 1983). The high occurrence of rhetorical questions by and to Kaluli (Papua New Guinea) children is explained by examining cultural preferences for indirect or "turned over" language (Schieffelin 1986). The early acquisition of semantically complex verbs by Samoan children is made comprehensible through an analysis of that culture's concern with the display of affect (Ochs 1986b; Platt 1986). And the first words that caregivers in different cultures attribute to children are demonstrated to be bound up with that culture's conceptions about the nature of children (Ochs and Schieffelin 1984).

In this study of language shift in Gapun, a focus on the villagers' language socialization patterns will be useful in two ways. First, as has been indicated above, caregiver–child speech is an important source of data for locating and understanding salient local ideas about what society is, what people are, and how they should behave. It is this type of fundamental and, for the most part, tacit knowledge that continually gets communicated to children and others in the language socialization process. Second, as was also noted earlier, Gapun parents say that the ongoing language shift in the village is the doing of their (often preverbal) children. "We haven't done anything," one village man explained when I asked him why village children don't speak the vernacular, "We try to get them to speak it, we want them to. But they won't. ...They're *bikhed.*" In order to understand the mechanisms behind language shift in Gapun, it is important to take seriously and try to understand the basis of this parental allocation of blame. What are the underlying assumptions about the nature of children, of learning, and of language that make it seem reasonable to the villagers to blame their babies for the demise of the village vernacular?

It will become clear in the chapters that follow that in allocating blame in the way they do, village parents are not being disingenuous or evasive.

The people of Gapun impute intentionality and strong wills to their children from a very early age, and given this, it is not surprising that they can believe babies capable of rejecting one language in favor of another. But since parents do not see themselves as having altered their linguistic interactions with children, a close look at the language socialization patterns in the village will allow us to determine if there is anything in the very structure of caregiver–child interactional patterns that is now favoring Tok Pisin without caregivers being aware of it. If this should be the case, such a finding would be of theoretical interest, not just for an understanding of the process of language shift, but also – if one follows Gal (1979: 4) in viewing shift as a "special instance of linguistic change" – for an understanding of the processes behind linguistic change generally.

Cultural reproduction and language shift: goals of this study

This book argues that the conceptions that people have about language, children, the self, and the place of these in those people's interpretation of their social world are central to an understanding of why they come to abandon their language. The emphasis in the chapters that follow will thus be on the villagers' own ideas about their world and on how the ways in which they have made sense of their changing world have come to affect the ways they use language.

Such a perspective should not be taken to imply that macrosociological processes are unimportant. It will become clear that a number of overarching social and economic factors, particularly the introduction of Christianity into the village and the fact that a large number of men used to leave the village for several years at a time as contracted laborers, are extremely significant in accounting for the language shift to Tok Pisin. The primary sense in which these factors are significant, however, is that they have become interpreted by the villagers in ways that have a direct bearing on language. This interpretive, or cultural, dimension is necessarily present in every case of language shift, but it is frequently missed or downplayed in research on this process, and it will be stressed throughout this book partly to highlight its absence in other work.[13]

Another reason for foregrounding the villagers' interpretations of their world in this study on shift has arisen to a large degree out of the empirical situation that I encountered in Gapun during my stay there in 1986–7. What is particularly striking about the village is that the changes which have affected the people there since the coming of white men in the early decades of this century are not primarily material changes, but rather ideological transformations, new ways of looking at the world and at themselves.

Gapun is difficult to reach and far away from any urban center. Partly because of this geographic isolation, villagers are only very marginally involved in the market economy. Everyone in Gapun is self-supporting through a combination of swidden agriculture, hunting, and sago-processing. Some villagers engage in cash-generating enterprises such as growing coffee or drying copra, but this is done on an ad hoc basis as a minor supplement to their subsistence activities. The amount of cash earned through such activities is not large, and it is quickly spent on store-bought items such as rice, sugar, batteries, or articles of clothing.

Out-migration from the village is negligible, consisting for the most part of young women who leave Gapun to reside in their husbands' villages. In 1986–7, four women and one man lived in other, more distant villages, but the man and three of the women returned frequently to Gapun, usually with their spouses and children, spending several weeks to several months visiting relatives and friends. A number of families from Gapun live in the nearby village of Wongan (a two-hour journey away by foot and canoe), where they feed and look after most of the schoolchildren from Gapun during the week. These families cannot, however, be considered to have left Gapun, since the close ties between the two villages and the relatively short distance between them allows the families to remain actively involved in most aspects of village life.

In-migration, too, is not yet significant. Aside from being adopted as a child, the only way for an outsider to establish him- or herself in Gapun is through marriage to a villager. In recent years, there has been a growing tendency for young men and women to choose their partners from outside Gapun, particularly from Wongan. The majority of marriages between those villagers living in Gapun, however, is still between fellow villagers. In ten of the sixteen married couples living in the village in 1987, both spouses were speakers of Taiap who had been born and raised in Gapun.[14]

In Gapun, we thus are confronted with a rural, fairly isolated community with little out-migration and still insignificant in-migration; an economically self-supporting village far removed from processes of industrialization or urbanization; a village where market economy penetration is negligible, where the majority of village parents both speak the vernacular and where all adults value the vernacular. And yet the village is in the process of shift from this vernacular to Tok Pisin. The relative absence of dramatic material and demographic changes means that the macrosociological factors which habitually are invoked to account for language shift in other societies have little relevance for Gapun. The usual explanations of language shift just do not fit this situation.[15]

From a cultural perspective, on the other hand, language shift in

Gapun can be understood as the result of what Marshall Sahlins has called a "structure of the conjuncture." The "structure of the conjuncture" is, according to Sahlins, "a set of historical relationships that at once reproduce the traditional cultural categories and give them new values out of the pragmatic context" (1985: 125). Sahlins' concern in his recent work (1981, 1985) has been to explain how people transform culture in the act of reproducing it, and he uses the idea of conjunctural structure to explain how, by drawing upon presupposed cultural categories to interpret and act upon new situations and events, people can, under certain circumstances, come to transform and revalue those very cultural categories by which they interpret and act. This idea of change through reproduction is the perspective from which I will approach language shift in Gapun. I will be arguing that the process of shift in the village is being brought about mainly because, in reproducing (through their day-to-day practices and their socialization patterns) the cultural categories through which they understand themselves and their world, Gapuners are transforming those categories. And those transformations are precipitating decisive consequences for how the villagers think about and use their languages.

One of the most important cultural transformations that has occurred in Gapun since the arrival of white people in their country at the beginning of the twentieth century has been a change in how the villagers view and express the self. As will become clear in the chapters that follow, two highly salient aspects of self receive a tremendous amount of elaboration in Gapun. The first of these is what the villagers call *hed* (lit. head). This is the dimension of self which is individualistic, irascible, selfish, unbending, haughty, and proud. Villagers express and find expression of *hed* in everything from a baby's first words, to women's harangues of abuse at villagers who have offended them in some way, to the now defunct custom of murdering an innocent maternal relative to display one's anger and shame. *Hed* in Gapun is a basic attribute of personhood. In each individual, however, *hed* is felt to coexist with another aspect of self that is named by the villagers. This second aspect of self is *save*, which means "knowledge." *Save* is the sociable, cooperative side of a person. All people, but especially men, are expected to use their *save*, their "knowledge," to "suppress" (*daunim*) their antisocial *heds* and cooperate with their fellow villagers.[16]

Although the display of *hed*, of personal autonomy, is considered necessary and uncontestable in certain social situations, it is admonished and devalued in village rhetoric. A man or woman who behaves in too *bikhed* (big-headed, willful) a manner is decried. Such an individual is seen in a very negative light and runs the risk of being struck dead by sorcery. *Save*, on the other hand, is extolled and praised. All good qualities – generosity, placidness, cooperativeness, willingness to work hard and to help others with their work – emerge from and are evidence of one's *save*.

This local understanding of self is essential to grasp in order to comprehend why the villagers of Gapun are shifting languages. The argument that will be made in this book is that while the villagers continue, in their socialization practices and in their interactions with one another, to reproduce and elaborate these two basic aspects of self, the introduction of Tok Pisin and Christianity into their society has thrown up a dramatic new series of oppositions, such as Christian: Pagan and Modern: Backward, that have affected the way in which villagers view and express the self. What was once a dual concept of personhood subsumed under one language has become a duality split along linguistic lines. *Hed* has become linked to the vernacular, which in turn has associations with women, the ancestors, and the past. *Save,* on the other hand, has come to be expressed through and by Tok Pisin, which in turn is strongly associated with men, the Catholic church, and modernity. This split can be diagrammed roughly as follows:

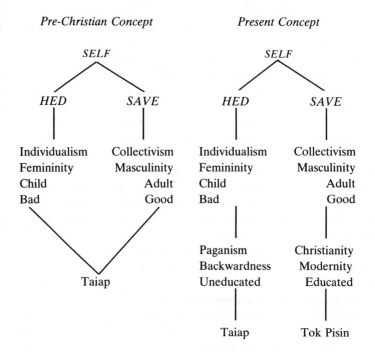

Pre-Christian Concept		Present Concept	
	SELF		SELF
HED	SAVE	HED	SAVE
Individualism	Collectivism	Individualism	Collectivism
Femininity	Masculinity	Femininity	Masculinity
Child	Adult	Child	Adult
Bad	Good	Bad	Good
		Paganism	Christianity
		Backwardness	Modernity
Taiap		Uneducated	Educated
		Taiap	Tok Pisin

Because Taiap has become associated with negatively charged values (relative to the dichotomies introduced through the white presence in Papua New Guinea), it is losing its ability to express positive aspects of self. At the same time, Tok Pisin, because it has become connected with *save* and the chain of associations bound up with that concept, has become a resource that villagers can draw upon in their interactions with one another to poignantly underscore their commitment to those values which everyone agrees are important, namely Christianity, modernity, collectivism, and so on. In using Tok Pisin, villagers are thus expressing an important and highly valued aspect of self; they are displaying their knowledge and social awareness, their *save*. But in doing this, they are also constituting a situation in which their vernacular is becoming less and less desirable and important. *In reproducing the self, Gapuners are changing the symbolic means through which the self can be reproduced.* The point to be made here is that it is this dynamic that is ultimately responsible for – quite without conscious effort or approval on the part of anyone – language shift in Gapun.

This argument is developed in detail in the chapters that follow. The first of these is a general ethnography of the village, describing the people who live there, their recent history, and their economy. Themes such as the villagers' notion of provocation and their understanding of development are outlined here. These themes are central to the conceptualizations that the people of Gapun hold of themselves and their world, and they play an important role in their daily lives and patterns of interaction and socialization.

The second chapter is about language. Beginning with a brief description of the vernacular language spoken in Gapun, the chapter moves on to detail the sociolinguistic situation in the village as of 1987. Here the exact character and nature of language shift is made clear, and the villagers' awareness of and reactions to the shift are discussed. After this follows a description of how the villagers use their languages in their day-to-day talk with one another. A characteristic feature of virtually every conversation that occurs between adults in Gapun is code-switching, which is a type of verbal behavior involving the alternate use of different languages within a single stretch of discourse or within an utterance. Most of the code-switching that occurs in Gapun is between Taiap and Tok Pisin, and the ways in which these two languages are switched in the villagers' speech is exemplified. Chapter 2 concludes with an examination of the connotations and values that are bound up with each of the villager's languages and discusses the strong associations that the vernacular language has with the villagers' past, with their land, and with women.

The two chapters that come next are concerned with exploring the villagers' concept of self. Both begin by considering different aspects of how young children are treated and spoken to, in order to make clear the ways in which these early interactional patterns are structured through the concepts of *hed* and *save*. The associations that give meaning and importance to *hed* and *save* are then documented through a detailed examination of the kinds of talk that villagers believe to be the embodiment of those two dimensions of self. In Chapter 3, the speech genre discussed is what the villagers call a *kros* (lit. cross, anger). It is characterized by the speaker – who is almost inevitably a woman – sitting in her house and screaming long monologues of abuse at people who have offended her in some way. In Chapter 4, oratories and harangues in the men's house are described and analyzed.

I have chosen to explore the villagers' notions of self by looking closely at their ways of talking to one another for two main reasons. The first is ethnographic. Although the information that we have on Melanesian societies is exceptionally rich and varied, one area about which we know comparatively little is that of discourse and patterns of language use. Although we now know a substantial amount about the structure of New Guinean languages, and although it is common in anthropological studies to be presented with summaries of myths, snippets of villagers' conversations with anthropologists, and with decontextualized words and sentences, it is still quite rare to be given extensive data about how Melanesians actually talk to one another.[17] Whenever speech in these communities is presented, it is usually in the form of political oratories delivered by (big) men. Everyday, mundane talk is usually not examined, and, as Goldman (1986) has recently pointed out, female discourse and speech patterns have been almost totally ignored by linguists and anthropologists. By presenting extended excerpts of speech from a variety of different contexts and speech genres, I hope in this monograph partly to convey an image of what sorts of things people living in a Papua New Guinean swamp say to one another and partly to contribute to awakening the interest of more scholars in the description and analysis of discourse patterns within Melanesian communities.[18]

The second major reason for concentrating on speech patterns in Chapters 3 and 4, and in this study as a whole, is theoretical. As was argued earlier in this introduction, in order to truly explain the process of language shift, it is necessary to understand the ways in which language is thought about and used within the language-shifting community. The analytical perspective from which an increasing number of researchers on language shift have begun to investigate this question is that of the ethnography of speaking. "By focusing on speaking as a

cultural system (or as part of culture systems organized in other terms),"
writes anthropologist Richard Bauman in his recent book on speaking
and silence among seventeenth-century Quakers, "the ethnography of
speaking seeks to elucidate the interrelationships among language, culture, and society at their source, in the culturally patterned use of language as an element and instrument of social life" (1983: 5). This is the
perspective on language taken in this study. Consequently, the speech
of the villagers is examined in detail as a means of making visible the
cultural assumptions that organize and are organized by language. Talk
is used as a lens through which salient ideas and beliefs are focused on
and made explicit. What is mainly of interest here is thus not so much
exactly what the villagers say, but rather what cultural assumptions they
are drawing on in order to be able to say what they say and expect
comprehension from their listeners. Viewing talk in this way means that
the study of speech events becomes an exploration of how male and
female are conceptualized, of how villagers deal with conflicts and express consensus, and of how they view language, knowledge, and personhood. As these conceptualizations are examined in this study, it will
gradually emerge that one dimension of self, *hed,* is linked closely to
Taiap, whereas the other dimension, *save,* has strong associations with
Tok Pisin.

Once the question of how the people of Gapun regard themselves in
relation to one another has been examined in Chapters 3 and 4, the
problem of how they see themselves in relation to the world beyond the
village is raised. Chapter 5 documents the villagers' ideas about Catholicism, schooling, and white people. This chapter examines various
expressions of the villagers' strongly held belief that the world as they
know it is soon going to become fundamentally transformed by the
power of the Christian God. This kind of idea, well-known to all researchers who have worked in Melanesia as "cargo cult" or "millenarian" thought, is absolutely basic to the way the people of Gapun
understand their world. Through an analysis of the villagers' syncretic
mythology, the stories they tell one another about the power of "the
Bishops," their participation in cargo-cult activities, and the printed
material that they choose to read, this chapter shows how the villagers'
interpretations of the world and their place in that world have come to
have a direct bearing on the current language situation in the village.

In Chapter 6, the focus of the discussion returns once again to the
concepts of *hed* and *save,* but this time the analysis centers on exactly
how these concepts structure and are structured through caregiver–child
interactions. The chapter explores how this structuring leads village
caregivers to use much more Tok Pisin than they realize in their inter-

actions with children, with the result that when children begin to talk, they do so in Tok Pisin.

In Chapters 2–6, my major goal is to illustrate the ways in which the villagers' thoughts on language, children, and self all work to systematically bias their language practices in favor of Tok Pisin. Chapter 7 diverges from this line of argumentation in that, here, the focus turns to those dimensions of village verbal interactions that are independent of language choice. If the rest of this book is an exegesis illustrating the ways in which *plus c'est la même chose, plus ça change,* then the point of Chapter 7 is to understand what in fact does remain the same while everything else is changing. The element of continuity in change is essential to account for in cases of language shift, especially in those many familiar cases in which people do not really seem to care very much that their language is dying out. In Gapun, for example, although villagers are aware that children are no longer speaking the vernacular, the salience of this awareness is not high, and for the most part, no one is overly concerned with their children's lack of Taiap. In order to understand the shrug-of-the-shoulder attitude that villagers have toward the demise of their language, it is necessary to determine whether there are any features of linguistic interaction that are considered to be more basic or important than the language through which those features are expressed. Another way of phrasing this question would be: What is the cultural basis of a community's acceptance of imperfect or "semi-" speakers?

Chapter 7 approaches this question through an examination of village practices of knowledge as these are revealed through the narrative conventions that Gapuners use in their informal talk with one another. In gossiping, amusing one another with outlandish tales, and telling one another stories of adventures in the rainforest during a pig hunt, Gapuners work together to construct a shared sense of community and a particular type of social reality, which they apply to interpret events, gauge the thoughts of others, and evaluate actions. As children in the village acquire the narrative conventions through which villagers construct their social reality, they acquire the knowledge they must possess in order to be considered competent members of society. In learning how to listen and structure their talk and interact with others, children become able to fully participate in village life, regardless of what language they speak.

The final chapter is a synthesis of the different aspects of language and self that emerge throughout this book. By teasing out the meanings that the villagers have come to assign their languages, and by exploring the ways in which those meanings have come to be tied to the expression of various dimensions of self, it becomes possible to understand the way in which Tok Pisin became incorporated into the villagers' verbal repertoire and the consequences that this incorporation has had and continues to have in Gapun.

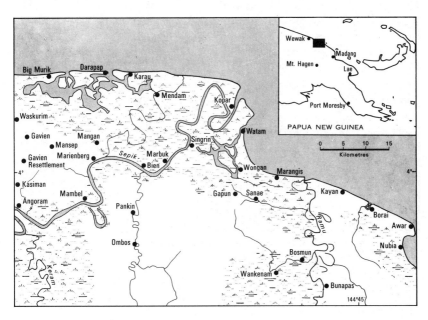

Map 1. Lower Sepik and Ramu regions.

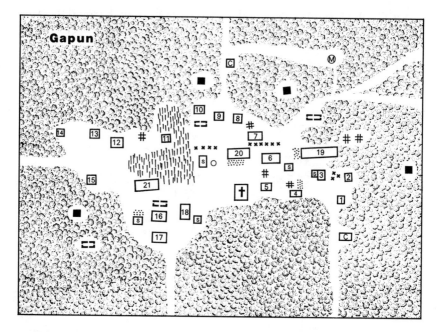

Platform for sitting and socializing
:::: Flower beds
||||| Long grass
ˣ Cultivated shrubs
⊞ Church
Ⓜ Coffee shelling machine

■ Maternity hut
© House for smoking copra
⊏⊐ House foundation
Ⓢ Roofed, unwalled shelter
○ Water tank

1 Kem and Wandi
2 Agrana
3 Reia
4 Mone and Sopak
5 Kapiru
6 Ambuli and Membo
7 Marame and Tambong
8 Visiting anthropologist
9 Allan, Sake, Jari, Sombang
10 Erapo, Aper and his wife Surum
11 Ajiragi, Arut and her husband Bowdi

12 Ariba and Paso
13 Anton and Ermina
14 Philip and Yamar
15 Kawi and Bit
16 Samek and Mairum
17 Samek's father Wanjo
18 Steven and Gerak
19 Kem's men's house
20 Kruni's men's house
21 Samek's men's house

Map 2. Gapun village.

1. The villagers and their village

Bonika emerges through the doorway of her house, balancing a large wooden plate of food on her head. With a pursed, serious look on her face, she begins to descend the narrow, notched pole that serves as the ladder to her house. Bonika is 6 years old and naked. The plate, shaped like a canoe and longer than Bonika's arm, contains a quivering mass of hot pink sago jelly, broth, and three small chunks of newly boiled pig meat. It is nearly dusk, and Bonika's mother, Membo, has just prepared the evening meal. She has instructed her two older daughters to carry some of the plates of food to various relatives, and Bonika's 7-year-old sister, Yapa, follows her out through the doorway. With another big plate on her head, Yapa shouts at Bonika in mock seriousness to hurry up or she'll turn the ladder on her. Bonika shrieks "*Ah Yapa!*" in a loud, accusing voice, reaches the ground, and laughs. She makes a quick move to turn the ladder that Yapa is now descending and screams as a small spurt of hot broth spills over the side of the plate and trickles down her bare back. Both girls laugh and shout at each other. When she is on the ground, Yapa raises her hand in a fist and tells Bonika "*Bai yu pispis nau*" (You're gonna piss now). Bonika laughs again, then screams, and scurries quickly in the direction of the far end of the village, which is the destination of her plate of food. Yapa starts off in the opposite direction: the plate of food she is carrying is for her father's sister's husband, who lives next door. "*Bai yu pispis nau,*" shouts Bonika back at her older sister, giggling, in a nyah-nyah voice as they separate.

The plate of sago pressed tightly against Bonika's head is for her mother Membo's older sister Bit. Bit lives in a small, dark, cluttered house on shaky supporting posts near the village graveyard. Until recently, this house marked a border of the village, but a while back Bit's eldest brother began to build a house directly behind it. This brother never got around to finishing his house and, after erecting the supporting posts and lashing together some runners for the roof, he abandoned the project. Now, after several months, the sun had bleached the exposed runners and posts, and the vines used to tie the whole construction together have become brittle and started to crack. The whole thing will have to be taken apart and begun again. In the meantime though, another of Bit's brothers and the in-married husband of her youngest sister have each built themselves a house behind hers. These three houses, together with the nearby house of another brother, form a kind of tiny hamlet in the small village.

To get to Bit's house, Bonika has to walk past the small unwalled men's house in the center of the village. This men's house belongs to Kruni, who, at around 60, is one of the oldest and most influential men in Gapun. Kruni lives in his men's house and he waits every evening, impatiently, loudly, hungrily for his old wife or one of his daughters to bring him his supper. Sometimes Kruni gets his food before it gets too dark. Sometimes, when his wife and daughters are feeling sick, or tired, or are "angry" (*kros*), or out of sago, Kruni gets nothing at all. Most often something eventually arrives, but not until well after nightfall. Thus, the evenings in Gapun are usually inaugurated as Kruni sits slurping sago and crunching on small, hard pieces of dried pig meat in total blackness, hurtling scathing interjections between mouthfuls at his wife and daughters for their laziness. Now, as he watches Bonika glide silently past him with a large plate of hot sago jelly on her head, Kruni loudly wonders why, if other women can manage to cook before dark, no one in his family can. In reply to this, Kruni's ancient wife, Sombang, hollers from somewhere deep inside her house, fifteen meters away: "*Yu tɔwɛr awtɛt! ŋa mnda yuwɔn mɔrasi aprɔnana!*" (You shut up! I'm sick of your complaining!).

A few hundred yards past Kruni's men's house stands Bit's house on its spindly posts. Nearing it, Bonika can hear that Kruni and Sombang have now begun shouting at each other in two overlapping monologues and that the couple's two adult daughters have also joined in and are shouting at Kruni, at Sombang, at each other. Approaching Bit's house, Bonika now also suddenly hears the brash voice of Paso, the wife of one of her mother's brothers. "*Bɔnika yu anakni?*" (Bonika where are you going?), Paso calls out from her veranda in the village's vernacular language. Bonika continues walking and motions with her eyes to Bit's house. "*Ah? Yu go we?*" (Ah? Where are you going?), Paso asks again, this time switching to Tok Pisin. Paso waits briefly for an answer, receives none, then asks one more time, "*Yu go long Bit ah?*" (Are you going to Bit?). "*Mm,*" says Bonika softly, still walking. "*Ey. Orait yu go*" (Ey. OK, you go), replies Paso. Then, suddenly spying the freshly boiled pig meat perched on top of the sago in Bonika's plate, Paso asks her, "*Papa i kilim wanpela pik ah?*" (Papa killed a pig did he?). "*Nogat*" (No), murmurs Bonika. "*Na husat i kilim?*" (Well, who killed it?), Paso asks, with interest. Bonika has now reached Bit's house, and with a straight back, she gingerly climbs up Bit's old, worn notched-pole ladder, seeing there the small white milk teeth of Bit's children that have been pounded into the notches to make sure their teeth will never fall out again. She doesn't answer Paso.

Bonika goes up into the house and sees her aunt Bit seated cross-legged on the floor near the hearth. In front of her is spread an array of plates: wooden ones like the one Bonika is carrying and a few chipped enamel ones with paintings of pink chrysanthemums and puffy orange goldfishes on the bottom. Bit has just "turned" (*tainim*/<u>nir</u>-) a large pot of sago jelly, and she is about to twist it – like one twists hot taffy – into each of the plates she has arranged before her. Having been informed of Bonika's coming by Paso's calls to her, Bit looks up as Bonika ascends the ladder and asks her who shot the pig. Bonika answers softly, hands her plate to Bit, and turns to go. "*Ah?*" Bit asks, louder, not having heard. "*Mone, Mone,*" snips Bonika, in an irritated voice. "*Ey,*" murmurs Bit in a gentle rise-fall tone.

From outside on her veranda, Paso has been listening hard to this interaction, but although she has managed to catch Bonika's answer, she is not quite sure what Bit's question was. "Mone killed a pig ah?" she shouts over at Bit in the vernacular. "*Awo*" (yes) comes the reply from inside Bit's house. This bit of news is immediately seized upon by another disembodied voice, this time rising from somewhere inside the house of Bit's brother Andon. "*Ey!*" comes the sharp cry of surprise, "Mone killed a pig?" "*Awo,*" reply Bit and Paso in one voice. "Where?" continues the voice of Andon. "Is it big?" "*Mipela i no save*" (We don't know), shouts Paso in Tok Pisin in an exaggerated tone of annoyance. "*Mipela i no save,*" she repeats to herself. Then, looking down from her porch at Bonika as the little girl skips back to her house, Paso muses quietly: "Down there they kill pigs and eat well. Up here we, poor things, starve to death." And she laughs throatily.

On her short trip from her own house to her aunt Bit's, Bonika has traversed most of Gapun. The village is only about five hundred meters long and a few hundred meters wide and is enclosed on all sides by rainforest. For most of 1987, there were sixteen houses and two men's houses in the village, but this number changes constantly as old houses are abandoned and new ones gradually built. Although it is not large, Gapun is considered by the villagers who live there to have two main sections, and Paso was expressing this division when she referred to the people "down there" and contrasted them with her own group "up here."

"Up here" is mainly the houses of Bit's large sibling group: Bit's own house, which she shares with her five children and her husband, who is also married to a woman at the other end of the village; the house of her younger sister Yamar, Yamar's in-married husband, Philip, and their young son; and the house of Bit's brother Andon, his in-married wife, Ermina, and their five children. Next to this cluster of houses is Paso's, which was built by her husband Ariba, another brother of Bit's. About fifty meters east of Paso's house, across a wide patch of tall kunai grass, stands another house occupied by one of Bit's siblings. Mairum, the oldest sister, lives here with her husband, Samek, and their four children. Samek's old father, Wanjo, lives in the house next door to them and is looked after by Samek and Mairum.

At the opposite end of the village stand the houses to which Paso refers when she talks about the people "down there." In the smoke-filled house at the entrance to the village live Kem, his in-married wife, Wandi, and their seven daughters. Kem is the only child of the former undisputed big man of Gapun, Masambe, who was mysteriously killed in the jungle in 1966. A tall, taut man with narrow features and a high voice, Kem is universally liked and respected in several villages because of his generosity and his ability to maintain friendly ties with people on several sides of a dispute. His dead mother and his wife, Wandi, both came from Sanae, a neighboring community feared by the Gapun villagers as an evil lair of malicious sorcery. Because of his links with Sanae, it usually falls to Kem to ply the Sanae villagers and take payments of money and pigs to them whenever anyone in Gapun falls seriously ill. Kem's neutrality in the numerous inter- and intravillage disputes that continually arise among villagers is structurally emphasized by the placement of his house, which is at the extreme end of the village, set slightly apart from the rest of the houses. For ten years after his father was killed, Kem and his family didn't live inside the village at all, but rather in a small house near his coffee gardens, a good ten-minute walk away from the village.

Kem's wife, Wandi, shares with him a reputation for generosity and hard work. The pair is often cited by men as the ideal couple, mainly because Wandi "isn't a woman who complains a lot (*toktok planti*); she just follows her husband," a situation about which most married men in the village can only fantasize. Wandi has the open, perfectly circular face characteristic of all Sanae villagers, light skin, and slender features. She possesses a quiet dignity, which over the twenty years of her married life in Gapun has been metamorphosing into a kind of matronly presence, and although she maintains close and tight ties with her relatives in Sanae, no one would ever dream of linking Wandi to the wicked deeds of her relatives and fellow Sanae villagers, who are known to be the cause of every death in Gapun. Wandi's status in the village is so secure that once, when she had been very ill for several weeks, the village men had a large meal prepared, assembled in the biggest, most powerful men's house in the village, offered food to their ancestral spirits, and at the same time roundly chastised them, demanding that they stop making Wandi sick. Three days later, she was back on her feet working sago.

Wandi is respected and liked for her generosity and her placid nature, but she is also silently pitied for her inability to give birth to anything but daughters. Her first child was a boy, but he died a few months after birth. Since then, seven girls have been born. Each time Wandi's slim figure swells with a new pregnancy, villagers wonder whether "this belly" will be a boy. Hopes were rather high during the final weeks of Wandi's latest (and probably her last – she's in her early forties) pregnancy, which coincided with a brief cargo cult that swept through the village. One young woman who had been catatonic for several days and who claimed to have Jesus in her stomach rubbed her hands across Wandi's distended abdomen and confidently announced that this "belly" would be a boy. Unfortunately for the credibilty of the cargo cult, the child turned out to be Wandi's seventh baby girl.

A few meters away from Kem and Wandi lives Agrana. Agrana's mother was from Gapun, but he was born and spent most of his early life in the neighboring village of Wongan. Agrana came and stayed in Gapun as a grown man at the insistence of Kem's father, Masambe, but he has also traveled to various New Guinea islands as a contracted laborer, and he worked for a while on the Sepik River as the *wokboi* (work boy) of a priest, driving him up and down the river in the priest's outboard-motor-powered canoe. Agrana returned from his job with the priest to marry Bonika's aunt Bit, but his voracious sexual appetite caused so much friction between the two that Bit's father and her brothers finally beat Agrana up and chased him away from her. Leaving Bit, Agrana spent three years away from Gapun, visiting relatives and fellow clan members in mysterious villages along the Ramu River, recounting for them his "shame" (*sem*/<u>*maikaraŋgar*</u>) at having been driven away from his wife. Villagers regard this extended trip of Agrana's rather anxiously because Ramu villages, which no one else in Gapun has ever seen, are feared for their powerful sorcery and *sangguma* men (*aŋgwar*). These *sangguma* men are considered to be especially horrific because of the way they kill their victims. First they ambush and mesmerize them. Then they rip out the victims' entrails with their fingers, which are long and clawed. The entrails are replaced with leaves and grass, and the still-dazed victim is sewn up and sent back to his or her village. Before the victim goes, the *sangguma* men whisper in his ear the exact day and time when he will die. And, at the appointed time, he dies.

A small, balding man with hunched shoulders and a wide, nearly toothless mouth, Agrana fancies himself as a kind of receptor of supernatural messages. After some significant event has occurred in the village, Agrana usually recounts, in hushed, meaningful tones, a dream he has had in which precisely that event was foretold. The spirits of the newly dead of several nearby villages often bang on Agrana's wall or blow out his kerosene lamp to inform him of their demise, and once Agrana alarmed the villagers by producing a large chunk of blackened wood that he claimed an invisible sorcerer had nearly succeeded in driving into his body the night before. When he informs the villagers of his encounters with spirits and invisible sorcerers, Agrana is generally believed and listened to attentively. For other reasons, though, he is the subject of a great deal of mirth in the village.

Agrana's renowned lust, which is narrowly and infamously focused on young unmarried girls whose breasts *sanap yet* (still stand) gives rise to countless lascivious jokes and innuendo. Agrana is also known for his temper. His sudden outbursts of ferocious anger – at Wandi for not sending him any food, at his pubescent daughter for spending too much time with her mother at the other end of the village, at everyone in Gapun for not supplying him with another wife – are smirked at by most villagers. His close associations with known sorcerers, however, and his occasional veiled threats to make use of such associations, help ensure that no one goes too far in their jests, at least not within his earshot.

Next to Agrana, in a large open house plagued by chickens, lives Raia, the self-appointed village historian and scribe. On small scraps of torn paper and in half-finished, discarded schoolchildren's exercise books, Raia tries to note down, in laborious arthritic script, events of major importance in village life, such as: "*1984 Desaba 24 25 26 27 28 pati ipinis birong Sake i wok rong em 3pera pik 2pera Boros birong pik i go rong Paso 2pera het birong pik i go rong Suni 1pera het birong pik igo long Samek 1pera bros igo long Mone*" (1984 December 24, 25, 26, 27, 28 Sake's funerary feast [which she sponsored for her dead father's mother's brother] is over. Three pigs and two pig-chests were given to Paso, two pig-heads were given to Suni, one pig-head was given to Samek, and one pig-chest was given to Mone). Since the 1960s, Raia has been carefully recording the date of every adult death in Gapun, including that of his wife, who died in 1974.

Raia suspects that his wife died because she had refused the advances of a village man named Guyam, who is widely regarded as the most sinister character in Gapun. Before she died, however, Raia's wife succeeded in magically inflicting him with the *sotwin* (short wind, i.e., asthma) that has gradually turned him, at about age 55, into a wraithlike invalid. Once a vivacious and tough worker and hunter – one of his favorite stories to tell is the time he single-handedly speared seven wild boars in one night – Raia now spends his days bent forlornly over his intricate carvings of small statues and masks, which he will sell to carving buyers, and caring for his crop of tobacco, some of which he sells to men and women from other villages.

The three houses built in a small cluster near Raia's house are another example of siblings living together. Sopak is a tough-as-nails woman with loud opinions on everything and dramatic gossip, often made up, about everyone. She lives in a cramped, dilapidated house next to Raia's with five of her children and her soft-spoken, pragmatic husband, Mone. Mone's sister, Kapiru, lives in a house only a few meters away with five of her children. Kapiru's husband, Kawi, is Sopak's elder brother, and although he is often seen at Kapiru's house, he generally sleeps at the other end of the village with Bit, whom he took as a second wife after Agrana was chased away from her.

A second brother of Sopak's, Ambuli, lives across a small cleared plaza with his wife and four daughters, one of whom is Bonika, the girl who delivered the plate of sago to her aunt Bit. Ambuli is the village *pre lida* (prayer leader), having traveled a few times to the Catholic mission station at Marienberg for short training courses. It is his duty to say mass on Sundays. Ambuli is short and powerfully built, like most village men, and he is quiet and discerning, speaking slowly and with carefully weighed words. These latter characteristics make him quite unlike his more flamboyant older sister, Sopak, and unlike his wife, Membo.

Ambuli's wife is Bit's younger sister, and she is the only one of her sibling group in Gapun who doesn't live together with her brothers and sisters at the "up" end of the village. Membo is larger than her husband and nearly as strong, but in most social situations she is restrained, even demure. Whenever Membo becomes angry, however, her harsh shouts rise in crescendos and are often punctuated by the throwing of plates and heavy pots, or by the striking of her husband or children with a handy piece of firewood. Utterly fearless, Membo will engage in virulent shouting matches with any village man, and she was once beaten up badly by her sister-in-law Kapiru's oldest sons after she had knocked Kapiru unconscious with a log, on the suspicion that she had helped to arrange a clandestine meeting between Ambuli and a young village woman.

Just behind Ambuli and Membo's house is the men's house that Bonika walked past on her way to Bit's. In many ways this men's house, and its owner, Kruni, are the center of village life. It is here that most of the village meetings take place, and since the house is strategically placed in the center of the village, most villagers have to walk by it on their way to work sago, hunt, fetch water, or visit people. Information from other villages often gets taken to and disseminated from Kruni's men's house, although in recent years this has been breaking down, to the anger and dismay of Kruni and the older village men. Kruni, from his seat by the hearth in his men's house, has views on most of the issues, arguments, and gossip that circulate in the village, and he is not hesitant to express these views, sometimes in a loud, booming voice heard the length of the entire village, and not infrequently accompanied by threats to descend and "hit" the person or persons who have offended him.

Although he doesn't possess one, Kruni is very much the village time-piece. His irritated early morning shouts of "*Sombang! Sombang!*" at his aged wife announce that he is hungry and that it is time or, more usually, past time for breakfast. His absence from the village during much of the day signifies time for work, and his late afternoon reappearance and cries at the children running around in the clearing in front of his men's house of "*Inap! Pinisim pilai bilong yupela! Inap nau!*" (Enough! Stop playing! Enough now!) announce the arrival of evening. At night, after his evening meal, Kruni sits by his small fire, usually little more than an ember, always ready to "story" (*stori/tik gur-*) and smoke with whomever happens to drop by. He is usually the last to crawl into his mosquito net at night, and he wakes up with the discordant screeches of the village roosters at the first light of day. Kruni and Raia, who is his younger brother, are the oldest representatives in Gapun of the main branch of the crocodile clan, and they are the sole repositories of myths and knowledge about their clan, about the now long discontinued male and female initiation practices, and about the history and ownership of village lands.

Kruni is a cautious, pensive man with a large, hooked Sepik nose, a broad face, gray, close-cropped hair, and no eyebrows. Two bluish spheres, faded with age, circle his eyes in a raccoonlike manner. This tattoo was cut into his skin in the 1950s by islanders with whom Kruni worked in the far-off town of Lae. Kruni has a full set of stubby white teeth of which he is very proud. He displays these frequently, attributing their existence and tenacity (a bit disingenuously, the other villagers wink) to the fact that he never "played around" with women in his youth. His back, once obviously muscular and powerful, is now arched with age and resembles a large, domed carapace. He bitterly blames his back problems on his mother's brother, who, during an initiation phase long ago, hit him so hard with a stick that a vertebra was knocked out of place. Kruni's bad back prevents him from walking far, working sago, hunting, or actually carrying out his threats to descend from his men's house and "hit" people. But he is still the nimblest and most tireless dancer at the traditional village *singsings*, and one morning in June 1986, Kruni awakened everyone in Gapun before dawn with roars of anger as he strode into the village with a bloody spear. He had just, he announced, impaled a village pig which had been sneaking into his garden at night for several weeks and devouring the tubers and vegetables that he spent his days planting and caring for.

Kruni's wife, Sombang, lives in a big house, newly built by one of her sons, about fifteen meters away from the men's house. Sombang is old, seemingly older than Kruni, and she is afflicted with a sickness that causes her speech to drawl and her "skin" to "shake": Her limbs jerk and twist independently of one another and out of sync with whatever task she happens to be performing. Sombang has tiny eyes like shiny beads, a pendulous nose, few teeth, no breasts, and extravagantly long earlobes, which are pierced and torn, and which are often pressed into use to hold cigarette butts or bits of betel pepper. Sombang is so emaciated that every bone in her convulsive body is visible. And yet, with a grace and strength that is natural and ageless in the villagers, she manages to lift huge, black, cauldronlike pots filled with water on and off fires, to chop fallen trees into firewood using a heavy dull axe, and, once, Sombang was observed carrying at least thirty kilos of bloody pig meat on her head, at night, with no moon, and with only the dim glow of her newspaper cigarette to guide her up and down the worn and slippery notched poles that serve as ladders to all the houses.

Sombang lives with her youngest daughter, Jari, who at 19 is unmarried and the mother of a young baby. Another daughter, Sake, also lives there. Sake is a small, tight woman with a bulbous nose and a blue daisy tattooed between her eyes. In her early thirties, Sake has breasts that are still defiantly upright and firm because of her inability to bear children. This, the villagers are convinced, is due to her having capriciously eaten too much of a magic tree bark used to prevent pregnancy. Despite her relative youth, Sake is the single most dominant woman in Gapun. She commands respect and vague feelings of fear from all villagers because of the speed and intensity with which she can hurl long monologues of abuse at anyone she feels has imposed on her in some way. Whenever Sake decides that another person's actions or words have infringed on her – and Sake decides this frequently – she lets her decision rip through the village in sharp, loud, vituperative, and obscene shouts that no one can escape hearing. These frequent *kros*es (lit. crosses; fits of anger) have won Sake renown in several surrounding villages. Her most spectacular display occurred during a quarrel with her older brother, when she marched over to her own brand-new house – the result of six months of heavy work by her husband and herself – and set it on fire, hacking at it in rage with an axe as it burned to the ground. On another infamous occasion, Sake provoked a major village battle by first slashing the forehead of her mother's brother's daughter with a butcher knife, then breaking the girl's father's arm with a well-aimed piece of firewood. Whenever Sake begins shouting at her in-married husband, Allan, men within hearing range inevitably advise him to "run away" before she gets too riled. And when Sake calls from her house for Allan to come, men likewise urgently whisper at him to go to her, even if that means doing something as unthinkable as leaving a meeting in the men's house.

Near Sake lives her younger brother Marame, who has a reputation for violence almost as formidable as that of Sake. Marame lives with his in-married wife, Tambong, and their three small children in a very old, leaky house that has been abandoned by its former inhabitants. Those inhabitants, another of Kruni and Sombang's daughters and her children, left their old house to move into a new one that this woman, Erapo, and her oldest son built next to Sombang's house.

Of the remaining two houses in the village, one is ostentatiously set apart between the cluster of houses associated with Kruni and those belonging to Bit and her brothers and sisters. This house belongs to Ajiragi, the victim of Sake's firewood throwing. Ajiragi is Sombang's youngest brother, but he is also half-brother to Bit and her large "line" of siblings, having had the same father. The placement of his house in a position between Sombang and his half-siblings is a spatial representation of these double ties. Ajiragi lives cramped and complaining in a very tiny house, together with his four children, one of whom recently married Kapiru's son Bowdi. Now he too lives with Ajiragi. Next to Ajiragi's house was at one time the nearly completed framework of a house being built by his older brother, Guyam. Guyam is old and alone, suffering from the same shaking sickness as his sister Sombang, and abandoned by his four daughters and by his first wife, whom he left to marry another woman, and whom he unsuccessfully tried to remarry when that woman later died. Guyam has a wild, sonambulic air about him; tangled, matted, graying hair; cross-eyes; and scaly skin stained chalky white by ringworm and grille. Other villagers are wary of Guyam and suspect him of knowing how to kill people through sorcery. He is usually vaguely implicated in many of the deaths that occur in the village, although his most serious outrage in 1987 was that he bewitched all of his brother-in-law's dogs, causing them to lose all their fur and turn blue. Guyam was held to have done this because this brother-in-law had neglected him when he distributed meat after a pig kill.

Guyam's house, which he laboriously constructed himself, managing somehow to carry heavy posts through the jungle to the site next to Ajiragi's house, had progressed a long way when one day he became angry at one of Ajiragi's young sons. Guyam shouted at his nephew and slashed up a pile of coconuts that the boy had stacked near his house.

Upon hearing about this later, Ajiragi insulted Guyam by calling h
"*bun as*" (bone ass), and he told him: "Take your house and go pu
somewhere else. You're a *man bilong kros* (bad-tempered man) anu
you can't live next to me!" Thoroughly shamed, Guyam began disman-
tling his house the next day, and he has since begun the long process
of reconstructing it on a site far outside village boundaries.

The remaining house in the village was once occupied by Guyam's
oldest daughter, Gerak, her three daughters, and her in-married husband, Steven. Gerak, like Sake and several other village women, has a
reputation for fierceness and for keeping her husband in line. On several
occasions she has snatched up an axe and chased Steven into the jungle
upon getting wind of one of his frequent infidelities. The house that the
couple lived in, a wreck in its last inhabitable stages, was abandoned
by them after Gerak publicly let it be known that her father, Guyam,
had reached his hand into her mosquito net and tried to grab her as she
slept with her children. This was interpreted as a clear sexual advance
by the disapproving villagers, and the incident was used by Gerak's
husband as an excuse to make off with an outboard motor claimed by
Guyam's brother Ajiragi. Leaving the village with this motor, and subsequently unable to return for fear that Steven would be killed through
sorcery, the couple appear to have left Gapun for the foreseeable future.

The "old place" and the war

Most of the people now living in Gapun have grown up in the wide
clearing that is the present site of the village. Older men and women
like Kruni and Sombang, however, can still clearly remember the "old
place," the original site of Gapun. Known simply as _Taiap num_ (Taiap
village), the "old place" was perched at the top of a small mountain,
about one hundred meters above sea level. The village afforded views
of the Sepik River and, on a clear day, of the perfect cone-shaped island
of Manam, poking up out of the sea, a hundred kilometers away. Old
men sometimes recall dreamily, especially when engaged in flattening
fat mosquitoes on their skin in the evening, the cool breeze that "always"
blew through the village, driving away the hated pests and allowing
people to sleep uncovered on their verandas. Another advantage of the
old place was its strategic mountaintop location, which afforded some
protection against enemy raids. Daily work in _Taiap num,_ though, was
hard. The rocky ground of the mountain meant that all gardens had to
be planted a fair distance from the village, down the mountain, and
essentials like water, sago, game and firewood had to be lugged up the
steep and often slippery mountain paths. Today, whenever an in-married
man is heard to complain about having to carry sago or pig meat long

distances from the jungle to the village, or whenever a tired woman is heard to argue with her adolescent daughter over which of them will fetch water, an old villager is always on hand and ready to tell them how lazy they are, asking them with polished rhetoric: "Your work is hard, ah? Your bones pain? You've never lived on the mountain. You've never seen how your ancestors worked. You think they just sat around? Man. If you had to carry things up that mountain every day, you'd cry."

It was the prospect of such hard work, however, that in the end prompted the villagers to move their village from the mountaintop. Sometime in 1943, Japanese soldiers appeared in *Taiap num* and instructed the villagers to build them a base camp at the bottom of their mountain. The Gapuners complied, and they maintained several months of cordial relations with the Japanese, supplying them with sago and vegetables from their gardens in return for small quantities of salt, money, or empty tins. The people of Gapun had never before had any kind of extensive contact with "white" people, and it amazed and pleased them to see that the Japanese attempted to communicate with them ("But their Tok Pisin, sorry, it wasn't good," remembers Kruni, "rubbish true") and that the soldiers ate food like sago, which villagers who had been on plantations had been told was food fit only for pigs. The villagers' friendly relations with the Japanese lasted until sometime in 1944, by which time the Allied offensive in the Pacific had succeeded in cutting off the soldiers' supply lines. As they grew sick and started to starve, the Japanese turned demanding and nasty. At the same time, rumors originating in villages further to the east of Gapun insisted that the Australians were "coming back" and would "punish" anyone discovered helping the Japanese. At this point the villagers followed the example of others in the area: They fled their homes and began living in simple shelters in the rainforest. This time is remembered by the older villagers as one of bitter hardship, mostly because of the many deaths that occurred during their time in the bush. Old Raia recalls that:

Plenty plenty plenty died in the bush, of this sickness. So many men we lost during the war. Women. Buried them in the bush. Like pigs and dogs. You think it was a good time that we could bury them in a graveyard? Buried them near the trunks of trees. Men's and women's bodies. You think only a few died? The Japanese sickness. Shit blood. And sorcery, too, it went inside this sickness and made people die.

When the villagers returned to their mountaintop after the war, they found their houses reduced to ash, razed by their traditional enemies, the villagers of Pankin, apparently at the command of the Japanese. Having lost a large number of adults in the sickness Raia named (probably dysentery[1]), the village men and women had neither the strength nor the energy to carry up the mountain the heavy house posts that would be needed to rebuild the village. Instead, they cleared an area of rainforest at the bottom of their mountain, near the base camp that they had built for the Japanese soldiers. Here the villagers rebuilt their houses, and they called their new village *Sambaiag*.

The villagers lived here from the end of the war until the late 1950s, when they moved again, this time in order to be closer to the mangrove lagoon, which since the war had gained increasing importance as the "road" by which money would enter the village. This lagoon, which connects with the Sepik River by means of a long, narrow, often clogged creek, was and still is the only way in which cash crops could be transported out of Gapun. Village men began growing cash crops in the mid-1950s, at the encouragement of Australian agricultural officers and of emergent *ol bisnisman* (entrepreneurs) from neighboring villages. The results of these early ventures were not encouraging. Raia remembers:

We planted rice, cut it, dried it, OK, we rolled and rolled it between our hands, poured it into a bag and rolled it and broke it up and collected it and we put it in [another] bag. We put it in a bag and went to Kopar [a twelve-hour journey by paddle-canoe]. We built a big house. Like a tradestore. But this company [which had promised the villagers that it would buy the rice], it didn't buy it. We took the rice to Kopar for nothing, we never got any money. And the rice, they never sent it to Wewak [the provincial capital]. It just stayed in Kopar and it rotted and they threw it out. Peanuts, too, we planted and sent to Kopar. Same as the rice, though – the company didn't buy them. Our hard work was all for nothing. There was no money in those two crops we planted.

After the utter failure of both the rice and the peanut ventures, the villagers' interest in these two crops withered. But what remained after these ventures was a large plot of cleared, level land that was an hour's walk closer to the mangrove lagoon than was *Sambaiag*. Gradually, individual families began building houses on this cleared area of land. By about 1960, the last villagers had moved to the new village, and *Sambaiag* was abandoned to the rainforest.

Gapun village

Today this village, no longer new, is a tidy, windless little slit in the jungle. The village area contrasts with the surrounding rainforest by being kept largely free from grass, and women spend several hours every few weeks bent at the waist hacking away with long, curved grass knives at the tufts of weeds that have sprouted up in the areas around their houses. Grass inside the village area is disliked, partly because snakes can hide and mosquitoes can live there, but also because the villagers consider it uncivilized – "pigs and dogs" are content to live in the grass, they say, people shouldn't be. Near their houses, some of the villagers have planted a few shrubs of orange and yellow daisylike flowers, which they think are "*nais*" (nice), and which they insert into their tight black hair whenever they feel in a particularly good mood or want to dress up. Varieties of a plant used in combination with magical chants are grown in patches throughout the village and in the surrounding bush, as are rows of slender betel nut palms and a few varieties of fruit trees. In the early 1960s, agricultural development workers came to Gapun with a large number of coconut seedlings and told the villagers about the market potential of copra. The seedlings were planted in and around the village, and today the fully-grown palms tower thirty meters over the roofs of the houses, providing everyone with a handy source of refreshment, food, and sometimes even income, but causing a great deal of anxiety among mothers, who fear that their children may be killed by a falling coconut. This is one of the dangers to life in a Papua New Guinean village. One of the loudest and most frequent cries heard in Gapun is the shrill warning shriek of "*AI! KOKONAS!*" (AI! CO-CONUT!), emitted whenever someone notices that small children are playing too near the base of one of the coconut palms.

Houses in Gapun are constructed entirely from bush materials such as vines and poles and sago-palm leaves, which are carried back to the village from the jungle. An average house is about twelve meters long and nine meters wide, and they are all built about one and a half meters off the ground, perched squatly on supporting posts that are planted at least a meter deep into the earth. The villagers consider it to be a man's responsibility to build a house for himself and his family, and the only help in this task that a man normally receives from other men is in carrying particularly heavy posts and rolls of floor bark from the bush and, sometimes, in roofing the house. Because house building must be interspersed between the days in which men hunt, work sago, or rest, it is a slow process that may take a single man a year or more to complete. Young men frequently delay building themselves a house until complaints from their wives and the relatives with whom they are living drive them to it – and even then they sometimes seek alternative solutions. Kruni's son Marame, for example, has been married for ten years, but he has managed to avoid building a house by squeezing his wife and three children in with his siblings and, whenever these siblings begin to *toktok planti* (talk plenty; i.e., complain), by moving them into rotting houses that other relatives have abandoned.

Since the end of World War II, when the villagers rebuilt their homes, most village houses have been only partly walled, with large sago-leaf shingles or airy bamboo screens placed at the far end of the house around the area surrounding the hearth. This started to change about ten years ago, when young village men began building tightly woven bamboo walls all the way around their houses in imitation of the plywood and corrugated-iron houses they saw at mission stations and in small towns like Angoram. Now the majority of houses in Gapun are completely walled in, and, often without windows, they are extremely dark at all times of the day. The only light that enters the houses filters through the open doorway and through the cracks in the bark floor.

Houses in the village have no furniture, and the first thing that one notices when one's eyes have adjusted to the interior dimness of someone's house is that virtually everything the household owns is strewn across the floor. Floors in these houses are made of the flattened bark of a species of what in Tok Pisin is called the *limbom* palm. The villagers prepare their floors by first felling this palm, chopping it repeatedly along the grain of the bark until it is thoroughly perforated, and then making a cut deep down the length of the tree. The tree falls open, and the inner mass is scraped out with a shovel. Only the outer bark remains, and this is rolled up like a carpet and carried by several men back to the house, where it is unrolled onto the runners that have been fastened with vines to supporting posts. About nine 1.5-by-3.5-meter bark rolls are needed to floor an average house. This type of floor is extremely functional because the chops made in the bark when preparing it widen and harden into thick cracks that run throughout the floor. These cracks are handy when it comes to sweeping scraps out of the house, and visitors always make sure they sit next to a good crack so they can easily spit out the bitter red juice that accumulates in their mouths as they sit chewing betel nut. The cracks in the floor also make it easy to deal with the waste products of small children, and whenever a baby urinates or defecates on anybody's floor, this is easily splashed through a crack with a glass of water. Floors in village houses last about three years, after which sections begin to break off, leaving large gaps in frequently traveled places throughout the house. Adults do their best to ignore these holes as long as possible, and they shout at their toddlers, "*Ai! Bai yu pundaun!*" (Ai! You're gonna fall!) whenever they notice them careening toward a hole in the floor. Despite these cries of warning, though, it is not uncommon for small children to occasionally fall through a hole and plummet 1.5 meters to the ground below.

Visiting, sleeping, washing babies, preparing food, and eating all take place on the floor in the village houses. No area of the house is reserved at all times for any particular activity. Influenced by what they have understood to be the way of white people, a few young men in the neighboring villages of Wongan and Sanae have begun building a wall in their houses to divide it up into a *rum bilong kuk* (cooking room) and a *rum bilong slip* (sleeping room). This is still unusual in Gapun, however, and in all but two of the village houses, a house consists of one large room with no inbuilt spatial divisions. Where somebody earlier on sat eating sago, spitting betel nut juice, pouring water over a struggling baby, removing midribs from tobacco leaves, shredding coconut, peeling taro, or squashing lice, you will now roll out your mat and sleep.

Sopak's house is typical of this kind of village house. Climbing up the worn, notched pole leading up into the murky house, one discerns the hearth at the far end. The hearth is a square hole cut into the middle of the floor on which a layer of clay has been slapped and supported on posts reaching down to the ground. The hearth and the area immediately surrounding it (*turɔ*) is considered the territory of the woman of the house, and it is here that Sopak often sits, cross-legged, with one hand on her baby or her cigarette and the other on a long pair of light wooden tongs that all women possess. These tongs are multipurpose tools. They are used to move burning logs, lift hot pots off the fire, hand embers to people wanting to light a cigarette, take tobacco from people to dry it over an ember, hit dogs, whack at children – outstretched, a pair of tongs can extend a woman's reach by over a meter.

Above the hearth in Sopak's house hangs a three-tiered series of small platforms made from small squares of the same bark that makes up the floors. These squares are suspended by vines from the roof and are greasy and black from years of smoke and fat. On the top level of this construction (*bed/tambrak*), plates and small pots are placed. The middle level is for meat, which women cure by laying it on this square of bark and keeping a small fire burning below it in the hearth. The lowest level of this *bed* consists of short, removable poles laid lengthwise between two supporting poles. On these the women place their iron hooks on which they hang their pots to cook.

Because of the lack of spatial divisions for different activities, and because of the constant traffic of visitors, dogs, chickens, and children who come into houses to visit, eat, sleep, or play, houses in Gapun give an impression of clutter and disarray. The floor in Sopak's house is black and old and pitted with large holes. It is strewn with shirts and skirts and frayed towels, an empty plastic sugar bag, half a coconut shell, a small knife, old green betel nut skins, spilled chalky-white lime, a few rusting batteries, clam shells from a meal eaten several days earlier, a hypodermic needle given to Sopak's children to play with by a nurse from Marienberg, and several empty plastic bottles used to hold kerosene or water. Because Sopak has not yet felt inclined to *brumim* (sweep) her house, the middle of the floor is alive with swarms of tiny black ants who are busy carrying away the remains of her children's breakfast of sago and coconut. Behind Sopak, near the far wall, stands a large plastic bucket, once white, filled with water. Unwashed pots containing the sticky remains of the sago breakfast are strewn on the floor beside the hearth, and a dog whom Sopak periodically smacks with her tongs is eating out of one of them. In another corner near her hearth, Sopak has thrown a large bunch of green cooking bananas, and the wide brown basket in which she carries food from her garden stands sagging against the wall, a few coarse stalks of tobacco poking out from it.

Roofs in the village houses are all made from sago thatch, and, like floors, they are extremely functional. The roof is one of the few places in their houses where villagers can hide objects from other people, and Sopak has at one time or another stuffed newly purchased bags of salt, files, betel pepper, newspaper for rolling cigarettes, balls of thread, and even small sums of money up into the thatch of her roof. Sometimes objects like these are forgotten or lost in the thatch, and not rediscovered until months later when someone else is crunching into the roof in search of something they've hidden there. Because it is one of the few areas of the house out of the reach of small children, villagers also use the roof as a storage place for objects they want to keep away from children. Adults in Gapun do not make any attempt to keep specific types of objects away from their children, and toddlers are generally free to explore around the house and play with anything they happen to find laying around. Plastic rice bags, rusty batteries, marbles, sticks, chewed betel nut skins, and butcher knives are all common playthings that parents hand to fussing toddlers in the hope of distracting and quieting them. The only things that parents try to keep out of the sight and reach of their children are particularly valued objects like an especially sharp carving knife. An object like this will be hidden because adults know that if a child sees it he'll want it, and the parent will have to give the knife to him to stop him from crying for it. Parents dislike giving objects like these to a child because they're afraid that the child will ruin them. This is always the reason shouted at children on those rare occasions when an object is snatched from them. "*Ai! Bai yu bagarapim samting bilong mi ia!*" (Ai! You're gonna ruin my thing!), a 2-year-old sucking a cigarette lighter might be told. "*Yu baim long moni bilong yu ah?!*" (Did you buy it with your money?!)

Along the sides of Sopak's house lie several mats of various sizes made of woven reeds and purchased in the small town of Angoram. These mats are spattered with small piles of clothes, and during the day they are either left spread out or are rolled up and pushed against the wall. At night, Sopak and her children hang their mosquito nets from spears and sticks pushed through the roof thatch, and they sleep on these mats, using bundles of clothes as pillows and blankets.

How people sleep in Gapun is up to each individual, but almost no one except old men and a few teenage boys likes to sleep alone. Usually a mother will sleep in one mosquito net with her baby and other small children, while her husband sleeps in another net with slightly older children. Sometimes though, a woman will make it known that she is "*les long slip wantaim ol mangi*" (sick of sleeping with kids), and these then usually crowd in with the father, leaving the mother to sleep alone with her baby. Occasionally, because they have only one mosquito net, or because they prefer it, an entire family sleeps together. Sake's brother Kawri sleeps quite happily every night with his wife and three children inside a mosquito net measuring no larger than 1.75 by 1.75 meters.

Villagers in Gapun do not have many possessions. Women generally own more than their husbands, and it is considered essential for a woman to possess a number of pots and plates with which to feed her family (the latter she may make herself out of sago-palm fronds), at least one or two spoons, a small knife for cutting meat, a *pambram* (a wedge of broken crockery on which sago pancakes are made – a few women have replaced these with aluminium frying pans bought in Angoram), and at least one cup or glass. Most women make their own fishing nets, with which they pursue small fish in the jungle streams during the dry season; those who do not know how to make the large baskets or netbags in which they carry food get other women to make them for them by appealing to kin ties and by collecting and providing them with the raw materials. In addition to these things, women usually own a towel, a few T-shirts, and one or two *laplap*s (bolt of cloth worn wrapped around the waist). For dress-up, most women have a Mother Hubbard or some other form of second-hand dress, and a few women own a brassiere, which is put on and worn uncovered on especially solemn occasions.

Men's possessions are much fewer in number and are concerned with hunting. Each man in Gapun is expected to own a number and variety of spears, which he makes himself out of bamboo and flattened and sharpened bits of metal, a sago pounder (*makɔr*), which he also fashions himself, a bush knife, and an axe, which is used by the man to cut down sago palms and the bones of pigs and by his wife to chop firewood. A flashlight is considered essential for hunting at night and all men own one, but they often have broken lightbulbs or no batteries. Like their wives, men own few clothes, usually possessing only a towel, one or two pairs of shorts, some T-shirts, and perhaps a pair of long pants and a shirt with some buttons on it for formal occasions like church or a trip to Angoram. Most men make small canoes out of tree trunks, and in these, they and their wives travel to Wongan. A few village men have acquired much sought-after tools like hammers, saws, and shovels. Both men and women usually own their own mosquito nets.

The money to buy possessions like mosquito nets or bush knives or flashlights is earned by the villagers largely through the sale of cash crops. A few years after the failure of rice and peanuts as a source of income, Australian agricultural development workers told the villagers about coffee, and Kem traveled to Angoram to obtain some seedlings. He returned to Gapun and planted these, and in 1966, the first coffee was harvested and sold. Since that time, most villagers have planted small plots of coffee, and the sale of coffee beans has become the most common way for villagers to earn cash. In 1986, for example, 38 percent of the total village income of 1,303 Kina (approximately the same in U.S. dollars) was from the sale of coffee beans. Besides coffee, a few villagers also sometimes process copra and sell it to buyers from large companies. Kem, always the economic innovator in the village, has begun to harvest and sell small amounts of cocoa beans, an example now being followed by several other village men, who have recently planted cocoa seedlings given to them by Kem. Some villagers sell to-bacco to men and women from other villages, and rarely, villagers will be persuaded to sell one of their pigs to someone from another village who wishes to kill it at a funerary or conciliatory feast. A few men carve masks or small figures out of wood and blacken them with a paste obtained from split batteries; these are bought by the white carving buyers who infrequently pass through Gapun. Women earn small amounts of money by collecting bamboo shoots or large red wildfowl eggs in the rainforest and selling them at a local market that occasionally forms in the neighboring village of Wongan. Once in a while, crocodiles are caught or killed by the villagers and sold to buyers in Marienberg or Angoram. The skins can sometimes fetch 50 Kina or more. Table 1.1 summarizes the villagers' earnings for 1986.[2]

Villagers do not attempt to keep track of each other's earnings, and unless they happen to remember that Samek, say, sold copra for 196 Kina at one point, they will have no idea or concern about what Samek and his family earned during the year. Earnings as such are not kept secret – when word reaches the villagers that coffee or copra buyers have come to Wongan, everybody who has coffee beans or copra to sell takes it there, and it is publicly weighed and paid for by the buyers. Villagers are always curious to know how much a particular crocodile skin or bag of coffee beans has fetched, and there is no stigma attached to asking a person how much money they have been paid. The person questioned will invariably respond truly, even quoting the exact number of Toea (cents) received, if he or she remembers it.

One reason why the villagers pay relatively little attention to their differences in cash incomes is because these differences, even though

Table 1.1. *Villagers' incomes in 1986 (in Kina)*

| | Household | | | | | | | | | | | | |
Source of income	Samek-Mairum	Kem-Wandi	Mone-Sopak	Allan-Sake	John*-Akwaria	Ambuli-Membo	Kapiru	Erapo-Aper	Ajiragi	Agrana	Ariba-Paso	Andon-Ermina	Bowdi-Arut	Kawi-Bit
Coffee	29	158	96	78	6	3	28	68	22	2		10		
Copra	193		61		68									
Cocoa		59												
Tobacco			5				48			28				
Carvings	14	17				19			27	17				
Pigs	65													
Crocodile skins		12				55								
Market				70										
Wage labor**					15						20		10	
Total	301	246	162	148	89	77	76	68	49	47	20	10	10	0

* Kawi and Kapiru's eldest son, married to a Sanae woman. In 1986, he and his wife oscillated between living in Sanae and staying in Gapun with Kapiru.

** Paid by a Japanese motorcycle company who sponsored a motorcycle race through the lower Sepik. A few villagers were hired to clear the jungle on the far borders of their land in preparation for this race.

they are in fact rather substantial (compare Samek and Mairum's earnings [301 Kina] with Kawi and Bit's [0 Kina]), have not yet begun to produce any other salient differences in Gapun. This is due largely to the fact that a great percentage of the cash earned by village men and women is earned in anticipation of a funerary or conciliatory feast. The money earned from the sale of cash crops or crocodile skins is ultimately redistributed among the villagers in the form of prestige foods like packaged white rice or Nescafé. In 1984, for example, Sake and her husband, Allan, earned a total of 150 Kina from the sale of copra. All of this money was used to purchase the rice, sugar, *tinpis* (tinned mackerel), Nescafé, and pigs that the two prepared and had distributed during the funerary feast that Sake sponsored for her dead *kandere* (father's mother's brother). The feast was so impressive that Sake was acclaimed owner of all the land, betel palms, coconuts, and sago palms that had belonged to her dead *kandere*.

Money in Gapun is in this way still being deployed mostly in traditional spheres, even if it is being use to inflate the terms of participation in these activities, thus compelling the villagers to earn cash to buy the necessary food items. Whereas in the past villagers impressed one another during feasts with large quantities of yams, bananas, betel nut, prepared sago, wildfowl eggs, and pork, it would be unthinkable nowadays to sponsor a funerary feast, for example, without at least two or three 25-killogram bags of white rice, several kilos of processed white sugar, at least six or seven tins of *tinpis,* and enough Nescafé to dilute in copious amounts of tepid water and serve at regular intervals to all the guests gathered in the village.

Ownership and provocation

Another reason why villagers are largely unconcerned with differences in their individual incomes is because outside of funerary or conciliatory feasts, money is not normally translated into ostentatious store-bought goods. Villagers buy durable objects only rarely, and when they make one of their extremely infrequent journeys into the settlements of Angoram or Bosmun to purchase some item of this kind, they may return empty-handed because the axe or the *laplap* they had intended to buy cost a few Kina more than they remembered it costing several years previously. Villagers will also resist buying certain items that they consider to be essential because they fear that other villagers will pester them to borrow them. On one occasion, after having calmly studied a new bush knife for several minutes at a counter in an Angoram store, Kem handed it back to the clerk and walked out looking weary. When I later asked him why he decided at the last minute not to buy the bush knife, which he, in fact, had traveled to Angoram with the express purpose of purchasing, Kem explained, "*Maski* (Enough), if I bought it then some people would see it and like it. They'd ask me to borrow it and they'd ask me ask me and ask me, and they'd end up ruining it. I thought of this so I didn't buy it. I know how people here are."

The question of borrowing and ownership is an infected one in Gapun. Villagers have a keen desire to be as self-sufficient as possible, and they consider that the ideal situation would be one in which they personally owned every object that they ever needed to use. As Kem indicates, however, villagers are at the same time often unwilling to purchase what they consider to be essential items, like new bush knives or shovels, because they know that if they do buy these things, they will have to loan them out to others. This kind of attitude, of course, actually promotes borrowing among the villagers because it ensures that valued items remain scarce. In fact, though, not only is loaning disliked, but the people of Gapun loathe borrowing from one another, and most villagers will resist borrowing a needed item, like a file or a saw, for as long as they can possibly hold out. When they finally decide that they absolutely must ask for the loan of some object, adults will inevitably make this request by sending a small child to do it, thus allowing the owner the option of easily denying the request by telling the child a quickly made-up lie. If worse comes to worst and an appropriate child cannot be found or refuses to go, then an adult will sometimes directly ask another adult for the loan of an object, but even in this case they will falsely attribute the request to someone other than themselves, as when Sake borrows Membo's grass knife with the lie that "the old one [i.e., her father, Kruni] is complaining about the grass so I guess I have to cut it now."

Sake explains the villagers' reluctance to ask other villagers for the loan of their possessions in this way:

Text 1.1

If you borrow something from another person, he'll complain (*toktok planti*). He'll give it to you, because you've asked him and you've given him shame. His mouth will say, "It's OK, you take it then." But his thoughts, that's something else altogether. I know. In his thoughts he really doesn't want to give you the thing. No, no way. You'll take it and leave and later you'll hear. A mouth will be heard later. Lots of talk will arise about this thing that you've borrowed.

The distinction that Sake makes here between thoughts and words is important because it captures the villagers' understanding that what a person says need not, and usually in fact does not, have any relation to what that person thinks or does. No one in Gapun is ever surprised when someone acts directly contrary to their statements, although some of the tension that is continually present in village relations stems from the fact that no one ever knows exactly what others really think or intend to do about things, because their statements on any matter are not expected to reflect their intentions. The gap between words and thoughts is most obvious when it comes to decisions reached in the men's house involving communal labor such as cutting grass along the path to the mangrove lagoon or repairing broken footbridges. These types of decisions are always reached after lengthy discussions about who needs to go work sago or hunt before they can participate in the work, and once this is finally sorted out, a day is decided upon. Most men present in the men's house always contribute a short speech or remark of support for the task to be done and for the appointed day. When this day arrives, however, it is not unusual for most or, sometimes, even for all men not to show up. Whenever this happens, big men like Kruni will bellow loudly from the men's house that everyone in Gapun is "*les*" (lazy), but no one is ever accused of "going back on their word" or of "breaking their promise" to work. That the disjunction villagers see between thoughts and words should be articulated by Sake while on the subject of borrowing others' possessions is not surprising, given the general importance that the people of Gapun attach to their possessions.

Possessions in Gapun are considered to be visible extensions and representations of the person who possesses them. The relationship between objects and people is constantly underscored for the villagers by the fact that no object of any use or value in the village is unowned. Every banana and every betel nut palm, every piece of firewood, stray strand of thread and empty beer bottle, every sago palm, plastic bag, and the land that these things are found on is owned by some person or group of people, and villagers defend their rights of ownership vigorously and relentlessly. Rare indeed is the day in Gapun not pierced at some point by the sharp accusatory monologues of a *kros* (cross) about possessions: Here Mairum is sitting in her house cursing at Bowdi, accusing him of having stolen three melons from her garden; here Guyam is roaring that his half-brother Ariba borrowed his shovel "*bipo bipo tru*" (a long time ago) and still hasn't returned it; here Kem's wife, Wandi, is shouting from her veranda, demanding 2 Kina in compensation from the unknown person who picked a cocoa pod off one of her trees and ate it. Gapun villagers speak the same tiny language, see each other virtually every day, have grown up together, and have known each other all their lives. Yet this familiarity does not extend to rights over each other's possessions, and even husbands and wives will sometimes argue violently if one of them uses some possession of the other without permission. *Bilong husat?/Animat?* (Whose?) is a question continually on the lips of every villager. It is a question that must be answered before anything can be used, borrowed, or stolen. It is one of the first questions a child learns to ask.

Links between possessor and possessed are so durable that they are even maintained when objects are discarded. Once, Sake's older sister Erapo spied an old, torn netbag tossed onto a rubbish heap at the edge of the village. Thinking the netbag had been made by her oldest married daughter, Erapo plucked it up, intending to unravel it and salvage some of the thread. Several hours later, however, Sake's raspy voice was heard rising from inside her house. Having been informed by Erapo's children that their mother had found an old netbag on the rubbish heap, Sake began to scream in two languages:

Text 1.2

Wanem meri i kisim bilum bilong mi igo?! Ah?! Ambin nɔŋɔr ŋaŋan mambaki̱ tarak kukuwɔkara?! Samting bilong yu na yu kisim ah? Yuwɔnkɛ ɔrak? Yu meri bilong givim tar long mi long wokim samting na yu kisim ah?! Samting bilong mi kisim i kam. I kam nau tasol. Kakat ŋayar.

What woman took my netbag?! Ah?! What woman took my netbag?! It was yours to take ah? Was it yours? You always give me thread to make netbags with so you can just take it ah? Bring my thing. Bring it now. Hurry up.

From inside her house, Erapo began a parallel monologue, shouting that the netbag wasn't Sake's at all, it was her daughter's, and she had removed it from the rubbish heap for that reason. Sake didn't know what she was talking about, Erapo yelled, she hadn't even seen the netbag. And besides, Sake was a "*meri bilong kros nating nating*" (a woman who always gets cross for no reason). After thirty minutes both women quieted down, Sake still demanding the netbag back and Erapo still denying that it was Sake's. A few hours later, the netbag was discovered by some children flung back on the rubbish heap. The children took it to Sake, who stuffed it up into her roof.

Because they are so unambiguously and continuously linked with their owners, possessions in Gapun are often deployed as messages emphasizing personal autonomy. A canoe promised several weeks in advance to transport seven people and their produce to the market in Angoram, for example, can be coolly withdrawn the night before the trip is supposed to take place because the owner is "*les*" (i.e., "doesn't want to" lend it). Another, much more dramatic expression of the idea that possessions can serve as symbolic extensions of their owner is the habit that villagers have of expressing their rage at what they consider to be infringements of their autonomy by destroying their own possessions. When Sopak discovered that someone had climbed up one of her betel palms and stolen a bunch of betel nut she had had her eye on, she had her son cut down the tree. When Sopak's husband, Mone, publicly berated Sake's brother Kawri for not helping the other village men cut the grass at the school in Wongan, Kawri answered by flying into a rage and chopping down all his own betel palms in the village. And when Sake's older brother Akupi argued with her and her husband, Allan, Sake – in what everyone in the village agrees was the most sensational eruption in memory – marched over to her newly built house and with great élan burned it to the ground.[3]

Villagers appreciate the message spelled out by felled betel palms and blazing houses, and although they may make sharp clicking sounds with their tongues to indicate their distaste over the waste of a good house or betel palm, they are not hesitant to lay the blame for the destruction not usually on the person who actually brought it about, but rather on the person or persons who are seen as having provoked the destruction.

Provocation in Gapun is regarded with horror. The villagers consider that to overtly attempt to influence the actions of another individual is one of the most serious offences that one person can commit against another. This idea is reflected in every type of relationship in the village, from the way parents coax and plead with their children to go ask a neighbor for a betel nut, to the ways in which village big men carefully monitor their oratorical speeches so as not to appear pushy. To overtly attempt to influence another person is to violate them and challenge them, and among adults, this will almost inevitably result in an argument or a fight, sooner or later. As Sake noted when she spoke about borrowing, to openly ask a person to borrow something is considered a provocation, for example, because the direct request will put the giver out by giving him shame, whereupon he will feel constrained to lend out his possession, even if he doesn't want to, and this will in turn lead to "*planti toktok.*"

Whenever the villagers argue or fight about anything, blame for the fight and its consequences is always placed in the first instance not on the person who is considered to be wrong or guilty of some offense, but rather on the person who is seen as the provocateur of the argument. Late one morning, Kem and Wandi's 7-year-old daughter, Eren, returned from a wash at a waterhole and made a hurried beeline for Sopak's house. From a distance, she could see that Sopak was at home, reclining and smoking on a pile of clothes, with her head propped up on an elbow and a breast tucked into her daughter's mouth. Eren scrambled up the ladder to Sopak and informed her that her neighbor Agrana was sitting with Raia a few hundred yards outside the village in a small house where Raia usually sat during the day working on his carvings. Agrana, Eren said, was loudly "talking no good" (*tok nogutim*) about

Sopak and her husband, Mone. Relations between Sopak and Agrana had been strained for several weeks because of the leading roles that Sopak and her husband had in the cargo activity that was taking place in the village at that time. Agrana was extremely critical of the cult, largely because one of the possessed cargo-cultists chased him away when he had tried to join in. Since then, he had been denouncing the cult as "Satan's work" whenever he could.

Kem's daughter reported that Agrana was complaining that Sopak had stopped "thinking of" him when she made food, and that she and Mone were lazy and only interested in making work for the Devil. Hearing this, Sopak's mouth dropped open and she let out a loud scream of disbelief. She yanked her breast out of her dozing daughter's mouth, jumped up, threw down her cigarette, and ran out of the village after Agrana.

She found him whittling at his carvings in the shade with Raia, and as soon as she saw him, Sopak began to shout. "You're mad at which woman?! Ah?!" she screamed at the old man, "You're talking no good about who?!" These rhetorical questions were followed by a bitter barrage of the most vulgar obscenities Sopak could think of. Then, without waiting for a response from Agrana, Sopak swung around and swept back into the village with bulging neck veins and flailing arms. She strode over to the small plaza in front of her house, and here she stood calling Agrana alliterative epithets like "*Yu bilak bokis BASTAD!*" (You flying fox BASTARD! – Agrana is a member of the flying fox clan) and shrieking that "*Ol i rausim yu long Wongan na yu smelim kan i kam long Gapun! Olsem dok! Harim?! Yu lapun long kaikai bilong mi! Tingim na yu toktok!*" (They threw you out of Wongan so you came to Gapun sniffing cunt! Like a dog! You hear?! You've grown old on my food! Remember that when you talk!)

By this time, everyone in the village had crowded around the plaza in front of Sopak's house to hear what she was screaming about, and they watched as Agrana now entered the village. Yelling at Sopak that the Devil had made her crazy, Agrana climbed into his house and began hacking at the walls with a machete. He then turned on a pile of wooden masks that had taken him several months to complete, which he had hoped to sell to any carving buyers who might happen by. One by one Agrana pitched these masks out through his door onto the ground, smashing off their delicately carved noses.

The argument continued in this way for twenty minutes: Sopak raging from the plaza in front of her house and Agrana wreaking havoc inside his house. In the end, Agrana left his wrecked house and stole away into the bush, where he remained until after nightfall. Sopak continued screaming for the better part of an hour, yelling at Agrana that if her hand weren't swollen she would break his skull and tear his eyes out of his head "like a hawk." She eventually wound down, finishing off her tirade by folding and rolling her flappy breasts into burlesque imitations of the kind that Agrana is widely known to lust after.

After this incident, everyone in the village was unanimous in blaming Agrana. He had, there was no doubt, provoked Sopak into becoming angry and screaming at him. Sopak, everyone agreed, "*i stap gut tasol*" (was just minding her own business). What did Agrana mean by provoking her anger? True, she hadn't given him food for a long time, but she was sick, her hand hurt she said. And besides, was Sopak Agrana's wife that he should "*tok hat*" (talk hotly) to her about food? Was she a "*kam meri*" (in-married woman) that he should shame her like that?

That provocation is the single most important element in blame assignment is also clear in those cases where people who aren't considered to be provoked join in an argument. Early one afternoon, Tambong, the in-married wife of Sake's brother Marame, sailed into the village from her garden. As she stepped from the jungle into the village, she began screaming at the top of her lungs that somebody had stolen her bananas. "Three bunches of my bananas!" she shouted, "My hard work has come to nothing!" Tambong was carrying two small bunches of spindly, green cooking bananas, which she tossed up into her house. Then she dramatically flung a cut banana stalk onto the ground in front of her and delivered a furious speech about how she wasn't a "woman from this place" (she is from Wongan), but that she worked harder than the "true" village women: She had planted a garden while all the other women ever did was "sleep." "Who," she kept repeating, "stole my bananas?! Who went and stole them? Yesterday I went and saw them there and now somebody's stolen them! You hear my children crying for food? Ah?!" Tambong continued like this for twenty minutes, then she climbed up into her house, smoked a cigarette, and went to sleep.

About three-quarters of an hour later, Tambong was awakened by the angry shouts of her neighbor Membo, who strode heavily into the village followed by a trail of children. Approaching Tambong's house, Membo threw her big carrying basket on the ground and shouted at Tambong to see that there were no bananas in it. She then marched up into her own house, knocked several large pots off the *bed* above the hearth, and continued screaming that she had not stolen Tambong's bananas.

After a few stunned moments, Tambong managed to call out that she hadn't accused Membo of anything, she hadn't mentioned her name. This was echoed by Tambong's husband, Marame, and by Kruni from their seats in the men's house. Even Sake began to get involved, hollering from somewhere inside her house that Membo had no reason to "give back mouth" (*bekim maus*) to Tambong. Tambong's anger had been "good," everyone shouted at Membo in separate monologues. Tambong's possessions had been violated, and she had exercised her legitimate rights in announcing this and being angry about it. "She was cross (*kros*) about her things that someone stole! She didn't call your name that you should give back mouth to her!" Membo was admonished. Apparently, Membo had been in the vicinity of Tambong's garden collecting wild greens earlier in the day, and when she returned to the village, her siblings at the "up" end told her about Tambong's *kros*. She felt herself accused and so she answered back. Even if they had known this, however, Sake and her relatives would not have cared. What was relevant to them was the fact that Membo was not considered to have been provoked here, so in "giving back mouth" to Tambong, she was out of line. People later indicated that they thought Membo, by "giving back mouth" to Tambong was, in fact, trying to provoke a fight with her and Marame. This may well have been true, since toward the end of this episode Membo suddenly shouted that Marame still had not repaid the 7 Kina that he had borrowed from her husband.

Of course, which person in an argument is the provoked and which is the provocateur is often an open question, but the fact that blame assignment is guided by ideas about provocation results in villagers attempting to structure their altercations with others so that they cannot be accused of provocation. It was probably for this reason – an attempt to portray himself as provoked – that Agrana destroyed his masks during Sopak's tirade against him. In another instance, Sopak and her family had been away in the jungle for over a week working sago and hunting. Returning to the village at dusk one evening, Sopak immediately noticed that the small pile of firewood under her house had grown even smaller during her absence in the bush. Standing in front of her house, she began to wonder loudly which village woman was "like a snake," without arms or legs, unable to go into the jungle to chop her own firewood but keen to send her children to steal Sopak's. These comments were clearly aimed at Sopak's sister-in-law Kapiru, who lived next door and who Sopak frequently accused of theft. After a few minutes of Sopak's accusations, Kapiru's high voice began to rise indignantly from inside her house. Sopak shouted over Kapiru's denials, asking rhetorically, "Why is Kapiru giving back mouth? I wasn't talking to you. Was I talking to Kapiru? Did I stand here and call Kapiru's name?" Then, after a dramatic pause: "You're giving back mouth because you stole my firewood."

"Coming up" in the village

The importance that the villagers in Gapun attach to their personal autonomy and to perceived affronts to that autonomy is at odds with a notion they name with the Tok Pisin word *kamap* (come up). In some of its senses, *kamap* can be translated to mean development. Just as the notion of development has several senses in English, so does *kamap* have a number of related meanings in the minds of the villagers. There are, for example, connotations of maturation: Children are said to *kamap*, beginning as ego-centered creatures who *nogat save/numbwan wakareŋa* (don't have knowledge) and developing into men and women who, in rhetoric if not in fact, are concerned with each other and with the common good. *Kamap* also has connotations of economic development, and the villages along the Sepik River that have several outboard motors and a few houses with corrugated-iron roofing are grandiosely said to be "coming up" by Gapuners. The most important aspect of *kamap*, however – one that encompasses these first two meanings and starkly differentiates the village understanding of development from standard Western views on the matter – is that the village concept of *kamap* signifies a transformation, in several senses of the word, toward the ways and beings of those whom the villagers call *ol kantri* ("the countries," i.e., the inhabitants of every other known country in the world except Papua New Guinea). Old Kruni, one of the most vocal advocates in the village of "coming up," explains the concept like this:

Text 1.3

Kamap, it's like we want to come up like all European countries. In the countries you've all changed. You all have faith and so you've all come up. We're the only ones who don't have faith. In the countries everyone lives well. There's no fighting, arguments; there's no spears or sorcery. Here we die from these
5   two things that I just named: spears and sorcery. But you, no. In the countries everyone lives really well, *wanbel* (in agreement, without conflict; lit. one-belly). And, too, you've got all kinds of factories to make all kinds of things: boats or ships or airplanes or cars or motors or money – whatever, all these factories are in the countries. There aren't any here among us in Papua New Guinea.
10   We're the last country. And the way of life, too. In the countries it's good. There's no work. Like what we do here – carry heavy things around on our shoulders, walk around through the jungle like pigs. No. You all just sit, drive around in cars. It's the same with food. White people just eat tinned food, everything comes in a tin – tinned fish or tinned meat or tinned crab or tinned
15   shrimp – whatever, it all comes in a tin. Houses. You all live in good houses. They have rooms in them, toilets. But us here, no. We haven't come up a little bit. God Papa hasn't changed us yet. We're still inside the Big Darkness. We still live the same way our fathers from a long time ago lived. Just like wild pigs.

When villagers like Kruni talk about coming up, their point of reference and their goal is *ol masta na misis,* i.e., white men and women. No one in Gapun has ever had close personal relations or even long conversations with any white person. Visits to the village since the 1930s by colonial officials, priests, and carving buyers have always been irregular and brief. The villagers' relations with the Japanese soldiers who occupied their land during World War II were based on the exchange of goods, not on verbal communication. And as "work boys" on plantations and on labor crews in the 1950s, older village men like Kruni have had white bosses, but differences in social hierarchy and race prevented the development of contact with these bosses or any other whites.

What the villagers know about white people and their lives, then, they know largely as a result of rumors told by other Papua New Guineans – almost all of whom have had as little contact with whites as the villagers themselves. Whenever it has been possible, villagers have keenly scrutinized whites, and their own observations have been used to confirm and elaborate on the stories they have been told by others. Nowadays village children go to school, where they are frequently told stories about white people and their ways. The reports about these things that the children sometimes volunteer to an adult become incorporated into the general picture the Gapuners have of how white people live.

Villagers have very definite ideas about how white people live, and they can without hesitation launch into detailed descriptions of the habits and lifestyles of *ol masta na misis.* One aspect of white life that the village men find particularly intriguing, for example, is the fact that white men and their wives never seem to have the loud arguments and fights about adultery that are so common in Gapun. "We fight over women," the men say soberly, echoing a statement heard from men all over Papua New Guinea. "Women are the cause of fights among men. But *ol masta,*" they continue, amazed, "don't fight over women." The explanation?

If a *misis* has sex with a *masta,* she always gets paid. The *masta* has money and he always pays her. When her husband comes back and finds out that another man has been with his wife, she will point to the money on the table. She'll show him the money and she'll tell him: "Look, there's the money. You can't get angry. You see the money?"

Village women, in a similar way, authoritatively account for why white women don't have maternity huts. "We black-skinned women," Wandi once explained, "when we have babies we can't go close to the Fathers and Mothers [i.e., old men and women]. If we did, our heat would give them asthma (*sotwin*). But when *ol misis* give birth," she continued, having heard this from Sopak, who had heard it from the wife of one of the schoolteachers in Wongan, "the nurse gives them a shot, gives them medicine to cool (*kolim*) them so that they can just walk around in their village and not give asthma to the Fathers."

Stories and images such as these have accumulated and been elaborated on in the villagers' discourse over the course of many years, and it is against these already more or less well known and established facts about white people that any new bits of information about them are judged. In addition to this kind of anecdotal knowledge, villagers in Gapun have also sought for and found confirmation of their beliefs about white people in a particular syncretic combination of the Bible stories with which they are familiar and their own traditional myths.

The most important myth in this regard is a long tale concerning the exploits of the first two beings to travel through the lower Sepik area – an older brother, Arena, and his younger brother, Andena. In this two-brother myth, the younger, unmarried brother allows himself to be seduced by his older brother's wife one day when the older brother is away fishing. The older brother discovers the details of this infidelity when he arrives home later that day, and the tale has it that he became so angry that he made plans to kill his younger brother. When the two brothers were later digging the hole for the gigantic supporting center post that would hold up the roof of their men's house, Arena told his brother to get down into the hole and dig. No matter how deep he dug, Arena kept shouting down to his younger brother to dig the hole deeper. Finally, when Andena had dug the narrow post hole so deep that "the beating of a slit-gong drum could barely be heard on the ground above," his older brother told him to stop. And with that, the older brother lifted the huge post high above his head and plunged it down the hole with all his strength.

Andena is the village's culture hero, the "smart" one, who was wise to his older brother. He had prepared himself in advance by taking with him down the hole a small parcel filled with red paint and bits of moss, which he placed at the bottom of the hole. Andena had also taken the precaution of digging himself an escape tunnel at the side of the hole, and into this he neatly slipped when he saw the base of the post plummeting towards his skull.

After apparently crushing his younger brother, Arena lifted the post back out of the hole and examined its base. The sight of sticky red liquid and bits of spongy matter satisfied him that he had indeed killed his brother. Andena, however, burrowed his way up to the surface again, far away from Arena. The myth continues, centering mostly on the younger brother and his exploits, one of which was the fashioning of two types of human beings: some made out of dark wood and some made out of the milky-pink pith of the sago palm.

In the end, Arena discovers that his younger brother is still alive, and he repents and sets out to find him. After a long hide-and-seek-like journey following his brother in a leaky canoe, Arena finally catches up to Andena, and the two paddle away into the sea, taking with them, it is said in some versions, the pale creatures that Andena had fashioned out of sago-palm pith. The two ancestors were never heard from again.[4]

This is the usual end of mythical figures in Gapun. The most significant mythical ancestors never died, and only one of them is said to still remain in Papua New Guinea. Almost always, the ancestors simply "went away." And where they went, the villagers have now decided, is across the sea to "the countries."[5] There the ancestors resurfaced and used their knowledge (*save*/*numbwan*) and their powers to *stretim* (straighten out, set right) the people there, and it is here that the traditional mythological figures mesh with Biblical characters. The most important female culture hero, for example, is a woman named Jari, who arrived in the lower Sepik area shortly after Arena and Andena. This woman was born from the belly of a snake, and her single most recounted deed was to create vaginas and breasts on women so that they could give birth without having to be split open (as had formerly been the case), and so that, having given birth and lived, they could nurse their babies. This had formerly been done by men, who had breasts. Jari removed these breasts from the men and gave them the women's beards in exchange. Jari, like Arena and Andena before her, also "went away." Later, she reemerges in "the countries" as Mary, mother of Jesus. Finding a large Byzantine portrait of the Virgin in the back pages of one of his yellowed religious books, Kruni's wizened brother Raia once traced over her elongated features and oval eyes with his arthritic hand and explained to me, "Here, this is Jari. You look at her pointy nose, her long fingers. We call her Jari. You all call her Mary."[6]

Like Jari, the two brothers are held to have gone away to "the countries" and "straightened out" the people there, giving them airplanes, factories, money, and white skin. A common version of the two-brother myth holds that when they had finished "straightening out" the countries, Arena and Andena *kisim wari gen* (became sad) and wanted to return to Papua New Guinea to "straighten out" the people there. They were prevented from doing this by the Australians, who didn't want Papua New Guineans to have the same knowledge, power, and skin as themselves.

That priests and other white people know about Arena and Andena, whom they call Cain and Abel, is proof to the villagers that their myths are accurate. And that Arena and Andena did, in fact, know about factories and so forth, is not doubted – the butt of their rifle and their "old car" are widely rumored and believed to still be preserved in Bangapura, a feared Ramu village that no villager except Agrana has ever seen.

The Arena–Andena myth is a particularly significant one in Gapun because it serves as a kind of framework into which information about the outside world is fitted. Upon hearing from me about subways, for example, Kruni nodded his head knowingly and looked around expansively at the other man seated in the men's house. "See," he intoned solemnly, "Andena knew how to dig tunnels under the ground. He had this power. He went and gave this power to the countries." In addition to providing the villagers with explanations for various aspects of the modern world, the two-brother myth also reinforces the villagers' perceptions of Papua New Guinea as what Kruni, in his explanation of "coming up," called "the last country" (Text 1.3; line 10).

Papua New Guinea as "the last country" has both geographical and developmental connotations. All villagers in Gapun, even those who have been to school for six years, have an image of the world as linear and flat. They know the names of some of the countries that make up the world, and even before World War II they had heard of Germany, England, and "*Kongkong.*" During the war, Gapuners learned of the existance of Japan, Australia, America, and India (a few village men saw some of the over 5,000 Indians that the Japanese had brought to Papua New Guinea as laborers during their occupation). Since World War II, the villagers have understood that there are "*planti ol kantri tumas*" (a great number of countries). Most of them can name "*Indonesia,*" "*Sina,*" "*Pilipin,*" "*Sautamerika,*" "*Rusia,*" "*Aprika,*" and "*Yurop*" as countries that exist together with Papua New Guinea. And in the villagers' conception of the world, these countries are all strung out in a line moving outward from Papua New Guinea ("the last country") to "*Beljum,*" which a Belgian missionary apparently once told some villagers was the "*namba wan kantri,*" an ambiguous phrase in Tok Pisin that can mean either "the best country" or "the first country." The villagers chose the latter interpretation.

Distance between Papua New Guinea and other countries is known roughly, and is expressed in phrases like "*klostu liklik*" (kind of close) or "*longwe tumas*" (extremely far). That Germans, whose country is known to be "*longwe tru*" (really far away), arrived in Papua New Guinea and colonized it before the Australians, who are "*klostu tru*" (very close), is mysterious and further proof for the villagers that the Australians did indeed prevent the two brothers from returning, and that they really don't want Papua New Guineans to "come up" at all.[7]

It is in the sense of "coming up" that the villagers also consider that they are "the last country." Everyone in Gapun "knows" that all other

Desire to be advanced / be industrialized

countries in the world are free from sorcery and have the factories, corrugated-iron houses, and tinned food that Kruni listed in his explanation of *kamap*. Only Papua New Guinea is left. The problem that the villagers in Gapun spend an enormous amount of time considering and elaborating is, then: How do we get what everybody else already has?

As Kruni indicates in his definition of "coming up," the solution to that problem is primarily religious. He echoes the opinions of all the villagers when he says that the basic reason for the gross disparity between Papua New Guinea and everywhere else is that "We're the only ones who don't have faith" (Text 1.3; lines 2–3). Gapun, the villagers frequently remind one another, is a *"kristen komuniti"* (Christian community) where everyone considers him- or herself to be a "Christian man/woman." But despite the fact that the villagers dutifully congregate every Sunday in their weatherworn *haus lotu* (church) and listen to a forty-minute mass said by Sopak's brother Ambuli, neither Kruni nor anyone else in Gapun considers that the villagers "have faith." People in the village aren't *wanbel* (cooperative), they tell each other. All everyone in Gapun ever does is "get angry, fight, swear, steal, lie, and talk behind people's backs." It is this kind of behavior, more than anything else, that the villagers portray as the obstacle to "coming up." If only everyone would just *tainim bel* (change their attitudes/become truly Christian), and if only women like Sake and Sopak would stop being so *bikhed* (stubborn, strong-willed), so the rhetoric goes, then everyone in Gapun could *kamap*.

Because of its essentially religious meaning, the villagers in Gapun do not see development as a process that they themselves can bring about in any concrete way. Hard work and the sales of large amounts of coffee beans or copra are constantly pushed by men in the men's house as an important ingredient in the "coming up" of the village, but everyone understands that even if they earn a lot of cash, the factories that manufacture the money and other goods that they have their eye on will still be out of their grasp. These things, the true goals of "coming up," will not be produced by the villagers themselves, but rather, they will one day appear as the reward for the villagers' piety and faith. For the villagers, then, "coming up" is not envisaged so much as a process, but as a sudden metamorphosis, a miraculous transmutation – of their bush-material houses into corrugated-iron blocks, of their swampy land into a webwork of highways, of their jungle food into rice and *tinpis* and Nescafé instant coffee, and of their black skins, most significantly, into white.

2. Language and talk in the village

Kem's Sanae-born wife, Wandi, is sitting cross-legged on her veranda, suckling her baby and chewing a large red wad of betel nut. She has been talking about language, contrasting her vernacular language, Adjora, with that of the Gapun villagers.

Text 2.1

You know [she explains, wiping a stream of crimson spittle from her chin with the back of her hand], our vernacular, what we speak in Sanae, it isn't hard. It's easy. We call everything straight. Things aren't hidden in our language. Everything is outside, it's there, just say it. Our language is really big – it goes all the way to the Ramu. One language, our language. It's all "*Sabu*" [Adjora]. Now Gapun, poor thing, no. There isn't any other village that speaks their language. Just them. And, too, their language is really hard. If you want to talk to a man, you have to talk to him in the men's language. You'll say "*wetet*" (come) and he'll *harim* (hear/understand) you and he'll come. Women, too. If you want to talk to a woman you have to say it straight in the women's language. "*Wetak*" (come), you have to say it like that. If you don't, the woman won't listen to (*harim*) you. It's too much for me. Gapun's language has all sorts of corners. Everything is inside, hiding. That's why I haven't really learned their language. I came here a long time ago and have stayed, but I've never really learned their language. I can understand it, but when I answer someone, I answer them in my language or in Tok Pisin. I can't speak their language. My tongue gets all hard.

The vernacular spoken by the villagers of Gapun is a language that they call *Taiap mer* (Taiap language). They are, as Wandi indicates, the only ones who speak this language, and in 1987, the total number of fluent Taiap speakers was exactly eighty-nine. By anyone's standards, this is a small language.[1] Not only is Taiap a small language, however, it also appears to be an isolate. The language has few morphological or lexical similarities with any of the other languages spoken around it, and from a linguistic point of view, Taiap is as different from the neighboring languages of Kopar and Adjora as Greek is different from Russian and Swedish (Map 3).

Taiap and these neighboring languages, Kopar and Adjora, are all

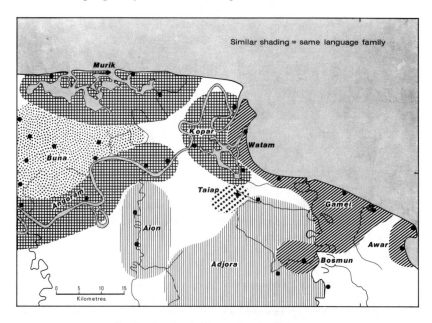

Map 3. Language distribution in the lower Sepik and Ramu regions.

what linguists working in Melanesia have come to call "Papuan languages." Papuan languages are spoken across the entire island of New
Guinea and on a few nearby islands. Although geographically limited,
they number over 700 and make up about ⅕ of the world's total number
of languages. The term "Papuan" languages deserves a short comment
because its meaning is rather unusual within linguistics. Usually, languages classified under the same rubric can all be traced back to a
common ancestral language. Thus, Austronesian languages, which number about 300 in Melanesia, are all descended from a common ancestral
language called Proto-Austronesian, spoken some 6,000 years ago. Papuan languages, however, are not related in this way. The rubric itself
is a kind of geographically based basket category into which all languages
spoken in Melanesia that are not Austronesian have been placed. There
is no "Proto-Papuan" language, and as far as is currently known, the
over sixty different language families that make up the Papuan group
may not be related to one another at all.[2]

The majority of languages spoken in the lower Sepik and Ramu river
basins, where Gapun is located, have been classified as belonging to the
Sepik–Ramu branch of Papuan languages. This is also the language
family into which Taiap was tentatively fitted by the Australian linguist

D. Laycock in 1973. On the basis of a short word list and a few verb paradigms that he gathered from two Taiap speakers in the village of Wongan during a fieldtrip in the early 1970s, Laycock observed that Taiap had certain resemblances to languages that he had classified under the rubric of the Sepik–Ramu phylum. For example, Taiap has a basic Sepik–Ramu phonological system (consisting of six vowels and fourteen consonants); like other Sepik–Ramu languages, Taiap usually places the verb in the sentence-final position; and again like these other languages, Taiap lacks the special morphological elements, called medial verbs, that are found in some Papuan languages and that express logical and temporal relations between sentences.

But beyond these very general similarities to other languages in the area, Taiap exhibits a number of peculiar grammatical features that led Laycock to classify it as an isolate.[3] The language's lexicon, first of all, is highly distinctive and unlike anything else encountered any-where in Melanesia. And unlike other languages in the area, Taiap employs ergative case marking, which means that it marks the subject of an intransitive verb in the same way (with a case called the ab-solutive, which in Taiap is expressed with a Ø-morpheme) as it marks the undergoer, or object, of a transitive verb. The actors of transitive verbs are marked differently and are inflected with suffixes that signify gender and number (-*ŋi* [masculine, singular], -*yi* [feminine, singular], -*gi* [plural]), for example,

Sɔpak-Ø   *pirɔk*
Sopak-ABSOLUTIVE laughed
'Sopak laughed'
Sɔpak-yi   *mum*   *nitukun*
Sopak-ERGATIVE   sago jelly prepared
'Sopak prepared sago jelly'

Another structural characteristic that clearly separates Taiap from its neighboring languages is its verbal morphology. Verbs in Taiap are constructed agglutinatively; that is to say, a verb is made up by chaining together morphemes that can be separated out by linguists and identified as carrying particular meanings. The fact that verbs are built up in this way means that the information that relatively isolating languages like English must express in an entire sentence can be expressed in Taiap by a single verb. For example, to say 'they are going to tell her,' speakers of Taiap use one verb: *namkrundakana*. This verb can be broken down into the following components:

nam	verb stem "talk"
-kru-	object marker "her" inflected to express a nonreal event (i.e., an event that has not yet occurred or may not occur)
-ndak-	actor marker "they" inflected to express a nonreal event
-ana	aspect marker expressing intention or an action that will occur in the immediate future

This type of verbal morphology is not unusual among Papuan languages. What distinguishes Taiap in relation to its neighboring languages, however, is the relative complexity of this morphology. Languages like Wandi's vernacular Adjora apparently do not inflect their verbs for object, actor, gender, or number.[4] All of these grammatical relations are marked on Taiap verbs, as are a variety of tense, mood and aspect relations, and relations of possession. In addition, Taiap possesses a highly aberrant feature known as discontinuous subject marking, which means that verbs in the language signal their subjects not through a single morphological element, but rather through the combination of two separate and discontinuous elements.[5] These kinds of differences in lexicon, case marking, and verb morphology distinguish Taiap so much from all other vernaculars spoken in the lower Sepik or Ramu area that it seems likely that the language has never been a relative of any of the languages that now surround the village.

The villagers of Gapun sometimes talk about their linguistic uniqueness, and they laugh about the fact that, whereas every other village they know of has "friend" villages (*ol ples bilong poromanim ol*) that speak the same language, Gapun, "poor thing" (*tarangu*), as Wandi says, is "*wanpis*" (lit. one fish or one piece), a loner.

For the villagers of Gapun and their neighbors, who of course know nothing about verb morphology or linguistics, the most significant characteristic about Taiap that sets it apart from all other languages is what Wandi in her remarks referred to as "men's language" and "women's language." If people from other villages know anything at all about Taiap, they know that the language "really" is "two languages": a "woman's" and a "man's." And these villagers are invariably appalled and amazed that a language as little as Taiap should be further "broken in two" in this way. There is a "two-language" mystique surrounding Taiap that is quite strong throughout the entire lower Sepik area. Some residents of neighboring villages even insist that Taiap is really *four* different languages: a man's, a woman's, a boy's, and a girl's.

The reason behind this "two-language" mystique is linguistically very simple. Taiap inflects its verbs for grammatical gender; neighboring languages do not. The way in which villagers who do not know anything at all about the Taiap language are confronted with this gender system is through hearing the imperative forms of intransitive verbs. Villagers throughout the lower Sepik area greatly enjoy knowing smatterings of other languages, which they sometimes use to be funny or to indicate familiarity with other groups. What these smatterings always consist of are what people refer to in Tok Pisin as *autsait tok* (outside talk), that is, single words and short commands that can be produced and understood without any deep knowledge of the language. Villagers in Gapun sometimes pass the time by testing each other's knowledge of foreign words for pig, dog, tobacco, sago jelly, and, inevitably, betel nut. Foreign imperatives for commands such as come, go, sit down, or talk are also frequently known by villagers who have only very slight contact with groups who speak those languages. Similarly, men and women from places like Watam or Sanae who know no Taiap appear to regard the language as slightly exotic, and in the same way that English speakers wishing to appear mysterious or esoteric may sometimes choose to pepper their speech with a word or phrase in French or some other foreign language, so do people from these villages occasionally add spice to their speech by inserting short formulaic phrases in Taiap, like *minjikɛ wakarɛ* ([I don't have] no betel nut).

People from other villages who come to Gapun for some reason, or who meet Gapun villagers in the settlements of Angoram or Marienberg, often quiz them at one point or another about what they call certain common objects like tobacco or betel nut, and they ask villagers how they tell people to go, come, sit, or talk. It is the forms of these imperatives that confound Gapun's neighbors because Taiap appears to be the only language in the lower Sepik region that marks gender on the second person singular forms of imperative intransitive verbs.

	Said to a man	*Said to a woman*
you come!	wɛ-tɛt	wɛ-tak
you go!	ɔ-tɛt	ɔ-tak
you talk!	nam-tɛt	nam-tak
you sit!	tutɔ-tɛt	tutɔ-tak

This system is very straightforward and uncomplicated, but when villagers who in their vernaculars use only one imperative form for both sexes become confronted with a language in which one must know two different forms to say exactly the same thing, they react with surprise and incomprehension. In this way, the "two-language" myth about Taiap gets perpetuated throughout the lower Sepik. And because the language really is "two languages" (or four, depending on whom one speaks to), Taiap is held by its neighbors to be an exceptionally "hard" language.

The Gapun villagers themselves accept this definition of Taiap as "broken in two," and they are, in fact, the first to describe their vernacular using Wandi's formulation that "if you talk to a man you have to talk to him in the men's language; if you talk to a woman, you have to talk to her in the women's language." On this basis, the villagers can agree with everyone else that their language is indeed "hard." This is a difficult concession to make entirely, however, given the symbolic weight carried by language in the lower Sepik and Ramu areas. Characterizations of language throughout this region are taken to be characterizations of the speakers of those languages. There is an isomorphism between language and identity that makes it almost impossible for anyone to ever describe his or her vernacular language as "hard." Wandi is typical here, and she goes to some lengths to stress that her own vernacular is "easy," qualifying this by saying that in Adjora, "everything" is called "straight," it's all "outside," nothing is "hidden." Taiap, on the other hand, is a "really hard" language. This implies, as Wandi explicitly remarks, that the language itself is crooked; it has "all sorts of corners." Furthermore, what is expressed by the language is all "inside," it is "hiding." The unflattering and even sinister implications of this kind of characterization do not escape the villagers, and when they are in the presence of men and women from other villages, Gapuners generally do not concede that their language is as hard and mysterious as others believe it to be. They do agree, however, even privately among themselves, that Taiap's "two-language" structure makes it *hat liklik* (a little bit hard), that is, harder than any other language they know anything about.

Tok Pisin and shift

1914 ⇐

In the village, the Taiap language coexists with the vernacular languages Adjora (spoken sometimes by Wandi and visitors from Sanae), Kopar (spoken sometimes by several in-married women and visitors from Wongan),[6] and most importantly, with Tok Pisin. Whereas both Adjora and Kopar have probably existed in Gapun as second or third languages for a very long time, the history of Tok Pisin in the village is relatively brief. Tok Pisin did not enter Gapun until sometime after 1914. A year or so before the outbreak of the First World War, word reached the villagers that white men were in the area searching for young men to work for them. These white men were German labor recruiters, and the men they were looking for were destined to be shipped off to the plantations that the Germans had established along the Madang coast and on various distant islands. Hearing about the presence of the recruiters, two adventurous young men from Gapun traveled to find them and work for them. These men were Kruni and Raia's father, Aiarpa, and Sopak's father, Waiki.

At this time, the villagers of Gapun knew next to nothing about white people. There had been only one brief contact between a villager and whites prior to this, and that had occurred several years previously, when a Gapun man named Ndair journeyed to the coastal village of Kaian to see for himself the white people he had been hearing rumors about and to exchange four large yams for a steel adze. When Aiarpa and Waiki went off to "sign on" as contracted laborers, all that was known for certain of white people was that they had desirable material goods that the villagers could acquire through trade or, now, it would seem, through labor.

Aiarpa and Waiki resisted the protests of their relatives and friends – who believed that the two men were going off to meet certain death – and they left with the recruiters. They were taken away to a copra plantation near the German settlement of Kokopo, located near the town of Rabaul on the island of New Britain. They remained on this plantation for at least three years, and during their time on the plantation they apparently witnessed the Australian occupation of German possessions at the outbreak of World War I. Raia recalls his father describing how the "*Inglis*" (that is, the Australians) rounded up the Germans and "put them into big crates. They put them inside, nailed them shut, and sent the Germans back to their country."

Sometime after the Australian takeover of German New Guinea, Aiarpa and Waiki were returned to Gapun. According to the stories that have survived them, the two men arrived triumphantly in the village, carrying with them the fruits of their labor: Each man had a small wooden patrol box filled with "cargo" (*kago*), i.e., steel tools, bolts of cloth, European tobacco, and small amounts of money. Even more impressive and long-lasting than this cargo were the stories that Aiarpa and Waiki recounted about their experiences on the plantation. Most impressive of all was the new language that the men had acquired while working for the white men.[7]

This language was Tok Pisin or, rather, the fledgling form of Tok Pisin being spoken at the time.[8] Like most other Melanesian groups did initially, everyone in Gapun, including Aiarpa and Waiki, assumed that Tok Pisin was the *tok ples,* the vernacular, of white people.[9] And like the other things that Aiarpa and Waiki had acquired from white people during their years on the plantation, the language of the white man entered the village's redistributive networks: Aiarpa and Waiki immediately set about sharing the language with their peers. The two men appear to have regarded Tok Pisin as a particularly valuable acquisition.

Several years after they had returned to Gapun, for example, a group of Australian labor recruiters suddenly appeared in the village. This was the first time any white person had actually come inside Gapun, and the villagers, the vast majority of whom had never before seen anyone with white skin, fled terrified into the jungle. The only ones who did not run away were Waiki, Aiarpa, and a few old men and women who had not been able to escape quickly enough. Seeing the village thus deserted, the recruiters resorted to what probably was a well-tested technique of persuasion: They gathered together the old people still left in the village and prevented them from slipping off into the jungle. They then waited until the anxious screams of these old people brought back a few young men. At that point, Aiarpa and Waiki apparently tried to convince a few young men to go off with the recruiters by telling them that, if they went, they would learn Tok Pisin. "We've taught you [some Tok Pisin]," they are said to have told the men, "but you don't know it good. If you go away to the plantation, you'll learn Tok Pisin well." Five men acquiesced and left with the recruiters.

A pattern of learning Tok Pisin thus became established in Gapun. Young men acquired basic knowledge of the language in the village; they then went off to work as contracted laborers to "learn Tok Pisin well"; and later, upon returning to the village, they taught the language to the young men who had not yet gone away. By 1942, when the Japanese bombed the town of Rabaul, thus drawing New Guinea into the Second World War, 13 village men (out of a total adult male population of, perhaps, 25) had spent three or more years away as plantation workers, and 7 of these had returned to Gapun.[10] Tok Pisin was being actively used in inter- and intravillage interactions between men, and the language was even being passed on to male youths. Kruni remembers that, as adolescents in the 1930s, he and his peers began learning Tok Pisin from the speech of his father Aiarpa and other men:

The Fathers told us, they called the names of things – betel nut, betel pepper, whatever – they called the names for us in Tok Pisin. And they told us to bring that thing, go, come, give it, put it, like that. And they spoke Tok Pisin, spoke it among themselves. They spoke it to men from Wongan, Watam, and we heard it. Then later we ourselves went away to work [on plantations] and we all learned it now.[11]

It was not until after the Second World War, however, that Tok Pisin "came up big" (*kamap bikpela*) in Gapun. Before the war, the language had been a male possession, acquired as a foreign language in adulthood or late childhood. After the war, Tok Pisin began to be used by females, and the age at which it was acquired began to drop. Although there are no written records in Gapun documenting the history of Tok Pisin's incorporation into the village, much of that history can be inferred from the present-day language capabilities of the men, women, and children now living in the village. The languages known by these villagers are shown in Table 2.1.

Like the speakers of other comparably small vernaculars throughout Melanesia, the villagers of Gapun command a good number of languages.[12] Virtually everyone over the age of 10 speaks at least two languages and understands at least one more. Multilingualism reaches a peak among the oldest generation of men, one of whom (Kruni's brother Raia) speaks five languages and has a good passive understanding of one more. This generation of men represents the traditional cultural ideal. Traditionally, multilingualism was both highly valued and necessary in Gapun. Because of the village's small size and the supposedly "hard" nature of its vernacular, very few outsiders ever learned Taiap. Before the advent of Tok Pisin as a regional lingua franca, this meant that Gapuners, in order to communicate with their neighbors, had to learn other vernaculars. The ability to do this was considered an integral part of Taiap identity. Senior men sometimes recount the tale of Kambedagam, the ancestral deity who founded Gapun. In their descriptions of Kambedagam, these men emphasize that he was unlike the ancestral founding deities of other villages in that he was multilingual. Stressing this, the men proudly note how they, by being multilingual, still follow "the way" established by Kambedagam.

"The way of Kambedagam" is not as apparent in the language capabilities of the men who succeed the village's oldest men in Generation II. With three exceptions, men's active competence in vernacular languages is reduced here to the point where they command only their own vernacular and Tok Pisin. Men in this generation still maintain a receptive knowledge of Kopar and, to a somewhat lesser extent, Adjora, but geographically distant languages like Watam and Bien (i.e., Angoram) have disappeared completely.

It is the women in this generation who, to a larger extent than their husbands, maintain the traditional pattern of vernacular multilingualism. Because there was only one senior woman alive in Gapun in 1987, it is not evident from Table 2.1 that in traditional times, village women, too, spoke at least either Kopar or Adjora in addition to Taiap.[13] Women in Generation II continue this pattern, and although they do not know any languages unknown to men, more women are actively multilingual than are men. Sopak, in her early forties, for example, speaks Adjora, whereas her older brother Kawi and her husband, Mone, only understand it. Differences like this directly reflect the history of Tok Pisin's incorporation into the village. Having been acquired in all-male contexts on the plantations, and having been brought back to the village by men,

Table 2.1. *Languages known by villagers living in Gapun in 1987*

Men			Women		
Age	Languages spoken	Understood	Age	Languages spoken	Understood
		Generation I			
65	T, A, K, TP	B	60+	T	A, K, TP
60+	T, A, K, TP	B, W			
60	T, A, K, TP	W			
55+	T, A, K, B, TP	W			
55+	T, K, W, TP	A, M			
50	T, K, TP	A, B			
		Generation II			
48	T, A, TP	K	43	A, TP	T, K
47	T, A, K, TP	W	43	T, A, K, TP	
42	T, TP	K, A	40	T, A, K, TP	
40	T, TP	K, A	38	T, A, K, TP	
40	T, TP	K, A	37	T, A, K	TP
40	T, A, K, TP		35	T, A, K, TP	
37	T, TP	K	35	T, P, TP	
37	T, TP	K, A	34	T, TP	K, A
36	T, TP	K, A, P	33	T, TP	K, A
34	Bu, TP	T	33	P, TP	T
34	T, TP	K	32	T, TP	K, A
30	T, TP	K	28	K, TP	T
26	Bu, TP	T	27	T, K, TP	
25	T, TP	K, A			
		Generation III			
23	T, TP	K	22	T, TP	K
22	T, TP	K, A	20	T, TP	
19	T, TP	K	19	T, K, TP	
18	T, K, TP	A	19	T, TP	K
16	T, TP	K	18	T, TP	K
14	T, TP	K	18	T, A, TP	K
14	T, TP	K	16	T, TP	K
14	TP	T	16	T, TP	K
14	T, TP	K	16	T, TP	K
14	T, TP	K	14	T, TP	K, A
13	T, TP	K	13	T, TP	K
12	TP	T	13	T, TP	K
12	T, TP	K	12	T, TP	K, A
10	T, TP		12	T, TP	K
10	T, TP	K	10	TP	T
			10	T, TP	

Table 2.1. (*cont.*)

	Men			Women	
Age	Languages spoken	Understood	Age	Languages spoken	Understood
		Generation IV			
9	TP	T	9	TP	T, A
9	TP	T	9	TP	T, K
8	TP	T	8	TP	T
8	TP	T	8	TP	T
8	TP	T	8	TP	T
7	TP		7	TP	T, A
5	TP		7	TP	T
5	TP		6	TP	T
4	TP		6	TP	T
4	TP		4	TP	
3	TP	?	4	TP	T
2	TP	?	4	TP	?
1	TP		4	TP	?
1	TP		3	TP	
			2	TP	?
			2	TP	

Note: Men and women in Generation II who do not actively speak Taiap are in-married from other villages.

Key: T = Taiap   TP = Tok Pisin   W = Watam
      A = Adjora   M = Murik   B = Bien (Angoram)
      K = Kopar   Bu = Buna   P = Pankin (Aion)

Tok Pisin remained a male language during the first decades of its absorption into the village verbal repertoire. This pattern is a familiar one in Papua New Guinea, and it is well known that languages learned on plantations first become established among men in a community before women begin to learn them. In some Melanesian communities, the associations between males and Tok Pisin are so strongly upheld that women have been observed to be "actively hindered" from learning the language.[14] No such extreme situation appears to have ever existed in Gapun, but regardless, no woman seems to have spoken or understood Tok Pisin before the 1940s, and those older women who did eventually learn the language did so after World War II.

    The Second World War and the years immediately following it brought a number of major changes to the village that contributed toward the spread of Tok Pisin. One of the most profound changes in Gapun as a result of the war was demographic: Five men and twelve women died during the war. This was at least 40 percent of the village pre-war adult population. The deaths of so many people, many of them elderly, left Gapun without a large number of non-Tok Pisin speakers. The overwhelming majority of villagers who survived the war had some knowledge of Tok Pisin, and many of the surviving men were relatively fluent speakers of the language.

2nd reason Another reason for the consolidation of Tok Pisin in Gapun at this time was the village conversion to Christianity. Gapuners had known about Christianity since at least the 1930s, but it was not until after World War II that any priest began making regular trips to the village, which was extremely difficult to reach at the time. Built far away from the nearest navigable creek, getting to Gapun entailed an arduous three- to five-hour trek through swamps often filled with chest-deep water and mud.[15] The first priest to make this journey on a semiregular basis was a Catholic missionary named H. Morin. He began coming to Gapun in the late 1940s, and by the mid-1950s, twenty-five villagers had been baptized. All talk about Christianity was conducted in Tok Pisin, and villagers learned to recite prayers, sing hymns, and listen to mass said in that language. Men and women themselves specifically name the visits of Father Morin and subsequent priests as one of the main reasons why Tok Pisin became consolidated in Gapun at this time.

3rd reason A final reason why Tok Pisin became so integrated into village verbal repertoires after the war was that during the early 1950s, virtually every single unmarried male in Gapun in his late teens or twenties (a total of 14 out of perhaps 17 or 18 young men) spent at least a year working as a contracted laborer on plantations on the islands of New Britain or New Ireland, as shiphands, or as road-workers in the town of Lae. These men all perfected their knowledge of Tok Pisin during this time, and when they later returned to the village, they continued the pattern established by their fathers of using that language in their interactions with one another and with their children.

Each of these changes resulted in more Tok Pisin being used in more contexts by more people in the village. Tok Pisin "came up big," as the villagers say, and this "bigness" made it available to women and girls, who began incorporating it into their own communicative repertoires. Once during a conversation concerning how women now in their thirties and forties learned Tok Pisin, Sopak summed up the postwar linguistic situation by declaring:

We just know it. Because Tok Pisin had come up big. After the war Tok Pisin wasn't scarce anymore (*i nomoa dia*). It was outside, it became like our vernacular. It wasn't scarce. And all we women in the village now, we're all born after the war. We grew up with Tok Pisin.

But even though females began using Tok Pisin after the war, large numbers of women and girls in other villages (especially Sanae) still spoke no Tok Pisin. So in their talk with neighboring villagers, in-married wives, and their own older female relatives, women continued to be dependent on vernacular languages long after men had already begun to use Tok Pisin in similar contexts.

It is in the following generation that women shift away from vernacular multilingualism to bilingualism in Tok Pisin and Taiap and passive competence in another vernacular (again, mostly Kopar). Women in general are thus lagging behind men in their language shift to Tok Pisin, exhibiting a pattern that is the reverse of that which is often found in language-shift situations in Europe.[16] This gender-based lag is even evident among the latest generation of children in the village. Here, a number of girls who do not actively command the vernacular at least sometimes use formulaic phrases and responses in their play and, occasionally, in their interactions with adults. No boy under 10 does this.

What stands out most clearly when the villagers' language competencies are considered from the perspective of a villagewide overview is that the addition of Tok Pisin into the villagers' language repertoires has resulted in the loss of other languages. Since the introduction of Tok Pisin into the village in the early decades of this century, the traditional pattern of multilingualism has rapidly lost ground with each successive generation. Tok Pisin has been incorporated into the villagers' linguistic repertoire first at the expense of other village vernaculars and now, ultimately, at the expense of the villagers' own vernacular. There has been a steady reduction in the number of languages that the villagers command, and the current trend is toward monolingualism in Tok Pisin. Although the vernacular remains in use among those villagers who learned it as children, a shift in acquisition patterns has occurred in recent years: For the first time ever, children born and raised in Gapun are not acquiring Taiap as their first language. As of 1987, no village child under 10 actively commanded the vernacular, and some of the youngest children (under 8) do not even possess a good passive knowledge of Taiap.

Awareness of shift

Villagers share an awareness that young children do not actively command the vernacular, but the salience of this awareness is not high. Very occasionally, big men like Raia or Kruni may suddenly shout at children who are laughing too loudly or playing too boisterously in front of the men's house that "You're all stupid in the vernacular! The vernacular of your ancestors!" Such explosions are more an expression of the men's general irritation than they are an attempt to influence the children's language production. Characteristic of these outbursts is that they are in Tok Pisin, and that they occur only when the big men are irritated because no one has thought to bring them dinner or when they are stressed because of a sickness or death in the village. Other reactions to children's lack of productive competence in the vernacular are more fatalistic. Tambong's cheerful agreement with her daughter that Tok Pisin is nowadays the "vernacular" of children (quoted as an epigraph to this book) exemplifies the matter-of-fact thoughts held by most villagers about their children's lack of competence in Taiap.

Beyond these kinds of comments, the current language situation in the village is not dwelled on or talked about. And even though the linguistic inabilities of village children in the vernacular are sometimes briefly focused upon in the speech of big men and others, men and women in Gapun rarely describe the situation from the perspective of a villagewide overview. It is highly unusual for villagers to consider the language situation in Gapun in terms of reduction and death. On a short stroll from one end of the village to the other, a villager might overhear Bit chatting in Taiap with Samek's brother's wife from Wongan, who responds in Kopar; Paso threatening her 6-year-old daughter, Kiring, in rapid spurts of Taiap and Tok Pisin; Kruni and Kem entertaining visitors from Watam in the men's house in a combination of Tok Pisin and the vernacular of the visitors; Sake's sister-in-law Tambong gossiping with her half-brother in Kopar, pausing to shout at her 4-year-old son in Tok Pisin to get out from underneath a coconut palm; Wandi and Sopak recounting a scandal about someone in Adjora; and Agrana and Raia, bent over carvings, muttering to one another in an idiosyncratic mixture of Tok Pisin, Taiap, Kopar, and Adjora. Immersed in this kind of multilingual cacophony, villagers have little occasion to consider their language situation as one characterized by reduced language competencies and change in a specific direction. Instead, from the perspective of individual villagers, communication in Gapun is richly varied and in a state of continual flux between different speakers and different languages.

Using languages in the village

The impression of variety and linguistic flux is continually re-created for the villagers by the way in which they use their languages in their talk to one another. Unlike some communities that have been described by linguists,[17] in Gapun, no stigma is attached to switching between languages within a single stretch of discourse, an utterance, or a constituent, and speakers make extensive use of both intra- and intersentential code-switching.

The single most important factor influencing villagers' language choice is their conversational partner. Gapuners have a strong sense of linguistic accommodation, and talk in most social situations is carefully monitored by all present. The topics and opinions that a person converses about with others are all finely adjusted to suit the general mood and opinions of those within hearing range. Accommodation of this type often extends to choice of language. Villagers are keen to accommodate others linguistically, and those who know other vernacular languages frequently use them, in stretches at least, when talking to men and women from other villages.

Ways in which vernacular multilingualism interacts with Tok Pisin can be seen in the following interaction, which took place in Kruni's men's house. Seated on the floor with a number of other men, Kruni has just heard a visiting man from Singrin (like Wongan, a Kopar-speaking village) call into the house in Tok Pisin for two men to leave and follow him somewhere. As one man gets up to leave, Kruni asks aloud which other man the Singrin man was calling to:

Text 2.2

Kruni:	*Mbi mɛnandi?*	K:	Who else?
Guyam:	*Em ia. Sɔŋɔr ia.*	G:	Him. Songor.
Kruni:	*Eh. Ah. Aria. Mi maŋgaw-* *na. Yu go pastaim. Ndi* *kawɔ amana.*	K:	Eh. Ah. OK. You go. You go then. Put that thing here.

Even though the Singrin man who called into the men's house to summon the two men spoke in Tok Pisin, Kruni asks his question in the Kopar language. His brother-in-law Guyam answers him in Tok Pisin, pointing to the other man, Songor, who had been summoned. Kruni then turns to Songor and addresses him in Kopar (*Mi maŋgawna*). Songor is a man from Sanae, however, and he does not in fact know Kopar. In telling Songor "You go" in Kopar, Kruni seems to be using language choice as a subtle way of speaking not to Songor, but to the Singrin man who had summoned him away from the men's house. Thus, although he is ostensibly talking to Songor, what Kruni appears to be doing here is reminding everyone present (especially the Singrin man who summoned Songor) that they are in his men's house and should defer to him. In choosing to speak to Songor in a language he doesn't understand, Kruni is giving permission to the Singrin man to take Songor *(handwritten margin note: Reasons for code Switching (examples))*

away from his men's house for a few minutes. Having told Songor to go in the Kopar language, Kruni repeats his utterance in Tok Pisin. Finally, he tells Songor to leave his basket while he goes, saying this in Songor's vernacular, Adjora.

In switching between languages in this way, Kruni is displaying a verbal pattern that is characteristic of the speech used by all but the youngest members of the village. Although not all villagers command additional vernaculars and, consequently, cannot switch between such languages with Kruni's dexterity, virtually everyone in Gapun over the age of 10 can code-switch between Taiap and Tok Pisin, and they do this continually. Villagers can separate Taiap and Tok Pisin, and they do so when speaking to people from other villages. But when they speak among themselves, villagers see no reason to keep the two languages separate. Taiap and Tok Pisin are constantly interspliced.

In their conversations with one another, Gapuners routinely incorporate elements from one language into the other within one and the same sentence. Certain words, especially nominals denoting everyday items such as betel nut, sago, fire, basket, water, dog, chicken, coconut, and so on are likely to be named in the vernacular even if the rest of the utterance is in Tok Pisin; for example,

Text 2.3

Painim wanem long sapwar bilong mi?!
'What are you looking for in my basket?!'

Text 2.4

Igo kisim airŋa tin bilong mi i kam.
'Go fetch my lime-tin and bring it.'

Most common objects like these also have equivalents in Tok Pisin, however, and these are sometimes used, even in vernacular utterances:

Text 2.5

ŋa basket-nɨ prukaku wakarɛ.
'I'm not working on a basket.'

Villagers also frequently insert Tok Pisin verbs into their vernacular utterances and inflect them with Taiap morphology:

Text 2.6

Masitɔ warak-a-kawt-rɛ,   yu   pasim maus   -aw-tɛt.
Masito talk-be-HAB-when/if, you   shut   mouth   be-2SG:IMPER
                'When Masito talks, you shut up!'

Text 2.7

ŋi Pɔtɔ-rɛ   *ɔ-ki-nɛt-a,*   *hatwok-ki-nɛt.*
He Wongan-LOC go-IRR-S:3SGmasc-CONJ hard work-IRR-S:3SGmasc
                  'He will go to Wongan and work hard.'

More rarely, villagers even affix vernacular verbal morphology to a Tok Pisin verb in a Tok Pisin utterance:

Text 2.8·

Yu kaikai-api,   *bai mipela go.*
You eat-CONSEC FUT 1PL   go
                  'After you've eaten, we'll go.'

Text 2.9

Yu wok. Yu wok. No ken toktok planti yu-yi   wokim wok tasol.
You work. You work. NEG can talk plenty you-ERG work work just.
      'You work. You work. You can't complain, just you do the work.'

Villagers do not reflect on the fact that they switch between languages in this way, and code-switching behavior as such is never spoken about. When pressed as to why they "change languages" as much as they do, the only explanation that anyone could come up with was a languid "If Tok Pisin comes to your mouth, you use Tok Pisin. If Taiap comes to your mouth, you use Taiap." Despite the fact that they have little to say about the subject, however, it soon becomes very clear to an observer that a main reason why the villagers switch between their languages the way they do is because of the great variety of rhetorical effects that can be achieved through code-switching. Kruni's nimble switch to the Kopar language to cast talk at the Singrin man without directly addressing him (Text 2.2) exemplifies only one of the many stylistic functions that code-switching is understood to be able to accomplish in the village.

One extremely common use of code-switching in Gapun involves self-repetition, where a speaker says one thing in one language and then repeats the same thing in another language. This type of repetition often serves to emphasize a command or a warning:

Text 2.10

Mother to daughter, who is playing with a baby:
ɔretukun. Ɛargarana. ɔretukun. LUSIM EM! Ɛnɛ nda tawairunak.
'Let her alone. She better not cry. Let her alone. LET HER ALONE! I'm gonna thump you now.'

Text 2.11

*Kisim buai bilong mi ikam. Harim ah? Kisim buai bilong mi ikam. ŋAŋAN
MINJIKƐ KUKUWƐ! KAKAT!*

'Bring my betel nut. Do you hear? Bring my betelnut. BRING MY BETELNUT!
HURRY UP!'

In the villagers' speech patterns, emphatic code-switching of this nature can occur either to or from the vernacular. Thus, it is not the case
that Tok Pisin, say, has more threatening connotations than the vernacular.[18] The emphasis or, in the examples given above, the threat,
lies in the *fact* of the code-switch, not the direction of the switch.

Another use of repetition is to convey emphatic agreement with a
previous speaker. In using two languages, agreement of this type can
be stretched to considerable lengths, as is evident in the following extract
from a conversation in Kruni's men's house concerning a rumor that
Sanae villagers had threatened a man from Wongan with sorcery:

Text 2.12

Kruni:	*I no gutpela.*	Kr:	That's not good.
Guyam:	*Ɛŋgɔn wakarɛ.*	G:	It's not good.
Agrana:	*Rabis.*	A:	Rubbish.
Kem:	*Supwaspwa ŋayar.*	K:	Truly bad.
Marame:	*Tru ia.*	M:	That's true.

In addition to repetition, code-switching in Gapun is also used to hotly
deny what a speaker experiences as an accusation:

Text 2.13

Sake (35 years) to her sister Jari (19 years):

Sake:	*Minjikɛ ana?!*	S:	Where's the betel nut?
	ŋaŋan minjikɛ ana?!		Where's my betel nut?!
Jari:	*Mi no save long*	J:	I don't know about
	minjikɛ bilong yu!		your betel nut!

Text 2.14

Erapo (45 years) to her daughter Tapu (23 years):

Erapo:	*Yu save mekim ol*	E:	You're always doing
	kainkain pasin. Mi les.		bad things. I'm sick of it.
Tapu:	*Mai! Yu tɔwɛr awtak!*	T:	Enough! You shut up!

Other ways villagers use code-switching are in rendering quotations (Text 2.15), interrupting a speaker and changing the topic (Text 2.16), and gaining the floor (Text 2.17):

Text 2.15

<u>*ŋi/Murimatɔmin Agrana nandɛnikɛ namnəŋgin:* "*Yu save lainim ol pikinini long poisin ia*"?</u>

<u>Did he/Muri's husband say to Agrana: "You teach the kids about sorcery"?</u>

Text 2.16

Sake: *Ol stilman. Nogat wanpela gutpela pasin i stap long bel bilong ol.*
        Stil tasol i pulap. Wanpela bilong ol i kam   *bai mi tokim em stret . . .*
Jari: <u>*Yu nam tatukun? Kɛm*</u>
    ŋan baranɨ bɔta . . . [continues in Taiap]

Sake: Thieves. There's not a good quality in them. They're full of thievery.
        If one of them comes,   I'm really gonna tell him . . .
Jari: <u>Have you heard? Kem went to his garden</u>
    <u>and . . .</u> [continues in Taiap]

Text 2.17

Kruni: *ŋayi nandɛ namrɨnɛt – pasim maus bilong yupela na harim mi.*
        <u>I'll tell you this</u> – shut your mouths and listen to me.

Still another use to which villagers put code-switching is in creating and highlighting dramatic contrasts. Yuki, a 60-year-old Gapun man who lives in Wongan, used code-switching between Tok Pisin and Taiap in this way when he found occasion to recount the story of his "death" for a number of men in Kruni's men's house:

Text 2.18

Yuki: <u>*Yu, ɛnɛ ambinɨnɨ ŋa ɛnɛ kut ainda? Wasɔnɛta bɔta, nɔŋɔr kiwɔk, ŋa*</u>
    <u>*kakun,*</u> *nau mi stap nau. Mi nogat sik moa. Nau mi stap olgeta, mi*
    winim taim. <u>*ŋa ɛnɛ kut inda.*</u>

Kruni: *Yu hap indai ia.*

Yuki: <u>*ŋa wasɔnɛtəŋa!*</u>

Yuki: <u>You, how is it that I'm alive today? Dying, I went and the woman took</u>
    <u>me and I ate</u> [some enchanted herbs], now I'm alive today. I'm not
    sick anymore. Now I'm completely alright. I'm beating Time. <u>I'm alive</u>
    <u>now.</u>

Kruni: You almost died.

Yuki: <u>I was dead!</u>

Here Yuki code-switches to highlight the drama of his "death," contrasting the fact that he died (in the vernacular) with his recovery (in Tok Pisin). Yuki also code-switches to emphatically complete and sum up his story: (. . . *mi winim taim. ŋa ɛnɛ kut inda/* . . . I'm beating Time. I'm alive now). In responding to Yuki, Kruni switches to Tok Pisin to signal emphatic agreement. But Yuki answers back in the vernacular, lending stress to his denial that he had not merely "almost died" – he was *dead*.

Meanings of language

When villagers like Yuki code-switch between languages, they rely heavily on the juxtaposition of separate codes to carry messages of drama, support, contradiction, etc. But in addition to this kind of rhetorical switching, there is another dimension of language meaning and use in Gapun that has to do with the variety of associations that villages attach to different languages. Like people everywhere, Gapuners evaluate languages in terms of beauty, power, appropriateness, and utility. Their opinions and ideas about different languages have consequences as to who uses the languages and the ways they are used in the village.

Kopar

The most central characteristic of the villagers' ideas about language is the isomorphism they see between language and language groups. Popular stereotypes about the people who speak a language are projected upon the villagers' ideas about the languages themselves. The Kopar vernacular, for example, spoken in Wongan and two other villages, is regarded as a slightly humorous language by Gapuners, who in grouchy moods stereotype people from Wongan as lazy, bumbling, and weak. Kopar is sometimes used by villagers to underscore a situation or story as funny or vaguely ridiculous, and the language is the only one that villagers have explicit aesthetic notions about: They think it sounds funny, as though speakers are "eating tongue" (*kaikai tang*).

Adjora

The villagers' opinions about Adjora, the language spoken in Sanae and the other vernacular with which they regularly come into contact, are highly contrastive to their ideas about Kopar and are linked to differences in social relations between the three groups. In the past, Gapun villagers maintained close ties with both Sanae and Wongan. But they considered themselves (and still think of themselves) as "forest people" (*ol man/meri bilong bus/miriŋa munjɛnum/naŋrɔ*) like the people of Sanae, not "water people" or "beach people" (*ol man/meri bilong wara/ nambis/awinŋa munjɛnum/naŋrɔ*) like the men and women in Wongan. The difference between these two kinds of people is expressed most saliently for the villagers in terms of diet ("water people" subsist mainly on sago and fish; "forest people" eat sago mainly with the meat of wild boars that they hunt with spears and dogs); mode of transportation (canoe vs. walking); techniques of leaching sago pulp ("water people" use an elaborate set-up constructed from the fronds of the sago palm; "forest people" leach the pulp in baskets); and general temperament ("forest people" are said to work harder and be made of tougher stuff than are "water people," who are often portrayed as whiny[19]). The ritual life and mythological traditions of Gapun were also more bound up with the Adjora-language groups, and although villagers had myths and some initiation practices in common with the people of Wongan,[20] the great bulk of their mythology and initiation rituals was shared with Adjora speakers. Even today, when senior men cannot remember a myth or do not know the name of some mythological figure, they defer without hesitation to Sanae and other Ramu villages, claiming that the men there are much more knowlegeable about their myths than they themselves are.

Since World War II, however, and especially since the late 1950s, when the Gapuners relocated their village to its present site, only an hour's trek from the nearest navigable creek, the villagers have increasingly oriented themselves toward the Sepik River and, hence, toward Wongan. This reorientation was prompted partly by the fact that villagers began growing small amounts of cash crops in the 1950s (Chapter 1) and had to transport them out of the village by way of water. Buyers often came only as far as Wongan, so it was up to the villagers to get their crops to Wongan to sell them. For the first time, village men and women learned to paddle canoes, which made travel to and from Wongan relatively easy (before the war, villagers were dependent upon the people of Wongan for transportation to and from that village). The opening of a government-run elementary school in Wongan in 1967 also strengthened the villagers ties with Wongan, for in addition to sending their children to school there, a few Gapun families moved to Wongan to be able to look after the Gapun children there during the week. Marriage between men and women from these two villages (especially between Wongan women and Gapun men) has become very common, and a consistent point of contention between senior men and people in their thirties and younger in Gapun is the large amount of time spent by the latter with their spouses and relatives in Wongan.

As they oriented themselves more closely toward Wongan, Gapuners became increasingly estranged from Adjora speakers. Visits between members of the two villages grew less frequent, and marriages between Gapuners and Sanae villagers all but ceased. Serious ideological alienation also set in. Unlike the villagers of Wongan, who perform no traditional rituals and who have very poor knowledge about, and little interest in, the traditional cosmology, Sanae villagers have a relatively strong sense of tradition. They maintain central aspects of the men's-house cult, such as the building of elaborate men's houses and the playing of the sacred flutes during funerary feasts. Gapuners know this, and because they try to be fervent Christians, their response has been to regard the people of Sanae with suspicion. As a group, the Sanae villagers are regarded as non-Christian and capable of great evil. Every death that occurs in Gapun is inevitably blamed on sorcery from Sanae. Women in particular feel uncomfortable when too many Sanae men are present in Gapun, and pregnant women, fearing that a Sanae man might shoot invisible missiles of sorcery into their bodies and "close" their birth canal, hide inside their houses until the men have gone. Also, despite periodic pressure from the senior men in Gapun, who (setting aside their anxieties over sorcery in this instance) would prefer young village women to marry strong "forest men" from Sanae instead of lazy weaklings from Wongan, no woman in the village would ever consider marrying into Sanae. The village is considered to be a bastion of sorcery.

Fear of the people of Sanae is projected onto the language spoken in Sanae. Gapuners agree that the Adjora language itself is potentially deadly. Adjora is strongly associated with magic and supernatural power. Villagers believe that Adjora-speaking men possess large arsenals of magic chants (*singsing/pɔisirŋa jɛm*) and that these include chants to kill people. It is felt that anyone knowing Adjora has potential access to the magic contained in that language. It is sometimes intimated, for example, that individual senior men in Gapun, almost all of whom speak fluent Adjora and are known to possess a number of chants in the language (most of them healing chants), are at least partly responsible for the death or serious illness of a villager in Gapun or Wongan. On one occasion during a gathering in Kruni's men's house, Sopak's husband, Mone, explicitly asked these senior men not to pass on any of their magic chants, including those used to cure illness, to any of their children. Mone feared that mere knowledge of the words would "make people sick." "When you all die, these chants must die with you," he told Kruni, Raia, and Kem. Everyone present in the men's house agreed with Mone. Raia scoffed at the idea that it would even be possible for young people to learn the chants even if the men wanted to teach them. Underscoring the relationship between the Adjora language and magic, he laughed and asked cynically, "What, our children know the vernacular? They know Adjora, ah?" The associations between Adjora and (evil) magic are a direct cause of the rapid decline in the number of active Adjora speakers in Gapun since World War II (Table 2.1).

Tok Pisin and English

Just as the villagers' perceptions of Adjora speakers have resulted in the contraction of that vernacular in Gapun, so have their attitudes toward those whom they believe to be the speakers of Tok Pisin contributed to the rapid expansion of that language in the village.

Ever since its entry into Gapun with Aiarpa and Waiki, villagers have believed that Tok Pisin was the vernacular of white people. This belief is still widely held, and only in the 1980s – due largely to my own presence in the village and my oft-repeated insistence that people in Sweden really do not know Tok Pisin – have some villagers come to suspect that Tok Pisin is not, in fact, what white men and women speak in "the countries." A new belief that the "true vernacular" (*tok ples tru*) of white people is English has led some enterprising villagers to take a keen interest in somehow acquiring that language. Kruni, for example, always wishing to be in the forefront of development, occasionally talks of traveling to Wongan and asking the schoolteachers there to give him a blackboard and some books so that he can teach himself English in his men's house.

Previously, English was widely regarded as an anomalous language of uncertain value or use. Even those young men and women who have spent six years in the local school in Wongan, where all instruction is in English, tended to hold this view. Unlike the vernaculars and Tok Pisin, English seemed to the villagers to have no native speakers. It existed solely as a language used in the school and, some villagers knew, on the radio. With no native speakers to evaluate, villagers were at a loss to know how to judge the language, and they have reacted to this state of affairs by simply ignoring it. The language has played almost no role in the villagers' understanding of development, white people, or the modern world, and as of 1987, the majority of villagers still had no opinions about English, other than to regard it as vaguely valuable because of its associations with the school.

Tok Pisin, on the other hand, by virtue of its generally accepted status as the vernacular of white people, has acquired a number of very definite associations. The most central of these is that the language, because it is understood to be the tongue spoken in "the countries," is better than any of the vernaculars. The superiority of Tok Pisin is not expressed by the villagers in terms of aesthetics or utility or instrumentality for social mobility, however; rather, Tok Pisin is better because it is more potent. Tok Pisin is powerful in the same sense that Adjora, for the villagers, is powerful.

For both languages, this power derives from the links that the villagers assume between language and nonhuman entities. Words in Gapun are understood to have power, and certain words uttered in certain contexts are seen by the villagers to have the ability to bring about certain outcomes. Words constitute direct links to spirit powers, which are expected to respond in desired ways if the proper words are said in the proper manner. The magic chants that village men know in the Adjora language, for example, are associated with particular ancestors or male cult deities (*tambaran*/m<u>ə</u>rip). These chants are potent and never uttered wantonly, for their power is such that to merely utter the words is to cause something to happen. During a language-eliciting session with Raia, I was once harshly reprimanded when I absentmindedly began whispering to myself the words of a chant to cause pregnancy that I had just copied down from one of the old man's papers. Raia shushed me sharply, pointed to a group of 7-year-old girls playing nearby, and asked angrily if I wanted the girls to become pregnant.

The power of Tok Pisin for the villagers lies in the connections that that language is thought to have with the spirit powers associated with white people. These powers are articulated in the idiom of Christianity, and villagers believe that they may obtain access to and eventually learn to harness the power of the Christian deities by knowing the language through which that power is evoked by priests and other white people.[21]

Taiap

Villagers have little to say about their own language. Apart from occasional remarks about Taiap's "two-language" structure, the people of Gapun find no reason to comment on the village vernacular. Like the rainforest, the village, and villagers' physical selves, Taiap just *is*. For this reason, my initial questions about whether individual villagers "liked" their vernacular were met with blank stares and puzzled expressions. A few villagers volunteered that the vernacular was "sweet." But most men and women responded to what they clearly considered to be a ridiculous question by explaining patiently that Taiap "is our language. It's the language of our ancestors. It's what we got from our mothers and fathers. They showed us and we speak it. It's like that."

Villagers in Gapun have no particular opinions about their language in relation to other vernaculars, except that they consider it to be "a little bit harder" than other languages. Also, relative to other vernaculars, villagers think that Taiap is valuable as a secret language. Even though the use of the vernacular to "hide talk" is a violation of the village principle of language accommodation to other speakers, villagers will sometimes deliberately use Taiap as a secret language, especially if they feel uncertain or threatened. A much recounted occasion when this happened was once during a large fight in Wongan that broke out between villagers from Gapun and Sanae. As the fighting grew more intense and began to involve large numbers of people, Sopak's husband, Mone, managed to achieve a temporary lull by blowing a whistle and crying out in Tok Pisin: "*Inap! Inap!*" (Stop! Stop!). Between his admonitions in Tok Pisin to stop the fighting, however, Mone also repeatedly slipped in the word "*ɔnɛmbrɛm!*," which is Taiap for "Beat the shit out of them!"

If Gapuners have little to say contrasting their vernacular to others around them, they do have ideas about how Taiap contrasts to Tok Pisin. Villagers consider that their vernacular has "little, little meanings" (*ol liklik liklik mining*) and a "foundation" (*as*) that Tok Pisin lacks. Both these "little, little meanings," which villagers exemplify with vernacular words for the flora and fauna of the rainforest, and the "foundation" they speak of are seen to be grounded in the land on which the villagers live.

Like other vernaculars, Taiap is understood by the people of Gapun to be inseparably bound up with the land (*graun/sumbwa*). Each village that the villagers know anything about is believed to have a founding ancestor (*kuskus/eŋgin*) who arrived at the site of each respective village after the land rose out of the sea at the beginning of time. All these founding ancestors are alike in every way except language. Sani, the mythical founding ancestor of Sanae, for example, differs from other mythical founding ancestors only in that he spoke Adjora. Sangginggi of Wongan spoke Kopar. And Kambedagam, the ancestor whom villagers say founded Gapun, spoke Taiap, in addition to being able to talk to Sani and Sangginggi in their respective languages.

The territorial boundaries of different villages are in this way seen to have been created with linguistic boundaries. And even though the founding ancestors all eventually "went away" (no one quite knows why or how or where), the linguistic stamp they imprinted upon the land remained fundamental. The rainforest and swamps that make up a village's land continue to be alive with that village's vernacular. The land is replete with a wide variety of supernatural beings that humans sometimes happen upon or see signs of. Some of these, like the tree-dwelling *kandap*, are mischievous, elfin creatures who can both help men in their hunting and, in nasty moods, snatch away the souls of babies. Others, like the water-spirits (*masalai/ɛmari*), are powerful and capable of great destruction. Assuming the form of gargantuan crocodiles, water-spirits have been known to overturn canoes, flood fields, and rise out of lakes to kill. In one frequently recounted myth in the village, the water-spirit Guyam once massacred every living member of the flying fox clan because they were gathering fish in one of his streams.

All beings that inhabit the rainforest live like humans. They all marry, have children, hunt, and construct houses. They also all speak. And like men and women, the beings of the forest all speak the vernacular of the village that owns the land. Those *kandap, masalai,* and other beings inhabiting the land owned by the Gapun villagers speak Taiap; those living on Sanae's land speak Adjora; and those on Wongan's land speak Kopar. So in the gestalt of these supernatural beings, villagers project their vernacular onto their physical world, defining it and delimiting it, as they define and delimit themselves from other groups, through language.

If the villagers' vernacular is projected onto their land, the land, in turn, is closely associated with the generations of Taiap-speaking ancestors who have lived on the land throughout history, and with the clans to which these ancestors have always belonged. Clans are the most important corporate groups in Gapun, and each villager is part of a clan (*kas* or *pamili/kandaŋ*). Clans are named after animals of the forest, and in 1987, the clans represented in the village were (in decreasing numerical order) the dog clan (*dok/jɛ*), the crocodile clan (*pukpuk/ɔrɛm*), the parrot clan (*karangal/karar*), the pig clan (*pik/bɔr*), and, with Sopak's neighbor Agrana as its only representative, the flying fox clan (*bilak bokis/jakɛp*). In a very loose way, villagers are sometimes associated with the clan of their father, and they can have ties created with several different clans by receiving special names from relatives or friends. But essentially, clan membership in Gapun is inherited matrilineally.[22] All of Sopak's children, for example, are "crocodiles" like their mother; not "dogs" like their father, Mone. Clans in Gapun have no founding ancestors, but they all have myths known to some of the most senior men, which tell of the arrival of the clan in Gapun, long ago, from areas along the headwaters of the Ramu River.

Clans are important in several ways. First, they distinguish whom a person can and cannot marry. Clans are exogamous, which means that two people from the same clan cannot marry: They are regarded as siblings and should not even ever have sex together. A spouse must always be from a different clan. In the past, when marriages were arranged with a frequency and finality that became uncustomary in the

1970s, villagers of both sexes regarded marriage as the exchange of sisters (real or classificatory) between clans. For a man to marry a woman and not supply the woman's clan with an exchange "sister" (*sens*) was an extremely grave offence, amounting to an invitation to the woman's disgruntled clan to murder someone through sorcery. Nowadays, even though it is generally agreed that young women and men should marry *long laik* (as they wish), clan membership continues to play an important role in the villagers' reactions to people's choice of a sexual or marital partner.[23] A union between a man and woman from the same clan is still considered incest and would be opposed by the villagers.

Second, clans are important in Gapun because they intertwine large numbers of people into networks that crosscut village ties. The clans represented in Gapun are said by the villagers to exist "everywhere," and one way in which they are important to individuals is that when traveling to villages where one has no close relatives, the only people who can be asked for food or a place to sleep are men and women who belong to the same clan as oneself. Before the villages of the lower Sepik were finally "pacified" by the colonial government in the 1920s, clans were also the most important groups in warfare. Warfare was primarily a clan, rather than a village, affair. The usual pattern was that men gathered together and went on raids of other villages, usually to kill a specific person – like a suspected sorcerer or a person from a particular clan, who would be killed as repayment for a death in one's own clan. In warfare, villagers strove to murder people from different clans, never, if they could help it, from their own. What usually would happen on a raid is that one or two men in the village being raided who belonged to the clan of the intruders would have been informed of the coming raid. The job of these men was to discreetly arrange things so that the attackers could get at their victim more easily.[24]

The final way in which clans in Gapun are of great importance is in their relation to the land. Clans own the land. Each clan represented in a village has rights over specific areas of land on which clan members born or adopted into the village can hunt, fish, work sago, gather firewood, find food, and plant gardens. Land rights are extremely salient for the villagers of Gapun, and every adult is acutely aware of what land is owned by which clan. Children learn this from a very young age as they travel through the rainforest with their parents to gather food and to work sago, and as they hear men and women recounting their adventures in various parts of the forest, the names of which (and thereby the ownership relations) are always specified exactly in village narratives. The rights to use clan land are energetically upheld, and if a man or woman were discovered to have worked sago or killed a pig or cassowary on another clan's land without having first obtained permission from the land's owners, a conflict would arise and retribution would have to be paid to members of the disaffected clan. Associations between land and the clans are so strong that "land" is often used in village discourse as a metaphor for "clan." To remark that "the land [of clan X] is coming up big" (*graun i kamap bikpela*) is to observe that the clan is populous and expanding because many children are being born.

Clan interests within a village are informally presided over by their most senior men. These individuals know something of the myths owned by their clan, and they use these to help settle the occasional disputes that arise between villagers over hunting rights or the rights to fell large trees for canoes. Sometimes old and knowledgeable senior women will be asked for an opinion or a piece of information on matters pertaining to the clan, but it is the senior men who from their seats in the men's house have the most say. Men, the men tell one another, "look after" (*lukautim*) and "boss" (*bosim*) the land, shaping its boundaries with their recital of myths and putting it to use to provide their families with food, materials for shelter, and gardens.

Clans, women, and Taiap

The same verbs, "look after" and "boss," are also used by men when they speak of women. Men in Gapun have complex views on women. Although relations between the sexes are relaxed and warm, and while men respect and even grudgingly admire "strong" women like Kruni's daughter Sake, who outdid all her brothers and sponsored an elaborate funerary feast for her dead father's mother's brother (Chapter 1), men also stereotype women as uncouth, antisocial, and destructive. And just as men see themselves molding and taming the land and putting it to good social use, so do they speak generally of male relations to females as ones in which the "wild" nature of women must be subverted and controlled by men.[25]

At the same time, however, women are also explicitly seen as the "foundation" of clan strength. Collectively referred to as "mothers" (*ol mama/mayaŋgrɔ*), women are talked about as the "base," or "root" (*as/ kandaŋ*) of the clan, and in abstract discussions men maintain that women are of more value than men. When a village woman in her twenties died after giving birth to a stillborn baby, Kruni lamented the loss and privately chastised the villagers of Sanae (who, it was taken for granted, caused the death) when he remarked, in conversation with a few village men in his men's house, that:

Women produce (*kamapim*) the clan. They're the root of the banana tree (*as bilong banana*). As long as the root of the banana tree remains, children will be born and grow. But you get rid of the root, how will children come to be? You [people from Sanae] can be angry, but [in appeasing your anger] you have to kill a man or a boy, not a woman or a girl.

Another time, shortly after the argument between Agrana and Sopak that resulted in Agrana smashing his carved masks on the ground outside his house (Chapter 1), Kruni's brother Raia recounted for a few men that during the fight Agrana had cursed Sopak, using the word "cunt" (*kan*). Raia disapproved of this. He explained that:

You can't talk bad about the cunt. The cunt is the Ancestor. The cunt produced (*kamapim*) the land/clans. True you have to have a cock, too, but this cock of ours can't produce anything at all.

This notion of women producing the clans is also the subject of an esoteric myth in the village that concerns what may be the first being in the world, the true ancestor of everything that is, an Ur-mother called Jenkenga Ojenata. The myth of Jenkenga Ojenata is not recounted extensively in Gapun today, partly because it is poorly known, and partly because senior men claim that the myth is powerful and used by Adjora speakers to eliminate people through sorcery. But what is known and told is that Jenkenga Ojenata was the ancestral being who probably gave birth to the two mythical brothers, Arena and Andena, and who originally "divided" (*skelim*) people into different clans.

Myths like that of Jenkenga Ojenata and comments like those of Kruni and Raia on the importance of women for the perpetuation of the clans are part of a discourse in Gapun that represents women as being very closely tied with the clans. Summing up the relations that villagers see among men, women, the land, and the clans, Sopak's husband, Mone, once remarked that "men look after the ground/clan, but women are the foundation." In fact, in calling women the "foundation" (*kandaŋ*), villagers are using the same word as they use for clan (*kandaŋ*). Women, the men are saying, *are* the clan.

There is thus a network of associations linking the vernacular to the land, the land to the clans represented in the village, and the clans to women. Within this network, women in Gapun come to be positioned in a special relationship to the Taiap language. This does not mean that women are imagined, even by one another, to generally speak "better" Taiap or have a more comprehensive grasp of the "little, little meanings" contained in the language than do men, especially senior men. In fact, both men and women remark occasionally that women tend to "foul up" (*poulim*/*bata-*) the vernacular.[26] But, notwithstanding their assumed linguistic inferiority, women in the village stand in a close metaphorical relationship to the vernacular. One instance in which this relationship is explicitly articulated is in the villagers' own explanation of why their vernacular is "broken in two."

The ancestral being who founded Gapun, Kambedagam, spoke Taiap, but Kambedagam left the area before any man had arrived to take up residence on the land. Sometime after Kambedagam had gone, the first human male to arrive in Gapun appeared on the scene. This man was named Kruni Maroka, and he made a camp on the mountaintop where the old pre-World War II village of Gapun once rested. Soon after arriving on the mountain, Kruni Maroka was approached by a woman. This was Akwer, a woman who had been living under the mountain since the time of Kambedagam. Kruni Maroka spoke to the woman in his vernacular, a language still spoken, say the villagers, in the upper reaches of the Ramu River.[27]

Hearing Kruni Maroka's speech, Akwer objected. "This vernacular will have to go," she told Kruni. "You'll learn to speak my language instead. My vernacular is Kambedagam's. It's the one that will remain from now on." With no argument or fuss, Kruni Maroka agreed to this and abandoned his language, acquiring instead the vernacular that Akwer then taught him.

Villagers who know this myth cite it as the reason why Gapun's vernacular is "broken in two" into a "man's language" and a "woman's language." Although they stress that Kambedagam spoke Taiap, Gapuners seem to accept the central role of a woman in passing the language on to men as accounting for why their language is really "two languages." Just as they are divisive in social life, so are women responsible for the "breaking" of the village vernacular into "two languages."

The metaphorical associations between women and the village vernacular are reinforced through praxis. Women in Gapun do speak more Taiap than do men. In their informal conversations with one another while chewing betel nut or doing work, women tend generally not to code-switch to Tok Pisin as much as men do. Whereas a relaxed conversation conducted in the vernacular with only very occasional, brief switches to Tok Pisin would be highly unusual verbal behavior for men, such a situation is not uncommon when women socialize together. Even more striking is the tendency for women who speak different vernaculars to converse for long stretches in their respective languages without using Tok Pisin. On occasions when Sake, her younger brother's wife, Tambong, and her older brother's wife, Luna, are alone together, the conversation among them can continue for a long time with Sake speaking Taiap; Tambong, Kopar; and Luna, who speaks both languages fluently, switching between the two. Although many village men are multilingual enough to have conversations in this way should they want to, a similar interaction among men with different, but mutually understandable, mother tongues would almost inevitably be conducted predominantly in Tok Pisin.

Another practical reinforcement of the metaphorical associations between women and Taiap is the fact that the only people in Gapun who are either not fluent speakers of Tok Pisin, or who simply prefer not to use it, are women (Table 2.1). Because villagers tend to accommodate these women by switching to the vernacular whenever they address them, they are frequently made aware of the fact that some women do not speak Tok Pisin. This gender-based difference, combined with the salient historical relationship that exists in the village between Tok Pisin and males, permits the maintenance of a stereotype in which all women can be portrayed as more or less incompetent in Tok Pisin.

That stereotype becomes strengthened even further because women in Gapun do not play leading or particularly prominent roles in those formal contexts in which a large public focuses its hearing on the display of Tok Pisin. Such focused hearings occur most commonly on those relatively rare occasions when the village is visited by carving buyers, government officials, policemen, or missionaries. All such contacts are handled by men. Women are often present throughout much of the talk that occurs on these occasions, but they tend to remain at the periphery of interaction. If a woman has something she especially wishes to communicate to the buyers or officials, she often chooses to speak through her husband or older children. The nonassertive role that women assume in their contacts with these representatives of the modern world serves to distort public conceptions of their competence in Tok Pisin. At the same time, it underscores the stereotype that women are less modern and, therefore, more traditional and, therefore, more bound to the vernacular than men are.

3. Having *hed*

Babies in Gapun are born in the jungle. When a woman late in her pregnancy feels her *bel kirap* (belly jump), she makes her way to one of the small clearings situated outside the village and there waits to give birth. Women never give birth totally alone; at the very least, older experienced women will take their young daughters to the clearing with them. Younger women are accompanied by mothers, sisters and friends, and any small children who happen to be around at the time. Boys over 4 are discouraged from trying to follow women into the <u>awinni tuŋgar iaw</u> (place of giving birth, lit. place of washing with water), and any boy over 6 who tried to attend would be chased away by the women.

Every woman in Gapun expects to begin having children soon after she marries, and if several years pass without a married woman becoming pregnant, the woman will begin to seek help from the men and older women in the area who are known to possess special magic chants, which they spit on betel nut and give to the woman to chew. In those cases in which a woman does not become pregnant despite periodic barrages of magic, it is gradually acknowledged that she *no save karim* (doesn't get pregnant). This is not considered to be a natural condition, but is rather the result of the woman's having eaten too much of a magic tree bark called <u>kip</u> to prevent pregnancy. Women routinely eat this bark before they marry, when they are expected to have a wide variety of sexual experiences. Some women are said not to appreciate the power of the bark, though, and they fail to understand that <u>kip</u> is not a temporary contraceptive; if <u>kip</u> is consumed too often, a woman will *never* become pregnant. No one in Gapun is childless, however, because adoption and fostering are practiced extensively, and women who cannot bear children will either *makim* (claim) or be given children by their siblings.

Birth in Gapun is an anxious time not only for the woman in labor, but for the entire village. In the course of the past fourteen years, three young village women have died frightening deaths during or soon after childbirth. Remembering this, everyone hopes for a quick delivery and

92

rapid expulsion of the placenta. Should a woman's labor last too long, word of this crackles through the village, and the big men and women are mobilized to spit magical chants on special leaves meant to "open" (*opim*) the woman. These leaves are then taken to the woman and rubbed on her body or else they are placed in cold water, which the woman is washed with and made to drink. In cases of especially long delays in giving birth or expelling the placenta, small sums of money are sometimes hurridly relayed to an old Sanae man who has a reputation for possessing chants that can "open" a woman who has been "closed" (*pas*) by particularly malicious spirits or sorcery.

Pregnancy, especially late pregnancy, is considered by the villagers to be an extremely vulnerable time for a woman, a time when sorcerers will not be able to resist the opportunity to kill her for some past wrong by shooting enchanted substances into her body to "close" her so that the baby or placenta will not be able to emerge. Alternatively, spirits of the ground might work similar magic on women who have offended them in some way. The prolonged labor of one young village woman was accounted for by recalling that she at one time several years previously had walked too close to a place in the rainforest where slit gong drums once were made. The spirit associated with these drums punished her by closing her. Only with the aid of her father, who happened to know the appropriate chant to "cool" (*kolim*) this spirit's power, was this woman able to successfully give birth.

While they are pregnant, women continue to work as usual, walking several kilometers over mountains and standing all day long leaching sago, carrying large bundles of firewood on their heads and backs, lifting heavy pots of water on and off fires. They believe that hard work during pregnancy eases the pain of childbirth. Marame's wife, Tambong, once explained:

It's good to walk around and work until you give birth. It feels good to feel your belly swaying when you walk. If you just sit down all the time, the *rot* [road for the baby; i.e., birth canal] will close and you'll carry big pain. When I had Bapong I worked until right before I gave birth – I walked up and down the mountain, it was really good. But with Bini I had a bad leg so I couldn't work much. And because of that, when I had Bini I carried a terrible pain.

When a child is born, its umbilical cord is held between a pair of tongs and cut by the mother with a razor blade. The afterbirth is dumped into a sago-frond container and placed in the branches of a nearby tree "so that the pigs and the dogs won't find it and eat it." The mother and the baby are washed, the child is wrapped up, and then both mother and child proceed to the maternity house (*haus karim/awinni tuŋgwar patir*), where they will both remain for weeks or months.

feminine blood issues of gen. + lang. life

Gapun villagers share with other Papua New Guinean peoples a great ambivalence toward blood, which is primarily associated with women. Too much blood in the body is considered debilitating and dangerous, and even today, whenever a village man feels that his "skin is tired" (*skin i les*), he will retire discreetly into the forest and jab the head of his erect penis with the sharp tip of a razor blade in order to release what is believed to be excess blood. This process of expelling what is considered to be feminine blood from the male body is regarded as desirable, and men maintain that they emerge from the treatment with renewed strength and vigor, and with handsome, firm, luminous skin. Blood itself, especially blood expelled from the female body, however, is thought to be highly polluting, and the vast amounts of blood and bodily matter flushed from the female body during birth is cause for alarm among many of the older village men. A woman who has recently given birth is "hot" (*hat/armbir*) and so dangerous that for an older man to even see her or tread on the same path as her would give him a potentially fatal attack of asthma. The need to contain the "heat" of postpartum women is the reason for the village's maternity houses.

Traditionally, maternity houses in Gapun were large and meant to accommodate several women and their babies. Because women remained secluded in these houses for over six months, and because three or four village women usually shared the same birth cycles, the maternity houses in the village were often filled with women and their newborn babies. Time in the *haus karim* was, and continues to be, the way by which women kept track of the relative ages of children. "Yapa is bigger [i.e., older] than Kama," Sopak will tell you, "because Yapa's mother was already in the maternity house with Yapa when I went into the bush to have Kama." The large maternity houses were places where young mothers could observe how more experienced women cared for their babies. Older women sometimes tell of how their companions in the maternity house could always be counted on to watch each other's babies whenever one of them slipped into the forest to wash or go to the toilet, and of how they would "help" each other with food whenever a woman's relatives neglected to supply her with enough to eat.

Despite the advantages of being together with other women while in seclusion after giving birth, the large maternity houses have gradually been replaced by more privatized and progressively smaller versions. At first, the smaller houses that individual men began building for their wives could be used at different times by the wife, sisters, and sometimes even sisters-in-law of the man who built them. Increasingly, though, women "complained" of this arrangement, and since the early 1980s, it has become established that each woman should have her own *haus karim*. This is the only real preparation that women and their husbands make for the arrival of a child, and when a woman's stomach swells to the size when she begins to think that *"taim i sot nau"* (it's almost time), she will begin preparing for her stay in the maternity house by chopping copious amounts of firewood. If her husband has not yet constructed a *haus karim* for her, she periodically "pushes" him to do so, often by publicly threatening to build it herself. Most often this is ineffective, and if a woman's husband simply has not built a maternity house for her, she then has no choice but to spend a few weeks in one belonging to another woman. This is done with absolute reluctance, because everyone knows that the owner of the maternity house will certainly, sooner or later, on the slightest pretext, begin to *toktok planti* about the arrangement.

The new type of maternity houses being built today are just big enough to accommodate a small hearth and a mosquito net. They are too tiny to stand up in and, because they are usually built hurriedly and crudely in a week or less, rain drips through holes in the roof and pigs snuffling under the house cause it to shake violently on its wobbly posts. And while the village women congratulate themselves that they have once again successfully defended their forever threatened autonomy by preventing anyone else from using their maternity house, they now complain of boredom and loneliness. After birth, one or two weeks of rest in the maternity house is enjoyed by all women, but the pleasure quickly turns to claustrophobia. Extended stays in these dark little huts, confined with their babies, unable to stand up or move around, are experienced by the women as suffocating and oppressive. If women have young children, these children will visit their mothers frequently and keep them informed about the goings-on in the village. Visits from other women are infrequent, though, and sometimes several days will pass without anyone coming to see the new mother. If a woman has her own mother or grown daughters living in the village when she gives birth, then these women will keep her supplied with firewood and food, and she can expect to be looked after fairly well. A woman who gives birth in a village where these female relatives are not present is in a precarious situation because no one may care to take responsibility for her. Sopak and Mone's eldest daughter, Basama, gave birth to her second child in Wongan, her husband's village, and spent the first two days after giving birth without food or water because Basama's maternal aunt (Sopak's sister) didn't "have" any food, and no other woman in the village took responsibility for her. In the end she had to be brought to Gapun by Sopak and Mone, who looked after her there.

The confining, dreary huts, isolation, and frequent hunger are reasons why women in Gapun nowadays refuse to remain in maternity houses longer than a month. After four to six weeks in the houses, women announce "*Mi les*" (I'm sick of this), and they return with their babies to the house in which they normally live. Here they rig up their mosquito nets near the hearth at the back of the house and remain as unobtrusively as possible for the next two to three months. During this time women consider themselves still in seclusion, but they all agree that it is preferable to be "secluded" in a large house with lots of people than to be cooped up and hungry in a leaky hut.

For several months after they give birth, women do not work or move around very much. To wash or go to the toilet, which they do only at night or when they are sure the village is deserted, women leave their houses through discreet back exits devised especially for them. They are aware that they cannot tread on the regular paths or be seen by any big men, lest their "heat" cause these men to become *sotwin* (asthmatic). In addition to these types of prohibitions on the behavior of women in seclusion, mothers and their babies are symbolically linked to one another in a number of ways, and women should observe certain taboos in order to protect the health of their infants. They should not eat certain foods, like red sweet potatoes, *aibika* (a kind of spinach that produces a viscous sap when cooked), or sugar cane, because these foods, even though it is the mother who eats them, would "stay in the baby's stomach and make his skin tight." Eating lizards would cause the baby's stomach to itch, and "heavy foods" like bananas or pumpkins, if the mother ate them, would make the baby's *as* (bottom) so heavy that it would have trouble learning how to stand and walk.

Young mothers nowadays are aware of at least some of these taboos, but few bother with them for any length of time. In general, the villagers of Gapun have calmly pragmatic views on taboos, and most taboos involving food or sexual behavior are breezily disregarded if individuals don't feel like observing them. "If your baby gets sick," explained Paso when she talked about why she doesn't observe the postpartum food taboos, "you know it's because you've eaten sugar cane or *aibika* or whatever. Alright, so you send word to whoever knows the right chant, and they'll spit on the baby and he'll get better." Older women like Sopak or Wandi consider that they've had so many children that the taboos don't matter much anymore, so they don't observe them strictly either. But at times they speak disparagingly about the nonchalance of the younger women. "These young women they don't hold the taboos. They eat anything, they screw around with their lovers. And look at their kids," Sopak exclaims occasionally, flinging her arm in a wide arc of distaste, "they haven't come up good. They're all gonna have short legs and little asses and their heads and their bellies are gonna get real big."

A woman's husband, too, has certain taboos that he should observe in order to ensure that the baby remains healthy. He should not, for example, carry heavy posts or dig holes, as this would make the baby's skin "heavy." And he, like his wife, should refrain from having sex until the baby can sit up by itself. If either husband or wife has sex before this time, the wife would surely become pregnant, since her *rot* is wide open, and the baby will become sick. A husband having illicit sex with a lover during his wife's seclusion would, in addition, risk being revealed by the newborn baby. "You can go and find your lover and sleep with her while your wife still hasn't come down [from seclusion]," Raia explained. "You can do that. But if you do, the baby will vomit up your sperm. And when that happens, where you gonna hide? [dramatic pause] The baby's exposed you now."

Because of the villagers' ideas about the heat and pollution surrounding birth, a newborn baby remains in seclusion with its mother, spending the first three or four months of its life in almost continual contact with the mother, lying on her lap during the day and sleeping at her breast at night. Other women and girls visiting the mother sometimes hold the baby for a few minutes at a time, but the baby never leaves the maternity house or, later, the darkened area of seclusion in the main house, and whenever it struggles or whines, the baby is immediately passed back to the mother, who silently presses a breast into its mouth. Conversations with the mother during her months in seclusion focus mostly on her health and news about the village and its neighbors. The mother's baby is sometimes spoken about, but it is not the subject of extensive attention or talk. More often, talk will be about babies in general, and women tell stories about their own experiences in childbirth and about the problems facing new mothers, such as how to protect the baby from sorcery. A mother will instruct her daughter to "Watch this baby" when it falls asleep and she sees an opportunity to slip away to the toilet, or she will sometimes wonder aloud, "What is tormenting this baby?" when the child cries too much. Beyond these kinds of comments, though, little talk is devoted to the infant. The only time babies of this age are spoken to directly is when mothers tell them "*Inap, inap*" (Enough, enough) whenever they cry, when they are fondly called "*liklik rat*" (little rat) because of their pinkish, pinched bodies, or when they are jokingly hit at and scolded as "*Blary longlong pik!*" (Bloody idiot pig) whenever they suddenly urinate or defecate on the mother.

Certain aspects of a baby's early expression of affect and growth of physical independence are noticed and remarked on by women, and traditionally, several of these developments had consequences for the actions and spatial placement of the mother. When a baby first laughed, a mother traditionally washed her hands with painfully hot water and was permitted to prepare her own food and eat with her fingers (before this her "heat," which was potentially dangerous even to herself, required that she eat using a small pair of wooden tongs, never touching her food with her hands). Likewise, the child's ability to sit up on the floor on its own was traditionally the signal for the woman that she could leave the maternity house. A baby's entrance into the village used to be a celebrated event in Gapun, involving the child's joking-kin (father's matrilineal kin, called *wanpilai* [one-play] in Tok Pisin; *jakum* in Taiap), who would decorate the baby with dog's teeth and carry it around from house to house along with a large plate of taro and yams. At each house people would greet the baby and take a piece of taro or yam to eat.

By the time a woman emerges from seclusion in her house and begins to reintegrate herself into village life, her baby has begun to focus and smile, and to reach out toward faces and objects placed before it. By this time, the infant has also been given a number of names by relatives. Before they are born, infants are not referred to as human at all. The unborn children of obviously pregnant women are simply called "the belly" (*bel/imin*). During the first few months after birth, babies remain nameless and are referred to as *bebi* or by the third person pronouns: *gu* (she/her) or *ŋi* (he/him) in the vernacular, *em* (he/she, her/him) in Tok Pisin. Even after they have received names most villagers continue using these words to talk about the babies until after the first year.

Naming a child is a sensitive and important business, because names, like everything else in Gapun, are owned, in this case by one of the five clans represented in the village. Names therefore signify clan membership, and it is essential not to make the mistake of giving a child a name belonging to another clan. This would be a serious provocation, an invitation to sorcery. To avoid this, important and knowledgeable men and women are always consulted before a name is given. There is a finite number of about 200 to 300 names that villagers choose from, and these are recycled approximately every third generation. Old people can thus often remember the last bearer of a particular name, and this assists them in remembering the clan affiliation of that name. Despite such safeguards, however, mistakes in naming are sometimes made, although these are not usually realized until after the death of the child or its close relative, when the villagers are trying to figure out why the death occurred. At this point someone may suddenly remember that the child had been given a name belonging to the wrong clan. In other cases, more knowledgeable men from villages closer to the Ramu River may visit Gapun and find occasion to correct the Gapun elders' understanding of a particular name. These men may insist that individuals "get rid of" (*rausim*) their old, "wrong" names and be given new ones, or else risk death by sorcery from someone belonging to the disaffected clan. Several villagers have suddenly found themselves in this position: The daughter of Sake's sister Erapo was compelled to "get rid of" her name Masepo and change it to Tapu at age 23, and Sopak's older brother's 19-year-old son suddenly was told to change his name from

Simbira to Ambang one day when a man from Sanae realized that the name Simbira didn't actually belong to the dog clan at all.

. Partly because a child belongs to the same clan as its mother, a woman has a great deal of say about what she wants to call her baby. Some women have special choices picked out even before the baby is born. Some reject the names given to them by relatives, holding out until they hear one they like. "When they wanted to give David a name," Paso once recounted, pointing at her 3-year-old son, "Mamma told me to call him Baik. I said, 'No (*Mi les*), I'm sick of rubbish names.' OK, Papa told me, 'call him Ainjari then.' That's an OK name, I thought. So I put that name on him." Even so, Paso later decided that she didn't particularly like "Ainjari" either, and so she herself decided to call her son David. This name caught on and quickly became what everybody else began to call the boy.

Villagers have a number of names, from two to more than five, plus, in most cases, a Christian name. Traditional names are divided into "big" names (*biknem*/<u>*nɔmb suman*</u>), i.e., those by which a person is most often called, and several "little" names (*liklik nem*/<u>*nɔmb mɔkɔp*</u>), which are not normally used by others. "Little" names can belong to any clan and are closely connected to the person who bestowed the name. Thus, if a barren woman, for example, wishes to take on some of the fostering responsibilities for one of her sibling's children, she will give the child a special name from her clan's stock. Ties of this nature entail mutual responsibility and obligations between the namegiver and the recipient. These ties may or may not be developed and activated, depending on the personalities and wishes of both persons. Villagers are occasionally heard grumbling, however, that namegivers don't take any responsibility for "their" children: Sopak's younger brother Ambuli frequently complained that his wife Membo's sister "just put a name" (*putim nating nem*) on his infant daughter and subsequently did nothing to help out with the baby. Similarly, in Raia's younger days, he once made a flamboyant speech wherein he demonstratively "threw away" one of his names that an old woman of the dog clan had given him as a child. He did this to protest the fact that no one from the dog clan would help him procure a classificatory sister whom he could exchange for a wife.

Interpreting children's behavior

When the child leaves seclusion with its mother and begins to be carried around the village and into the houses of friends and relatives, it gets passed around and fondled by little girls and boys, and by the mother's sisters, in-laws, and close friends. Women who do not fall into these categories are hesitant to handle small infants because they fear that they might be accused of "giving sickness" to the child should it later fall ill. Men and most adolescent boys disdain to hold infants under about 10 months because of the likelihood that the baby will suddenly spray them with urine or feces. Older men dislike coming into contact with infants at all until the child can at least walk.

As a baby gets carried around in the village and passed among people, its actions and vocalizations become the subject of comment by others. Villagers begin attributing intention and specific emotions to the child. Most often, these imputed intentions and emotions are either aggression, anger, or dissatisfaction. When Sopak's 8-month-old baby, Masito, reaches out toward a dog lying beside her, Sopak comments: "Look, she's mad (*kros*) now, she wants to hit the dog." Thrusting Masito closer to the dog, Sopak lifts the baby's hand onto its fur and tells her: "That's it, hit it. Hit it!" Children's babbling sounds and noises are also interpreted as expressions of dissatisfaction or aggression. A child cooing softly in its mother's lap is likely to be shaken suddenly and asked: "*Ai! Yu belhat long wanem? Ah?!*" (Ai! What are you mad about? Ah?!). Imputed aggression in babies is frequently matched by anyone tending them, and the most common mode of face play with babies involves the caregiver biting her lower lip, widening her eyes, thrusting out her chin sharply, and raising the heel of her hand in a threatening manner, swinging it to within a few millimeters of the child's face and then suddenly pulling it back again. After pulling several of these punches, the woman or man doing this laughs at the baby and nuzzles its face and body with her or his lips.

As soon as a baby can focus and hold on to objects, its actions and reactions begin to influence the behavior of everyone around it. Women in Gapun evaluate each other as mothers on the basis of whether or not they *lukautim gut* (look after well) their infants. A baby who is being looked after well is first of all "fat" – the bigger the better – and healthy. Any sickness that befalls a child under 2 is usually considered in the first instance to be a consequence of the child's mother having broken a postpartum taboo. Mothers are also judged on how well they can interpret the needs and wants of their infants, and a crying or fussing baby is a sign that a mother is not performing her role well. Babies are not considered to "just cry" (*krai nating*) unless they are ensorcelled. Otherwise, they are always crying because they want something. Mothers should know what their babies are crying for, and they should respond to the cries by immediately acting on their interpretations and giving the child whatever it wants. Women in the village are constantly interpreting the cries, moans, and noises that their babies make, and since most of these sounds are considered to express distress of some sort, mothers are quick to give the child whatever they think it wants in order to quiet it down. Once babies can no longer be stifled simply by pushing a breast into their mouths, mothers begin supplying them with objects to pacify them. Virtually nothing is withheld from a crying child, and 6-month-old babies frequently find themselves suddenly holding betel nut, soggy cigarette butts, glass bottles, plastic rice bags, or butcher knives just because they started to whine.

Children in Gapun seem to learn very early that their nonverbal expressions always result in some sort of response from caregivers, be it a breast or an object snatched away from an older sibling and handed to them. One consequence of this immediate, casual relationship between a child's nonverbal actions and the responses of others is that children have little need to verbalize their desires. A large number of village children do not begin constructing simple three-word sentences until they are nearly 3 years old. Before this (and, if a child's mother has no new baby to look after, well after this), increasingly loud screams will without fail get a child whatever it wants.

Gapuners consistently interpret much of their infants' prelinguistic and nonverbal behavior as expressions of dissatisfaction and aggression because of their thoughts on the nature of children and of self. An essential aspect of the self in Gapun is referred to by the Tok Pisin word *hed* and in the vernacular by <u>kɔkir.</u> Both these words mean, exactly, "head." Each individual, the villagers believe, "has *hed*." Each individual, they mean by this, has a fundamental sense of personal will and autonomy. Even before they are born, during the time they are not even referred to by a human pronoun but still called "the belly," babies' *hed*s are sometimes a topic of discussion. When Wandi's abdomen swelled to tremendous size and weeks went by without her feeling any contractions, men and women openly wondered why "the belly" didn't "want" to "come." When the child finally was born, several women scolded it indirectly, publicly commenting later that it shouldn't have been so *bikhed* (willful; lit. big-headed) about being born.

After birth, babies continue to be talked about and treated as stubborn, big-headed individualists. Preverbal infants are frequently shaken lightly by their mothers and chastised playfully that their *hed*s are too "strong" and "big," and that they "never listen to talk." Imputed assertiveness in children is also reflected in the first words that are attributed to them. Villagers pay little attention to children's early babbling sounds unless the child whines and shows signs of distress. Very early in their development, however, babies are believed to utter certain words. A child's very first word is generally held to be *ɔki* (go + IRREAL STATUS). This is a Taiap word meaning, approximately, "I'm getting out of here." Attributed to infants as young as 2 months, this word encapsulates the adult belief that babies will "do what they want" (*bi-*

hainim laik bilong ol yet) and go where they will, regardless of the wishes of others. The two words that villagers consider to rapidly follow ɔki̵ also underscore the notion of a baby as an independent, aggressive individualist with a "strong" *hed*. These words are *mnda* (I'm sick of this) and *aiata* (stop it).

Each villager in Gapun is considered to possess *hed,* and the display of personal autonomy is considered necessary and correct in certain social situations, such as in response to provocation. In general, however, *hed* is admonished and devalued in the villagers' talk to one another. In anyone but small children, *hed* is officially condemned. In village rhetoric, the word is used to signify egoism, selfishness, and maverick individualism. *Hed* is bad. It is antisocial and stubbornly autonomistic. It is held up in stark contrast to development (*kamap*), which, as Kruni explained (Chapter 1, Text 1.3) is a group pursuit: Development will occur only if everyone joins together, "suppresses *hed*" (*daunim hed*), and makes the village into a *kristen komuniti* (Christian community). *Hed* is what is preventing development from coming about, everybody agrees. It is the plug blocking the metamorphosis that one day will occur and change their village, their material living conditions, and even their physical selves.

But from the perspective of the individual, the *hed* that is preventing Gapun from "coming up" is not one's own. Individual villagers consider themselves to be "good" men and women (*gutpela man/meri / munjɛ/ nɔŋɔr ɛŋgɔn*) who *are* cooperative and Christian, and who *do* "suppress" their own *hed* for the public good. The problem, as the villagers see it, is everybody else's *hed*. There is a deep-seated anxiety among Gapuners that the *hed*s of their fellow villagers really are not very "suppressed" at all and that these *hed*s, brazen and selfish, are constantly poised to wantonly violate one's own sense of personal space and autonomy.

This is resisted fiercely. The people of Gapun maintain a finely elaborated concept of provocation, which is continuously being brought into play in village life. Provocation is considered to be any action by an individual that causes somebody else to feel put out, exploited, insulted, wronged, violated, or mistreated. It is known in the village by the Tok Pisin verb *pusim* (push) or, more to the point in the vernacular, as *kɔki̵r ikru* (to "give head" to another person). Because each person in Gapun is felt to already have *hed,* to have a sense of personal autonomy, any overt attempt to influence someone else, to attempt to "give head" to him or her, is considered an extremely serious offence. This understanding of interpersonal relations is one of the central dimensions of village social life.

Like most Papua New Guinean societies, Gapun is acephalous and politically anarchistic. The "big men" (*bikpela man*/*munjɛ suman*) in the village are not leaders in the usual sense of the word. Men like Kruni and Kem are "big" because of their age and experience, their compelling personalities, their ability to maintain a wide range of social relationships, and their skills in hunting and oratory (traditionally, prowess in warfare was also an essential component of the big man status). There are no formal or hereditary underpinnings to the big man role, and people listen to them or follow them to the extent that they want to. For their part, big men cannot order anyone to do anything. They can suggest and cajole and harangue, but they cannot command. The big men are acutely aware of this, and their zesty oratories in the men's house urging others to repair bridges or cut grass are frequently punctuated by the eager reassurance, "but I'm not pushing you." To "push" somebody is to challenge them, and among adults, this will almost inevitably result in an argument or a fight, sooner or later.

This type of relationship permeates the entire society. No relationship, not even that between adult and child, is understood by the villagers to involve legitimate power to order another person to do something against his or her will. No man supposes that he can make his wife do anything she strongly opposes doing, for example. And parents will entreat and nag and threaten their recalcitrant children in order to get them to go fetch water or deliver a message, but only exceptionally rarely will a child's refusal to carry out a certain task (a refusal usually signaled by a growled "*Mi les!*" (I don't want to!) or by the child's running away) provoke a parent to pressing the matter. Almost inevitably, the parent will turn to another child or available person to carry out the desired task, or will do it him- or herself. Nonobedient children, especially girls, are sometimes smacked hard by their mothers with wooden tongs or a handy piece of firewood, but this is more an expression of anger on the mother's behalf than it is an effort to get the child to carry out an order, since the smacked child will invariably run away screaming and crying or fall down screaming and crying, leaving the mother to carry out the task herself or enlist somebody else to do it.

The concern that villagers share about infringements on their autonomy has led them to develop a number of dramatic ways to announce provocation and deal with it, such as flying into a rage and destroying their own possessions, like Sake did when she burned down her own newly built house in the course of an argument with her older brother. In performing this kind of action, the villagers seem to be signaling, in effect, "Look what you have pushed me to do." Destroying one's own possessions in this way is thus a concentration of the themes of *hed*, provocation, and causality. These themes found their most extreme expression in the traditional custom of *ɔndir*. This custom, last enacted in Gapun in the late 1920s, prescribed that a man whose wife had left him for another man would murder an innocent matrilineal relative, i.e., one of his own clan members. The cultural logic that this deed drew upon and set into motion demanded that the wife's new husband then murder one of his matrilineal relatives. This second death was considered to have "settled" (*stretim*) the matter, and the wife would remain with her new husband.[1]

Having a *kros*

By far the most common way in which Gapuners deal with what they perceive to be infringements on their autonomy is by loudly announcing them to the entire village, using the specific verbal genre they call *kros* (lit. cross; anger). *Kros*es are public proclamations of conflict. They are characterized by insults, vulgarity, direct threats, and by persistent repetition of accusations. There is no attempt on anyone's part to "talk things out" or come to any kind of agreement. *Kros*es announce to the village that something reprehensible has happened and that someone is dissatisfied. They are explosions of anger. And more than this, *kros*es are dramatic declarations of self-display. They are occasions when villagers assert themselves and their personal autonomy by broadcasting that these have been violated. Self-display is such a central aspect of *kros*es that the recipient of the *kros* does not even have to be present while the *kros* is being held. Sake's sister-in-law Tambong, for example, frequently *kros*es her husband, Marame, when he is far out of earshot. One day Marame suddenly decided to help some men make a canoe instead of going with Tambong to work sago as had been planned. After he had gone off into the jungle to work on the canoe, Tambong sat on her veranda and screamed for thirty minutes at Marame that her "belly" was "hot" because they had no food and she and her children had slept hungry the night before. "Did you see the kids crying in hunger this morning?!" she shouted through the village at an absent Marame:

You know why they were crying?! What are we – your pigs that we should just stay hungry all the time?! I'm taking the kids and going back to my village [Wongan]. You can't come after us, following us like a dog, and bring us back here! . . . You can't come and finish my kids' food. It's our food. Did you go and get any food or earn any money for us?! You can't come here and say you're hungry. You think of us and go find food for us, ah? I won't lose this talk. This talk's gonna remain. In the afternoon I'll still be talking . . ..

*Kros*es in the village can and do occur at any time during the day or night, but the majority take place in the late afternoon when the villagers return home from working sago or hunting in the rainforest. Gapuners walk up to twenty kilometers a day in the swampy rainforest, to and from their sago palms or in pursuit of a wild boar that has been speared. Their work in the jungle – chopping and leaching sago or carrying fifty kilos of pig meat on one's head or shoulder – is extremely hard. Despite this, though, men and women rarely take food with them when they leave the village, and they often go off to work in the morning without having eaten at all. Throughout the day, they smoke and chew betel nut to dampen their hunger pangs, but by the time they return to the village in the late afternoon after a long day of hard physical labor with nothing to eat, they are exhausted and short-tempered. In this state, almost any infraction – a teenage daughter who has neglected to fetch enough firewood to cook the evening meal, the news that someone who is not a close relative shouted at your child during the day, noticing on the way home that someone has stolen a papaya that you had been planning on picking when it reached your favorite degree of ripeness – is liable to provoke a sharp, prolonged *kros* in which the antagonist's name is "rubbished" and past disputes are dredged up with bitterness.

*Kros*es can be extremely vituperative, and partly because of their volatile nature, they are structured by precise rules to which all villagers adhere as long as they want the conflict to remain a shouting match.[2] Two rules are paramount: The *kros* should take place in the immediate vicinity of, or preferably from inside, one's house; and the protagonists, while they may shout at each other, should do so in two overlapping monologues. If either of these two rules is broken, and one of the antagonists either begins directly replying to the other's accusations or moves down from her or his house onto the ground, then the *kros* runs a great risk of escalating into a fight in which fists, sticks, sharp objects, and even axes may be used.

*Kros*es are recurring and abundant in Gapun. The frequency with which *kros*es occur in the village is, in addition to being linked to notions of provocation, also bound up with village understandings of causality. In Gapun, as in most Melanesian societies, most things don't just happen. They are made to happen by somebody or something. Rain doesn't just fall in the village, for example; it is made to fall by somebody who wants water for a tobacco crop or who wishes to "bugger up" somebody else's work plans. Likewise, the villagers do not consider that dogs just track down and corner wild boars. Dogs are enabled to corner boars through appropriately applied magic. Conversely, the eyes and noses of dogs can be "closed" and made unable to find boars – also through magic. People in the village don't just get sick; somebody's malevolence or a big man's dissatisfaction with them causes them to be ill. And villagers, the men and women of Gapun all stress tersely, "don't just die" (*ino indai nating*/*sapkini wasɔkɨ wakarɛ*), they are always, without exception, killed – murdered by sorcerers in revenge for some "wrong" committed by themselves, a spouse, child, parent, or matrilineal relative.

Gapun villagers thus contextualize all types of changes, and they find explanations for them in their social relationships. From the perspective of the individual, this means that the actions of other people are seen as having the potential to infringe directly, and potentially fatally, on the self: on one's health (if my sister's son steals betel nut from an old man with knowledge of sorcery, then *I* may be killed), one's crops (a young woman entering my newly planted garden will cause my tobacco to be devoured by insects and my yams not to grow), and one's hunting ability (if my wife doesn't send food to the big men, they may magically "close" the eyes and noses of my dogs). The actions of others may even "push" one to do things against one's will, such as destroying one's own possessions in a fit of rage.

A consequence of the villagers' certainty that someone else is always responsible and that sudden changes are invariably caused, at some level, by human action is that the number of things for which people can be blamed is quite considerable. This, in turn, augments the potential for conflict in the village to an extravagant degree. And, in fact, this potential for conflict is fully realized in Gapun, where hardly a day goes by without some new quarrel being aired or an old contention rising to the surface. The majority of these conflicts concern theft, laziness, suspicion of adultery, and suspicion of magic directed against one's garden or hunting dogs, in that order of frequency. But any action by another person that can possibly be interpreted as a violation of personal autonomy is liable to provoke a *kros*.

One dark evening about ten o'clock, the baby of Sake's 19-year-old unmarried sister, Jari, began to cry loudly. As the crying continued, Sake and her mother, Sombang, from inside their mosquito nets, began hissing curses at Jari to quiet the child. As it happened, though, Jari was nowhere to be found, and Sake screamed out for her to return to the house and take care of her baby. Five minutes later, when Jari still hadn't arrived, Sake called out again. At this point, she also began a public *kros* at her sister:

Text 3.1

Sake: Where are you walking around looking for cock?!
           Where are you walking around looking for cock?!
           It's time to sleep. There's no noise in the village, everyone's sleeping =

5 Sombang: = I'm sick of this, not being able to sleep. I'm sick of it.

Kruni: = If I come down [from the men's house], she's gonna bugger up!

Sake: Bloody idiot bastard you.

You Jari are gonna do this, if you're gonna come here [to the
10   house] you better think twice when you come down. You're
gonna get knocked down good =
[Jari arrives]

Sombang: You don't have something? You don't have a baby? You're out
walking around like you don't. Who are you prowling around
for?

15 Sake: = I'm telling you here you're really gonna die. You bring your
head up this step, that head of yours is gonna get broken in two.

Jari: We were walking around looking for something. We weren't
prowling around to fuck.

Kruni: You're doing good things.

20 Sake: What are you prowling around for? You go and stay up there. . . .
You don't have a baby? You don't have a baby so you go and stay
up there, ah?

Sombang: Why did you go and stay away?

Sake: Why did you go and stay away for such a long time up there?! What
25   kind of story were you telling?

Sombang: What were you up there for?

Sake: What kind of talk/story were you up there telling?
Bloody no good stinking nose of yours, it's rotted away!

Sombang: Prowl around for this [i.e., sex], I'm sick of it. I'm sick of it.

30 Kruni: This kind [of woman], hit her upside the head. When she tastes
blood, she'll understand.

Sombang: You alone. . . . Who's wife were you walking around with? [sar-
castic; i.e., you were out with a man]

35   Enough.

Sake: Is she a child who stays at home?! Is she a child who stays at home?!
What were you prowling around for?!

Sombang: You don't have any responsibilities, you just prowl around for this
[sex]. Enough. You, I have lots of nasty words. I'm gonna start
40   cursing at you now.

Sake: Why did you go up and stay up there?! Ah?! Why did you go and
stay up there?!

Sombang: Hold him [the baby]! I'm sick of this. I'm sick of it, sick of it.

Sake: Who's the woman who stays here and gets a pain in her mouth?
45   You always go away, my mouth pains bad from shouting for you.
You don't have a baby?! You're a single woman, ah?! You should
prowl around like that?! Mine, my mouth is really stinking here
[with curses].
I'm gonna let you have it . . . never mind. [pause]
50   What did you go and stay away up there for?! You stayed up there
for what?! You were looking for what that you went and stayed
away for so long?!

Jari: Shut up! Enough!

Sake: I'm gonna whip you and piss is gonna bugger you up.

Kruni: You stay where you are. Stay where you are. Tomorrow I'm gonna
55   see the face of this kind of child. You stay put. I'm gonna sleep
           first.

Jari: He's jealous so he's complaining.

Sake: He's jealous. He's jealous so he's complaining here. You see the
           time?! Is it time to be out?! Ah?! You see all the big men sleeping?!
60   You got a watch?! You see the time?! What time is it, tell me then.
           What time is it?! It's still afternoon, ah?! Ah?! Is everyone still out
           around the village? They're all out talking?! Idiot, you're out prowl-
           ing around like a pig. You're a pig. Do you hear? You're a real
           pig-woman. You don't have a head. Call out, she just stays away
65   and stays and stays. If you're a human being you have knowledge
           (*save*). [pause]
           You don't have a baby so you go and stay away. He cries, if we
           call out to you, the old one [i.e., Kruni] gets up and crosses us. Is
           it time to be out that you go and stay away?

70 Sombang: I'm sick of this.

Jari: You shut up!

Sake: Mm, she'll shut up. Mm. Right. She'll shut up for you. You do
           good things so everyone is just going to shut up for you.
           ⎡ Yanga, your head is really good, it has a lot of fat.
75 Kruni: ⎣ You sleep now-o. I'll come looking for you tomorrow.

Jari: You all go on and talk. I'm gonna beat this baby and he's gonna
           die.

Sake: Your head is full of fat. I'm gonna split it open and eat it. [pause]
           What did you go and stay away for?! Who told you to go and stay
80   away? Ah?! Did we send you on an errand that you went and stayed
           up there? You're a pig, prowling around, snuffling around, going
           and just staying away. The men are all sleeping, [if we] call out
           they're all gonna get up and be mad. They're gonna get mad at
           (*krosim*) us.

85 Kruni: Bloody idiot head.

Sake's outpouring of abuse at her sister is immediately recognizable
to any villager as a *kros*. The spatial placement of the antagonists is
appropriate: Sake and Sombang were seated at opposite ends of their
house, and Jari, once she arrived and had to enter the house to quiet
her baby, took a position well away from, and with her back turned
to, her mother and her sister. Kruni shouted his interjections from
his seat in his men's house, about fifteen meters away.

Numerous cultural assertions are made in this *kros*. By initiating and
prolonging the *kros* in the first place, Sake announces herself to be the
victim of Jari's misbehavior. This is the spark that ignites all village
*kros*es: Somebody feels put out, exploited, insulted, wronged, violated,

or mistreated by somebody else. Villagers are careful always to establish the precise nature of their victimization fairly early on in the *kros* in order to make it clear they aren't just "showing *hed*," but that theirs is a "good *kros*" (*gutpela kros*/<u>*nam εŋgɔn*</u>) and that they have ample reason to be angry. Sake begins her *kros* by appealing to a general sense of victimization, shrieking at Jari in a loud voice across the – until that moment peacefully sleeping – village that "everyone's sleeping" and implying that her baby will wake everybody up. Sombang joins in on this note, establishing her right to shout at Jari by proclaiming that she's "sick of" not being able to sleep.

Sake seizes upon this conflict with her sister as an opportunity for self-assertion. What is wrong about Jari's behavior is not so much her absence as such, but rather the fact that her neglect of her motherly duties imposes on Sake. Sake declares herself to be "the woman" who always stays at home and "gets a pain in her mouth" from having to call out to an absent Jari whenever her baby cries. Besides that, whenever she has to call out to Jari at night, Kruni and the other big men in the village get angry at *her* for waking them up. Jari is thus not only, or even mainly, guilty of negligence and unseemly promiscuity; the conflict has arisen because she has impinged upon Sake's sense of autonomy and independence by putting her in a position to do things she doesn't want to do.

The penalty for this infringement is scathing public abuse. Sake warns her sister that she is going to "whip" her and "split open" her head. She shames Jari several times by referring unflatteringly to her physical features. In line 28, Sake shouts at Jari that her nose is "stinking" and "rotting away." This is a highly insulting reference to the fact that Jari is sometimes referred to by others as "rotting nose" because the villagers think that her rather pug-shaped nose looks as though it has begun to decompose. Another blow is struck by calling Jari "Yanga" in line 74. Yanga is the name of an ugly bald man from another village; in calling her sister by this name, Sake is mockingly referring to the fact that Jari has unattractively short hair after having cut it off to get rid of lice.

In addition to personal insults, Sake also pointedly uses vulgarity to humiliate her sister. The extended pig metaphor (lines 62–81) is intended to shame Jari into realizing that the mother of a young child is expected to remain close to home at night so she can attend to her baby if the need should arise. Even if she isn't married, a mother should not be out "snuffling around" at night "looking for cock," like a "single woman," leaving her baby in the care of others who may not feel like watching him.

In a fashion characteristic of village *kros*es, Sake, Sombang, and Kruni all structure their contributions as part of an announcement or monologue about Jari's behavior. Their abuse operates on two levels: It is meant to be interpreted both as *talk to* Jari and as *talk about* Jari. One of the ways in which this is signaled is through the use of different pronouns to address Jari. Sake and her parents alternate between addressing Jari directly ("Why did you go and stay?") and in the third person ("Is she a child who stays at home?"). Jari is thus fictionalized in her own presence and must listen to others insult her and publicly evaluate her behavior as though she weren't there. This form of discourse has a distancing function: Jari is directed here to see herself as others see her. It is also an effective shaming technique. One of the worst experiences a villager can imagine is to find her- or himself suddenly the object of other people's public scrutiny. The basis for this fear is established early in childhood, as caregivers shame disobedient children by looking at them with lips curled in surprise and disgust and announcing loudly, "*Ye lukim em!/Yɛ rarɛtukun/rarɛtəŋgin!*" (Ye [exclamation of distaste] look at her/him!).[3]

Even when the direct form of address is used, the point of calling out "you" to Jari is clearly not to elicit speech from her or draw her into a dialogue. All the questions in this *kros* are rhetorical: Jari is not expected to reply at all. When she does actually respond shortly after her arrival in the house, saying, "We were walking around looking for something. We weren't prowling around to fuck" (lines 17–18), she is ignored, and Sake, Sombang, and Kruni all continue as though Jari had not spoken. Jari's excuses are not relevant; she has already been proclaimed guilty.

By answering at all, Jari risks escalating this *kros* into a fight. The participation of both her mother and her father in Sake's *kros* makes it clear that she cannot hope to seek support from them, and it is perhaps for this reason that Jari resorts to a threat to assert herself through the destruction of her baby (lines 76–7). In replying directly to Sake's abuse, Jari risks being interpreted as implying that Sake has no right to be angry. It is important for the object of a *kros* to know when it is appropriate to speak and when to remain silent. The villagers do not consider *kros*es in themselves to be attempts to negotiate blame assignment. Blame has already been assigned, and the *kros* is a public announcement of that fact. The person being blamed is free to begin a *kros* of her own in which she can assert herself by denying the accusations being hurled at her and by producing a barrage of insults and accusations of her own. This must be structured as an independent and overlapping monologue, however. Any attempt to negotiate blame assignment by providing excuses or trying to engage the accuser in a dialogue is considered "giving back mouth" (*bekim maus/sik ɛp-*).

"Giving back mouth" is a serious challenge indeed, since *kros*es are primarily occasions of self-display. Within this frame, any attempt to disrupt a person's *kros* is understood by the villagers not only as a challenge to the accuser's perception of the action that provoked the *kros,* but, more outrageously still, a challenge to the accuser's status and right of self-assertion. Children over 7 who are verbal enough to attempt to respond to their mother's angry chastisements at them begin to be confronted with this idea when they are shushed and told to "just hear my talk." If a child ignores this warning and persists in trying to argue back, he or she is shouted down with a sharp cry of "*AH!*" and threatened with a piece of firewood. Such a maternal reaction is a small-scale enactment of what usually does happen when adults begin "giving back mouth" during a *kros:* This is seen as an escalation of the conflict, and if it continues for any length of time, it will lead to the disputants leaving their houses and confronting each other on the ground. This, in turn, usually leads to violence.

In asserting themselves and in accusing Jari, Kruni, Sombang, and especially Sake make heavy use of particular discursive features such as loudness, overlapping talk, and especially repetition. Repetition is the single most important and frequently employed rhetorical device in the villagers' speech, and it figures prominently in every type of oral performance in Gapun. One of the main things that villagers do through repetition is emphasize points. Since *kros*es are always sparked off by some offense that someone has committed, this offense usually stands out as the backbone of the *kros,* and it gets recycled continually throughout the accuser's talk. Sake and Sombang consistently return to Jari's misbehavior, stressing repeatedly that she has been out "prowling around" and wondering cynically why she had to "go and stay away so long" with her friends at the "up" end of the village. The rhetorical question, "You don't have a baby?" which means "You have a baby!" is also peppered throughout the *kros.*

Repetition occurs both within a turn and between turns. In both cases, repetition is either exact repetition, where a previous utterance is repeated verbatim; paraphrase, where the sense of the words is repeated but the words themselves are different; or repetition with variation, where a previous utterance is modified in some way, such as changing a question into a statement. All of these ways of repeating are common in village speech. But in addition, one of the most widely used forms of repetition used in Gapun is repetition through code-switching. A reorganization of the way in which a short extract of the *kros* (lines 20–28) is displayed can illustrate the form and functions of this latter type of repetition involving two languages.

	TAIAP	TOK PISIN
Sake:	What are you prowling around for? You go and stay up there .... You don't have a baby?	
		You don't have a baby so you go and stay up there, ah?
Sombang:	Why did you go and stay away?	
Sake:		Why did you go and stay away for such a long time up there?!
		What kind of story were you telling?
Sombang:	What were you up there for?	
Sake:	What kind of talk/story were you up there telling?	
		Bloody no good stinking nose of yours, it's rotted away!

With the exception of the insult about Jari's nose, this entire stretch of speech consists entirely of repetitions. Sake's rhetorical questions about prowling around and about the baby are repetitions of earlier utterances (lines 1–2, 12–14), and the rest of the talk consists of repetitions on the topic of why Jari remained so long with her friends. Sake's repetitions are prompted both by her own utterances (lines 21–2, 25–6) and by Sombang's contributions (lines 23–4).

A great deal of the code-switched repetitions in the villagers' speech follows a call–response pattern in which the speaker calls out an opinion, threat, warning, or thought, and the respondent (or the speaker her- or himself) echoes that utterance in another language. The fact that the template for the code-switched response is frequently the surface structure of the immediately preceding utterance/call makes it clear that villagers pay close attention to the structure of the talk they are producing. And a striking characteristic of much of the code-switching that occurs in Gapun is that it appears to be motivated more by the surface features of the previous utterance than by any underlying social principle. Indeed, the salience for the villagers of this kind of oscillation between languages appears for the most part to be not so much the evocation of the different values associated with their languages, as is commonly argued in studies on code-switching[4] (one would be hard-pressed, for example, to identify the aspect of the values associated with Tok Pisin to which Sake is alluding when she suddenly switches to that language in lines 21–2), as it is the construction of a rhythmically patterned discourse. There is an aesthetic, almost musical, quality to much of the speech that villagers produce. It is as though they continually monitor their own speech and that of others in order to collaborate to produce talk that contains a measure of balance between Taiap and Tok Pisin.

The effect of balance between languages that villagers like Sake manage to achieve through their patterned repetition and code-switching may be the linguistic manifestation of the more general concern with social balance that is a central issue in the life of every villager. Together with the majority of other Papua New Guinean communities, Gapuners have a strong sense that all social relationships should be reciprocal and balanced, and much of what the villagers do is directed toward maintaining a balance, or spitefully and pointedly upsetting it. In the past, the institution of sister exchange and the tit-for-tat pattern of warfare practiced by the villagers maintained a very real sense of balance between different clans. Sorcery today is considered by the villagers to serve much the same function. Between individuals, balance is embodied in reciprocal exchange relationships and in notions such as the belief that one's matrilineal relatives can die because of one's "wrongs." It seems as though the pervasiveness of these kinds of ideas about balance in social relationships also plays a role in shaping the ways in which the villagers use their languages in their talk to one another. In maintaining an acute sense of social balance, bi- and multilingual Gapuners have developed a keen sense of linguistic balance as well.[5]

Talk like that which occurs in Sake's *kros* is not only a matter of aesthetics, however; it also serves pragmatic functions. By repeating through code-switching, villagers extend and stress their arguments. Between turns, this type of repetition allows speakers to express their support and approval of an argument with great linguistic economy but without simply parroting. Instead, by repeating through code-switching, a supporter is, in effect, taking the words out of the original speaker's mouth and making them her or his own.

An important by-product of these kinds of overlapping aesthetic and pragmatic considerations about discourse is that speakers often convey the same information in both Taiap and Tok Pisin.[6] In the extract from the *kros* displayed above, virtually every utterance is said in both the villagers' languages. Adults listening to such speech are likely to evaluate and appreciate it in terms of the aesthetic sense and pragmatic information it is conveying. For children, the fact that speech produced in the vernacular very frequently is repeated in Tok Pisin means that they have the opportunity to follow and understand oral performances by adults even if they do not command the Taiap language.

Women, children, *kros*es, and *hed*

A great deal of the villagers' time and talk is spent defending their autonomy. Gapuners argue so frequently and vigorously that Sake's husband, Allan, in-married from a community near the Marienberg mission station, once felt compelled to characterize Gapun acidly as "a little village with big conflicts" (*liklik ples na planti wari i save kamap*). Judging by the prodigious number of these conflicts, it sometimes seems as though Gapuners find it uncomfortable crowding together in the same little village. Many men and women, vociferously "sick of" the fact that other villagers steal from them or impinge upon their autonomy in some other way, periodically threaten to leave the village and move away forever with their families into the jungle. During the dry season of June to September, a number of families do move deep into the jungle to their bush houses for a month or more at a time. But they always come back, and immediately a new cycle of self-assertion is begun, in the form of fights, *kros*es and the ostentatious destruction of personal property. It is as though the villagers have decided that the only way they can live together at all is by making sure that everyone else is constantly aware of their rights. And so these get loudly proclaimed whenever some sort of violation provides the opportunity to do so.

All of the ways that villagers have developed to do this proclaiming both reflect and reinforce their view of themselves as "having *hed*." "Having *hed*" is a critical concept for the people of Gapun. Harshly devalued in public rhetoric as bad, selfish, and uncivilized, *hed* is nonetheless held to be a fundamental and uncontestable attribute of the self, signifying personal will and autonomy. Talk of an individual's *hed* often begins before that person is born; so in a sense, a person exists in the village as an autonomous, willful individual even before he or she emerges from the womb. After birth, babies continue to be treated as aggressive individuals with strong *hed*s of their own. They are in a perpetual state of anger and dissatisfaction, ready to cry and be *kros* when their desires are not met, demanding attention and accommodation from their caregivers. In children up to 3 years old, aggressive behavior is expected, encouraged, and regarded with amusement. When mothers visit one another, they sometimes hold their babies close together and encourage them to fight. "Kamik," Paso will tell her 10-month-old daughter, dangling her in front of Jari's baby, Kunji, "Go hit him. Go on. Hit him." Babies in Gapun finding themselves near a dog are encouraged to hit the dog, not pet it. And a child observed whacking at a chicken with a stick or raising a knife at an older sibling will be rewarded with smiles and and cries of "Watch out, he's *kros* now." Young children in Gapun embody *hed*.

But if young children are always showing *hed* and acting cross, the same is true of women. Whenever Sake or some other woman has a loud *kros,* those village men not directly involved in some way make clucking sounds of recognition, shake their heads disparagingly, and mutter knowingly that "this kind of rubbish talk is the habit of women, it's their way" (*desela kain rabis tok em we bilong ol meri, pasin bilong ol*). Women are collectively held by village men to be more *bikhed* than are men. In ways similar to most Papua New Guinean societies, women in Gapun are associated with individualism, atomicity, and antisocial behavior. Traditionally, men, through their common residence in the men's house and through their perpetual preparations for and acting out of funerary feasts, initiation rites, and war raids represented and embodied cooperation and society. The collective actions of men were considered the "bones" (*bun*/<u>*niŋ*</u>) of society. The actions of women, even though these were sometimes collective in nature,[7] do not appear to have been accorded the same type of cultural significance as those of men, and women were and continue to be represented as divisive troublemakers whose selfish actions constantly threaten the solid, manly group. It is remembered that Arena's wife seduced his younger brother, Andena, in myth, thus precipitating the great rift between the two brothers. When men in Gapun say "we fight over women," they are saying that they would not fight if there were no women; i.e., women, with their sex,[8] their *kros*es, and their unwillingness to "suppress" their *heds,* are the root of all conflicts.

Women in Gapun do not share this view of themselves as destructive troublemakers. Women who have *kros*es do not interpret their own behavior in reference to the stereotype. When Sake, for example, has a *kros,* she does not consider her own behavior to be divisive; she is legitimately defending her rights and autonomy from attack. When another woman has a *kros,* however, then Sake will often be quick to sniff that the woman is "a woman who always gets angry for no reason" (*meri bilong kros nating nating*).

The existence of a culturally elaborated stereotype of women as quarrelsome means that such a role is available for any woman to act out. And as a stereotypically female role, it is unattractive for men. The most striking global characteristics of *kros*es – the fact that they occur inside or in the close proximity of houses (which the villagers associate, in distinction to the men's house, with femaleness), and the fact that they are overtly divisive and inflammatory in nature – underline the *kros* as a quintessential female activity.

Because men in the village like to pretend that they have no conflicts with others, they dismiss *kros*es as *samting bilong ol meri*/<u>*naŋrɔma ɔrak*</u> (what women do). The village stereotype of ideal male behavior puts pressure on the men to be more sociable, generous, dignified, and temperate than their wives, who are expected to fly off the handle and have a *kros* at the slightest excuse. In most cases, a married man is able to uphold this stereotype and simultaneously announce infringements by simply informing his wife about some slight or infraction that he has been subjected to (such as somebody not returning a borrowed axe or shovel). The wife, always anxious to defend her own autonomy and that of her family, takes it from there and, in doing so, reinforces the stereotype of bickering women through her behavior.[9] Almost invariably, *kros*es in Gapun are conducted by women. All those villagers who have acquired a reputation for being perpetually prepared to break out into a *kros* at a moment's notice – Sake, her sister Erapo, Paso's sister-in-law Mairum, and Sopak – are women. And even on those occasions when men publicly *belhat* (get angry, shout), this anger is usually directed at that man's wife or his close female relatives. So public arguments almost inevitably involve women at some level. Both men and women blame (other) women for making trouble and "showing *hed.*"

Both women and young children are thus considered to embody *hed,* and certain types of verbal behavior are remarked upon by the villagers as indications of this *hed.* For women, it is *kros*es. For children, it is their first words. The first words attributed to children between 2 and 7 months – *ɔki* (I'm getting out of here), *mnda* (I'm sick of this), and *aiata* (stop it) – are clear expressions of *hed* for the villagers. No one imagines that any of these words have been *learned* by children. They all are attributed long before a child begins to repeat fragments of the speech of others or interact verbally with anyone else. Instead of repetition or invitations to interaction, Gapuners view these first three, fundamentally nonsocial words as pure manifestations of the child's nature. The 5-month-old baby who is held to declare "I'm getting out of here," who is seen as ordering others to "stop it," and who is believed to obstinately announce "I'm sick of this" is considered to be truly expressing her or his self. It is revealing that this expressing is thought to be done with Taiap words. This is not an indication of parental expectations that their children "naturally" speak Taiap first because it is the village vernacular; in fact, all language used by children after these first three words is interpreted by parents as speech in Tok Pisin (Chapter 6). Instead, the fact that the villagers consider that a child's first, fundamentally antisocial linguistic expressions are uttered in the village vernacular suggests that Gapuners perceive a link between the expression of *hed* and the Taiap language.

This link between *hed* and the vernacular is amplified by the associations that Taiap has with women, by virtue of their perceived ties to the land, the clans, and to traditional lifestyles. Because women, in addition to embodying salient dimensions of the vernacular, are also collectively stereotyped as big-headed, unwilling to suppress *hed*, short-tempered, and divisive, a dense web of associations crystallizes in the village. And within this framework, *kros*es – that distinctively female speech genre – come to be seen primarily as something done in the vernacular.

Actually, *kros*es are not conducted only in Taiap. The rhetorical power that code-switching makes possible is available to all bilingual villagers in all their talk. And because *kros*es are occasions for public self-assertion, they are rhetorical events par excellence. Skilled and experienced *kros*ers like Sake do not hesitate to blast their antagonists with the full force of their rhetorical arsenal, using code-switching between Taiap and Tok Pisin[10] to stress, interrupt, highlight, and contradict.

But in spite of the code-switching that occurs during the course of a *kros*, the *kros* as a verbal genre is understood as a vernacular occurrence, and there is a marked preference in the villagers' speech to use the vernacular when they have or become involved in a *kros*. In Sake's *kros*, for instance, even though Sake continually code-switches for rhetorical effect, the other participants speak almost exclusively in Taiap. The result is that the bulk of the *kros* is conducted in Taiap.

For the villagers of Gapun then, *hed*, although it is a fundamental aspect of every villager, is linked most strongly with childishness, femaleness, divisiveness, *kros*es, and the Taiap language. When one "supresses *hed*" (*daunim hed*) in order to be regarded as a "good" man or woman, one supresses all of these things.

4. Showing *save*

Sake is combing her hair. In the village, this is a solemn, careful, severe practice. Sake sits in the sun on her veranda, straight-backed, with her head bowed over a shirt that she has spread out between her legs. Inserting the wide Afro-style comb at the back of her head, she yanks it violently through her hair, ripping out tangled knots and splashing tiny black lice out onto the shirt. After she has done this several times, Sake pauses and examines the contents of the shirt. Then, looking intent, she begins to exterminate the vermin in front of her, slowly and methodically squeezing them between the fingernails of her forefinger and thumb. Sometimes the larger ones explode like a berry with an audible pop. When all the lice on her shirt have been squashed in this manner, Sake begins the combing process again. After about ten minutes of combing and pinching, satisfied that most of the lice in her hair have been ousted and destroyed, Sake will lift the shirt full of torn-out hair and dead lice, and she will shake it out onto the floor of her house.

As she sits tugging the comb through her hair, Sake keeps an eye on her sister Jari's 10-month-old baby, Kunji. The child has been left in Sake's care while his mother collects wild greens from the jungle. Kunji has recently learned to propel himself across the bark floor by scooting himself in a sitting position with one leg; moving along in this way he has come across a large, battered metal dish set down in the middle of the floor. In this dish, Sake always tries to keep some embers burning so that she can dry bits of tobacco and light her cigarettes without having to get up and go to the hearth. Three meters away, Sake watches as Kunji puts out his hand to touch the embers glowing in the dish:

Text 4.1

<u>Ai. That's fire. Fire.</u>	[pause, Kunji looks at Sake]
You see it too?!	[pause]
Fire. It's fire.	[pause, Kunji reaches toward the embers]
<u>Tsk. Fire, it's fire, fire.</u>	[irritated]

118

You don't have ears, ah?!	[pause]
Tsk. Fire! Fire! Enough,	
the fire's gonna burn you now.	[Kunji pays no attention]
The fire's gonna burn him.	[to Kunji]
Fire *ario.*	[threatening exclamation calling out to the fire to come and get Kunji]
Fire *ario.*	[pause]
Tsk.	[Sake throws down her comb, gets up, goes over to Kunji and lifts him up. She is irritated.]
You don't have a little bit of	
save in that big head of yours, ah?!	

Kruni has just finished his dinner. It is late and it is dark, and the meal that his wife, Sombang, finally brought to him after much cursing – a dry, burned sago pancake and a small strip of hard pig skin – has left Kruni unsatisfied and in a bad mood. He sits disgruntled in his men's house, chewing betel nut and sweating as his young granddaughter builds a fire underneath the men's house to drive away mosquitoes. Now, as his eyes and mouth fill with the smoke billowing up through the cracks in the floor, Kruni announces his opinion about women:

Text 4.2

Women, they're always doing bad things. Before women didn't used to show these kind of ways, *bikhed, kros,* get angry and shout, complain all the time. Only once in a while, because they were all afraid of sorcery, of the spear, too. If they showed these kind of *kros* ways, *bikhed* ways, they knew that the men would kill them. Now all the spears are locked up, now is the time of Europeans. Good time, [but] the women they still keep the heathen ways. They don't do good things. They don't suppress their *hed* a little bit. No way. Talk *kros,* bad talk, that's the way of the women, their habit. They don't have any *save.*

The people of Gapun have a great deal to say about what they call *save* (pronounced "sáv-ei"). For the villagers, this word has a number of intertwined connotations. In its most basic sense, *save* signifies knowledge: the knowledge of facts and being able to learn from experience and through doing. But it also means more than that. *Save* is knowledge about appropriate behavior and speech, awareness of social obligations and roles, cognizance of the consequences that one's own or someone else's actions or words can have. *Save* is a metaphor often used in Gapun to mean social sensitivity and solidarity. When Kruni, in the middle of a tirade about not getting his dinner, screams at Sombang from his men's house, shouting that she *"nogat save"* (has no *save*), he means that she is not fulfilling her role as his wife and as a good Christian; he means that she is "showing *hed,*" flaunting her autonomy, being selfish. *Save,* as Kruni implies in his criticism of women, is the knowledge that one sometimes must "suppress *hed,*" i.e., compromise, fulfill social obligations, and accommodate others even if one doesn't want to. It is the existential quality that male villagers frequently contend most plainly differentiates men from women and that all villagers consider most clearly differentiates adults from children. Adults have, and should continually demonstrate that they have, *save.* Children don't. When a toddler suddenly plummets through a hole in the floor despite warning shouts or when a baby burns himself by plunging his hands into a plate of hot sago jelly that his mother has just prepared, he is comforted, told not to have such a strong *hed* and laughingly chided, "You're really stupid. You don't have a grain of *save* in that big head of yours." Similarly, when children up to about 7 years steal, break, or lose objects belonging to others, they are scolded and then immediately forgiven because they *nogat save* (don't have *save*).

But despite frequently heard admonitions like this – that young children who show no sign of comprehending what words like "fire" mean or of understanding rights of possession *nogat save* – villagers conceptualize *save* as already present in even the youngest babies. Attaining *save,* coming to know, is not something that the villagers think children can be taught. Children can be taught certain things, like the names of objects and of relatives, but *save* itself is not taught; *save,* in the villagers' view, "breaks open" (*bruk*/*krarara ɔ-*) inside the child, like an egg. Sake's sister Erapo described how the villagers view their children's learning process and the adult role in it:

We teach kids to call the names of things, like, um, what . . . like pig, dog, betel nut. Or coconut, or *kandere* [mother's brother], that's what we teach them. We'll call it, and they'll repeat it. [pause] Later now, when their *save* breaks open now, then they'll start to learn everything really fast.

Erapo highlights the villagers' view that teaching and learning are two distinct processes and that the one can occur independently of the other. Parents consider that they can tell their children to "call the names of things," but that the children will only "start to learn" once their *save* breaks open inside of them.

Viewing the emergence of knowledge in this way has two main consequences. First, such a view determines the kinds of talk that village caregivers provide for their children. Because villagers believe that children will learn on their own once their *save* cracks open, they see no reason to be didactic in their interactions with children. When Sake sees her 10-month-old nephew about to grab hold of a burning coal, she warns him – not by explicitly ordering him not to touch the ember – but by insistently repeating the word "fire" in an irritated tone, implying that he should understand the meaning of the word and the consequences of reaching into the fire. Kunji's lack of comprehension is taken as evidence of his lack of *save*.

Caregivers in the village are also notably unconcerned with aspects of language such as referent identification. Only occasionally and incidentally do adults explicitly link names and referents for their children. For example, the earliest verbal routines enacted between a mother and her child are distraction routines, begun whenever the child cannot be quieted by a breast or an object. In these interactions, which continue until the third year, a mother swoops a crying child off the floor, takes it to where it can see outside, and extends her arm, pointing at the distance. Early versions of this routine consist mainly of the key Tok Pisin word *em ia* (there/over there), said in a steadily rising singsong intonation, followed by the name of some object or person, e.g.,

Text 4.3

Em ia pik ia, pík. Pik ia, em ia. Yu lukim tu?

Pik, pik ia. Lukim wanpela pik i kam ia. Em ia . . .

There pig there, píg. Pig there, there. You see it?

Pig, pig there. Look at the pig coming. There . . .

The heavy use of repetition and stress on the word "pig" might seem didactic, and sometimes this kind of repetition is used by caregivers to teach a child to say something. The purpose of these distraction routines is not primarily to link an object with its name, however, since more often than not the object being pointed at and named will not actually be visible anywhere. Mothers engaging their children in these routines are not concerned with teaching the children; they believe that the routines will stop the child from crying. Later, when children themselves begin to respond to and initiate these routines with caregivers, they will be corrected if they point to a house or a tree and call it a pig ("Where's a pig? Ah? Where? That's not a pig, that's a tree, *sia* [exclamation of surprise] you're stupid (*longlong/babasak*), that's a tree, tree"). Until then, the primary purpose of the distraction routines is to distract the child away from its own concerns and focus its attention outside itself. For the child, it must often be unclear what a prompt to look at actually refers to, since the referent will either be obscure (as when a mother points towards a mass of trees in the distance and tells her child *"Em ia, pisin ia"* [There, a bird]), invisible (as when children are told to look at spirits whom caregivers claim are coming to get them), or something completely different from what is being pointed at, as here, where a mother points toward the rainforest and urges her child to look at a (nonexistent) pig.

2nd

The second major consequence of the villagers' view that *save* is something that "breaks open" inside the child is that villagers wait for and remark on signs that indicate that a child's *save* has begun to emerge. Children in the village are thought to show evidence of *save* when they start, at between 20 and 30 months, to use language by themselves to engage others in verbal interactions. Gapuners thus conceptualize a break between what they hold to be a child's early language – words like *ɔki̯, mnda*, and *aiata*, which are considered to be blunt declarations of the child's true aggressive *hed* – and their later verbal utterances, which are observed to be interactive in nature and expressive of *save*. Language used in interaction with others is understood as both an indication and a result of *save* "breaking open." In recognizing such a link between verbal interaction and *save*, villagers are asserting their belief that language is one of the chief means through which an individual expresses her or his social competence.

Talking consensus

In informal interactions, this belief is expressed through the work that villagers do to accommodate others verbally. Speakers demonstrate their *save* by accommodating others in language choice and in the opinions they express. Villagers are keen to accommodate others linguistically, by speaking to them in their vernacular languages and by being careful to express opinions and choose topics they are sure will suit their interlocutors.

The most powerful expression of the villagers' concern with displaying *save* through speech, however, is the verbal genre of oratory. Oratories in Gapun are occasions on which the village men engage in speeches that downplay tension, smooth over disagreement, stress consensus, and, in doing so, create contexts in which they and others may publicly demonstrate their *save*. Oratorical speeches have always taken place in the men's cult houses, and they generally concern matters pertinent to the orchestration of male group activities. Anthropologists observing Papua New Guinean societies have noted that the relatively few occasions during which a group identifies itself as a collective "society" are those characterized by the synchronic participation of large numbers of men, such as warfare, ceremonial exchange, or initiation.[1] Collective male actions like these have traditionally constituted visible pageants of male consensus and solidarity, put on display for the villagers themselves and for the benefit of those groups with whom they fought and traded or whom they entertained at funerary feasts. The kind of talk used in the men's house to debate and organize these group displays has come to be associated with the values of consensus and solidarity that underlie those actions.

In the past, the only places in the village where conflicts were specifically forbidden to occur were the men's cult houses. To argue or fight under the eyes of the ancestors or, worse still, in the presence of the *tambaran* (the men's cult deity), would call forth their wrath upon one's clan and possibly upon one's entire village. Anyone foolhardy enough to break this taboo would be forced to ritually "buy back the shame" (*baim (bek) sem*) of the ancestors by killing one or more large village pigs and distributing the cooked meat, along with impressive quantities of betel nut and tobacco, to the men in the men's house. Some of this offering would get presented to the ancestors and/or the *tambaran,* and long speeches would be made to appease the offended spirits and ask them not to vent some terrible retribution on the villagers.

Even though most of the cult activities have not been practiced in over forty years, the links between the cult houses, the ancestors, and the *tambaran* are still extremely salient and strong. Open disagreement and fighting in the men's house remains forbidden, and the kind of talk traditionally associated with the cult houses endures today. One reason for the persistence of oratorical speech is that the men's house is still where village meetings are held and major issues discussed. Today, such meetings usually take place on a Sunday afternoon or in the early evening of other days, and they are usually called by the village *komiti.* The *komiti* (from the English "committee") is a village man who has been elected to a post of leadership instituted by the Australian colonial government and later continued by the independent Papua New Guinean government. This man is supposed to be the village's *maus man* (representative/speaker; lit. "mouth-man") on those rare occasions when the village receives a visit from the police or a government official, and he is supposed to be the one who settles all intravillage disputes. In addition to these duties, which in Gapun are more nominal than real, the *komiti* is the one who is supposed to be responsible for organizing the villagers to do communal work in and around the village, so that it is kept clean and tidy.

When he wants to call a village meeting, the *komiti* announces this by beating several times on an old slit-gong drum. This beating is repeated 20 to 40 minutes later, and at this time the village men are expected to make their way to the men's house.[2] Men and women are almost always up enough on the state of village affairs to know what the meeting is being called for, and the men go to the men's house or remain at home, depending on their desire to participate or "hear the talk." If the meeting has been called to discuss a subject that requires the participation of women, such as certain types of communal labor, women will be shouted at from the men's house to come and "hear the talk." Those who want to will gather with their small children around the men's house, sitting on the ground in front of the house or standing against it resting their elbows on the men's house floor. Even when the women aren't summoned to hear the men make speeches, those women like Sake or Membo who live close enough to the men's house to hear what is going on inside sometimes entertain themselves by settling in on their verandas with their betel nut and cigarettes to listen to the oratories. To the annoyance of the men, these women "have no shame" about laughing raucously if they hear something that amuses them, or about contributing loud exclamations of agreement or distaste as the speeches continue.

Meetings are called in the men's house to announce the need for labor to clear overgrown paths or repair rotten footbridges; to work out the arrangements that have to be made for funerary feasts; to try to find out who or what is causing a villager to be sick; to discuss the meaning of messages and news items that villagers bring back from other villages, from trips to Angoram or Marienberg, or from the schoolteachers in Wongan; or to arrange to help a village man and his wife in some task that requires a number of laborers, such as carrying house posts, roofing a house, or clearing the forest to plant a garden. If the meeting is called on behalf of a particular individual or couple, then that man and his wife will normally send a few plates of sago and pig meat or banana or yam stew to the men's house, to be eaten by the men before the meeting is formally begun. By eating this food, men commit themselves to performing the work requested by the couple. Before, during, and directly after such a meal, men sit together in small groups in the men's house, chatting, eating from the same large, canoe-shaped plates, and sharing betel nut and tobacco. Once the oratories begin, the atmosphere in the men's house becomes more formal in that attention becomes more focused on the speakers, who address the entire congregation of men and, if they have been called to the men's house, women.

Gapuners have no word in their language for oratory. The villagers do not explicitly recognize the structural and rhetorical features of oratory as something specific or unique enough to warrant a particular label of its own. The vernacular-language name that the village men give for oratory if they are pressed – *ambagaiŋa nam* (men's house talk) – indicates that the salient feature of oratories for the villagers is the spatial and social context in which they occur and not the details of how they are performed.[3]

Because they are so strongly associated with the men's house, oratories, by definition, are male. Only men in Gapun are considered to orate. There is no rule or explicit consensus in the village that women cannot orate,[4] and strong-willed women like Sopak, Sake, and her sister Erapo do occasionally speak in public gatherings that concern both men and women. Women's speeches contain many of the same rhetorical features, such as repetition, that are predominant in oratories, but they differ importantly in that they are much briefer than most men's speeches, and they never contain any of the particular formulaic tags that the men use to mark their speech as oratorical. Furthermore, women, who are not allowed inside the men's house, obviously cannot speak from there, and so their contributions to a discussion have a peripheral character that is underscored by their spatial placement. Because of these factors, and because of the historical and symbolic relationship between men and oratorical speech, women who make short speeches at public gatherings are not considered to be orating; they are, rather, "complaining."

Not even all men can legitimately orate, however; this privilege is restricted to married men and widowers. Usually, men do not begin making speeches in the men's house until they are married and at least in their late twenties. Some village men, to whom the other villagers sometimes refer as "closed-mouth men" (*ol mauspas man*) grow old and die without ever orating. There is no formal instruction in oratory techniques, and young men seem to learn to orate through a lifetime of lounging around in the men's house listening to the speeches of other men. During the meetings in the men's house in which oratory occurs, unmarried men and boys from the age of 15 are free to cast short comments or suggestions into most discussions, but they never make long speeches. If and when a married man decides that he wishes to begin orating, he will do so in his own time and on his own accord, because oratories are never invited or prompted; they are announced by the speaker with formal markers such as, "Ah, excuse (me), I have a little something to say to you all" (*Ah, eskus, mi gat liklik tok bilong tokim yupela*) or by first thanking the previous speaker for having spoken ("Thank you very much . . . " [*Tenk yu tru . . .*]). A speaker may even rise from his sitting position and remain standing throughout his speech. When finished, speakers usually conclude with the formulaic "That's it, my little talk" (*Em tasol liklik tok bilong mi*).

An average speech lasts about fifteen minutes. Some of the village men can continue for greater lengths, sometimes talking for up to forty-five minutes. During these long speeches, the attention of the listeners waxes and wanes. At times almost everyone in and around the men's house will be carrying on private conversations, laughing, offering each other betel nut or tobacco, and joking while someone is making a speech. At other times during the same oratory, attention becomes refocused on the speaker, and any loud laughter or joking will be censured by the senior men.

In oratory, stress is not placed on solving problems or actually achieving concrete results, although this is one potential outcome of the meetings in the men's house, and it is occasionally realized. More often, however, when the time comes to perform the activity that had been agreed upon, the consensus that had been arrived at in the men's house during oratorical speeches is ignored by some or even most of the individuals who had been present and took part in making the decision in the first place. No matter what they say or agree to during a formal meeting, everyone in Gapun knows that men and women will, in the end, do what they want (*wokim long laik*). Even if it turns out that everyone actually shows up to work on the appointed day, no one in the village attributes this to feelings of obligation toward "keeping their word." Rather, the villagers note airily, they and others decided to participate in the work because they "felt like it" (*laik i kirap*) at the time.

The cosmetic nature of any consensus reached during a session of oratorical speeches is a manifestation of the way villagers consider that speech should be used in interpersonal interactions. Like all groups, Gapuners have firm, if unspoken, ideas about how linguistic interactions should be managed. Whereas in some cultures speakers are encouraged to use language to express their opinions, feelings, or thoughts, in Gapun, cultural stress is placed on using language to show *save,* and that means using language to accommodate and facilitate agreement. This particular emphasis on how language should be used has two major consequences for the speeches that are delivered in the men's house.

First, it means that talk during formal village meetings is expected to be and is interpreted as being consensus-oriented. Unlike the *kros,* which is the sole village speech genre in which conflict is explicitly foregrounded, open disagreement is not possible within the framework of oratorical speech. The only way of truly disagreeing in a social situation dominated by oratory is to say nothing at all. Meetings such as the yearly parent–teacher meeting in Wongan, which are always pockmarked with long silences on the part of the villagers and by anxious urgings of one or two men to *"Toktok! Toktok!"* (Talk! Talk!), are meetings in which most of the participants are very much opposed to the general direction that the talk in the meeting is taking.

Second, the expectation that speakers will use language to express *save* means that the particular facts under discussion and the specific points made by speakers in their oratories are not as important as the evocation of a general feeling of agreement. It also means that a person's statements on any subject are expected to reflect not their true opinions on the matter, but rather their willingness to exhibit their *save* and agree. And *this* means that no one in the village can ever be sure of what anyone else is really thinking.

[handwritten margin note: lying + intention]

Villagers are aware, however, that there are many ways to agree and that people may agree with their "mouth" but not with their "thoughts." So they are always on the lookout for the "true" meaning of a person's words in any given context. The fact that language, besides being a means of agreeing is also a subtle instrument that can express many meanings simultaneously, does not escape anybody. On the contrary, in a system where one should not explicitly say what one means, the attention of both speakers and listeners becomes focused on ways of not saying what one means.

One striking way in which orators in Gapun are able to create an atmosphere of consensus – or, at least, one in which open disagreement is suppressed – while they simultaneously convey a range of opinions that conflict with that consensus is by continuously reneging on and dissociating themselves from the talk that they produce. This rhetorical strategy frequently results in talk that is so confusing that it is no longer clear to anyone exactly what opinion is being expressed. A typical example of this occurred when Sopak's husband, Mone, the village *komiti* at the time, informed the villagers during a large meeting concerning the school that the owners of the only outboard motor in the village had decided to begin charging people to use it.

Text 4.4

Mone:	. . . wherever you go, ah, tell about this, that the motor costs four Kina now to go. [pause] And come.
Marame:	We have to spread this news everywhere =
Mone:	= everywhere. Whoever goes anywhere has to tell people this. There's a charge now for the motor. [pause] Not for us. For us as well, whoever has [money] can give it. If not, he can go free, supply petrol.

There are several unclear messages in Mone's short announcement. Because he pauses noticeably between the words "to go" and "And come," it is not clear whether the price of 4 Kina is for a round trip or whether a passenger must pay 4 Kina to go and 4 Kina to come back to the village. Also, at first, Mone states that the new charge for the motor applies only to people from villages other than Gapun. The 4-Kina fee, he informs everyone explicitly, is "not for us," i.e., the villagers. In his next breath, however, he contradicts this statement by first telling the villagers that the new fee is in fact "for us as well," but he then clarifies that to seemingly mean only those villagers who have money. He then mystifies the matter further by explaining that those who have no money can "go free," *if* they "supply petrol." In fact, this means not going free at all, since petrol must be purchased, and, moreover, the cost of petrol to Marienberg or Angoram would be at least five times the cost of the 4-Kina passenger fee. Mone's last statement also raises the question of what the 4 Kina is actually for, and of whether those who pay the fee would also be responsible for supplying petrol for the trip.

The reason for Mone's use of this type of rhetorical strategy was his realization that he was making an extremely controversial announcement. Outboard motors in Gapun are a deep and dependable source of conflict. In the late 1970s, Sake's brother Akupi and another village man, Samek, decided to buy an outboard motor each. Each managed to pool together approximately 400 Kina from relatives, and they went to the bank in Angoram with this money and explained that their village needed an outboard motor or two. The bank gave each man a loan of 400 Kina, and the two traveled to the town of Wewak and purchased two 15-horsepower outboard motors for the money. Neither of these motors lasted very long. Akupi's motor pulled loose from its bindings and plunged to the bottom of the Sepik River soon after it was purchased (because, it was said, people from Mangan, the Sepik village from which Sake's husband, Allan, comes, were angry at Sake); and Samek's motor "buggered up" after a few years because of rust and inadequate care. So by 1987, Gapun had been without any outboard motor at all for a number of years. This fact was loudly bemoaned almost daily by someone in the village. The rapid loss of both these expensive motors had also generated bitterness among the relatives who had contributed to their purchase. These people felt that they hadn't received their money's worth from the deal.

One day, the news spread throughout Gapun that somebody from a Sepik village who knew about outboard motors had helped Samek and that his old motor was suddenly running again. No sooner had villagers begun to consider the possibilities of this happy event, however, than Samek and his wife, Mairum, decided to charge for the use of their motor, as they knew was done in other villages. Upon hearing that Mone had called a general village meeting that evening to discuss why some of the village children had run away from school, Samek and Mairum asked him to convey their decision to the other villagers. Mone understood well enough what the general reaction to this announcement would be, and so in order to dampen the conflict he was certain would arise, and also to make it clear that he himself had no part in the announcement itself, he chose a strategy of dissociation. Mone's meta-message was not lost on anybody, and the villagers all agreed afterward that the "meaning" of the announcement was that Samek and Mairum were "greedy about their motor. They don't want anybody to use it."

A similar strategy of rhetorical dissociation was consistently adopted by the leaders of the village *yut* [*grup*] (youth group) over the issue of payment to the group for its work. *Yut* is a government-instituted village work force to which, despite its name, all village adults and adolescents ideally belong. In early 1986, a young *yut kodinata* (youth coordinator) made a brief appearance in a village near Gapun and explained that something new, called *yut*, had "come up." The purpose of *yut* was to keep young men from leaving their villages, drifting into the towns, and becoming *raskol*s (petty-gang members). *Yut* was designed to strengthen ties in the village by providing an organizational basis through which the villagers could perform communal labor like cutting grass, cleaning around the village, or growing communal cash crops. In addition, *yut* was to constitute a work force that individual village entrepreneurs could hire to do work that would help them earn more cash, i.e., a man could hire the village *yut* to clear his garden, harvest his coffee, and so forth. The main attraction of *yut* for the villagers of Gapun was the youth coordinator's promise that the government intended to give money to all villages that formed youth groups.[5] So the villagers complied willingly and formed a *yut grup* in their village, duly electing, on the instructions given by the youth coordinator, a *presiden, namba tu presiden* (vice-president), *kuskus* (secretary), and *tresara* (treasurer).

Since its inception, however, there had been confusion about how people who wanted to hire the youth group for a specific job would pay for its services. Some villagers wanted to be able to pay for communal labor in the traditional manner, which involves sending large plates of sago and pig meat to the men's house to announce the work and decide on a day to perform it, supplying the workers with a lunch of sago and coconut soup while the work is being performed, and feeding the workers with a large meal of sago and pig meat at the end of the day. Others, particularly those who had been elected to positions of leadership in the *yut*, insisted that all *yut* work should be paid for with money.[6] Others maintained that both money *and* food should be forthcoming.[7] This was an inflamed issue, because some villagers asserted that they had no money. The matter was raised at least six times at various meetings in the men's house during 1986–7, and each time it was brought up, lengthy oratories were made and a consensus was seemingly reached. Still, no one in Gapun was ever sure about what kind of payment their own youth group would accept. Confusion surrounding this issue led the villagers to ignore their own *yut* and instead get the youth groups of other villages to come and do work for them.

The reason for the confusion was due largely to the oratorical strategy of dissociation. The problem was that the youth leaders considered that they understood the purpose and function of *yut* better than the rest of the villagers, and they wanted to "fill up the youth group's bank" (*pulamapim benk bilong ol yut*) with money, as the *yut kodinata* had told them to do. They intended to do this by insisting that all work done by the *yut* had to be paid for by money. To push this standpoint too strongly would, however, have resulted in an open conflict, since several villagers (the most vocal of whom was Sake) had let it be known that they strongly opposed such a thought.

Once, after a long period of inactivity during which the village *yut* had all but ceased to exist, the youth leaders called a general meeting to find out who still wanted to be a *memba* (member) of *yut* and who wanted to *stepaut* (withdraw; lit. "step out"). An announcement had been made the previous week that the meeting would be held, and when the slit-gong drum was beat, summoning the villagers, almost all of them showed up: men drifting up into Kruni's men's house, women sitting or standing on the ground below. But one villager who refused to attend was Sake, who instead of coming sat in the back of her house a few meters away and had a *kros* about the fact that despite repeated requests and plates of food sent to the men's house, the *yut* of Gapun had not helped her and her husband, Allan, carry and raise the posts for their new house (the one she later burned down). Sake and Allan had had to get Wongan's youth group to help them, and they had paid them with food. "I ask for help to build the house, food gets sent to the men's house I don't know how many times, bellies get filled up, and do they help to build the house?!" Sake screamed vehemently from somewhere deep inside the back regions of her house, "*Wakarɛ!* (No!) *Wakarɛ wakarɛ wakarɛ wakarɛ wakarɛ wakarɛ!* No man helped build nothing! You all just work for money!"

The response of Marame, the president of the village youth group, to Sake's shouts displays his skill in the practice of rhetorical dissociation:

Text 4.5

I've announced to everyone, everyone knows about this. It [youth work] is not just done for money, no. If you don't have money, make food. If you don't have food and you have money, put that. I've already told you all. Alright, as for all us young men, youth work won't be done without money. That's for the big men. Youth will give service [i.e., work for food]. But all us young men have enough strength to find money. This is the law we've got. If you have no money, then make food.

This kind of speech is extremely difficult to argue against, since it is not at all clear what Marame is saying. Can one pay for *yut* work with just food? Or does one need to pay with money? Are there special rules that apply only to the big men? Or do the same rules apply to everyone? Villagers holding completely opposing viewpoints on these issues could all interpret Marame's speech as supporting their point of view. Conflict is denied in these kinds of speeches because the speaker interweaves the conflicting opinions or statements into the same utterance without indicating in even the slightest manner that they are, in fact, conflicting. By treating contradictory propositions in the same breath and in a tone and a context suggesting agreement, village men are stressing that there really should be no disagreement at all. In other conversations, this strategy is used between turns as well, and the men frequently give speeches to "support" (*sapotim*) another speaker in which they say things that totally contradict the speech of the speaker whom they declare themselves to be supporting.

Another way village men underline consensus in talk in the men's house is through the heavy use of repetition and supportive interjections from listeners. The uses to which these features are put are illustrated in a conversation that occurred one evening in Kruni's men's house. The men had been discussing a fight in Wongan that had broken out several days earlier. The fight, which began when a man hit his wife and her relatives and clan brothers rushed to support her, ended when one of the main aggressors bellowed loudly that his arm had been broken. As a result of this fight, both sides were reportedly getting ready to *kotim* (court) the other, i.e., travel to the local administrative seat in Angoram (eight hours away by motor-powered canoe) and have their case tried in the local court. A few young men from Gapun had taken part in the fight, but the majority of the village men were relieved that any court action would not involve them.

Text 4.6[8]

Kruni:	We're just gonna stay quiet and listen.
Marame:	Ah we/we're not involved here, let's just listen to their talk.
Ambuli:	It's their business in their village.
Marame:	Their business. And if they take it to [Angoram to] court, you don't think one side will return and one side will be put in jail. No. Both sides =
Kruni:	= all of them =
Marame:	= all of them.
Kruni:	You know the law was buggered up between them.
Marame:	We're not involved, it's their business . . .

All but one of the turns in this stretch of conversation are explicitly linked to one another through repetition and repetition with variation. This is made clearer when the repetitions in this transcript are circled and linked:

Kruni: We're just gonna stay quiet and listen.

Marame: Ah we/we're not involved here, let's just listen to their talk.

Ambuli: It's their business in their village.

Marame: Their business. And if they take it to [Angoram
           to] court, you don't think one side will return
           and one side will be put in jail. No. Both sides ⇒

Kruni: = all of them ⇒

Marame: = all of them.

Kruni: You know the law was buggered up between them.

Marame: We're not involved, it's their business . . .

As in *kros*es, there is a delicate sense of balance in how the men intertwine their contributions through code-switching. When a man repeats a statement in a language different from the one in which the statement was made, he is not just parroting, he is subtly conveying his own understanding and reformulation of the original statement. Repetition and repetition with variation also play an important role in a more general sense. By repeating certain key words and phrases, villagers work together to structure their discourse around those aspects of a situation that immediately are perceived to be the least controversial. In discourse terms, it is clear that this kind of repetition drives the conversation forward by providing the men with a framework around which they can build their talk. In the above conversation, it is the fact that "we're not involved" that provides the basis for individual contributions and elaboration.

In extended oratorical speeches, men combine features like repetition, code-switching, and dissociative rhetorical strategies in order to stress certain points on which everyone can voice agreement. In this way, skilled speakers effectively lay the foundation for consensus and, in doing so, demonstrate their *save*.

As the village meeting about the *yut* group toward which Sake had directed her *kros* continued, Kem stood up in the men's house and delivered a forty-minute speech. The main reason for calling the meeting in the first place was that the village *yut* group had been inactive for quite a while, due to conflicts among the villagers. It is this situation that Kem addresses as he begins his speech:

Text 4.7

Yes, thank you
And
I'm going to tell you all a little talk.
Sorry true, it's not a big talk.
Talk/Your work is good.
Good now, there aren't any complaints.
The work you're doing now is good.
The way of *yut,* you've understood it.
And
A little problem arose
Last month.
This little problem is here
I haven't straightened it out.
And
Maybe that's why there are a few complaints around.
And
So I'm saying this:
A sickness has got [my] wife
And
So I'm still getting ready.
I don't know what time what day I'll be able look after this problem from earlier
... [continues in Tok Pisin].

Kem's speech is typical of the majority of oratories produced in the men's house. Several specific characteristics of that speech stand out here. First, there is the formal structure of the talk. Kem begins with the formulaic phrase *"Yes, tenk yu." Yes, plis* (please), *tenk yu* (thank you), *eskus* (excuse [me]), and *sore tru* (pardon me) are oral markers of formality that men habitually use to begin their speeches. They are usually followed by statements announcing that the speaker has "a little talk" (*liklik tok*) or "a little worry" (*liklik wari*) to deliver to his audience. These opening phrases are discourse-framing devices that function partly to mark what follows as a formal speech and partly to announce the speaker's intention to assume the floor. These phrases are never used by women.

A second feature of Kem's speech is his use of indirection and reneging to dissociate himself from the talk he is producing. After announcing his intention to make a speech, Kem hurries to stress that the work of the village's youth group is "good," employing both code-switching and repetition to emphasize this, and stating at the same time that "there aren't any complaints." Once he has established this, Kem then goes on to reveal that there are, in fact, "a few complaints" about the youth group after all. Kem uses extreme indirection here, and he is careful not to assign blame to anyone but himself. Kem criticizes no one. Nothing in his speech could possibly be interpreted by any villager as aggressive or "pushy." By first saying there are no complaints and by then leaving unstated who has the complaints, Kem is indicating that *he* is not accusing anyone of being antisocial and harboring complaints; he is merely noting the fact that complaints "are around." Here Kem dissociates himself from his talk in the same way that Mone dissociated himself from his talk about the motor (Text 4.4). In both cases, the discursive strategy used conveys the impression that the speaker's words have been generated from a source outside the speaker and that the speaker is merely reporting something.[9]

This dissociative strategy is tied to another characteristic aspect of Kem's talk. Throughout this entire stretch of speech, Kem displays a guise of self-effacement. He consistently tones down his status and role as a big man. The speech is delivered in a placating tone that suggests "I really have nothing to say and perhaps shouldn't be wasting your time talking at all." His consistent use of diminutives emphasizes this: He explains that his talk is not "a big talk"; he speaks of a "little problem" and "a few complaints."

This self-effacement is purposeful. One of the things that Kem is doing with his talk is reaffirming his intention to sponsor a large conciliatory feast to compensate another village man who had been injured in a fight that had been started by Kem's 20-year-old daughter. Kem chose this context to mention his plans because that fight had at the time generated a series of other spin-off fights, one of which constituted the reason why villagers no longer would cooperate in the youth group. In reaffirming his intention to go through with the conciliatory feast, Kem is requesting help. To perform the feast, various people on Kem's "side," that is, his kin group and the matrilineal clan of his daughter, must help him by contributing prestige food like white rice and sugar and garden food like bananas and yams to the prestation of food that will be delivered to the injured man. Kem cannot and should not amass all of this by himself. Here he is indicating that others should begin collecting money and thinking about the state of their gardens so that they will be able to assist him in carrying out the conciliatory feast.

This dimension of Kem's talk is what the villagers call "hidden" (*i *hait/ambugar*). Kem supplies no explicit information regarding his intention to sponsor the feast (except to say, obliquely, "I'm still getting ready" [he doesn't say for what]), he gives no background information, and his referents are unspecified (he mentions only "this [unnamed] problem"). In order to grasp the meaning "underneath" Kem's words, his listeners must be intimately acquainted with village affairs, and they must connect their knowledge of these affairs to Kem's one brief clue: his sudden mention of his wife's illness. By introducing the notion of sickness, of inability, Kem blithely alerts the villagers that he is unable to carry out all the preparations for the feast by himself and that those listening should begin thinking about helping him. This is as close as Kem comes to a direct request for help. It was effective, however, because shortly after this talk, several of Kem's relatives did indeed begin making small preparations for the conciliatory feast.

Kem is able to leave this entire, central message "hidden" in his speech because he can rely on the village understanding that the discovery and comprehension of the meaning of speech is the responsibility of the listener. While speakers in Gapun hasten to accommodate listeners in terms of language choice, opinions, and topic, considerations of *save* place them under no burden to make themselves clear or facilitate listener comprehension, and concern about appearing provocative makes it advantageous for speakers to formulate themselves as vaguely as possible. For the villagers, the ideal communicative situation is considered to be one in which an individual apprehends meaning and understands the needs and desires of another person with as little verbalization as possible of those needs. The responsibility of successful communication in the village is seen to lie primarily with the listener, and this is a structuring principle of all communication in Gapun.[10] It is applied to all interactions – from oratories like Kem's to child–caregiver interactions, in which caregivers feel that it is their responsibility to constantly interpret the cries and whines of their babies.[11]

In assuming that his listeners will be able to "get behind" his words and understand what he is really saying, Kem remains, in the structure and content of his talk, firmly in line with the villagers' ideas about the expression of social sensitivity and of not "giving *hed*." By portraying himself as a poor man with a sick wife, Kem lays the foundation for a reaction based on sympathy. The response from Kem's listeners will not arise out of any sense of threat or force. Instead, it will be generated from within themselves. Those who listen to this speech will extract the "hidden" meanings from Kem's talk and will feel moved to help him out of their own sense of social solidarity and goodwill. By successfully interpreting his speech in the first place, and then by acting on that interpretation and coming to his assistance, Kem's listeners are provided by him with an opportunity to use and display their *save*.

Writing consensus

These ways of using language to show *save* and not give *hed* have been carried over to the villagers' uses of literacy. Command of the written word has existed in the village since the mid-1950s, and since 1967, when a government-run grammar school was opened in Wongan, the majority of children in Gapun have become acquainted, at least, with the idea of literacy skills. Outside school, these skills are almost never used, and few boys and virtually no girls who these days become literate in school make any use of their reading and writing abilities outside the classroom. After they leave school at age 14 or 15, many of these young people may never read and will almost certainly never write again. There are few opportunities in the course of normal village life to read or write. The only type of literature that regularly enters the village, for example, is the *Sydney Morning Herald,* but this is purchased in loose sheets by the villagers and used to roll cigarettes; it is never read.

Nevertheless, one of the few ways literacy skills have become incorporated into village life is in the writing of notes. Villagers sometimes write short notes to other villagers (or get somebody else to write the note for them) in order to request something. In these notes, the ways of using language that are particular to oratory have been carried over to a written form. Notes in Gapun are oratories compressed and written down. This is exemplified by a note sent to me by a village couple in their thirties (see Figure 4.1). The note was delivered about a week before Kem's large conciliatory feast (the one he alluded to in his speech) was due to be held.

Text 4.8[12]

Dear Don
Yes Don
I have a little worry to tell you.
Yes Don
I want to tell you that I'm sick
And
I don't have time to get ready to go to the market [to sell produce in order to earn some money].
So Don
I want to ask you.
Can you help me to buy a little rice for me.

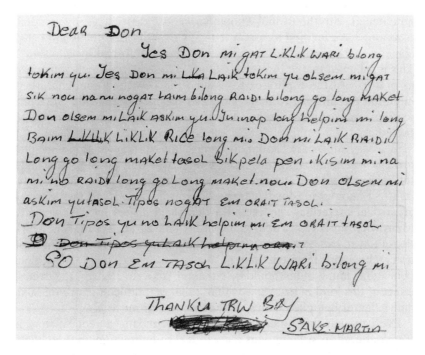

Figure 4.1. Letter to the author from Allan Kasia and Sake Martin.

Don
I wanted to get ready to go to the market but a big pain got me so I didn't go to the market.
Don
It's like, I'm just asking you.
If no [i.e., if you don't want to]
That's just alright.
Don
If you don't want to help me,
That's just alright.
Don [crossed out]
If you want to help, alright . . . [crossed out]
So Don
that's it, my little worry.
Thank You Truly
By
Allan Kasia [crossed out]
Sake Martin

The parallels with Kem's speech in the men's house are striking. The note begins with the formulaic opening phrase that villagers with some schooling have learned to use in letters: *"Dear."* But directly after that comes a new opening, this time the oral marker of formal speech *"Yes."* This is followed by the formulaic "I have a little worry to tell you." Just as orators use these phrases to assume the floor and announce their intention to deliver a formal speech, so they are used in the villagers' writing. The recipient of this note is not being written to so much as orated at.

In a way markedly similar to Kem's, the authors of this note first make a statement – in this case, a request – only to then dissociate themselves from that statement/request and diminish its implications by in effect apologizing for having made it at all. Like Kem, who uses a great deal of verbiage to establish that the villagers' work "is good" when what he is really addressing in his talk is the fact that the work doesn't even exist anymore, Sake and Allan spend more words in their note telling the recipient that he doesn't have to "help" them than persuading him that he should help them. Like Kem's words, the overall effect of this kind of discourse is that it makes it difficult to accuse Sake and Allan of being assuming, presumptuous, or pushy.

Even though this note is more direct in making a request than is Kem's speech, it still contains a great deal of indirection, and no background or contextual information is explicitly given. But in order to respond to the note in an appropriate manner, the recipient must be familiar with village affairs. The note assumes that I not only am aware of the impending conciliatory feast, but that I also know how much rice Sake and Allan are expected to provide. In this case, the request for "a little rice" is a somewhat forced diminutive, since both the sender and the receiver of the message know that for Sake and Allan to adequately fulfill their social responsibilities during the feast, at least 25 kilograms of rice are required. Furthermore, the reader of this note is expected to be able to get "behind" the words and understand that Sake and Allan are not requesting a contribution to help them buy rice – as they explicitly state – what they want and expect is that the entire 25 kilograms of rice will be bought for them.

The final point of similarity between Kem's talk in the men's house and this note is the amount of work done on self-effacement and the creation of a context in which the listener/recipient can demonstrate his *save*. As in Kem's talk, this is built up partly through the use of diminutives ("a little worry;" "a little rice") and partly by the introduction of the notion of inability. Again, the authors of the note are seeking to avoid, just as Kem did in his talk, giving the impression of forcefulness and insistence. They are not really making a request, it is implied, they are merely bringing some compelling facts about sickness to the attention of the recipient of the note, leaving him to act on those facts. How he reacts is up to him. He can respond on the basis of his *save* and display social solidarity with the afflicted person, or he may not. In any case, the decision is his. He cannot claim at some point to have been "pushed" into doing something he didn't want to do.

The voice of truth

The plying and self-deprecating tone of Kem's speech and village notes is typical of the bulk of public language that the village men produce. Sometimes, however, this language can become more aggressive and take on the character of harangues. Whenever this happens, specific rules apply.

Because harangues take place in the men's house and in the context of consensus that exists there, they are never directed at specific individuals. To target an individual in a harangue would be considered a gross provocation and would result in violence. Harangues in the men's house can only be aimed at age- or gender-based groups. A harangue can be directed at "all you young people" or "you women," but never at kin or clan groups; a man could never harangue "all you people of the dog clan," for example, because this would be tantamount to inviting retribution from dog clan ancestors or dog clan sorcerers in Sanae.

Also, while harangues usually begin as a result of some concrete action performed by someone or some group, they should quickly move beyond that specific action and address general truths instead. So, for example, instead of dwelling on the fact that a number of village men and women didn't feel like carrying Sister Mariana's heavy patrol boxes full of medicine from the village to her canoe, a harangue prompted by this event would dwell on the lazy and uncooperative nature of Gapuners in general.

This is an aspect of the final rule governing the appropriateness of harangues in Gapun. They can occur only against the backdrop of ideas for which a broad consensus has already been established. Harangues tell people what they already should know. They are the voice of Truth, the explicit pronouncement of central values that are unassailable and presumed to be shared by everyone in the village.

Whereas any married man can make a speech in the men's house, only men with status can legitimately harangue. Big men like Kruni, Raia, or Kem are always free to harangue. Younger men who can lay claim to temporary status in specific situations may also harangue – Mone, not quite considered a big man, may harangue in his role as the village *komiti,* and Marame, in his late twenties, is free to harangue villagers at youth meetings in his capacity as president of the youth group. Agrana, who has no real status in the village, occasionally harangues in his speeches in the men's house, but these usually only evoke sniggers from most people.

As the youth meeting at which Kem held his oratory progressed, Marame and his brother Akupi, who at that time was the village *komiti,* asked each villager present whether they wanted to remain a member of the *yut* or whether they wanted to *stap autsait* (be outside). Each villager responded in turn that they had no disagreement with anyone, of course they wanted to remain "inside" the youth group. After eleven people had been asked, a young unmarried man dared to upset the consensus that had been established by replying that the wanted to "withdraw" (*stepaut*) from the youth group. The tension that this announcement created was soon heightened by Sake's husband, Allan, who remained silent and refused to give an answer to the question when it was posed to him. Finally, Sake's *kros* about her house caused tempers to flare. Shortly after Marame's reply to Sake, quoted above (Text 4.5), old Kruni began a harangue from his seat by the hearth.

Text 4.9

I'll tell you this, shut your mouths and listen to me.
     If you young people are going to stay in this village
     and show this kind of *hed*,
          I'm gonna throw you out.
5   I'm telling you.
          I'm gonna throw you out.
          You're gonna run straight into the swamps.
     When you're here under my eyes, you make good work.
I'm telling you that.
10   If you want to make heathen ways,
     argue and fight, man,
          I'm gonna chase you.
          I'll chase you to the swamps.
          I'll chase you off my ground.
15 I'm telling you here.
          To me, in my village, you can't make bad *hed*.
I'm sick of it.
          Look out, I'll chase you.

Stand on the ground, woman, man, make good work!
20   If you come and bring a trade store here,
            I'll praise you!
        If you want to bring *kros*es and fights all the time,
            I'll throw you all out!
I'm sick of this.
25   You have to be a true man!
        You're a man with education!
        Now you're standing on your own two feet, man and woman!
        Don't bring a lot of problems!
        Good work, you smell it and leave it.
30   Make bad bad *hed* like the ancestors,
            I don't want that.

        All you standard six men and women, you do these things
        under my eyes,
            I'm gonna throw you out of this village.
35 I'm telling you all.
I'm sick of all kinds of ways in my village!
            Lots of *hed*.
I'm sick of it.
            Cross, cross!
40 I'm sick of it!
I'm sick of it.
        Good head, good ways can remain.
        Just work, play, eat.
            That I like.
45   I don't like this laziness.
        The *komiti* can hit the drum [to summon everyone to a
        meeting], [but] you just ignore it!
            I don't like that.

        This is the time now,
50   Papua New Guinea, you're standing on your own feet –
        make your country.

        This isn't the time of big men and big women.
        This is the time of you young people.
        You all know about school,
55   know how to read, write, speak English.
        This is yours.

        That's it, my little *kros*.
I'm sick of this.

You all can't lose out to other villages!
60   You're all the same group.
All you young women went to school together!
Young men, young women, you've been to school together.
This knowledge (*save*) you received . . .
to develop your village.
65   Fill up your village's bank.
Bring in money.

In this speech, Kruni follows a number of oratorical conventions. He frames the speech as oratorical by announcing his intention to take the floor and, near the end of his speech, he announces its closure with the phrase "That's it, my little *kros*" (*Em tasol liklik kros bilong mi*), which is an original variation of the formulaic oratorical tag "That's it, my little talk" (*Em tasol liklik tok bilong mi*). In ways similar to Kem in his speech, Kruni relies heavily on repetition and code-switching to stress his main points.

Unlike Kem's oratory, however, Kruni's talk is belligerent and provocative. His speech is remarkable for its agressiveness in a social context otherwise characterized by the absence of open displays of anger and hostility. The speech begins in a calm, even tone, but it rapidly develops into a harsh harangue delivered in furious, booming shouts and punctuated by sweeping gestures of threat and disgust. One reason why Kruni has the freedom to harangue so aggressively is because of his status as a big man. Here, though, Kruni subtly cues his listeners that he is temporarily laying claim to another, even more auspicious, role. In the first part of his speech, Kruni repeatedly threatens violence to villagers who "show *hed.*" He shouts that he will throw such villagers out of "his" village and chase them "into the swamps." Everyone in Gapun realizes that Kruni's age and his bad back would prevent him from ever really carrying out such a threat. Moreover, in a society like Gapun, where one should never attempt to overtly influence the behavior of another individual, and where every centimeter of ground is vociferously owned by someone, Kruni's claims that the entire village is "his" and that he has the right to chase people away depending on his evaluation of their behavior would normally be considered preposterous and highly inflammatory.

Kruni, however, is not just speaking as himself. He is also assuming the voice of his mythical namesake, Kruni Maroka, the first man to settle in Gapun (Chapter 2). As the oldest living member of the crocodile clan in the village, and as one of the few repositories of clan myths and knowledge, Kruni sometimes takes it upon himself to speak in the name of his ancestor. When telling the myth about Kruni Maroka's arrival in Gapun, long ago in the shrouded past, Kruni frequently takes the perspective of his ancestor, describing his adventures in the first person: "I arrived at the mountain . . . ," or "I beat the slit-gong drum summoning other men. . . . "[13] Other occasions at which Kruni sometimes speaks as his ancestor are in oratories and harangues like this one, where the development of the village is under discussion. On these occasions, Kruni cloaks his own desires to see Gapun "come up" in the words of his ancestors, speaking thereby in a voice weighty with potency and sanctioned by the villagers' understanding of their own history. In doing so, Kruni asserts a distance between his person and his words: In a way similar to Kem, who carefully selects his words so that he may not easily be seen as their source, Kruni here portrays himself as a channel of ancestral authority and knowledge. This, in characteristic dissociative style, allows Kruni to both condemn the ways of the ancestors as "heathen ways" (line 10) and "bad bad *hed*" (line 30), even as he simultaneously draws on the authority of the ancestors to appeal to the villagers to abandon ancestral ways so that the village might "come up."

In this harangue, Kruni typically never explicitly cues the villagers that he is addressing them on two levels. Instead, he relies on the outlandish nature of his threats and the harshness of his tone to alert listeners to the fact that he is speaking to them both as himself and in the voice of their common founding ancestor.

Yet another reason why Kruni is so aggressive in his harangue is because he is voicing a consensus opinion that no one in the village could possibly dispute. Throughout his speech, Kruni repeatedly decries the villagers' *hed*s, linking these with "laziness," "*kros*es and fights," and "heathen ways." All these qualities are distressing, but they are absolutely enraging when they are connected with "standard six men and women;" that is, young men and women who have gone to school. These men and women have "received knowledge (*save*)," which they should use to "develop [their] village" (*kamapim ples*). There is no excuse for educated men and women to "make bad, bad *hed* like the ancestors." Young men and women in the village "know all about school, know how to read, write." They should use this knowledge to "bring money" into Gapun and "fill up [their] village's bank."

Kruni's argument is unassailable. No one in Gapun could argue in favor of laziness, fighting, and heathen ways. No one would object to a trade store being established in the village. No one wishes to see Gapun "lose out to other villages," remaining the same while others become rich. And no one would ever consider that the purpose of education might not be to "fill up your village's bank." All these truths, for the villagers, are self-evident. In pointing them out to his listeners,

Kruni's anger and aggression can be seen as attempts to reinforce consensus, not destroy it. Just before this outburst, the fragile consensus that had been so gingerly established during the youth meeting was threatening to shatter. By choosing to harangue at this point, Kruni manages to remind everybody that there are certain values on which the villagers all agree, no matter what. In the face of these common values, Kruni is advising Sake and others that their attempts to sabotage the consensus are "bad *hed*," that is, a display of the kind of behavior that everyone agrees is wrong.

Men, Tok Pisin, and *save*

After thoroughly abusing her sister Jari and screaming out over the village that Jari is "a real pig-woman" (*wanpela pik-meri stret*), Sake, during her *kros* about Jari's baby, pressed home this pig metaphor even further by caustically reminding her sister: "If you're a human being you have *save!*" (Text 3.1; lines 65–6). Like the truths enumerated in Kruni's harangue, this carefully chosen reprimand to Jari is an expression of a fundamental axiom shared by all villagers.

The self in Gapun is conceived of as a duality. Just as every individual in the village is held to "have *hed*" and be stubborn, willful, and autonomous, so is every human being considered to be born with social sensitivity and awareness – *save* – encapsulated somewhere inside her or his person. But unlike *hed*, which is shared by "pigs and dogs" and other animals, and which is evident from birth in human babies, *save* emerges only gradually as children mature and become integrated into the social life of their community. Without any assistance or interference from caregivers, a child's *save* "breaks open" in its own time. All others can do is wait for this to happen. When it does, children will begin to listen to others, understand the import of warnings and words like "fire," and will begin to use language interactively with those around them.

Save is the villagers' way of naming the social skills, competence, and sensitivity that children are expected to demonstrate as they assume a place in village life. *Save* is the uniquely human attribute that makes it possible for people of decidedly differing opinions and temperaments to live together, cooperate, and maintain social relations. The conceptual basis of the villagers' understanding of *save* is the notion of accommodation. In their actions, relationships, and speech, villagers should accommodate. How well one accommodates other people is an indication of how much *save* one has. Inability to accommodate is interpreted as lack of *save*, and insensitivity to the needs of others or unwillingness to accommodate them is taken to be evidence of provocation, of *hed.*

In Gapun, *save* can be displayed in a variety of ways. Hard work, generosity, a placid temperament, frequent attendance at the village's Sunday mass, and impressive fulfillment of social obligations are all considered to be evidence of *save.* The earliest and single most common way for an individual to show *save,* however, is through language. And just as particular types of language use are remarked on as expressions of *hed,* so do the villagers consider that other types of language behavior are clear demonstrations of an individual's *save.*

Villagers demonstrate their *save* by being outwardly self-effacing, accommodating, and agreeable. They strive to accommodate others in terms of language choice, topic, and opinions. Even the notes written by villagers strain to convey a tone of self-deprecation and awareness of the autonomy of others. These notes are patterned on the epitome of *save:* oratorical speech.

Oratorical speech is *save* on parade. Through their skillful manipulation of a wide variety of paralinguistic cues (e.g., speakers are called and assembled under the same roof), metalinguistic cues (e.g., speakers address their talk to a general public, use politeness markers to assume and relinquish the floor), and linguistic cues (use of diminutives, supportive repetition), villagers who orate are given credit for drawing their listeners together into a consensus. Good orators manage to downplay the tensions that continually infect daily life in the village, and through their talk, they promote an illusion that everyone is in agreement and that there really are no conflicts at all. In creating this illusion and bringing the villagers together in this way, orators demonstrate their own *save,* their own social awareness and skills, even as they work to structure a context in which others can demonstrate their *save* by listening and contributing to the buildup of the consensus by repeating and agreeing.

In all of this, it is men who play a leading role. From the point of view of everyone, it is men who, through their oratories and their exhortations to work together, to be more Christian, and to bring money into Gapun, are the builders and maintainers of village cohesion. Because women do not orate, it becomes possible to cast them in the role of antiorators, as those who are somehow constantly poised to threaten the consensus that the men continually work so hard to establish.

This image of women is applied to and reinforced by what is considered to be a specifically female verbal genre – the *kros.* In almost every way, oratories, even oratorical harangues like Kruni's, are inversions of *kros*es. *Kros*es emanate from inside or near private houses; oratories occur in or near the communal men's house. *Kros*es are organized as two competing monologues; in oratories, the people being orated at are free to contribute sympathetic interjections throughout the speech and follow the orator by producing a speech or a summation in which they "give support" to the orator. *Kros*es are meant to shame a specific, named person or a specific unknown, unnamed culprit; oratories are intended to generalize and address people as members of a group: Even if the topic of an oratory is some sort of transgression committed, blame is diffused and generalized, and everyone is reminded that others in the village (though not necessarily they themselves) are just as lazy or unchristian or big-headed as the (unnamed) person or persons who committed the transgression. For both men and women, *kros*es are associated with (other) women and divisiveness; oratories, on the other hand, are seen as concrete evidence that men in Gapun really are more consensus-oriented, sociable, and Christian than are their forever bickering wives.

There is clearly an understanding among the villagers that, whereas all people have some *save,* some people have more than others. *Save is an idiom used in Gapun to signify difference.* Generally speaking, adults have more *save* than children, and men have more than women. Although individual women, like Kem's wife, Wandi, who rarely has *kros*es and who is held to work hard and help her husband, are not usually said to lack *save,* women are collectively stereotyped in this way, as Kruni asserts when he complains that "women don't have any *save*" (Text 4.2).

But beyond being correlated for the villagers with age and gender, *save* is also linked to modernity. Those who have acquired knowledge about and familiarity with the modern world have more *save* than those who have not managed to gain such knowledge and who, therefore, still "follow the ways of the ancestors" (*bihainim we bilong ol tumbuna*). Villagers occasionally enjoy telling stories about "the people of the upper Sepik" (*ol man bilong Sepik antap*), who they have heard lack clothes, access to schooling, cash crops like coffee, contact with white people, "the word of God" (*tok bilong God*), and Tok Pisin. Sometimes the villagers express pity for these people, calling them "poor things" (*tarangu*) and wondering why they are so backward. On other occasions, though, the same villagers laugh derisively at such people (whom no one has ever actually seen), calling them "wildmen" (*ol wailman*) and authoritatively recounting that the "upper Sepiks" "live like pigs," without houses or clothes, eating "any kind of food" (*ol kainkain kaikai*), and are little and stunted "like children." Anxious stories are told about how these people "have lots of ancestral stories," and, consequently, "lots of sorcery." Gapuners claim that these people are "rubbish men who only like to hurt other people," and they say that they would "run away" if they ever came across one. Like children and (other) women, the "upper Sepiks" are considered by the villagers to *nogat save* (not have *save*).

This dimension of modernity is a critical element in all village oratories. Yet another difference between *kros*es and oratorical speeches is that, whereas the former only address intravillage relationships and local affairs, oratories link these relationships and the actions of villagers to "modern" processes and institutions that have their locus far beyond the scope of the village. The need to repair rotten footbridges will be justified by pointing out that villagers must have a way to get their coffee beans out of the village to the buyers, and discussion concerning the organization of a funerary feast will center on the ability of the dead person's relatives to dry enough copra to earn the money that must purchase the white rice, sugar, *tinpis,* and Nescafé that will be consumed during the feast. At some point during each village meeting, no matter what the original reason for the meeting happened to be, somebody will inevitably extol Christian ideals, mention the value of education, devalue the ways of the ancestors, and urge the villagers to show *save* so they all can "come up." The men's house has thus become an important arena in which individual men can publicly assert their familiarity with the modern world by reminding others that the Church, school, "Papua New Guinea," and *bisnis* (cash-generating enterprises) have altered the nature of village relationships and must be accorded a central role in village life – as Kruni makes explicit in his harangue when he shouts at the villagers that "this isn't the time of big men and big women. This is the time of you young people" (Text 4.9, lines 52–3).

There is a strong preference for making these assertions in Tok Pisin. Although men use a great deal of rhetorical code-switching in their speeches, the overwhelming bulk of all oratories is conducted in Tok Pisin. Kruni's harangue is an illuminating instance of this phenomenon because not only is his speech mostly in Tok Pisin (in marked contrast to his participation in Sake's *kros* [Text 3.1], which, with the exception of one insult to his daughter Jari, is conducted entirely in Taiap), but the information that Kruni wishes to convey in the harangue is delivered in Tok Pisin. The vernacular, on the other hand, is used very markedly as a kind of phatic punctuation, almost entirely lacking informational substance aside from making clear Kruni's feelings of dissatisfaction about the villagers' *hed*s. The use of Taiap is heavily redundant, since what Kruni for the most part uses the language to express ("I'm sick of this!") is clear anyway from his tone of voice and expressions.[14]

Another example of Tok Pisin dominance in oratory is Kem's speech (Text 4.7), which, after some initial code-switching employed to gain the floor and emphasize points, continued for forty minutes almost entirely in Tok Pisin. The only other domain in Gapun where as much Tok Pisin is consistently used is that of Christian worship.

This preference for Tok Pisin in oratorical speech is related to two important aspects of village life. First, it is tied to the fact that the men's house and the activities that occur there have increasingly come to be defined in opposition to traditional society and values (what the villagers refer to as "the ways of the ancestors" [*ol we bilong ol tumbuna*]). "Now," as Kruni often points out, "all the spears are locked up, now is the time of Europeans." Men in Gapun no longer congregate in their cult houses to debate the organization of raiding parties or to perform collective initiation celebrations. These days, the men are summoned to the men's house by the village *komiti,* the *yut presiden* or by the village prayer leader; and they gather to orate about the status of the youth group, the need to "fill up [the] village's bank" with money, or to complain that the villagers' *heds* are preventing Gapun from "coming up."

Second, men are able to substantiate their claims to knowledge about the modern world by choosing to orate in the language through which that world is understood to be constituted. Men use Tok Pisin to claim authority in these domains, employing a strategy similar to the one utilized by Kruni in his harangue. Just as Kruni artfully and powerfully signaled to the villagers through his metalinguistic communication that he was claiming the authority to speak in the voice of his mythical ancestor Kruni Maroka, so can speakers convey to their listeners a claim to wider authority and knowledge by choosing to orate predominantly in Tok Pisin.[15]

But, although the reasons for Tok Pisin's ascendance in the men's house could be analyzed as being largely "historical," having to do with the decline of the traditional men's cult and the "secularization" of the men's house, and although the reasons for the men's contemporary preference for Tok Pisin in their speeches could be seen as being largely "social," having to do with their desire to claim authority in domains connected to the modern world, none of these reasons is separable from the "cultural," which has to do with the villagers' ways of structuring their experience and interpreting their world. Because oratorical speech and the context in which it occurs embodies those qualities of self that all villagers value and wish to be associated with, the language in which this speech is articulated has itself become available as a symbol for the values it is used to express. Through its close associations with oratory, men, consensus, and modernity, Tok Pisin has become incorporated into the villagers' verbal repertoires not just as one more language, but rather as a ripe and meaningful symbolic resource that villagers can draw upon to assert their social competence and to show their *save*.

1. "Gapun is difficult to reach and far away from any urban center." (Introduction, p. 17)

2. "The village area contrasts with the surrounding rainforest by being kept largely free from grass...." (Chapter 1, p. 39)

3. "Despite these cries of warning, though, it is not uncommon for small children to occasionally fall through a hole and plummet 1.5 meters to the ground below." (Chapter 1, p. 41)

4. "Men's possessions are much fewer in number and are concerned with hunting." (Chapter 1, p. 44)

5. "From a distance, she could see that Sopak was at home, reclining and smoking on a pile of clothes, with her head propped up on an elbow and a breast tucked into her daughter's mouth." (Chapter 1, p. 51)

6. "There is no formal instruction in oratory techniques, and young men seem to learn to orate through a lifetime of lounging around in the men's house listening to the speeches of other men." (Chapter 4, p. 125)

7. "After birth, one or two weeks of rest in the maternity house is enjoyed by all women, but the pleasure quickly turns to claustrophobia." (Chapter 3, p. 95)

8. "Hard work, generosity, a placid temperament, frequent attendance at the village's Sunday mass, and impressive fulfillment of social obligations are all considered to be evidence of *save*." (Chapter 4, p. 145)

9. "Bapong was a very verbal 4-year-old who frequently talked and sang to himself, sometimes loudly, in adult company." (Chapter 6, p. 210)

10. "In these peer groups, children of both sexes practice and develop their language skills as they play, explore their environment, recount stories, and argue with one another." (Chapter 6, p. 217)

11. "In these relaxed, informal settings, the villagers of Gapun sit, chew betel nut, sweat, spit, swat at mosquitoes, and engage in a specific speech genre they call *stori* (*tik*)." (Chapter 7, p. 234)

12. "I could follow his gaze as he looked away from me . . . past the rickety village church where a picture of an ivory-skinned Jesus, donated by a missionary, hangs on the wall next to the altar . . . ." (Conclusion, pp. 266–7)

5. Preparing to change

"In the beginning," explains Agrana, as he slides a mashed up wad of betel nut into his nearly toothless mouth and settles in to tell an epic,

all the children of God were inside a big enclosure (*banis*). In Paradise. All the prophets were there. Yeah, the mission calls them "prophets." And we call them *eŋgin*. *Eŋgin*. Kambedagam, Mongema, Sangginggi, Sani – they were all inside. And some other ones too; Moses, the one with the stick, he was there. They were all inside that enclosure. Alright, God made the ground. He pulled back the water, and the ground came up and appeared. He made the ground now, and he opened the fence, told everybody: "You all go spread out now. Go spread out over the ground." He sent them all away now.

That's it, all the prophets went and spread out now, but two of them stayed inside the fence. Adam and Eve. The two of them stayed and they committed a big wrong. The missions, they always tell us that Adam and Eve ate the seeds of a tree and God got *kros* because of this and threw them out. This isn't true. We know that this is a lie. They're hiding talk. We know that Adam and Eve had intercourse, and God saw this and He got *kros* about this and threw them out. Because they broke a taboo (*tambu*). Broke a taboo. Alright, God saw them and was *kros* now, and He told them: "You two get out. You can't stay in Paradise anymore, you've broken a taboo. Get out." And in the spot where the two had had intercourse, God shattered the ground and made a big hole. This hole is still there. It exists. When we die we'll go to this hole and go inside like this [gestures like a diver] and go into the Place of Dead Souls (*Daiman Ples*).

Alright, they committed a wrong and Papa threw them out. He sent them to go follow (or succeed [*bihainim*]) the prophets. He sent them to straighten out the earth (*graun*) so that we would have a good way of life. He had already sent the prophets, but they didn't do anything. Alright, God saw this, so He sent Adam and Eve to come after them and do this work. They were sent to straighten us out. Give us *save* and make us *kamap* and have white skin, and have the ways of the Europeans and books/read books, all kinds of ways, ship/ manufacture ships, airplanes, whatever, this is what they were sent for.

But the two of them didn't do this work. They came, just looked around and went back again. They didn't show us well. They just left us with nothing. You see how we live: eat with our hands, live in no-good houses – sago-palm thatch, that we ourselves have to make. You all have white skin and so you have lots of *save*. But us, we're the only ones who live like rubbish. [We're] stupid. We're the last country.

Alright, they [Adam and Eve] want to go back to Heaven now. Went, followed the road back to Papa now. They went, were going back and a pregnancy came up along the way. Papa Himself blew into the belly of Mary/eh, what Mary? Mary? Yes Mary. Mary. The mission calls her "Mary," but her true name, the one that God gave her is Eve. And we call her Jari. On this ground: Jari. Alright, in Heaven on top: Eve.

Alright, a pregnancy came up along the way, and Eve feels like she's gonna have the baby now. It's night now, and she's gonna have the baby now. Alright, the two of them go and ask the ones who look after the sheep and the goats, they want to sleep in this house, she's gonna have a baby. [But] no. They say no. The man who looks after the sheep and the goats says, "Oh, sorry. There's no room. Everything is asleep. All the shepherds are asleep. There's nowhere for you to go inside and sleep."

Alright, the troughs for putting food for the sheep and goats, their troughs, this man he saw them, and he went back and told the two: "Come with me." They went, and that's it, she went to the trough. In this trough, in this little house she had the baby, in this trough. And they put the baby in this trough, which was for the food of the sheep and goats.

Put him in the trough, dawn, morning now, that's it, they wanted to go now. The two wanted to go back to Heaven now. They went, and went through all the villages along the road to Heaven. Alright, they went, went went went went went went, they came to the village of the Jews (*ol judaman*). They're all killers. Rotten people. Rubbish people. And, too, they had a king. Adam and Eve came to this king's village, this king who ate children. He used to eat children. His name was . . . ah . . . I . . . wait, I'll think of it . . . King David. King David, yeah, that's it. A child-eater. A bad man.

Alright now, they came to the village of this no-good king now, and they were afraid. "It wouldn't be good if this king eats our baby," the two of them said. Alright, they took him, put him in a basket, alright, they hid him, hid him. Now, the daughter of King Herod, Martha now, she came. She came and went to the place where the baby was hidden and she saw him. She saw the baby floating around. She took him up, went to her father now. Alright, King David he wanted to eat the baby, but King Herod told him no, it's his baby, he found it on his road. That's it, he raised the baby for a long time. Alright, Eve went and told him now: "It's mine. I left him in the basket. This king here who eats children, I was afraid of this, and so I left him in the rushes there." There's a picture of this in the Bible. A little basket that they put him in.

Alright, Eve and Adam escaped the king with their child. And they said, "We haven't had sex with one another. We haven't slept together. And this pregnancy, it just came up."

"It isn't your pregnancy" – this is God talking – "It's not your pregnancy. You two committed a wrong. It's my child. It's my child."

Alright, the two of them thought about this: "Oh yes."

Time went, alright, it went, went now, the child he grew, Jesus, he grew up and started to teach. He got [his teacher's] decorations now, he taught school. He taught people. Jews, disciples, he taught them now.

Time went, he, Jesus himself, he told some priests – they call them "disciples," but they're priests – he told them to walk around with him. They walked around with him, went went went went went. That's it, and Jesus, he worked all kinds of miracles. He put all the stars in Heaven, he made them and he put them on top of all the clouds. All the stars. The moon, too. Alright, he made factories now. All kinds of factories: factories to make cars and ships and airplanes and money; all different kinds of big, big factories, he filled up the countries. And these factories, what did they run on? They ran on the Glory of God (*Ol i save wok long glori bilong God*).

He made these miracles and everybody saw this, and some no-good disciples, they saw this and they said: "Oh, he's surpassed (*winim*) us now. He's surpassed us now." Alright, they all got together and they were going to kill him.

Then Papa Himself spoke: "I'm going to straighten the wrong now. The mother and father [i.e., Eve and Adam] I didn't kill them, I didn't turn my back on them. They've come back [to Heaven]. Alright, the child is mine. From her womb. Alright, I have to kill him. Pay for the wrong that the two committed. Alright, put him on a cross."

The disciples wanted to kill him, but God spoke: "No, don't kill him. Put him on a cross. The picture of this will remain." Alright, they put him on a cross. Here, here's the cross [Agrana points to a picture in a religious booklet called "*Jisas i Karim Hevi Bilong Yumi*" (Jesus Bore Our Sins)]. That's the cross. It still exists.

Alright, they put him on the cross now, nailed him, but he didn't die. Night, day, he remained alive. He wouldn't die. Papa gave him pain, his mother and father committed a wrong, alright, for this reason he was put on the cross and given pain. He gave him pain, time went went went went, alright, God Himself spoke now: "Alright it's almost over," He told them: "You can kill him. His soul (*sol*) will come to me. His body, put it in a hole."

Alright, He came now, Papa God came and Jesus saw Him. He looked at Him for a long time, and then he cried out now: "Oh Papa! What is this all about?! My skin pains! Why do I have to stay like this?!"

Alright, God Himself spoke to the priests: "You get salt, alright, get this poison and give it to him. When he cries out for water, give him the poison and he'll die." No, they didn't give him enough poison and he didn't die. He stayed alive. And God said: "Oh man! He's winning (*Em i win yet*)! He's winning!" Alright, He spoke again now: "Get a spear." Some of the no-good disciples got a spear and speared him. Speared him in the side like this, pierced his lung. That's it. It was over.

It was over now and time went. Friday night, Thursday night, his mother went and took him down from the cross. Took him down from the cross. She took him off the cross. She took him and went down to the place I named before, the Place of Dead Souls. She took his body there. And the mother and father, God said to them: "He was your payment. You two committed a wrong, alright, the child from your womb, he finished this wrong of yours. He paid for your wrong. I'm not *kros* anymore. The anger (*bel*) is finished." God Himself told them this. Alright, He told them now: "You two stay with his body and look after the Place of Dead Souls."

That's it, that's where they are now. And Jesus's soul is on top in Heaven with Papa. Now God is moving aside, He's letting Jesus take things over now. And he's talking about coming back again to straighten us out. This prophet of Jesus, they call him the Pope, he just came to Hagen [Mount Hagen, in the New Guinea highlands[1]] to prepare the road for Jesus's return. He told everybody: "Oh, the time is near now, he's coming. The time is near now, he's coming." Alright, he came with this talk and then he went back. He said: "This year will finish, then the next, then the next year, he [Jesus] will come." He's gonna complete (or destroy [*pinisim*]) all the places in Papua New Guinea. All the jungle, beaches, water, everything. We've heard about this now, he himself is gonna come down. He'll come down and say: "I'm not here because I'm angry or to kill you or do anything like that. I'm here to establish another kind of order (*mekim narapela kain lo*)." All the villages where we have black skin, he's going to change us. We have to ready ourselves. Change will come up. That's what he says. That's the talk.[2]

Trying to find the road

Unlike those communities around the world that dislike and resist change, the villagers of Gapun welcome change. Indeed, they anticipate it. "Change," as Agrana explains, "will come up" (*Sens bai kamap*), and the villagers are concerned with "readying themselves" for that change and with doing what they can to bring it about as quickly as possible.

The change that Gapuners are awaiting is not just social or economic. It is total. Villagers believe that one day – soon – their own black skins and those of their fellow Papua New Guineans will buckle and crack, and "like crabs," everyone in the country will step out of "these old rubbish skins," emerging with milky-white flesh and silky-straight hair. With these new skins will appear money, automobiles, airplanes and roads, telephones, steamships, the factories in which all these things are manufactured, and the *save* that is required to keep those factories running. This particular understanding of "change" is fundamental and shared by all villagers. It is an understanding upon which they base their interpretation of their world and their place within that world.[3]

Whenever this change is spoken about, it is done so in the idiom of Christianity. Since the end of World War II, through brief and sporadic visits from Catholic priests, "catechists" from other Sepik villages, through rumor, and, since the late 1960s, through the local school,[4] villagers have become familiar with fragments of Biblical stories. They are reminded of these stories through the prayers they recite during the church service held every Sunday morning in the village and in the short Bible passages that the local "prayer leader" reads during this brief mass. These stories and the faith they illustrate have come to provide the people of Gapun with a framework for interpreting their changing world, and they are given a prominent place in the villagers' lives.

Unlike traditional stories and myths, however, which were recounted and enacted in the cult houses during initiation ceremonies and funerary rites, Biblical tales and Christian doctrine are never explicitly spoken about in Gapun. Villagers do not tell each other Bible stories or ask anyone about the reason for a particular Christian belief. Gapuners never discuss Christianity, partly because they do not consider that they have enough *save* to do so, and partly because there is no natural forum in the village for such discussions to occur. The only existing forum with the potential to serve this function is the church service held each Sunday in the village. But this is a strictly patterned ceremony in which the villagers participate by singing predetermined hymns and by chanting formulaic responses to the set cues provided by the prayer leader. There is no opportunity during mass for spontaneous speech or discussion to occur.

Yet another reason why villagers never discuss the content and details of Christian doctrine is because they believe that such things are, by their very nature, secret. This belief has its roots in the villagers' pre-Christian understanding of sacred religious knowledge, which was owned and elaborated on by recognized ritual specialists and based on firmly-maintained secrecy. The modern equivalents of traditional ritual specialists are the Catholic missionaries with whom the villagers occasionally come into contact, but villagers never discuss theology with them because they are certain that the missionaries deliberately "hide" from them the knowledge they require in order to understand Christianity and get it to work for them. For similar reasons, Gapuners will not discuss Christianity with one another. They reason that even if another villager did manage to discover some profound new truth about Christianity, that person would surely stubbornly refuse (*bikhed*) to share his secret knowledge with anyone else. So the covert nature of Christian knowledge has led the villagers to consider that they will never learn about Christianity through discussion and talk. Instead, they believe that stealth, cunning, careful reticence, and the close observation of the words and actions of others (especially priests and white people) may lead them to stumble onto the "true meaning" of Christianity.

Because of these factors, talk about Christianity in Gapun is largely confined to talk about morality and proper behavior. Harangues like Kruni's (Text 4.9), in which hard work, knowledge, obedience, and generosity are explicitly linked to Christianity, are heard almost daily in the village. But the only other times the villagers overtly discuss Christianity is when they complain or gossip about the behavior of individual priests or when they recount for one another tales of the awesome powers of "the Bishops," whom the villagers fear because "the Bishops" are held to be able to destroy whole populations with a single prayer: The volcanic explosion that killed over 400 people in and near the town of Rabaul in May 1937, for example, is believed to have been caused by the Bishop of Wewak, Leo Archfeld, who was angry because workers in Rabaul charged him too much to repair his boat.

Doubts about their religious knowledge, lack of an agreed-upon forum, and considerations of secrecy mean that, although the moralistic aspect of Christianity is highly salient in village life, the details of the Christian pantheon and the internal coherence of Christian mythology are never talked about. There is no standardized version of Catholicism in Gapun, so individuals are free to cobble together their own more or less coherent theology. Those with a philosophical bent like Agrana do so by constantly incorporating new experiences and discoveries into their understandings of Christianity.

Agrana's version of Genesis and the death of Jesus is thus unlikely to be held in exactitude by anybody else, and several of the most important details in his long narrative have arisen directly out of his personal experiences. His opening image of a large enclosure containing the "prophets" was suggested to him when he once overheard a priest telling some villagers in Angoram that God looks after people like men look after their domestic animals. Likewise, the centrality of what Agrana calls the Place of Dead Souls (*Daiman Ples*) in his tale is the result of an out-of-body experience that he had as a young man, when he was "murdered" through sorcery but then quickly revived as a result of a marriage dispute among his matrilineal relatives. Yet another idiosyncratic detail in Agrana's story is the reason he gives for Jesus's death. In claiming that God had Jesus killed as "payment" for the "wrong" committed by his "mother and father," Agrana, in a gentle Gapunesque twist, structures his tale around the village dictum that nobody ever "just dies": Every death in the village is murder, brought about "by sorcery or spear" as a result of some "wrong" committed by the individual her- or himself, by her or his parents, children, or spouse, or by some matrilineal relative.

This particular version of why Jesus died contrasts with the much more widespread opinion (to which Agrana himself subscribes at other times), which holds that Jesus was killed because he wanted to come to Papua New Guinea and "straighten out" (*stretim*) the villagers there. Sake's brother Kawri, who holds this view, explains that:

Jesus straightened out all the countries. He straightened out all the countries, then he went to Australia. He straightened out the Australians, alright, he wanted to come to us in Papua New Guinea now. But the Australians, they didn't want that. They didn't want the Papua New Guineans to *kamap* like them. They had this thought, so they killed Jesus. Gave him big pain, poor thing. Beat him with nettles, whipped him, nailed him to a wooden cross and he died. Now his body is still around. If you go to Rome, you'll see it.

While the details of Agrana's understanding of Genesis and the death of Christ may not be held by everybody else in the village, the major themes running through his tale are assertions of basic truths held by all villagers. Agrana's delicate interweaving of traditional mythological personae (such as Kambedagam, Mongema, Sani, and Jari) with Biblical characters, settings, and intrigues reflects the way Christianity has been incorporated into the villagers' traditional cosmological thought.

Christianity has not so much displaced the traditional belief system as it has encompassed it. Villagers have interpreted Christianity as providing them with a framework into which their traditional cosmology fits. This fit permits the villagers to discover that their traditional beliefs both illuminate and are illuminated by the modern world. The people of Gapun now understand, for example, that their ancestors didn't just disappear into the ocean, as their forefathers believed. They now know that the ancestors left New Guinea and traveled to "the countries," where they "straightened out" the people there. And villagers can make sense of strange tales they hear about "the countries," such as stories about subways, through reference to their traditional mythology (Chapter 1).[5]

The second recurring theme in Agrana's narrative with which all villagers would agree is his assertion that Papua New Guinea is the "last country," the only place in the world where everybody still has black skin and where the prosperity and overabundance of goods found in "the countries" is absent. Everyone would also agree that the reason for this unsatisfying situation is that somebody didn't do his job. At several points in his narrative, Agrana stresses that Christian deities have the power to "straighten out" Papua New Guinea and make the villagers "come up and have white skin . . . and the ways of Europeans." The original prophets "didn't do anything," and Adam and Eve "just looked around and went back [to Heaven] again." Now hope has been pinned on Jesus, whom several villagers sometimes refer to approvingly as "our man," who is said to be "talking about coming back to straighten us out." This notion of Biblical figures having the power to "straighten out" the villagers is the most central theme in everyone's understanding of Christianity: It is why the villagers are Christian and it is what Christianity is all about. Christianity is the "road" (*rot*) that will lead to the metamorphosis they all anxiously await.

The coming of the Word

The villagers' first meeting with Christianity was a shock. In the late 1930s, a renegade Catholic priest named Heinriech Luttmer suddenly arrived in the neighboring village of Wongan and demanded that the men there reveal their sacred flutes to women and children. This demand was met with the same sense of horror that a devout Christian would feel if ordered to urinate on a crucifix. Traditional cosmological thought in Gapun, as in other Sepik and Ramu villages, centered around these sacred flutes, which were the embodiment of the most revered of the men's cult deities, the *tambaran (mərip)*. The *tambaran* constituted the organizational and ideological basis of Gapun society: of the perpetual warfare that existed throughout the area (heads from victims [*kwai kɔkir*] were "fed" to the *tambaran* and remained in the cult house), of the initiation cycle through which all males had to pass, and of the elaborate funerary feasts which were held after the death of village men or women.

The sacred flutes were, and still are, among the most profound symbols of the male cult. The flutes are the voice of the *tambaran,* of the Gods; they manifest the power and glory of malehood in general and of the clan in particular. They are hidden from all except initiated males, and they are played inside a cult house traditionally shrouded in mystery and fear. Women and children are said to have trembled and fled into the bush at the sound of the flutes. Boys panicked and fainted when first taken into the men's house to be confronted with them. For women to even speak of them was traditionally punishable by death. And now a white priest was insisting that the men remove these sacred objects from hiding and play them in full view of all women and children.

Father Luttmer had sent men to fetch the people of Gapun, and a large contingent of villagers was brought to Wongan to witness the exposure of the men's cult sacra and the playing of the flutes. Kruni was a child at the time. This is what he remembers:

Kr: All the men, women, children, they all went up into the men's house. All the Fathers, they didn't want to do this, they were crying. Alright, two big men, the *luluai* and *tultul* [two positions of village authority instituted by the colonial powers], Game and Sarimbe, the priest ordered them and they played the flutes. Played them as they cried.

DK: But why didn't the big men tell the priest that they couldn't play the flutes in front of the women and children?

Kr: He was a white man! (*Masta ia!*) He was a priest! Which man is gonna talk back to him, dispute his talk?! They were all afraid. They did what he told them to do. All the mothers took their children and the priest made them go up into the men's house. They all sat down like this [with bowed heads]. They all closed their eyes. They didn't want to see this thing [i.e., the flutes]. They were making a big cry too. They were afraid of sorcery. They knew that if they looked at this thing then the men would kill them through sorcery. But this priest ordered them, shouted at them, told them to look at the two flutes.

DK: And did they look?

Kr: Ah hah, they looked at them. And sorcery got them all. They're all dead now. Not one of them left alive. The Fathers finished them all off.

The day after his exposure of the men's cult sacra, Fr. Luttmer left Wongan. The villagers never heard from him again.[6] The people that

Fr. Luttmer left behind him were thoroughly traumatized. The flutes were immediately hidden away again, and everyone waited numbly for the wrath of the *tambaran* and the sorcery of the elder men, now totally exposed and shamed, to begin striking down the women who had laid eyes on the sacred objects.

In one fell swoop, the men's cult, the backbone of Gapun society, was broken. The cult had already been considerably weakened during the previous twenty years by the lack of interest of the village's young men. A number of these men had already spent three or more years away from Gapun working as contracted laborers on faraway copra plantations for the Germans and, after 1914, for the Australians. The experiences and goods that these men obtained on the plantations appear to have impressed them much more than did the traditional men's cult. Kruni's old brother, Raia, remembers that, "All the Fathers" [i.e., all the men in his father's generation, the generation from which the first contracted laborers were drawn] "didn't know any stories about the men's house [i.e., about the men's cult]. All they ever wanted to tell stories about," Raia recalls with a pucker, "was their time on the plantation." This situation and Fr. Luttmer's visit were enough to end the cult practices. After Fr. Luttmer's visit to Wongan, the traditional initiation cycle was abandoned and never revived.

After Fr. Luttmer, the villagers of Gapun had no direct contact with Christianity until after World War II. A few years after the villagers returned from their hiding places in the rainforest and rebuilt their village on a spot near the abandoned Japanese base camp, a Catholic priest began making brief but semiregular visits to Gapun. A small church was built in the new village. In 1949, several villagers were baptized.

The establishment of Catholicism in Gapun coincided with and was in all probability reinforced by a period of cargo-cult activity that swept throughout the lower Sepik–Ramu area. The first of these was a movement inspired by stories of the Rai Coast cult led by the well-known cult leader Yali.[7] No one in Gapun ever saw or heard Yali, whom they call "Yaring," but based on the reports they received about his teachings and powers, the villagers began to spend entire nights chanting prayers and flying into violent *extase*. They became convinced that their ancestors were about to return from the dead, bringing with them all of the cargo that white people had. Men and women from Gapun and Wongan had sex with each others' spouses, and several villagers occasionally slept in the graveyard, waiting for money to appear there. During this time the villagers destroyed or buried, and subsequently lost, the few traditional cult items that remained from before the war because they were told that these items were "blocking" the road of return for the ancestors, who wanted to come back to the village laden with cargo.

This cult apparently lasted several months but was finally disbanded when it failed to produce the desired results and when it was heard that the colonial authorities had jailed "Yaring" and would "punish" anyone who persisted in performing cult activities. It was soon followed by another millenarian cult led by a man named Ninga, who came from the lower Sepik village of Bien. This movement revolved around a combination of intensive prayer and the imitation of life on a European plantation. Praying took place in the evenings, with all villagers gathered together to repeat their limited repertoire of supplications over and over. Early each morning, a *garamut* (slit-gong drum) drumbeat signaled to all villagers that it was time to gather in the center of the village and stand in orderly rows. Lined up in this way, men and women were then assigned jobs (such as clearing underbrush around the village or hunting) by the village *luluai*. A patrol officer visiting villages near Gapun also influenced by Ninga wrote this report in 1950:

In some villages there is strict discipline – a morning roll call by officers and apportioning of tasks. These parades sometimes have their amusing sides. At Dongon, on the arrival of the patrol, after an honest but poor rendition of the national anthem, at the command from the luluai, all natives from aged women to toddlers executed a smart right turn, gave a snappy salute, and dismissed.[8]

Villagers themselves found nothing amusing in these activities, and even today people speak with a glowing seriousness of the period when they followed Ninga's teachings. During this time, they recall, the village was clean, free of grass and of animal excreta, everything was efficient and well-organized, and no one was *bikhed*. Ninga is believed to have had "power": He had "a light" and could perform feats like turning the tides and controlling the behavior of crocodiles and other wild animals. Europeans, the villagers claim, were all too aware of Ninga's "power." Agrana recalls that: "The government and the priests called Ninga to Angoram and tested him. With their own eyes they saw him make money appear, and they said 'This is true.' But they stopped him. They told him to stop using his powers. Otherwise they would put him in jail." Several villagers report that they felt almost ready to "change" during this period, but the cult broke down after about ten months, again partly because no cargo appeared, partly because the colonial administrators kept putting pressure on Ninga and threatening him with jail in case a full-scale cargo cult resulted, but mostly because the wife of the *luluai* in the village of Pankin ran off with Ninga, causing a scandal and resulting in Ninga himself losing interest in his "work."

From its very beginnings then, Catholicism in Gapun has been closely linked with notions of the coming of cargo and the millenium. Since the

1950s, there have been two more outbreaks of overt cargo activity in the village: once in 1965–6, and the other as recently as 1987.

The millenarian activity in 1965–6 was relatively short-lived and was inspired by a young man in the Adjora-language-speaking village of Tarengi. This man, Raphael, managed to convince the villagers from a wide area that he repeatedly traveled to Heaven in an airplane and had learned there how to produce money and cure sickness by glaring at people through a pair of magic spectacles (these were later discovered to be a pair of cheap sunglasses). This is the most blatantly fraudulent of all the cults, and senior men in Gapun burst out laughing now when they recount how they were fooled as they gathered expectantly outside the house of the Tarengi man, listening in awe as they heard the motor of a large airplane starting up inside the house (this was Raphael blowing into a large bottle) and then the voice of the angelic spirit who was said to possess Raphael's body while he was occupied in Heaven (the angel's voice was produced by Raphael holding his nose and speaking loudly). Until Raphael was exposed as a fake several months after he began, villagers believed him and paid him most of their savings in order to become "members" in his "work." Once they paid him, villagers expected Raphael to use his powers to make money appear under their bedding mats.

The most recent spate of millenarian activity in Gapun, in 1987, was directly sparked off by rumors that the village of Bogia (about a 1½-day walk from Gapun along the coast) had received a letter from God that informed them of the exact time the world would end. For weeks, Gapun villagers talked excitedly about traveling to Bogia to see this letter for themselves. Although no one actually ever made that trip, bits of information contained in the letter from God did leak out and eventually reach Gapun: The world, it was said, would end at "three o'clock" on "day ten." This would be a Thursday, in "year thirteen."

Nobody in Gapun understood what "year thirteen" could possibly mean, but many of the villagers, including the village prayer leader, began to "ready themselves" for the End anyway, expecting it to arrive at any moment. Instructed by villagers from the coastal village of Marangis, young men and women in Gapun constructed a series of elaborate altars that they decorated with brightly colored flowers, big orange seeds, yellow sago fronds, and flashlight-sized plastic statues of the Virgin Mary. Every evening for several weeks these villagers held charismatic prayer meetings, sometimes lasting most of the night, and several times resulting in many of those present falling into violent, shaking *extase* in ways that led the older villagers to draw parallels with the "Yaring" cult from the 1950s. A few young members of this "spirit movement" claimed to be able to see into people's "stomachs" (*bel*) and spot evil anti-

Christian thoughts there. There was also talk that the villagers' mentors in Marangis could raise newly deceased men and women back from the dead. Villagers reported enthusiastically that the cult leaders in Marangis had begun to feel their skins "blister and crack," in anticipation of the "change" to white skin, and some people began to recount apocalyptic dreams in which they had seen their spouses or children grinning at them with white skin and living in houses with corrugated-iron roofs.

The role of literacy

An important characteristic of this latest bout of millenarian activity is its ties to the written word. That the cargo-oriented activity of 1987 was directly related to a written product, from the pen of no one less than God Himself, is an indication of the prominent role that literacy has come to play in the villagers' perceptions of how they can bring about their "change."

Historically, literacy in Gapun – like virtually everywhere else in the Pacific region – was introduced by missionaries. The first village man to acquire literacy skills did so on a Catholic mission station in the mid-1950s. This man, Kruni, worked hard to learn how to read and write, learning these skills by sitting in on lessons held for local children:

I learned my ABCs, and after a while I could read and write now. I knew now. I went and read the Bible, the prayer book, the hymn book. . .

The social setting in which Kruni became literate and the uses to which he subsequently applied his literacy skills illustrate the tight connection that has existed between literacy and Catholicism ever since villagers began acquiring the written word. When Kruni returned to Gapun from the mission station, he used his newly acquired literacy skills to say a simple mass on Sundays. He shared his knowledge of letters with other village men, and a few of these learned enough to follow along in hymn booklets and perhaps to write their names. In the early 1960s, several of the village men and women who are now in their forties were sent by their parents to another mission station for schooling. Harsh punishment drove these boys and girls to run away before acquiring any literacy skills beyond perhaps learning the alphabet.

In any case, from the introduction of literacy in Gapun in the mid-1950s until the late 1960s, any villager who became literate did so in a context directly associated with the Catholic Church, be this through Kruni, the village prayer leader, or on a mission station. This link between literacy and the Church was reinforced further by the fact that there was a total absence of any literature except booklets and pamphlets addressing Catholic beliefs and liturgy. When villagers learned to read, they did so in order to be able to read Christian literature.

Just how closely literacy and Christianity have remained intertwined in Gapun is perhaps best illustrated by the type of literature the villagers actually possess. To discover this, I conducted a survey by going from household to household and asking the villagers to show me all the books and papers they possessed. Discounting loose pages from old exercise books and calendars, and the vaccination booklets that Sister Mariana, the nurse who occasionally comes to the village, sometimes gives to parents for their children, eighty-four specimens of printed matter were found in Gapun.

There were huge differences in who possessed this literature: The household of Sopak's brother Ambuli, the young man who usually said mass on Sundays, accounted for 40 of those 84 specimens of literature. The great bulk of Ambuli's printed material consisted of moldy old liturgical pamphlets in Tok Pisin that nobody ever looked at. The households of the two other village men who assisted Ambuli in saying mass contained 18 books or pamphlets, again, all concerning the Catholic liturgy. Thus the households of the three men directly responsible for conducting religious services in the village accounted for almost 70 percent of all literature possessed by the villagers. Of the remaining households, one contained 8 pieces of printed matter, six possessed between 1 and 4 items, and five households possessed no printed material at all.

Of the 84 specimens of printed matter found in the village, all but 2 were directly connected with Christianity. One of those was an automobile maintenance manual in English that one of Sopak's sons had somehow come by during a trip to the provincial capital of Wewak. The other was a small booklet called *Daisy Sing-Along*. It contained a number of evergreen songs like "Yellow Rose of Texas" and "O Du Lieber Augustin." The automobile maintenance manual was frequently passed around in the household that owned it, as adults and children enjoyed tracing their fingers along the line drawings of gears and sockets and wondering how they all fit together and made a car run. The *Daisy Sing-Along* book was never read.

All the rest of the literature in Gapun was religious. The most common printed item in the village is the small paperbound hymn booklet called *Niu Laip* (New Life). If a household possesses only one item of literature, this will be it. The next most common item is the soft-covered *Nupela Testamen na Ol Sam* (New Testament and the Psalms), which several households keep in a plastic rice bag up in the rafters of their roof. The remainder of the religious matter consists of various booklets and calendars containing Bible stories, prayers, and liturgical instructions, always in Tok Pisin.

With the exception of the hymn booklet, which the villagers take with them to mass and sometimes look in while singing, most of this literature is almost never read. Only printed matter containing pictures or line drawings is ever really looked at. Nobody ever actually reads the Bible, for example, but sometimes schoolchildren or an adult and several schoolchildren page through it together and comment to each other about the abstract line drawings of figures they find there. This paging through printed matter and commenting to one another about the pictures found there is how villagers most often "read."

One extremely popular item of literature in the village is a single copy of a moldy booklet without a cover called *Bel Bilong Man* (Man's Heart; lit. Man's Stomach) by the villagers. This booklet contains line drawings of various animals, which the Tok Pisin text explains personify different sinful behaviors: A bird of paradise represents Vanity and *Bikhed;* a dog symbolizes *"pasin bilong pamuk"* (Promiscuity); a cassowary is meant to stand for Aggression, and so on. The story that the booklet tells is that men must work to drive these sinful ways from their heart and replace them with Christian qualities, symbolized iconographically by a smiling mouth (for a Christian conscience), an open eye (for seeing the Light), an open Bible, a burning bush, and a crucifix. If one does not replace sinful ways with Christian ways, the text warns, then one's soul will be dragged to Hell. This fate is rather dramatically illustrated in a drawing in the booklet reproduced in Fig. 5.1.

Village schoolchildren have added to this drawing, writing *sinman* (sinner) on the soul destined for the Flames, and labeling the horned figures as *seten* (Satan). An interesting iconographic detail of the drawing is the appearance of a book, in the hand of the man who is standing near the top of the picture. This book, even though it has no label, is immediately understood by every villager to be the Bible, in a manner suggesting that the very concept "book" is essentially Christian in nature. The man holding this book, neatly dressed in a button-down shirt and standing poignantly apart from the dead sinner, is interpreted by the villagers as representing the village prayer leader.

Another drawing later on in the booklet depicts the death of another man – possibly this same prayer leader (Fig. 5.2). The text on the page opposite this illustration explains that it depicts "the death of a believer" (*"Indai bilong man i bilip"*). Details in this drawing, such as the European-style window in the man's house and the emphasis of the husband–wife relationship over that of extended families (signaled by the absence of any mourning relatives) subtly remind the villagers that there is an isomorphism between Christian and European styles and values. The prominence, once again, of a book is also striking. The book in this drawing is again unlabeled, but it is clearly not representing a *Daisy*

Figure 5.1. "The death of a sinner."

Sing-Along book or a car repair manual. This picture is an uncommonly apt and powerful encoding of what the villagers in Gapun believe to be the relationship between literacy and Christianity. Especially noteworthy is the color of the rising spirit's hair (and, by association, of his skin). Because they do not actually read religious texts, it is from illustrations such as these that villagers extract a great deal of their knowledge about Christianity. And in illustrations like this, the villagers continually find proof that they are correct in believing things such as that their skin "changes" and becomes white when they die.

Gapuners actively and creatively attempt to exploit the links they perceive between the written word, Christianity, and cargo in order to bypass the priests and find their own "road" to the millenium. In Sep-

Figure 5.2. "The death of a believer."

tember 1986, word reached the village that a new "road" had been discovered by their neighbors in Wongan. Returning from a brief visit to that village, Sake's brother Marame sat in Kruni's men's house and explained to the men gathered there that the villagers of Wongan had been informed by relatives and friends from other villages along the Bogia Coast of a new "bank" called "Innovative Finance." For 50 Kina, explained Marame, Innovative Finance will send one the address of a place in America where "big amounts of money just lie around. Like shells. Money there is like leaves on a tree. If you write to them," he told the men, "however many thousand million Kina you want, they'll just send it to you. Whatever you want, they'll send it. This big money is there in America to help all us poor people. You don't have to pay anything back. The money is there to be given away."

Several months after first hearing about Innovative Finance, a man from the Bogia Coast village of Borai made a short visit to Wongan and informed the villagers that Innovative Finance works like this: You send away 10 Kina to the address of Innovative Finance in the town of Madang. This 10 Kina enrolls you in the *Moni-program* for one year. You are also promised a *membasip kit* (membership kit) that according to the coupon that the Borai man produced at this point, you can return within thirty days for a full refund if you are not satisfied. What one, in fact, receives as a "membership kit," however, turns out to be ten more enrollment slips. These must be used to enroll new members (*kisim ol nupela memba*) at the cost of 10 Kina each. When this is done, you send the 100 Kina, plus 40 Kina of your own to Innovative Finance, and in return you receive a "receipt" that you have paid them 50 Kina (observe, *not* 150). On this receipt there is a number. Villagers were impressed by this, and everyone agreed on its significance: "If you lose this number, it's all over. They don't know your name. Just the number."

With the receipt for 50 Kina, you also receive a *Gran Pom* (grand form or grant form). Here you fill in the amount of money you want. Each "member," the Borai man explained, has "her or his own 1,000,000 Kina waiting for her or him," so one can decide to receive all the money at once, or to portion it out, taking "1,000 or 10,000 at a time, whatever you want."

After you have sent away this *Gran Pom,* the next time you happen to be in the settlement of Bogia, where Innovative Finance has an office (and where, incidentally, the letter from God was to be delivered several months later), you collect 250 Kina. The first time you collect this, you keep 50 Kina and give 100 Kina to two of the ten people who paid you 10 Kina to be enrolled as a "member." This gift of 100 Kina finishes off your obligations to those whom you enrolled in the "money program." Next time you go to Bogia to collect "your" money, you keep it all. The two people you've given the 100 Kina to, in the meantime, must now also get ten more people to give them 10 Kina each, and they also pay 40 Kina for their own *Gran Pom.* They then get a receipt for 50 Kina, and later they get 250 Kina, which they give to two of their members, and so on.

Innovative Finance is clearly a derivative of the chain letter or "pyramid" money-making schemes that regularly make short-lived appearances in many Western countries. The background against which the villagers of Gapun interpret such a scheme is different, however, from Western interpretations, and the differences are instructive of the way the villagers perceive "the countries" to exist and function. Several key concepts were foregrounded in the way the villagers presented and discussed information about Innovative Finance.

First, there is the belief that Innovative Finance is a "bank." For the villagers, banks are institutions that control access to the cargo. By depositing money in a bank it is believed that one thereby becomes a "member" of that bank. This membership enables one to begin tapping into the cargo. Several villagers attempted to do this in the mid-1970s, making the long journey to the provincial capital of Wewak in order to deposit 2 or 5 Kina in the bank. Having thereby become "members" of the bank, these men returned to Gapun to wait for their money to "work" and "get big." They were resentful and deeply suspicious when they returned several years later to withdraw their money and only received what they had deposited. Nobody could explain why the bank didn't give them any "free money" like it routinely gave, the villagers "knew," to members like Joe Kenni (a prominent Papua New Guinean businessman in Angoram). The reason for this deception, the villagers agreed, was that someone had "hidden" from the villagers the knowledge of how one *really* becomes a member of the bank.

Another key concept to which the villagers often return in their discussions about how to obtain the cargo is the idea of a *Gran Pom,* which they only have to fill in to receive vast sums of money. One of the newest innovations in the literacy–cargo nexus has been the recent discovery of "forms" (*ol pom*). These days, instead of repeating a string of memorized *Hail Marys* like their fathers, male "standard six leavers" devote time to wondering how they can obtain the "forms" that they have heard will bring the cargo if one fills them in correctly. One of these young men in his early twenties once expressed with great bitterness and indignation his conviction that someone had stolen "seven million Kina" from him. It turned out that he had obtained a lottery form from one of the schoolteachers at the local school. He filled in the form and returned it to the teacher to be sent off. He was certain that he had won the money because as he understood it, "If you write in your name and address without any mistakes at all then you win." He had, he explained, taken great care when completing the form, and he was certain that he had made no errors. The fact that the seven million Kina never turned up could therefore only be explained by thievery and fraud.

The written word plays an extremely prominent role in all recent village schemes to obtain the cargo. In order to get money through Innovative Finance, for example, one gets written receipts for money, one is given a "number" of great significance, one fills in forms. In addition, the bulk of the transactions are handled by mail. The discovery of the postal service and the recent understanding that villagers can use it to get things delivered to them has currently strengthened their belief that they have found a way around the priests and that they are now poised to begin direct communication with the distant powers that control access to the cargo. This discovery occurred simultaneously with the acquisition by a village man of glossy, brightly colored brochures from American mail order companies, passed on to him from friends in another village. These brochures caused a commotion in Gapun, and villagers poured over them in excited groups, marveling at the abundance of goods that the brochures seem to be offering. Proclaiming triumphantly that they had finally found the "road" they have been seeking, young men sat down and wrote brief letters to the addresses they found in the front of the brochures, requesting that the cargo be sent to them forthwith.[9]

The role of the school

Villagers' ideas about literacy, the millenium, and Christianity form a framework into which all aspects of the modern world are fitted. One domain in which all these themes coalesce is in the villagers' understanding of schooling. Gapuners have known about schooling since at least the mid-1950s, when Kruni traveled to the mission station to learn how to read and write. As soon as they could, some villagers attempted to put their children in school, sending them either to a mission school near the Ramu River or, in the early 1960s, to a series of government-run schools located near or on the Sepik River. Parents preferred these latter schools because Sepik villagers were not considered as likely to ensorcell their children as were the Ramu villagers, but the distances between these schools and Gapun village were too great, and parents found it difficult to keep their children supplied with food while they attended school.

One day in the mid-1960s, the ground under the government-run school in the Murik village of Mendam suddenly gave way, causing the entire school to slide into the sea. Seeing his chance, Kruni, who was Gapun's *kaunsil* (village representative) at the time, moved quickly and succeeded in convincing the local authorities that the school should be transplanted to Wongan, which he insisted was the *namel ples* (village in the middle). Villagers from Gapun, Wongan, and Sanae and their relatives from other villages cleared a large area of land and built the classrooms for the school. In 1967, Wongan Community School was opened, and since that time the great majority of children in Gapun have attended between three and six years of school. These children oscillate between living with relatives in Wongan during the week and

:turning to the village on the weekends, and making the almost two-
our trip between Gapun and Wongan daily.

A belief shared by all villagers is that school, introduced by white
people, is one of the main "roads" to European knowledge and ways
of life.[10] Like the literacy skills that children learn in school, school itself
is linked extremely strongly with Christianity. In his tale of Genesis, for
example, Agrana points out that Jesus was "a teacher." And the teachers
at Wongan Community School, in a bid for more respect or perhaps
because they believe it themselves, strive to reinforce parental perceptions of schooling as linked to Catholicism. A lightly disguised threat
commonly repeated by the headmaster to parents is: "Jesus was the first
teacher. He himself invented education. If you parents don't send your
children to school then when you die, I don't know, will you be punished
[by being sent to Hell]?"

Comments such as this by people in positions of authority, like the
headmaster, strengthen the villagers' firm belief that the ultimate purpose of school is to teach their children the secret of the cargo. They
think that once children "learn to read and write and get a big *save*,"
they will be able to "save" (*sebim*) their village by writing letters to
"banks" like Innovative Finance and by establishing *bisnis* (economic
enterprises) in the village, thereby opening the "road" to the cargo.

These ideas are most frequently expressed in quiet talks and in harangues in the men's house. Whenever school is spoken of in those
contexts, several themes are bound to emerge. The first will be that no
Gapun child has ever passed the grade six examination and gone on to
high school. Harangues often dwell on the fact that "every other village"
has sent some of their children to high school. "But our little village,
nosiree (*nogat tru*). Nosiree. None of our kids have acquired any *save*.
Nosiree, nosiree."[11] This is a sore point that inevitably leads first to a
suggestion that "somebody" should collect money from each villager so
that a large sum can be given to "the Bishop" together with a request
that he pray to God to give the children of Gapun more *save*, and then
to a distribution of blame.

Parents never blame themselves for their children's failure in school
because as they see it, they have done their part. They have, first of
all, "pulled" the school to Wongan and constructed the classrooms with
their own hands. In addition to this, parents pay school fees (2 Kina
per child plus 3 Kina per family per year), they see to it that their
children attend school regularly, they try to be present at the yearly
Parent and Citizens meeting (which consists of several hours of teacher
complaints at parents that they should be more generous toward the
teachers by supplying them with food and betel nut, and that they should
organize themselves to come to the school and cut the grass more often),

they go to the school at least twice a year to cut the grass on the playing field, and they remain up on gossip about the teachers' private lives.

Although men never blame themselves in any way, they frequently chastise children for not working hard enough at school. Parents do not know how to evaluate their children's schoolwork, and there is little opportunity for them even to attempt to do so because they never receive any type of evaluation of their children's work from the teachers. On the rare occasion when a child brings a completed workbook back to the village, a parent or older sibling may leaf through it delicately and briefly without comment, then hand it to a baby to play with and shred. Parents never ask their children about schoolwork: Talk about school, even between schoolchildren themselves, centers exclusively on the fun or scandalous events that occur there. School experiences are shared, but the work done in school is never discussed by anyone, unless it occurs in the context of a story about something else ("We were doing maths when the teacher got mad at Jipa and boxed her ears"). Because parents never hear talk about schoolwork or ever actually see children doing any schoolwork (homework is never assigned in any grade), they assume that the children aren't working as hard as they should, especially not compared to white children, who senior men like Kruni claim do nothing except sit alone and read and write all day long. This occasional realization sometimes leads to sudden loud cries from the men's house that, "You're all slack about school! Just play, play. All you all want to do is play!" The games that schoolchildren acquire at school from other children and bring back into the village, such as marbles, are particularly galling to the men, who regularly seize upon them as the "root of stupidity" (*as bilong longlong*/babasakŋa kandaŋ). If an old man is in a grouchy mood, any child playing such a game within sight of the men's house is likely to provoke an outburst.

The harshest criticism for the children's failure in school, however, is reserved for the teachers. Like Catholic priests, successful business-men, bank officials, and members of the government, Gapuners believe that teachers are concealing truths from them. Teachers (in 1986–7 these were three men from Sepik villages, two of which – Bien and Mendam, – are located in the lower Sepik not too far from Gapun; the third, Kambaramba, is located in the middle Sepik), who attended high-school and then teachers' training college, are imagined to be working against the villagers, withholding from their children the secrets they need to know in order to be able to "win" their exams and go on to high school. Whenever parents in Gapun criticize these teachers in their conversa-tions with one another, they never say that teachers in the school can't do their job or don't teach the children well. Instead, employing a language rooted in their millenarian conceptualization of the world, villagers complain darkly that "the teachers hide knowledge (*save*) from our children," thus suggesting obstructive intent or conspiracy.

Parents send their children to school assuming that they will learn skills and secrets that they can use later to repay those who have worked hard to provide them with school fees and, eventually, to "save" the entire village. The structure and organization of education in the school, however, makes it hard for village children to find connections between the work they do in school and their lives in the village. Instruction in school, for example, is in English, a language almost never heard or used by anybody outside of the classroom.[12] While the esoteric and mysterious nature of this language reinforces parental beliefs that the purpose of school is to reveal millenarian secrets to their children,[13] it results in children learning very little during their first two or three years, in large part because of their inability to cope with instruction in English.

But even beyond language, there is an overall lack of fit between the classroom and life in the village that appears to be a widespread characteristic of schooling throughout the country. Many observers of schooling in Papua New Guinea have noted that what is taught to village children in rural schools has little or no relevance to their own lives, except to make them dissatisfied with them. Nelson Giraure, a Papua New Guinean, could be describing the current curriculum in Wongan Community School when he writes of his own experiences in primary school:

Social studies became not the study of our village community but the study of communities in other countries. We learned of the Red Indians, how they hunted, how their houses were built, their legends and songs. We learned of the Eskimos, of their igloos, their hunting methods, and the animals which lived in their land. We learned of the great powers like Russia and America and the way in which people there lived. All this was new to us so we sat back and listened and listened and still listened. At no time were we taught about our own people. The way we lived was considered unimportant. Our legends and myths were never told to us. Our customs were never discussed. The big men in our village did not compare with the big men from overseas.[14]

Instruction in school is based on repetition and rote. Classroom time is spent copying into notebooks, repeating in unison what the teacher says to repeat, and, sometimes, answering a question with a single word or by correct use of a "pattern." Children never ask questions or speak spontaneously during a lesson. No opportunity is given for children to creatively use their knowledge or to connect their knowledge to any aspect of village life.[15]

A typical school exercise in Wongan Community School began in the grade two classroom when all the children suddenly were ordered by Pita, the teacher, to "stand." After a pause, during which Pita finished off the letter he had been writing (to an American mail order company) while the children had been copying dictation words off the barely visible blackboard, he told them to go to the front of the class and stand in a circle. Sopak's 11-year-old son, Gom, was told to stand in the center. Pita asked "Where is Gom?" The first two girls he called on to answer that question bowed their heads and said nothing. The third responded shyly and metallically, "He is in our middle." "That's right," said Pita. He then asked the children if they remembered the "pattern" that they had recited the previous day while they had looked at a line drawing on the blackboard. The drawing had been erased from the blackboard, but Pita still had it in mind. "Where is the Aid Post?" he suddenly asked the children. "On the other side of the river," he answered himself, reminding the children of the "pattern" from before.

Everyone chorused "Yes" to Pita's question whether they remembered this "pattern," so he again posed his question, "Where is Gom?" The first child to whom the question was now asked answered promptly, "On the other side of the middle." Pita became annoyed. "Forget about 'on the other side,' " he told the children. "Just say, 'In the middle of the circle.' " Each child was then called on in turn to repeat: "Where is Gom? In the middle of the circle."

When it was Ume's turn, he began by repeating the question "Where is Gom?" and then started to answer it with "He's middle of the . . ." He was interrupted by the teacher, who told him, "No, not 'He's' or 'She's' or 'It's.' Just say, 'In the middle of the circle.' " Ume began again: "He's the middle . . ." "No!" shouted Pita, "Not 'He's'! Now: Where is Gom?!" Ume repeated this, then hesitated. "What are you waiting for?" Pita asked, irritated. "I'm not going to tell you all the answers. Say it." Ume stared straight ahead with glazed eyes and was silent. After a few seconds, Pita turned to the child next to Ume, who responded in the way the teacher wanted.

This excercise was not successful. That many of the children did not understand the meaning of "middle" was clear when they said things like, "Gom is in front of the middle," a few minutes later when Gom had been placed in front of the blackboard facing them. The general confusion was not lessened by the teacher's insistence that in their replies the children not use "He's," even though many of them spontaneously did so. Even if everything else in their response was correct, if they began with "He's," Pita stopped them, said "No," and made them begin again. Like Ume, several other children did not seem to comprehend what they were supposed to say, and they kept beginning their answer with "He's." After a few times of this and repeated reprimands from Pita of "No, not 'He's'!" he told one of the children to repeat the "pattern." The child did so, and those who had begun by saying "He's" repeated the "pattern" like parrots.

Later, all the children were divided into groups of four and told to ask each other, "Where is Gom?" The children all answered either "In the middle of the circle" or "In the front of the classroom," despite the fact that Gom (who was also asked the same question – "Where is Gom?" – and who answered in the requisite way) at this point was in neither of these positions. The children repeated, mindlessly and ritually, the "pattern" until the teacher sent them out for a break.

The way instruction is organized and carried out in school contributes to the formation of a self-perpetuating circle. Children, unable first of all to follow instruction for the first few years because of their inability to cope with English, and then, later, finding themselves unable to relate anything they learn in school to anything they do outside the classroom, become bored and lose interest at an early age, applying themselves only enough to ease their tedium. After they leave school they quickly discover that nothing they learned there is particularly useful for "filling up the village's bank," as the big men constantly exhort them to do. "Standard six leavers" see that even those without any education at all are capable of earning money through their coffee or cocoa gardens, and they wonder what it was that school was supposed to have given them to make them able to "save" Gapun. The only skills they acquired that seem to be of any value at all are literacy skills. And so ambitious young men set about attempting to apply their skills, and they spend much time trying to find the "forms" and the addresses to mysterious places in America that they have heard will open a "road" to the cargo. When these attempts do not result in the arrival of any cargo, these men gradually come to blame their teachers and then themselves for having missed out on the secrets they were supposed to be learning. Later, they send their own children to school thinking, as their parents before them did, that the new generation will acquire the *save* that they themselves glimpsed but somehow missed.[16]

White skin and *save*

The villagers' belief that the school is a "road" preparing their children for another way of life, a life not concerned with the here and now, but with a life that will be, is thus not contradicted, but confirmed and perpetuated by those who have been to school. The mysterious way of life that the village children learn about is the way of life of those with white skin.

Coexisting with and reinforcing the understandings that villagers have about Christianity, the millenium, literacy, and school are the conceptions they have about white people. For the villagers, white men and

women have "changed" (*sens pinis*). With their airplanes, cars, corrugated-iron roofs, money, tinned food, and pale skin, whites represent
not only everything that the villagers are not, but also everything that
the villagers one day will become.

Stories about the ways of *ol masta,* as white people are generically
called, abound in Gapun, and villagers take a certain pride in knowing
even minute and intimate details such as why white people don't have
lice (their hair is so straight and slick that the vermin can't get a grip
on it and slide off). All dimensions of white behavior are considered
superior to that of the villagers. Even hard to understand actions, such
as what white women do with their newborn babies ("Mothers, they
don't hold the baby a little bit. They throw it in a dish as soon as it's
born and wash it with soap. Then they put a 'rubber breast' [i.e., pacifier]
in its mouth and take it into another room") are regarded as expressions
of superior, albeit opaque, values, and village men and women recount
all such behavior with glowing approval.

The "villages" from which *ol masta* come are imagined to be opulent
metropolises overflowing with every kind of imaginable and unimagin-
able cargo and riches. The villages of the white people are thought to
be crammed with goods: "Every space is filled with things – cars full of
cargo (*ol kago-kar*), houses, all sorts of things – it's all filled up." That
walking is not possible is no problem, since whites never walk anyway:
"Wherever you want to go, cars take you." The factories in these countries are in constant, heated production, churning out so much cargo
and money that it "lays around on the ground and just rots, like leaves."
The only drawback to life in "the countries," according to some, is the
noise: The constant chugging of generators and factory motors creates
such a din that many white people become slightly deaf. This is Raia's
perhaps somewhat too congenial explanation of why so many *mastas*
have the habit of shouting loudly at their Papua New Guinean servants
and laborers.

Villagers, especially older men, also have firm ideas about how white
people raise their children, and they periodically harangue mothers from
the men's house that they should treat their children differently. Kruni
frequently complains that:

The kids here just play around all the time like pigs. That's not the way of the
white people. I've seen them on the plantation. The children of whites, you
think they go around and play, shout everywhere they go? Man, no way. They
just stay in their house, their parents lock them (*kalabusim ol*) inside the house.
They just sit there. There's a big taboo on playing. If they play, their father
and mother beat them on the behind with a stick. And no other kids go to see
them. No way. They just stay in their house. If they want to go somewhere,
alright, put them in the car and go. That's good. They all develop (*kamap*

wantaim) big *save*. Become clear. And our kids – the parents teach them to go into other people's houses, hold other people's skin. They're gonna be stupid.

But although villagers admire and try to emulate white people, their opinions of them also contain a firm, if often unexpressed and deeply buried, strand of resentment. This resentment is a result of incomprehension on the part of the villagers as to why whites do not seem to want them to "change" and "come up." Nobody doubts for a second that white people, especially "the Bishops," and probably the priests, have the knowledge to "change" the villagers. So why, everyone wonders, do they insist on "hiding" this knowledge? Nobody quite knows the answer to that question, but a number of stories familiar to everyone in the village touch on the topic. The village understanding that Jesus didn't come to Papua New Guinea to "straighten out" the people there because the Australians killed him to prevent him from doing so is a typical expression of this theme. Another popular story in this genre involves what the villagers call a *Kumu* (or *Kumul*) *Karamap*. The *Kumu Karamap* is a small book that was given to selected Papua New Guinean soldiers who fought alongside the Australians in World War II. The book had the power to make objects materialize out of nowhere. Raia explained that:

If you don't have food and you want to eat, then you hold this thing [the book] and open it. A page with food will appear. This page will appear now and you'll look and see a table and a chair, and all kinds of good food will appear. Rice and coffee, sugar, tinned meat, tinned prawns, tinned crab . . . what . . . ham, cordial to drink; all this kind of food will appear. When you've finished eating, your stomach is full, then you'll close the book now, and the table chair, everything, where did it go? [i.e., it all disappeared]

Another page in the book made guns and ammunition appear in the same way. Another page produced money.

Raia went on to recount that when the war was over, the Australians demanded that the Papua New Guineans relinquish their *Kumu Karamap* books. "Some people cried," he said, when it became known that the "little books" had all been taken away from the Papua New Guineans. "Plenty of us died in the war. Why didn't they want to leave us keep these things?!"

Today, priests and other white people are suspected of possessing these little books and producing cargo with their power. As far as is known, the only Papua New Guinean to possess one is Michael Somare, the first Prime Minister of the country. He received his, villagers say, from the Pope during his visit to Rome. But like other government officials who have become privy to white secrets and power, Somare is believed to be "hiding" his book from his fellow Papua New Guineans.

Sparking even more resentment in some villagers is the suspicion that the "power" whites have was acquired by appropriating it from Papua New Guineans in the first place. The two-brother myth, which ends with Arena and Andena going to "the countries," "straightening" them out, and then being prevented from returning to Papua New Guinea (Chapter 1), is interpreted by villagers in this way. A story, brought into Gapun in 1986 by a 19-year-old youth, that much of the Australians' "power" during World War II was generated from a little netbag given away to Australian soldiers by a Papua New Guinean in some faraway village is another extension of this theme.

Attitudes like these do not mean that the villagers have any less desire to become white themselves; they just mean that Gapuners regard white people with a certain amount of caution and some distrust.[17] But in general, villagers assume goodheartedly that the resistence of white people to their "coming up" and "changing skin" must be a result not so much of white meanness as of their own unworthiness and moral/ Christian failings. Also, villagers are convinced that regardless of what individual white people think about it, everyone in Gapun will "change skin" anyway, if not before then at least after death. This process is detailed in a story often told by Raia and well known to everyone in Gapun:

A man from Madang went [to school] and became a policeman. Alright, he married a woman from a village near Madang. He married her and he left her. He went to [Port] Moresby to work. He went by himself. He didn't take his wife along because the government didn't give him a house to live in. They told him to wait first, "You work for awhile, then we'll give you a house." Then he would go back and get his wife or tell her to come on the telephone, I don't know.

That's it, he went to Moresby to start work as a policeman now, and all the villagers back home, they hurried up and ensorcelled his wife and killed her. News of this reached her man and he was really sad now. He got an airplane and came to Madang, went back to the village. That's it, he cried now. Made a big, big cry. Cried and cried and cried. He didn't do any work or anything at all, he just stayed at home and cried. He just stayed at home and cried.

Alright, that's it, he went to see the bishop now. He went to the bishop and said: "I don't have a wife now. I don't have a wife to make me food. I'm all alone now." The bishop thought about this, worried about him and he spoke: "I'm gonna send you to Rome. Your wife is there."

Alright, the bishop made a big case and told the man to go inside and sit down. He gave him some biscuits to eat. And too, he gave him a paper. On this paper the bishop had written a note to the Pope. He said to the man: "When you get to Rome, give this paper to the Pope. When you give it to him he'll know that I myself sent you." Alright, closed the case, put it on an airplane and sent it to Rome.[18]

It comes to Rome and the Pope sees the case and opens it. That's it, the man he gets out and gives the note to the Pope. The Pope reads it and says: "You were sad about your wife and so you came." "That's right." Alright, the Pope says to him: "Your wife is here. Now she's in school, getting knowledge (*save*). If you wait here you'll see when she comes on this big road."

The man waited, waited, waited, waited, waited now, he sees his wife coming up on the road. She had changed skin and was white, like a European. His wife saw her husband standing there and she asked him: "How did you get here?" "The bishop sent me." "Mm." Alright, his wife took him to her house and she told him: "This is where we'll stay." She said: "We can eat together, but we can't sleep together. You'll sleep in this room and I'll sleep in another. During the day, I'm going to go to school." And she told him that later she would mark a day when her husband would change skin. Alright after this, the two of them could go to God Papa.

Alright, his wife told him this and she told him about a taboo. All the rooms in the house, he could go inside them. Only one, his wife told him, he couldn't go inside. A big taboo. But this wife she didn't take the key to that room with her when she went. She just gave the key to him.

Alright, time passed and the two of them lived like that: During the day the wife would go to school and her husband would wait for her. When she came in the afternoon, they would eat together. When they slept, they slept in separate rooms. Time went and one day the man took the key and opened the door that his wife had tabooed.

That's it, he wasn't in Rome anymore, he appeared in the graveyard of his village. Oh, sorry, he cried now. In the afternoon his wife finished school and came back to the house. And her husband wasn't there. "Eh, where did my husband go?" That's it, she saw the door, the one she had tabooed, it was open and she knew her husband had broken the taboo. That's it: "That's your problem" (*Wari bilong yu*), she said.

And the husband he went again to the bishop. The bishop saw him and asked him: "Eh, how did you get here? I sent you to Rome, to your wife." That's it, the man told the bishop his story and the bishop got angry at him: "That's it. You think I'm going to send you again? Enough. You go back to Moresby and find a job. Your road is closed. I sent you once. I'm not going to send you again. Get out of here!"

In addition to making explicit the villagers' beliefs concerning the interrelationship between skin, school, and religion, Raia's story also illuminates village conceptions of geography and afterlife. It is an expression of the belief held by all villagers, even those with six years of schooling, who have seen maps and globes of the world, that "the countries" lie either in Heaven or along the road to Heaven, which stretches out from Papua New Guinea (the "last country") in an upward arc into the sky. This "road" can be traveled only in airplanes, huge steamships, by magic, or in death.

This geo-metaphysical placement of "the countries" in or near Heaven – and, consequently, under the dominion of God and the Pope – implies that no *pasin nogut* (bad ways) exist in the countries. In their private talks and their harangues, villagers frequently stress that "in the countries there's no *kros*, fighting, lying, stealing, and there's no talking behind people's backs!'" Most importantly, villagers maintain that "in the countries," there is also "no sorcery" (*nogat poisen/pɔisir wakarɛŋa*). Because the only way any villager can die, aside from being cold-bloodedly murdered, is by sorcery, this belief that sorcery doesn't exist in "the countries" means that no one there ever dies. And this is what the villagers often tell themselves. "White people don't die" (*Ol masta i no save indai*) is a truth in Gapun, and it is a belief consistent with their contention that they themselves become white when they die: Having died once, one cannot die again.[19]

Raia's story about the policeman and his wife also makes explicit the villagers' ideas about the relationship between white skin and *save*. In the villagers' conceptual hierarchy of *save*, if children have least and adult men most, then the *save* of Papua New Guinean men and women is still minute when compared to that of *ol masta*. This is reflected in multiple ways. The vernacular-language name for white people, for example, is the same name as that by which the original prophets sent to the ground by God are called: *ɛŋgin munjɛ/nɔŋɔr* (lit. prophet, or ancestral man/woman). And villagers tirelessly point out for one another, in the same way that Agrana does in his epic about the death of Jesus, how stupid (*longlong/babasak*) they all are, living "like pigs and dogs." During a quiet conversation in the men's house that touched on school, Kem once felt compelled to remind the men present that "*Ol masta* have full *save*. Us no. Just a little *save*. We just have half-*save*. Half.'" Again in his epic, Agrana explains, in a phrase that gets repeated ceaselessly in village conversations and that encapsulates the villagers' view, that "You all have white skin AND SO you have lots of *save*." The one, in the villagers' understanding of the world, necessitates and makes possible the other.

Change will come

Papua New Guinea has become famous among scholars of many disciplines because of the abundant number of cargo cults that have been observed to occur there. Usually, these cults have been analyzed as confusions or aberrations that disappear once villagers understand that airplanes and ships are not in fact obtained through magic or praying. A point that is sometimes overlooked in discussions of cargo cults is that the cults themselves are merely the "activist" manifestations of the beliefs.[20] The beliefs that generated the cargo cults do not just disappear with the cults. They can remain strong; indeed, they can remain fundamental, without any overt millenarian activity taking place at all, although this is likely to erupt from time to time.[21]

This is what has happened in Gapun. Despite the passage of time and several unsuccessful cargo cults in the village, the cargo-oriented world-view held by Gapuners has not been replaced by another way of looking at life. The villagers' millenarian framework, with its emphasis on finding secrets and on being deceived by everyone, is flexible and encompassing enough to account for the failures of the past cults. Nobody questions that certain people like "the Bishops" have the "power" to bring on the millenium if only they should choose to do so. And nobody doubts that certain pious, wise, and gifted villagers like Ninga or "Yaring" also have that power. As is commonly the case in millenarian frameworks throughout Melanesia, the failure of the movements that grow to surround people like Ninga or "Yaring" is interpreted as a moral failing of the followers or as caused by preventive steps taken by the government or the missions. The failure is never attributed to the beliefs themselves. On the contrary, the demonstrable failure of the cults merely reinforces the villagers' view of their world as conspiring to keep them from "changing" and becoming white. From this perspective, the only effect that social or technological innovations can possibly have on the villagers is to provide them with additional means by which they might succeed in bringing forth the cargo. And literacy, schooling, and increased knowledge about institutions like banks have all been incorporated into village thought in precisely this way.

Villagers do not lament the changes that have occurred in Gapun since the arrival of the white men. No one wishes even for a moment to return to a way of life without factory-produced clothing, metal tools, cash crops, outboard motors, knowledge of letters, and access to medicine. Changes like these are thought of by the villagers as symbols of material advancement. But because all change is also interpreted within a religious framework, such material advancements are, in addition, signs of something more meaningful.

Changes in the village are not imagined to be random or haphazard. Each innovation seen as having its source in the outside world of school, church, or "the countries" is viewed as a significant step further along the "road" to the final transformation. Even social innovations that people like the village big men do not approve of and periodically condemn, such as the waning of the custom of bringing news from other villages first to the men's house, seem to the villagers to be somehow meaningful, leading to something else, pointing the way toward even more momentous changes that are yet to come.

At the end of his epic tale of the beginning of the world and the death of Jesus, Agrana recounts "talk" that reveals that Jesus "is talking about coming back to straighten us out." This "talk" summarizes an elaborate conception of the world in which Christian deities, bank officials, priests, "the Bishops," members of the Papua New Guinean government, mythological ancestors, white expatriates, and the villagers of Gapun are all implicated and have a role to play. The "talk" is a condensation of the conceptual framework that each person in Gapun draws upon to make sense of the world and of his or her place within that world.

The language in which the "talk" Agrana refers to is necessarily expressed is Tok Pisin. Tok Pisin is the language understood by the villagers to be used by all institutions and persons that have any role at all in the "coming up" of the village. All contacts with people outside the village whom Gapuners regard as agents or representatives of development, such as carving buyers, coffee and copra buyers, politicians, and missionaries, are carried out in Tok Pisin. And parents know that their village vernacular is not only not used, but is expressly forbidden to be used in the local school. The ideological message implied by this interdiction is not lost on the villagers, and they understand it to be a not so subtle sign that their language has no role to play in the "coming up" of the village. In fact, Tok Pisin is also formally forbidden in the schools, but in reality it is the language used by the children in their conversations with one another both inside and outside the classroom. Tok Pisin is also used between teachers and students outside the classroom and, in bursts, inside the classroom as well. In addition, the language is also used by the teachers in their speech to one another outside of school hours, when speaking to their families and their children (a fact not missed by the sharp-eared Gapuners), and when socializing with village parents. Villagers thus associate teachers more with Tok Pisin than with English, and some Gapun parents who have not been to school themselves think that their children are taught in Tok Pisin, learning English only as a subject like any other.

Beyond being the language of school and of contact with people who give them money (such as carving buyers), Tok Pisin is also the language of literacy and religion. Although children these days learn their literacy skills in English, they are able, without any instruction, to transfer their reading and writing skills to Tok Pisin, thus becoming functionally literate in that language. Outside the classroom, villagers never use English, and on those relatively rare occasions when individuals do read or write, they do so in Tok Pisin. The link between Tok Pisin and literacy is further strengthed by the fact that the overwhelming majority of all literature found in the village is in Tok Pisin. The exceptions to this are sheets of the *Sydney Morning Herald,* which are smoked, not read, and the brochures from American mail order catalogues, which are examined for their flashy pictures, not their textual content.

This link between literacy and Tok Pisin has a special significance in light of the strong associations that the villagers, in turn, perceive to exist between the written word and religion, which is also expressed only in Tok Pisin. Tok Pisin has become so tightly tied to religion that it is the only domain in the village in which the otherwise prevalent patterns of code-switching to Taiap *never* occur. All aspects of Christian worship – mass, talk about religion, even private prayer – are verbalized exclusively in Tok Pisin. Even the cargo cults that have occurred in the village or involved villagers have been in Tok Pisin: Raphael, possessed by an angel of God and speaking through his nose, spoke Tok Pisin, not his native language, Adjora, or some other vernacular. And during the 1987 cult, during which villagers of all ages chanted and convulsed and rolled on the ground in ecstatic trances, possessed by the "holy spirit," not a word of Taiap was heard from anybody.

Although villagers profess not to know what language is spoken after death or in Heaven, their actions and stories indicate that they at least suspect what that language may be – and it isn't Taiap. Agrana, for example, once recounted a dream for the men in Kruni's men's house, in which his long-dead mother, Makri, appeared to him with white skin. Makri, who while alive commanded a respectable number of vernacular languages, but no Tok Pisin, spoke to her son in that latter language. Raia's story of the policeman and his wife in Rome also has the two conversing in Tok Pisin. And in an especially telling gesture, men, when they directly address their long-dead ancestors in the men's house, asking them for luck in hunting or chastising them for "giving sickness" to a village man or woman, often speak to these ghosts in Tok Pisin, a language none of them would have known in life.

In contrast to Tok Pisin, the village vernacular has no structural or ideological buttressing to strengthen its position in Gapun. "Taiap," anyone will respond when asked why the language is valuable and why children should continue learning it, "is the language of our Mothers and Fathers. It's the language of our ancestors." Since the coming of the white men and, especially, since the coming of the missionaries, however, the ways of the ancestors are not regarded highly, and any reference to the "Fathers" in everyday speech is likely to be in the context of signifying something or some action that is old-fashioned, unchristian, selfish, and stupid. The loss of the old men's cult is not mourned in the least by anyone in the village, and no one romanticizes the way their parents and grandparents lived before the "pacification" of the area by missionaries and Australians. Men and women in their forties and younger occasionally sit together and recount for each other stories of the *taim bilong bipo* (the past) that they have heard from others. But even when these younger villagers laugh and revel in the luridness and grizzliness of ritual killings, the feeding of heads to the *tambaran* and the pain of initiation rituals, they always disdainfully conclude at the end of such sessions that the ancestors really were *longlong man* (crazy, stupid), and they would not like to have been around then.

The village vernacular has become conceptually tied in the villagers' thoughts to the past – a past they devalue and strive actively to be free of. The entire emphasis in village rhetoric, idioms, actions, and imagination is an emphasis on the future: on the "coming up" of the village and the "changing" of the villagers. In this much anticipated future, the village vernacular simply has no place. Because of the associations that the vernacular has taken on in village thought, it must inevitably be abandoned one day, along with the bad habits, heathen ways, bush-material houses, and black skins that are currently locking the villagers to their ancestors and to their past.

6. Becoming monolingual

Gapun villagers do not own radios, read newspapers, or have access to other depersonalized sources of information, so whatever they know about other people and other places, they know through their own experiences or through the stories of others. In this way, information is always contextualized, and it is always tightly bound up with whoever passes it on. Villagers' talk is not taken up with discussions of *issues* like politics, religion, or economy. People in Gapun occasionally talk about the Papally bestowed "power" of Michael Somare (Papua New Guinea's first Prime Minister), or the miraculous happenings linked to a statue of the Virgin Mary in a Ramu village, or they may discuss why the price they get paid for their coffee beans keeps going up and down for no discernible reason. But these topics are never discussed apart from the fact that someone has seen or experienced them her- or himself or has heard about them from someone else. Talk about anything in Gapun is ultimately anchored in the talkers and the social contexts in and about which they speak.

The villagers' continual embedding of talk in social relations and contexts both reflects and influences their notions of what language is and what it is for. The local concept of language emphasizes its interactional character. For the villagers, language is a collaborative activity primarily concerned with the elaboration and manipulation of social relationships, and consequently, with the demonstration of *save*. This conception of language focuses more on discourse and on pragmatic effect than on individual words or isolated sentences, and it foregrounds a view of language as something done together with other people or something done to affect the actions of other people.[1] During speech, listeners are expected to react to speakers with talk of their own: with interjections of support, with repetition, and with help in structuring the discourse. By responding in this way, and by intuiting and adjusting their verbal and nonverbal reactions to the talk that the speaker produces, listeners demonstrate their *save*.

This kind of conceptualization of language entails the expectation that

190

speech will occur in the presence of an audience of socially competent and potentially responsive listeners, of listeners who themselves have *save* and who can collaboratively participate in the construction of a discourse. This expectation, in turn, automatically disqualifies certain potential recipients of speech as listeners. Domestic animals such as the scabies-ridden dogs the villagers keep to hunt with are, for example, not regarded as audiences in the villagers eyes, and they are never spoken to except to be brusquely ordered to "get out of the way" or to "come."

Likewise, babies, who "have no *save*," do not qualify as conversational partners, and one of the most characteristic features of adult talk to babies and young children in Gapun is the relative lack of it. For the first six months of their lives, village children are seldom spoken to at all except when they start to cry and mothers tell them "*Inap, inap*" (Enough, enough) or "*Susu, susu*" (Drink the breast, drink the breast), or when they are playfully called by animal-inspired vocatives such as "little rat" or "bloody stupid pig." If a mother is bored or alone with her baby, she may occasionally repeat the child's cooing sounds and engage in face play, but these interactions seldom last more than thirty seconds at a time, and they are immediately abandoned if somebody more interesting to talk to happens along. No caregiver ever attempts to engage an infant in any kind of sustained conversational activity, and even actions involving the physical handling of a baby's body, such as feeding, washing, or piercing boils, are performed without any comment to the child at all. At this age, child vocalizations are always treated as expressions of hunger and dissatisfaction, and as soon as a baby begins to fuss or struggle, a breast will be squeezed, firmly and wordlessly, into its open mouth.

It is only when children from about 8 months start to resist being quieted by the breast or by having an object suddenly placed in their hands that mothers begin talking to them. This is the point at which the *em ia* distraction routines begin (Chapter 4), when mothers point into the distance and with singsong intonation direct the child to attend to an object or occurrence that may or may not be present. As with earlier speech to the child, distraction routines do not engage the child in verbal interaction. On the contrary, their goal is to get the child to stop crying and be quiet.

The distraction routines are the beginning, however, of extensive verbal input addressed directly to the child. Throughout an *em ia* routine, caregivers work to keep the attention of the child by speaking directly to it, by pointing, and by orienting the child's body outwards toward the object of the talk, the village. As the child grows older and less likely to be distracted for long by simple calls to look at a pig or a dog, *em ia* routines become lengthy and increasingly complex. Caregivers interweave calls to look at pigs and dogs with threats, asides, and general comments about the child's behavior. A large number of these communicative conventions, which are typical of caregiver speech to children between the ages of 8–12 months and 3 years, are evident in the following monologue by Sopak. Sopak's daughter Masito (2;1) has been crying insistently for several minutes, and despite several attempts to quiet her by offering her a breast, her favorite butcher knife, and a crimson wad of betel nut that Sopak had been chewing, Masito won't stop. Her temper growing short, Sopak finally swoops the child off the floor and tries once again to silence her with a breast:

Text 6.1

Drink it, drink it [the breast]. Drink it and swallow. Sss. Quiet. Quiet. Quiet now. Eye, her eye is hurting. Enough, Kama [Masito's 6-year-old sister] that sago head [Kama's nickname] just left again. Enough! Baso! [Masito's 16-year-old brother] Baso, Baso, *Sia* [an exclamation]. I haven't washed, her dirty skin
5   [Masito's] is gonna mess me up. Drink the breast. Tsk. Oh, Kama died. Ah! I'm gonna box your ears now! Why are you doing this? Your tears are gonna block your eyes now. Drink the breast. Drink the breast. Ding bes. [baby talk] Eh, Uh, Father's child [exclamation of exasperation]. *Asapɔi* [term meaning nonkin] I call out to their kids and they're *bikhed*. [Sopak means here that she
10 calls to her mother's sister's children to come and amuse Masito, but they treat her like someone with whom they have no kin obligations and don't listen to her.]

Look at the pig! Yo, the pig died.
Look, at it.
15 Look Obrɨwa's gonna spear a chicken.
Look. Obrɨwa's gonna spear a chicken now. Ah. [Masito stops crying.]
Priest. Priest. Priest here.
The priest is coming.
Nurse. Mariana [the nurse's name] here.
20 Mariana is coming.
Priest. Father Pita is coming.
Over here, he's sitting in Kruni's men's house. [Masito begins to whine.]
We're gonna go see him. [Masito stops.]
The priest is going with the nurse. The nurse is coming.
25 Oh, a couple of these hermit crabs [in a bag on the floor] are crawling away. Yesterday they went to get hermit crabs, but there were none at all. [Masito starts to whine.]
Enough.

Uncle's baby is gonna fall down and die. She's sleeping in the house and every-
30   one's gone. Yapa [the baby's older sister] went somewhere.
Michael's-eh-Gom's chicken here.
I haven't seen Basama's. [Masito whines louder.]
There. Gom's chicken.
Gom's chicken. There.
35   It has a nice color. [Masito stops whining.]

Sopak begins her talk with a series of directives ordering Masito to
nurse and be quiet (lines 1–2). When this is ineffective, she continues
first by interpreting Masito's behavior aloud as a sign that her eye hurts
(line 2), then by telling her to stop crying (line 2). She then announces
loudly to nobody in particular that Masito's 6-year-old sister, Kama, has
run off again and is nowhere around to help distract Masito (lines 2–
3).

Sopak's next move is to shout, first at Masito ("Enough!") and then
into the distance after Masito's adolescent brother Baso (lines 3–4). In
calling out in this way to her son, Sopak's goal is not to summon Baso,
who Sopak knows is not in the village anyway. Her calls to Baso are
intended to distract Masito and make her forget whatever it is she is
crying about. Voice modulation of the type used here by Sopak is regularly employed by mothers to startle their crying children and get them
to stop crying, if only for a moment. If a child persists in crying too
loudly and too long, a caregiver may respond by attempting to shout
the baby down with a prolonged, loud scream in the child's ear. Before
this point is reached, however, it is common for mothers or other caregivers to bark short, sharp, loud sounds into the child's ear, sounds like
the names of relatives with reputations for short-temperedness or the
sound of startled fear: "*Yɛ!*" These sounds are accompanied by sudden
jolts or by the caregiver hugging the child tighter to her or his body as
though offering protection from some threatening presence.

Distracting children in this way is also sometimes done by directing
their attention to dramatic actions, like a fight or an accident, which are
often not really happening. A mother will point urgently into the empty
distance, clutch her baby close to her body, and tell it excitedly: "Yo
look! A fight! Ye! Kruni's hitting Sombang! Look!" In her talk to Masito,
Sopak uses this ploy when she points and directs the child's attention
to the pig (line 13) and to the girl who she says is about to spear the
chicken (lines 15–16). None of this is in fact happening, and no pig, girl,
or chicken is visible in the direction in which Sopak is pointing.

Just as frequently, startling children involves suddenly announcing the death of a close relative, as when Sopak tells Masito that her sister Kama has died (line 5), and when she later says that Masito's baby cousin is going to "fall down and die" (line 29). When the death of her sister has no effect on Masito, Sopak continues trying to scare her in to silence by looking out into the (once again, empty) distance and telling her that the priest and nurse from Marienberg are arriving in the village (lines 17–24). These two figures are frequently used by caregivers to frighten children since they are both strangers and have white skin. Parents know that every village child is especially terrified of Sister Mariana, who in addition to being a white stranger also squeezes their boils and gives them injections.

As Sopak's talk to Masito continues, she digresses and comments to herself that two of the hermit crabs she had planned to roast as a snack are crawling out of their burlap bag (lines 25–6). Turning her attention back to Masito when she starts to whine, Sopak attempts once more to divert her attention away from herself by startling her with the imminent death of her baby cousin (lines 29–30). In the end, Sopak initiates another *em ia* routine, this time involving a chicken that actually is visible in the grass below the houses (lines 33–4). Once this routine is begun, Masito stops crying for several minutes.

Taiap and Tok Pisin

Throughout her talk to Masito, Sopak oscillates between the village vernacular and Tok Pisin. Just as the two languages are not separated in adult speech in the village, so are Taiap and Tok Pisin never kept strictly separate in caregiver speech to children. The way Sopak intersplices the languages in her monologue is reminiscent of the ways adult villagers code-switch in their conversations with one another. But even though the fluid manner in which adults continually switch between Taiap and Tok Pisin is carried over in talk to children, one convention stands out and differentiates adult–adult talk from that of adult–child.

Sopak begins speaking in the vernacular and continues this way throughout the first half of the monologue, switching only briefly to Tok Pisin to startle Masito with a loud shout of "Enough!" (line 3); to frighten her by telling her that her sister Kama is dead (line 5); and to comment on the tears blocking her eyes (lines 6–7). Throughout this part of the speech, Masito remains crying. She stops only after Sopak initiates an *em ia* routine, signaled by the high rise–fall intonation on her utterance "Yo, the pig died" and by a switch to Tok Pisin (line 13). Once Sopak successfully captures Masito's attention with a series of urgently enunciated directives in both languages (*rarɛtukun/lukim* = Look at it; lines

14–16), Masito actually stops crying. When this happens, Sopak, in her continuing talk to Masito, switches exclusively to Tok Pisin, except when she voices observations to herself in a lowered voice about the hermit crabs (lines 25–6) and her daughter Basama's chicken (line 32). The only other vernacular utterance here directed to Masito is "Gom's chicken" (line 33), but this is immediately translated into Tok Pisin.[2]

In choosing to use Tok Pisin in talk addressed directly to Masito, Sopak is displaying a pattern of speech common to all village parents. Although villagers speak their usual mixture of vernacular languages and Tok Pisin in the presence of their children and in their talk to children, there is an overwhelming tendency for caregivers to switch to Tok Pisin when they especially want a child to attend to their talk, and when they see that they have the child's attention, as Sopak does here (lines 17*ff*). This tendency is so strong that even those village women who rarely speak Tok Pisin to anyone else tend to switch to this language when they directly address their children.

After a child's birth, a pattern becomes established very quickly wherein a mother speaks to adults and others in her usual combination of the vernacular and Tok Pisin, but tends to switch to Tok Pisin whenever she directly addresses her infant. In a typical instance, Paso and her husband Ariba have been sitting on their veranda chewing betel nut and chatting with Ariba's brother's wife, Ermina. Although Ermina understands Tok Pisin and speaks it well, she is one of the few village women who tends not to speak much Tok Pisin to other adults in Gapun. Out of deference to her, the bulk of the conversation has been in Taiap:

Text 6.2

Ariba:	. . . *Ermina*	A:	. . . Ermina
Ermina:	*Ah?*	E:	Ah?
Ariba:	*Tret wukkɛ?*	A:	Do you have any thread?
Ermina:	*Takwat ɛnda. Yundi. Em wari bilong yu. Yuwɔn nunuk mɔsɛrkukubɛtəŋan.*	E:	What a joke. You're too much. That's your problem. You bought yours after I bought mine. [i.e., you should still have some left]
Ariba:	*Sitbed taman aŋgɔ krararawɔk.*	A:	[My] whole blanket is coming apart.
Ermina:	*Gu nil anakapɛ?! Yuwɔn ɔmínyi nil dabaipiatan nil iati wakarɛ.*	E:	What needle are you gonna use?! Your wife lost the needle I lent her and she never gave me another one.

Ermina's 7-month-old baby, who has been sleeping on her lap, wakes up suddenly at this moment and starts to whine and struggle.]

Ermina:	*Ey, inap inap inap inap.*	E:	Ey, enough enough enough
	Slip yu slip.		enough.
	Ey, susu nau susu.		Sleep, you sleep.
			Ey, drink the breast now, drink the breast.

[Ermina presses her breast to the baby's mouth and continues her conversation with Ariba and Paso in Taiap.]

In another household, Sake sits chewing betel nut and holding her sister Jari's 13-month-old baby, Kunji, on her lap. Sake has just watched her old mother, Sombang, take some yams over to Kruni in his men's house. Sombang carried them over in a sago-frond bucket; when she climbs back up the pole to her house, Sake informs her in Taiap:

Text 6.3

Sɔmbaŋndɨ gumɛ kɔndɛw ɔrak	Sombang that bucket you put those
parkunŋa ɛŋgɔn wakarɛ. Yɛwɨr	things [the yams] in isn't good. You
warəŋgar kɔndɛw aŋgɔ yuyi kukuprɪɛk	put them in the one used for putting
warakkukubɔk. Yɛwɨr warəŋgar kɔn-	animal shit in. That's the one for put-
dɛw aŋgɔ.	ting shit in.

[Kunji grabs hold of Sake's jar of powdered lime.]

Ai! Yu no ken bagarapim kambang bi-	Ai! Don't you mess up my lime! Let
long mi! Lusim yu. Yu Kunji yu no	it go you. You Kunji you never listen
save harim tok liklik. Yu man bilong	to talk a little bit. You're a *bikhed*
bikhed.	man.

One reason why caregivers switch to Tok Pisin in this manner when speaking to children is because of their beliefs about that language in relation to Taiap. Villagers hear the evaluation of their vernacular by others and know that everybody else considers Taiap to be an unusually "hard" language. This characterization of their vernacular on the basis of the language's "two-language" gender system has influenced the villagers' own perceptions of their vernacular, for even though they know all too well the sinister undertones of saying that a language is "hard," they admit to one another that Taiap is in fact "a little bit hard" (*i hat liklik*). No one ever suggests that Tok Pisin is a difficult or sinister language, and the fact that virtually everyone in Gapun and all surrounding villages has learned Tok Pisin as a second language underscores its straightforwardness and accessibility. Only *ol buskanaka* (country bumpkins) and *ol longlong man* (idiots) do not know Tok Pisin.[3]

This perception of the vernacular as difficult is coupled with an adult appreciation of the limited processing and productive capabilities of young children. Villagers observe and comment on the fact that children

Table 6.1. *Baby-talk lexicon in Taiap*

Adult form	Baby-talk form	Meaning
mambrag	*mamak*	spirit
kakamatïk	*kakam*	millipede
mərïp	*ŋwaŋu*	tambaran
min	*mimi*	breast
yɛwïr	*pipi*	excrement
nɔk	*sɔsɔ*	urine
bɔrsip	*sisi*	pig meat
gɔmar	*mar*	fish
yamïŋɛ	*amɛi*	wildfowl egg
min atukun	*mimi maka*	drink the breast
atïtïŋgarana	*pupərəŋgarana*	[you] better not fall

have difficulty pronouncing certain sounds and that they often don't listen to or understand adult conversations. These limitations are explained in terms of the child's *save* not yet having "broken open," and they result in villagers sometimes modifying their speech to children, in the same way that adults strive to modify their speech and choice of language in conversation with others so as to accommodate them verbally. Sopak and a few older villagers claim that there used to be a special baby-talk register in the vernacular, called <u>*biɔngima mɛr*</u> (lit. infants' language). These villagers state that this register was extensive and widely used whenever caregivers, particularly women, spoke to infants and young children (<u>*biɔngi*</u>). Today it is difficult to assess how accurate these claims are because although they say that the register was large, the total number of items belonging to the register that anyone could recall was 11, consisting of 9 nouns and 2 verb phrases (Table 6.1).[4]

The items on this list are all common words that mothers, especially, would use when talking to their children. The first three objects are frequently named to frighten small children, and the remaining nouns name the child's bodily functions and common foods that children eat. The two verb phrases on the list similarly have obvious relevance for small children, who are continually being silenced by breasts, and who live in perpetual danger of suddenly falling off the side of a house or through a hole in the floor.

The derivitive morphological and phonological processes involved in the reductions (e.g., *gɔmar* > <u>*mar*</u>) or the reductions and reduplication (<u>*min*</u> > <u>*mimi*</u>) of the baby-talk items are similar to those processes through which baby-talk lexicons are derived in many of the world's languages.[5] One word – <u>*ŋwaŋu*</u> (*tambaran;* male cult deity) – is an onomatopoetic rendering of the sound made by the flutes played in the men's house when the *tambaran* is there. Two of the words on the list that are not obvious derivations of their adult forms (*sɔsɔ* [for *nɔk*; urine] and *maka* [for *atukun*; drink; imperative form]), plus the word for pigmeat (*sisi* [for *bɔrsip*]), appear to be borrowings into Taiap from Austronesian languages.[6] That the villagers have borrowed in this way suggests that even before Tok Pisin entered the village, Gapuners considered certain items in foreign languages to be somehow more appropriate for children than equivalent elements in their own language.

Since Tok Pisin entered the village, however, this vernacular baby-talk register has been virtually abandoned. On very rare occasions, a mother might use the word *mamak* (spirit) to frighten a child, after she has repeatedly tried with the adult form (*mambrag*), and on one occasion in 1986, a 35-year-old man who had been trying for several minutes to coax his 2½-year-old son to swallow a malaria tablet was heard to tell the boy in exasperation: "*Marasin maka!*" (Drink the medicine!). Beyond this, however, none of the vernacular baby-talk forms are used anymore by most villagers. Sopak, the woman who supplied the list in Table 6.1 and the only villager who actually does, although very rarely, use some of the items in that list (e.g., in line 7 of her monologue to Masito; Text 6.1), claims that the baby-talk register has only just been abandoned by the current generation of village mothers, that is, those women under 45 years of age. According to Sopak and others, her mother and the women in that generation knew the entire register and used it when talking to children. These women were also the final generation of village women who would not have spoken Tok Pisin fluently (Chapter 2, Table 2.1). If what Sopak and others say is correct, then it seems that the vernacular baby-talk register was the first entire register in the language to disappear as a result of the villagers' incorporation of Tok Pisin into their verbal repertoires.[7]

No real baby-talk register exists in the villagers' Tok Pisin, perhaps because the language itself has taken on connotations of a kind of "baby-code," and switches to that language serve the same accommodating function as switches to the vernacular baby-talk register did in the past. Certain individuals, however, do sometimes alter their speech even in Tok Pisin for short periods when they engage in verbal play with a child or when they imitate her or him. These alterations are rule-governed reductions in which consonant clusters are deleted ([*bloŋ*] > [*boŋ*] [=posessive lexeme], [*gutpla*] > [*gupa*] [=good]); medial liquids are deleted ([*tarangu*] > [*tangu*] [=poor thing], [*bagarap*] > [*bagap*] [=ruin, destroy]); silibants are articulated as plosives ([*suruk*] > [*turuk*] [=move over]); and reduplicated adult forms are reduced by deleting the final consonant of the first syllable, thereby also altering the stress (*wáswás*

> *wawás* [=wash], *pékpék* > *pepék* [=defecate/excrement], *sáksák* > *sasák* [=sago]).

There is a great deal of variation among villagers as to whether or not they alter their speech in this way when speaking to children. Some women such as Paso almost never use any of these simplified Tok Pisin forms, doing so only to explicitly imitate a child's pronunciation.[8] Others, like Sopak and her older children, use these forms occasionally, especially if their child interlocutor produces an incomplete or reduced form, such as [*boŋ*] (for [*bloŋ*] =posessive lexeme). Men do not generally use these forms at all, and even women like Sopak who do use them do so only sporadically and inconsistently. Beyond these phonological modifications, there are no systematic syntactic or morphological simplifications or alterations specifically for children in either Taiap or Tok Pisin, although the allative/directional lexeme *long* in Tok Pisin (as in *Kama i go long Wongan* [Kama went to Wongan]) is omitted more frequently in adult speech to children than in adult speech to other adults.

Sibling caregivers

That adults tend to switch to Tok Pisin when speaking directly to young children means that from an early age, the linguistic input that these children receive is unbalanced. Children hear both Taiap and Tok Pisin spoken around them constantly, and the vernacular is often used when speaking to them, as is clear from Sopak's talk to Masito. But the great bulk of the talk that gets addressed directly to children and to which the children are expected to attend is in Tok Pisin.

This input in Tok Pisin is augmented by the kind of talk that a child hears from his or her older siblings and their friends. These older children are a major source of linguistic input for a child, because caregiving responsibilities in the village are not confined to mothers, but are distributed among all female relatives in the household.

Villagers consider that a mother should never stray far enough from her nursing baby that she cannot be on hand to feed the child should it begin crying incessantly – that Jari did this was one of the reasons behind Sake's *kros* (Chapter 3; Text 3.1).[9] But beyond this responsibility, mothers are free to delegate caregiving tasks to others. Since the advent of school, which removes girls between the ages of 8 and 14 from the village for much of the time, these tasks have come to fall heavily on a woman's preschool daughters. From the moment a woman gives birth in the jungle, all her daughters over 4 years of age will provide her with continual assistance in the care of a new baby. While a woman remains in the maternity house with her baby, her daughters run errands for her, bring her bits of news, and look after the baby whenever she leaves to wash or go to the toilet. When the mother leaves the maternity house and returns to the house in which she normally resides, these daughters are expected to be constantly on hand to hold the baby when a mother is preparing meals, to amuse it while the mother is leaching sago pith in the forest, or to simply take it off the mother's hands and away when she is tired or in a bad mood.

Sharing caregiving responsibilities in this way results in babies and young children spending as much time (and in some cases more time) in the company of their preschool sisters and their playmates as they do with their mothers. And on the backs and in the laps of these girls, infants and young children are the objects of extensive physical and verbal play. Whereas adult–child interactions with children under 2 tend to be brief, formulaic, and designed to distract and quiet, preschool girls can amuse themselves and their infant charges for up to twenty minutes at a time with songs and word play. In the following example, Bonika (6 years) is sitting alone with her little sister, Armambwira (7 months), on the porch of their house.

Text 6.4

Bonika: [bouncing Armambwira up and down on her lap]

. . . *bús mangi bús mangi*	. . . búsh kid búsh kid
bús mangi	búsh kid
bús bús músh músh búsh	búsh búsh músh músh búsh
yu bús mangi bús mangi yu	you búsh kid búsh kid you
bús mangi músh músh	búsh kid músh músh
bús mangi músh músh	búsh kid músh músh

[Seeing their 7-year-old sister, Yapa, emerging from the forest, Bonika slaps Armambwira lightly on the face and points to Yapa:]

Yapa ia Yapa ia	There's Yapa there's Yapa
em ia em ia em ia	there there there
Yapa tata ia	there's older sibling Yapa
lukim tata	look at older sibling
Yapa	Yapa
apa apa apa	apa apa apa
em ia Yapa Bapa ba pa	there Yapa Bapa ba pa
pa pa pa	pa pa pa

[Bonika suddenly puts Armambwira belly-down on the floor and spanks her bottom to the rhythm of:]

Yu sindaún	You sit dówn
sindaún	sit dówn
sindaún	sit dówn
sindaún	sit dówn

[Bonika lifts Armambwira up and lays her across her lap.]

Nau bai yu slip.	Now you're gonna sleep
Sip sip bebi.	Seep seep baby.
Bebi! Sip sip sip.	Baby! Seep seep seep.
Bebi! Bobi bobi	Baby! Bobi bobi
bebu bebu	bebu bebu
wo wo wo wo wo wo . . .	wo wo wo wo wo wo . . .

This interaction lasted for fifteen minutes and engaged Armambwira both physically and verbally in ways that do not occur between adults and children. Although Armambwira remained silent for most of this interaction, the babbling sounds of babies and young children are frequently incorporated into such play, providing a framework for the older children's rhymes and songs. This type of word play often consists for the most part of isolated syllables and nonsense words. But whenever language does occur, that language is always Tok Pisin. Like adults, older siblings talk to their young charges in Tok Pisin. But unlike adults and those children who have cared for infants in the past, the use of Tok Pisin by the present generation of child caregivers is no longer based on choice. The current generation of children who assist their mothers in the care of new babies does not actively command Taiap. This ensures that all those babies now growing up in the village hear only Tok Pisin spoken to them by their sibling caregivers in all verbal interactions.

Interpreting children's speech

In addition to the adult tendency to switch to Tok Pisin when directly addressing young children, and the amount and kind of input in Tok Pisin that children receive from their preschool sisters, there is a further factor in village communicational patterns that weights the language acquisition process in favor of Tok Pisin. This is the way in which parents interpret infant vocalizations.

The only vocalizations by infants that anyone ever interprets as utter-nces in the vernacular are the first three words a child is considered to utter: *ɔki* (I'm getting out of here), *mnda* (I'm sick of this), and *aiata* (Stop it), plus the directive *gaw* (*Wait*), which some villagers listed among a child's first words. Following these initial vocalizations, which are recognized only a few months after birth and underscore the aggressive nature of babies, there is a long period in which caregivers do not attribute linguistic meaning to a child's sounds; they are either ignored or dismissed as incomprehensible "rubbish talk" (*rabis tok*), "nothing calls" (*gar sindɛr*), or "bird talk" (*tok bilong ol pisin/tamma nam*).

Only at about 18 months do some mothers begin once again to interpret their child's vocalizations as words. But now, without exception, these words are no longer interpreted as Taiap. From this point, all a child's "talk" is considered to be in Tok Pisin. When Gerak heard Mangia (1;8) utter to herself in private speech [*ta'tai*], for example, she turned to her daughter Saror and said, "That's it. She said to you: "Older sibling is leaving (*Tata i go*)." Using the same interpretive strategy, Sopak, when she saw Kama giving Masito (1;6) a betel nut and heard Masito murmur "*mama ka* (inaudible babble)," announced, "She's talking about betel nut: "Kama has chewed betel nut" (*Kama i kaikai buai pinis*). This is the same point in the child's development at which caregivers start to remark that the child's *save* is beginning to "break open." This eruption of *save* thus coincides with and is concretely manifested in the attribution of Tok Pisin in the child's speech.

At the same time that children are considered to be showing *save* through their vocalizations in Tok Pisin, they have also begun to walk. This physical independence allows caregivers to test the child's emerging *save* and put it to use; and at this stage, the nature of caregiver talk to children changes. Although distraction sequences remain common when the child starts to cry, caregivers now begin increasingly to use directives in their talk to children. These directives function to involve children in social life. Rather than just tell a child, "Sleep, sleep" or "Drink the breast," caregivers now begin to command toddlers to give betel nut to their visiting mother's brother, to pass an ember to their grandmother so that she can dry her tobacco leaf, to fetch a knife from across the room from an older sibling. By successfully carrying out a command to fetch betel nut, tobacco leaves, embers, knives, or tongs, children demonstrate their *save* at the same time that they, for the first time, become active participants in the social interactions occurring around them.

The increased amount of talk to children at this stage in their development is in effect an increased amount of input in Tok Pisin. Because they are believed to be producing it, parents now assume that children understand Tok Pisin, but not Taiap. One evening, Sopak was sitting near her hearth with Masito (1;6). She had made dinner and had just

given a plate of sago to her husband Mone, who was sitting a few yards
away. Not hungry herself, Sopak sat swishing around water in an empty
sago pot.

Text 6.5

Sopak:	*Sia. ŋa ruru sɛnɛ ia kirawmbrɨ wakarɛ. Ɛndɛkarɛ, ɛndɛkarɛ.* [turns to Mas] *Mm. Masito.*	S:	<u>*Sia*</u> [exclamation]. <u>These two poor kids I just don't know</u>. <u>Hungry, hungry</u>. [turns to Mas] Mm. Masito.
5	*Kisim spun i go givim papa.* [hands Mas a spoon] *Spun.* [points spoon at Mone] *Papa. Kirap nau.* [tries to lift Mas to her feet]		Take the spoon and go give it to Papa. [hands Mas a spoon] Spoon. [points spoon at Mone] Papa. Get up now. [tries to lift Mas to her feet]
10	*Ap. Kirap. kirap.*		Up. Get up. Get up.
Mone:	*Da kukuwɛ.*	M:	<u>Bring it now</u>.
Sopak:	[lifting Mas to her feet] *Aop.*	S:	[lifting Mas to her feet] Uup.

[Masito walks over to Mone and hands him the spoon.]

Mone:	[taking spoon] *Ta.*	M:	[taking spoon] Thanks.

[Masito goes back and stands near Sopak.]

Mone:	[to Masito, who doesn't respond] *Ta kukuwɛ.*	M:	[to Masito, who doesn't respond] <u>Bring the knife</u>.
Sopak:	[looking at Masito] *Ta.* [impatiently:] *Naip. Naip.*	S:	[looking at Masito] <u>Knife</u>. [impatiently:] Knife. Knife.
15			
Mone:	[points at the floor near Masito's feet] *Em ia.*	M:	[points at the floor near Masito's feet] There it is.
Sopak:	*Kisim ta.*	S:	Get <u>the knife</u>.
Mone:	[points] *Klostu long lek bilong yu. Em i stap.*	M:	[points] Near your foot. There it is.
20			

[Masito looks down at the knife, then at Mone.]

	Em. Kisim i kam. Aŋgidɛ tarak kukuwɛ		Yeah. Bring it. <u>Bring that</u>.
Sopak:	[picks up knife, points at Mone with it]	S:	[picks up knife, points at Mone with it]

25

Uh. Pap<u>ana</u>na. [pushes knife toward Mas] <u>Ta, ta.</u> Em ia naip ia. <u>Aŋgodɛ, ta aŋgodɛ.</u> Kisim.	Uh. <u>For</u> Papa. [pushes knife toward Mas] <u>Knife, knife.</u> Here, knife here. <u>Here, knife here.</u> Take it.

[Masito takes the knife from Sopak, walks over to Mone and gives it to him.]

Here Sopak and Mone characteristically use both languages in the course of this short interaction, switching between them in their talk to Masito in the same way that they switch between languages in their talk to one another and to other adult villagers. The ways in which the languages are used, however, indicate that both parents consider that Masito, at 18 months, already commands Tok Pisin but does not know much Taiap. With the exception of Mone's initial formulaic command "*Da kukuwɛ*" ("Bring it now"; line 11), the first part of this interaction, concerning the spoon, is conducted by Sopak entirely in Tok Pisin, and she displays once again the village pattern of switching to Tok Pisin when addressing a child directly (lines 4–5). In the second half of this interaction, the Taiap word *ta* (knife) is treated as a new word. Masito's failure to respond to Mone's request for the knife is treated by Sopak as a failure to comprehend what is being asked for, and she defines *ta* for Masito by giving its Tok Pisin equivalent in a curt, impatient tone that implies that Masito should know that *ta* is another word for the already familiar *naip* (lines 15–16). The information that Masito has to have about the knife in order to carry out her father's request, in this case its location, is also in Tok Pisin.

At the time this interaction took place, Masito was using language only very rarely. For the most part, she communicated with Sopak and other members of her family by pointing, grabbing, crying, and whining. But despite her lack of productive competence, both of Masito's parents had already decided that she commanded Tok Pisin, but not the vernacular. This was continually made clear in interactions like the one above. It was also occasionally made explicit in talk such as this recorded around the same time:

Text 6.6

Sopak:	*Don i kam yu mas "gut nait."*	S:	When Don comes you must [say] "*gut nait*" [i.e., "good evening" in Tok Pisin].
Masito:	*Mm.*	M:	Mm.
Sopak:	*"Gut nait."*	S:	"*Gut nait*."
Masito:	*Mm.*	M:	Mm.
Sopak:	*Ikur ɛŋgɔn.* [pause]	S:	*Ikur ɛŋgɔn.* ["Good evening" in

Yu no save long <u>ikur</u>	Taiap]. [pause] You don't know
<u>ɛŋgɔn</u>. "Gut nait."	*<u>ikur ɛŋgɔn</u>*. [So say] *"Gut nait."*

The assumptions that Masito's parents had about her language capabilities at around age 2 are shared by the parents of other young children, and even though the great majority of village toddlers resemble Masito in that they do not yet speak, they are believed by caregivers already to have a good comprehensive knowledge of Tok Pisin. This belief is reinforced each time a child correctly carries out an order in Tok Pisin. And because adults continue to switch to Tok Pisin whenever they speak directly to their children, the bulk of the directives to children are in that language.

Once children begin responding to and carrying out directives, parents begin to become aware that children tend to react much more frequently and readily to speech in Tok Pisin than they do to directives in Taiap. This results not only in even more Tok Pisin being used in speech to children, but also in Taiap utterances being increasingly systematically translated into Tok Pisin whenever the speaker wants to elicit a response from the child. This translating will be done by either the speaker her- or himself (Text 6.7); by one of the child's older siblings (Text 6.8); or, especially in the several village households in which mothers speak a great deal of Taiap, by the child's father, whenever he is present (Text 6.9):

Text 6.7

Gerak > Mangia (1;11) as she plays in the hearth:

Maŋgia kɔsim batarɛngarkɛ.	<u>Mangia don't mess up the</u>
Maŋgia kɔsim ɔretukun.	<u>ashes. Mangia leave the</u>
Mangia! Draipela hed yu no	<u>ashes</u> alone. Mangia! Big
ken bagarapim sit bilong paia!	head don't mess up the ashes!

Text 6.8

Ermina and Giang's older sister, Gut (10 years), want Giang (3;8) to come away from the cake of sago he is playing with and sit down near them, but for several minutes he has ignored their calls to "come." Now Ermina flicks her head in the direction of the visiting anthropologist:

Ermina:	*Wɛtɛt. Munjɛ tutɔtɛt.*	E:	<u>Come. The man is sitting</u>
	Ariɔ.		<u>there. He's gonna get you.</u>
Gut:	*Giang em bai ronim yu ia.*	G:	<u>Giang he's gonna come after</u>
	Giang kam.		<u>you</u>. Giang come.
Ermina:	*ŋi nda ɔrunɛtana indɛ.*	E:	He's gonna shoot you now.

	Kɛmbatik aŋgudɛ.		There's his bow.
Gut:	*Giang kɛmbatik[10] bilong em ia. Em bai sutim yu nau.*	G:	Giang there's his bow. He's gonna shoot you now.
Ermina:	*Kam. Wɛtɛt.*	E:	Come. Come.
Gut:	*Em bai sutim yu nau.*	G:	He's gonna shoot you now.

[Giang runs over to Ermina and Gut laughing.]

Text 6.9

Bit and her husband Kawi sit chewing betel nut when their youngest son Yur (6 years) comes up into the house, grabs a large machete, and turns to leave again:

Bit:	*Yu ambin nirkwankut pətiŋar-rɛki?*	B:	What are you doing with the machete?
Kawi:	*Yu bai mekim wanem samting?*	K:	What are you gonna do?
Bit:	*Yu anakni?*	B:	Where are you going?
Kawi:	*Yu laik go we?* *Yu bai go we?*	K:	Where are you going? Where are you going?
Yur:	*Kimərik.*	Y:	Sago grubs.
Kawi:	*Kimərik wantaim husat? Yu nɛkɛr ɔkitɛt? Maski yu stap yu no ken igo.*	K:	[Go gather] sago grubs with who? Are you going by yourself? Enough, you stay, you can't go.

[Yur ignores them and walks off into the jungle with the machete.]

Another way Tok Pisin is frequently foregrounded in caregiver–child interactions at this stage is through the increased use of Tok Pisin verbs in vernacular utterances:

Text 6.10

David (3;3) holds up a bit of string to his mother, Paso, and whines:

Paso:	*Katim ah?*	P:	Cut it ah?
	[David whines.]		
Paso:	*Anakŋa katim-kru?*	P:	Cut it where?
	[David whines.]		
Paso:	*Anakŋa katim-kru?*	P:	Cut it where?
	[David whines.]		
Paso:	*Katim em ah?*	P:	Cut this ah?
	[David whines.]		

Paso:	*Ambukəni katim-kru?*	P:	Cut it how?

[David whines.]

Paso:	*Orait, yu gɔ lusim-tukun.*	P:	OK, you let it go then.

[Paso cuts the string and David stops whining.]

The most common switch point to Tok Pisin in speech to children of this age is when the child either doesn't respond as in (Texts 6.7–6.10) above) or asks "Ah?":

Text 6.11

Masito (2;3) is holding a marble, which Sopak tells her to put in the pocket of the short pants she is wearing:

Sopak:	*Bakni waritukun.*	S:	Put it in [your] back pocket.
Masito:	*Ah?*	M:	Ah?
Sopak:	*Bakni waritukun.*	S:	Put it in [your] back pocket.
Masito:	*Ah?*	M:	Ah?
Sopak:	*Trausisŋa bak. Aŋgɔdɛ. aŋgɔdɛ.*	S:	The back pocket of the trousers. There, there.
Masito:	*Ah?*	M:	Ah?
Sopak:	*Bak ia putim! Haitim long Yapa. Nogut Yapa lukim, yu putim long bak.*	S:	The back pocket here, put it! Hide it from Yapa. Don't let Yapa see it, you put it in your back pocket.

That caregivers are so willing to translate their vernacular utterances into Tok Pisin means that children come to understand that whatever is said to them in Taiap will be repeated in Tok Pisin, sooner or later. They learn that they can influence and even determine the surface forms of caregiver utterances by not responding, by whining (as Masito does when Sopak speaks to her in Taiap toward the end of her monologue in Text 6.1, and as David does in order to get Paso to cut his string), or by responding with "Ah?"

The types of communication patterns described above combine continually in caregiver–child interactions in Gapun, and work together to result in a language rich in Tok Pisin but relatively poor in Taiap. This can be seen clearly in the following interaction involving Paso, her husband, Ariba, her adolescent sister, Kiki, and two of her children: Kiring (6 years) and David (3;4 years). It is early in the evening, and everyone is seated on the floor in Paso and Ariba's house. Paso is cooking dinner, and a few minutes prior to this interaction, she had asked loudly where the salt was. Nobody answered her at that point, but now Ariba tells Kiring, who is sitting near a small basket, to fetch the salt.

Text 6.12

Ariba:	Ɔtaka saimnɨ kawat tarkru.	A:	Go to the basket and get the salt.	
	[Kiring doesn't respond.]			
Ariba:	Go kisim sol long saim Kakat!	A:	Go fetch the salt in the basket. Hurry!	CODE-SWITCH TO TOK PISIN AFTER NO RESPONSE
Kiring:	Mi les long go i kam.	K:	I'm sick of coming and going.	
Ariba:	[pointing] Aŋgidɛ mɛnjikan.	A:	[pointing] It's there close to you.	
	[Kiring grunts and remains where she is.]			
Kiki:	Kiriŋ yu ɔtak kawat tarkru!	Ki:	Kiring you go and get the salt!	
Kiring:	Mi les!	K:	I don't want to!	
	[pause]			
Kiki:	Dɛbid mɛmɛtet igo painim sol long saim.	Ki:	David get up and go find the salt in the basket.	CODE-SWITCH TO TOK PISIN WHEN ADDRESSING CHILD

[When Kiki says "David get up," Kiring rises and goes over to the basket. Now David also gets up, goes to the basket, and sits down next to Kiring, who is rummaging through it. He begins to look, too, but Kiring hits him.]

Ariba:	Ganɔkaw ɲiɲi amainukun. Yu suman. Debid painim=	A:	Let him find it. You're big [older]. David look for it=	CODE-SWITCH TO TOK PISIN WHEN ADDRESSING CHILD
Paso:	=Painim- tukun.	P:	=Look for it.	TOK PISIN VERB STEM WITH TAIAP MORPHOLOGY
	[Kiring hits David again and he begins to whine.]			
Ariba:	[threatening Kiring] ŋa mɛmkɨn- ɛtrɛ niŋg	A:	[threatening Kiring] If I get up little bones	

<u>mɔkɔp</u>	are <u>gonna get</u>	
adɨdiɔkindak.	<u>broken</u>.	

[Kiring pushes the basket at David with a disgusted grunt and pretends to hit him on the head with the palm of her hand. She moves away and David remains whining.]

Ariba:	*OK, Debid*	A:	OK, David look	CODE-SWITCH TO
	painimpainim.		for it, look for it.	TOK PISIN WHEN
	Kisim <u>saim</u> i		Bring the <u>basket</u>.	ADDRESSING CHILD
	kam.			

Starting to talk

This mass of input in Tok Pisin that children receive during their early years occurs against the background of the villagers' understandings of *hed* and the nature of children. Gapuners' concern about accommodating and not infringing on the personal autonomy of others is extended to their interactions with children, and it manifests itself in a tendency to refrain from making a child do anything against her or his will, including talk. Adults and older siblings speak to young children in the village, but they neither encourage or expect the children to talk back. At no point in her long monologue with Masito (Text 6.1), for example, does Sopak try to elicit any type of verbal reaction from the child.

Caregivers sometimes tell young children to call out the name of a relative, and they may ask "What?" (*Wanem/Ambin*) if the child vocalizes especially loudly. But if the child doesn't call out the relative's name or respond to the "What?" after two or three prompts, then the matter will invariably be dropped. By the age of about 2, children have been observed to have said a few words, and, as adults comment that their *save* has begun to "break open," they are increasingly prompted to respond to directives in ways similar to those in which Masito was urged to give the spoon and the knife to her father (Text 6.5). Children of this age are not, however, expected to be actively using language to communicate. Until they are 6 or 7, and sometimes even older, parents asking children questions or giving them directives accept either no verbal response at all or extremely minimal responses such as the grunts and moans that David uses to get Paso to cut his string (Text 6.10). Children are not expected to really begin talking until they are 5 or 6 years old.[11] A child who is especially verbal at a young age will be encouraged by adults and older children, who will engage the child in short exchanges and try to get her or him to answer information questions. A talkative child is somewhat unexpected, however, and whereas no one would remark on a 4-year-old who said very little and who still relied heavily on whines and groans to communicate with his mother, villagers notice and occasionally express surprise at and annoyance with a loquatious child. Bapong was a very verbal 4-year-old who frequently talked and sang to himself, sometimes loudly, in adult company. More than once on these occasions he was suddenly shushed in half serious tones: "*Sia! Liklik man na maus tasol i bikpela olgeta!*" (*Sia!* Little man, the only thing big on you is your mouth!)

The villagers' dispreference for prompting children to speak is a characteristic feature of every type of caregiver–child interaction. Adults do not play games with their children very often or for very long, for example, but when they do engage a child in play, this rarely includes verbal interaction. For a few months after Ermina's 10-month-old daughter, Bogua, died, for instance, Sopak occasionally initiated a brief game with Masito by asking her, "Masi, how did Bogua look dead?" The expected response to this was not verbal, but for Masito to close her eyes and pucker her face, to the general amusement of Sopak and anybody else who happened to see it.

In another typical instance, Gerak picked up a deck of cards she found lying on the floor and called to her 6-year-old daughter, Saror, "Come, let's play." Saror sat opposite her mother, and Gerak began dealing the cards. The game rules were that, whatever card the other person put down, one had to put down the same suit, or the same number, in which case the suit to play changed to that of the card just put down. If one had neither the same suit or number as the card just played, then one had to pick a new card from the deck. None of this was explained to Saror, and the two played by Gerak's looking at Saror's hand and choosing an appropriate card, then telling her, "Put that one," or "Pick." Saror quickly grew impatient, and when it was her turn, she began to immediately throw down a card. Unless it happened to be right, which it usually wasn't, Gerak threw the card back at her, saying, "Not that one" (*I no em*) or "You're stupid, you're a pig" (*Yu longlong, yu pik*), and she picked an appropriate card from Saror's hand. Three-fourths of the way through this game, Gerak suddenly decided to change the rules, so that when Saror did in fact put down a correct number, thereby changing the suit, Gerak flung it back at her and played her own cards, which matched the previous suit. She said nothing about this, and Saror, who was making little effort to understand the game, didn't care. But no verbal interactions occurred during this game, and Gerak continued to simply pick from Saror's cards when it was the girl's turn to play.

Partly because they are not encouraged or expected to talk, and partly because the bulk of linguistic input addressed directly to them is in Tok Pisin, by the time village children do begin to use language in their interactions at about 1;6–2;3 years, the language they produce is Tok Pisin.[12]

Children begin speaking by picking up and repeating parts of words and phrases they hear in conversations around them. This repeating is not normally noticed or commented upon by caregivers. Bini (1;11), lying across his mother's lap, demonstrated this kind of early speech as his mother, Tambong, recounted for a group of listeners her reaction when she, staying in Wongan, heard the slit-gong drum signaling the death of a village woman:

Text 6.13

Tambong: *Mipela harim garamut na mipela no moa*
istap, ⌜ *mipela olgeta i kirap tasol igo* ⌜ *nau,*
Bini: ⌊ *itap*   ⌊ *go go*
Tambong: *mi na papa, Bometa, man bilong em, orait Kaimbang,*
⌜ *meri bilong en, Apusi, mipela olgeta i go wantaim.*
Bini: ⌊ *kaiba*

Tambong: We heard the slit-gong drum and we didn't
stay ⌜ another minute, we all got up and went ⌜ now,
Bini: ⌊ tay   ⌊ went went
Tambong: me and Papa, Bometa, her husband, alright, Kaimbang,
⌜ his wife, Apusi, we all went together.
Bini: ⌊ kaiba

Children do not appear to spontaneously repeat or produce the vernacular in this way. When adult conversations or narratives like this occur primarily in Taiap or some other vernacular language, children most often simply remain silent. If they do repeat to themselves during such talk, they do so with sounds that do not have their source in the adult talk.

The most common linguistic situation for village children to find themselves in, however, is one in which both the vernacular and Tok Pisin are used in the course of the same interaction. In these cases, even those young children who have hardly begun to talk show themselves to be adept at focusing on those elements in the conversation that are either Tok Pisin or are Taiap nominals habitually used in Tok Pisin speech (such as the vernacular words for betel nut, sago, coconut, chicken, tobacco, and other common objects). Always, it is these elements, to the exclusion of all others, that the children repeat and incorporate into their own private monologues. David (2;8) employs this kind of selective repetition as he listens to and tries to participate in a conversation between his mother, Paso; his father, Ariba; and his 7-year-old brother, Yaman.

Text 6.14

Ariba: *Sore, pɛsaw ŋaŋan aini* ⌜*Mɔnim tankunŋan* =
David: ⌞ *payo pik bong mi. Pa pik bong mi*
Yaman: = *Draipela nogut tru* =

Ariba: ⌜ = *Pasɔ pɛsawmat nɛr aŋgɔdɛ nipis. Miŋan. Kɛmɛm.*
David: ⌞ *Payo. Payo pik. Pik bong mi.*

Yaman: *Soti kisim i kam ia, em sotpela* =
David: = *Soti*
Paso: *Wanem samting?*
Yaman: ⌜ *Em ia, pɛsaw.* ⌜ *Soti kisim i kam.*
David: ⌞ *Soti kam.* ⌿ *Payo soti soti soti igo igo igo kisi kam.*
Ariba: ⌞ *Pɛsawmat nɛr anini Mɔnim yam rarkukatɔtrɛ.*

Yaman: *Na mipela i kam olgeta long pilaipilai i stap, mipela i go waswas long Ambibwar. Mipela igo waswas istap istap istap/*
Paso: *Sɔtiŋi pɛsawŋan kukubɛt?*
Ariba: *Aniŋi?*
Paso: *Sɔti.*
Ariba: ⌜ *Wakarɛ.*
Yaman: ⌞ *Em kisim i kam. Em kisim i kam i go olsem ia. Em ia em holim long han i kam ia.*
         Em ia em karim i kam igo. Pɛsaw. Liklik pɛsaw.
Ariba: *Em, wanem ia, kɔpiwɔk.*
Yaman: ⌜ *Ey kɔpiwɔk.*
David: ⌞ *kɔkɔk kɔkɔk*
Yaman: *KɔpiWƆK. Wanem kɔkɔk?!*
                    [Paso and Ariba laugh.]

1   Ariba: You wouldn't believe it, my bird of paradise[13]
                    ⌜ that I saw over in Monim =
    David: ⌞ Payo [Pa + vocative "yo"] my pig. Pa my pig.
    Yaman: = [It was] huge =
5   Ariba: ⌜ = Paso that bird of paradise's tail feathers were this long.
             ⌞ A male. Long.
    David: ⌞ Payo. Payo pig. My pig.
    Yaman: The one that Shorty came with, [its tail feathers were] short =
    David: = Shorty
10 Paso: What?

Yaman: ⌈ That, the bird of paradise. ⌈ The one Shorty came with.
David: ⌊ Shorty came. ⊢ Payo Shorty Shorty Shorty went
                                          went went came
Ariba: ⌊ The bird of paradise's tail feathers
15   over at Monim when I went to look
                                          at the sago palm.

Yaman: And [then] we came back and we were playing, [Yaman is continuing
       a narrative that Ariba had interrupted with his talk of the bird of
       paradise] we went to wash at Ambibwar. We went and washed washed
20   washed/
Paso: Did Shorty come with a bird of paradise?
Ariba: Who?
Paso: Shorty.
Ariba: ⌈ No.
25 Yaman: ⌊ He came with one. He came with it and went over there. He
       held it in his hand and came. He carried it and came here.
       Bird of paradise. A little bird of paradise.
Ariba: That was a, what, black cockatoo (*kɔpiwɔk*).
Yaman: ⌈ Eh, black cockatoo (*kɔpiwɔk*).
30 David: ⌊ chicken chicken (*kɔkɔk*).
Yaman: Black COCKAtoo (*kɔpiwɔk*). What chicken (*kɔkɔk*)?!
       [Paso and Ariba laugh.]

David here pays close attention to the speech progressing around him throughout this exchange, and even though he is unsuccessful in his attempt to break into the conversation and gain the floor, he continues to follow the talk, latching onto and repeating nominals and parts of verb phrases that occur in the talk of his father and his brother. It is clear, however, that David is not just repeating random chunks of speech. Although both Taiap and Tok Pisin are used throughout this talk, David ignores the Taiap and repeats only Tok Pisin or Taiap nominals that are frequently used even in the villagers' Tok Pisin speech to one another. The purposefulness and systematic way David is already able to hold the two linguistic systems apart is most apparent in his initial utterance "Payo my pig. Pa my pig" (line 3). This possessive phrase appears to be not just a repetition, but a repetition–translation, based on a mishearing of Ariba's opening noun phrase *pɛsaw ŋaŋan* (my bird of paradise). In the same way that David later mishears the unfamiliar word *kɔpiwɔk* (black cockatoo) and interprets it as *kɔkɔk* (chicken; line 30), here he seems to interpret the unfamiliar Taiap word *pɛsaw* (bird of paradise) as the Tok Pisin *pik* (pig). David's mishearing may have arisen because Ariba opened his talk with the Tok Pisin word "*Sore*" (You wouldn't believe it); a word that David would have noticed because it was marked with exaggerated rising intonation similar to that used in *em ia* routines. It seems likely that David heard *pɛsaw ŋaŋan* (my bird of paradise) as *pik ŋaŋan* (my pig) and that, wishing to attract his father's attention, he countered Ariba's claim to the "pig" by playfully claiming it for himself, doing so by translating the Taiap possessive pronoun *ŋaŋan* to its Tok Pisin equivalent *bilong mi*.

David's language behavior is typical of the talk produced by every child currently growing up in the village and is illustrative of the fact that even though these children live in a multilingual community where Taiap and Tok Pisin are continually interspersed in the speech of all adults, they do not go through a period of mixing languages in the way that studies of bilingual children have shown to be common. Instead, by the time they begin using language, children in Gapun appear to have already managed to separate the two linguistic systems from one another. And they use only Tok Pisin.[14] This is clear both from their repeating patterns and from the private speech that children of this age also engage in. One day as they were rummaging around near the outskirts of the village, Bini (1;11), his 4-year-old brother, Bapong, and a few older boys managed to wound a bright green tree lizard (Taiap: *gɔgrɔdak*; no equivalent in Tok Pisin) that they discovered scuttling up a coconut palm. They carried the lizard around with them until it died, letting it run and struggle on the ground as they threw small spears at it and laughed. A week later, Bini reenacted this experience while engaging in play by himself in the corner of his house:

Text 6.15

[pointing toward roof]:

Mia, gɔgɔ mia. Gɔgɔ gɔgɔdia   There *gɔgɔ* there. *Gɔgɔ gɔgɔ* there

[points toward wall]:

Mia gɔgɔ mia   There *gɔgɔ* there

[looks toward floor]:

Mía gɔgɔd gɔgɔ gɔgɔ!   Thére *gɔgɔd gɔgɔ gɔgɔ!*

[stabs stick at imaginary lizard]

Here, although Bini uses the vernacular word for the lizard, the structure of his speech is a Tok Pisin *em ia* routine.

Once children begin using Tok Pisin themselves, the village convention of accommodating other speakers in their own choice of language becomes activated continually, with the result that parents switch to Tok Pisin even more systematically when they talk to their children. It is at this point in the child's language development that parents may realize that their children do not, in fact, speak the vernacular, and some mothers may make fleeting attempts to get the child to speak Taiap.

At age 2;2, Masito suddenly began spontaneously using language to a much greater extent than she had ever done previously. Shortly after this began, her mother realized that everything the child said was in Tok Pisin. For two weeks, Sopak sporadically tried to get Masito to speak the vernacular, through interactions like this:

Text 6.16

Masito picks up a betel nut she finds on the floor and holds it up:

Sopak:	*Wanpela buai ah? Eh/*	S:	A betel nut ah? Eh/
	Nambarkɛ?		One?
Masito:	*Ah?*	M:	Ah?
Sopak:	*Nambarkɛ?*	S:	One?
	Masitɔ: Nambarkɛ?		Masito: One?
	Minjikɛ nambarkɛ?		One betel nut?
	Masitɔ namtak: minjikɛ		Masito talk: betel nut.
Masito:	*Jikɛ.*	M:	Beenut.
Sopak:	*Nambar.*	S:	One.
Masito:	*Namba.*	M:	One.
Sopak:	*Minjikɛ sami wakarɛ.*	S:	Not a lot of betel nut.
	Minjikɛ sami wakarɛ.		Not a lot of betel nut.
	Nam/		Talk/

[Masito bites into the betel nut.]

Sopak:	*Mi no tok long kaikai*	S:	I didn't say to chew
	buai.		betel nut.
	ŋa namnak: minjikɛ sami		I said: not a lot of
	wakarɛ.		betel nut.
	Yu wanpela longlong mangi		You're one really
	tru [laughs].		stupid kid [laughs].

Short-lived attempts like this to get children to speak the vernacular have no effect other than underscoring the fact that parents regard their children as Tok Pisin speakers. Although parents at this point begin explicitly blaming their children for being *bikhed* and refusing to speak Taiap, the association between children and Tok Pisin is, in fact, so strong that adults will address children in that language even if a child should actually happen to answer in Taiap:

Text 6.17

Kapiru, from inside her house, calls to her daughter Bup (7 years), who is playing with Kama (6 years) in Kama's house:

Kapiru:	*Bup!*	K:	Bup!
Kama:	*Aŋgɔdɛ.*	Ka:	Here.
Kapiru:	*Yu ambin nirkwankuk?*	K:	What are you doing?
Kama:	*Gu ɛmrariakuk* [laughs].	Ka:	She's playing [laughs].
Kapiru:	*Go kisim sampela buai moa.*	K:	Go fetch some more betel nut.

Text 6.18

Sopak holds out her hand to her brother's daughter Bup (7 years), who is cutting coconut meat out of a shell with a small knife:

Sopak:	*Kisim naip i kam.*	S:	Bring the knife.
Bup:	[loud voice] *ŋaŋan aŋgi!*	B:	[loud voice] It's mine!
Sopak:	*Sha! Sem bilong yu.*	S:	Sha! [Feel] shame.
	Yu bikpela meri ah?!		You're a grown-up woman ah?!

This association between children and Tok Pisin feeds back on itself so that it influences how parents talk to even very small children. Also, as it now becomes clear to caregivers that their children only speak Tok Pisin, the vernacular begins to assume the character of a secret code that caregivers use to talk about the children in their presence. On one occasion, for example, Wandi wanted to go work in her coffee garden without having to take along her 3-year-old daughter, Ampamna. She gave Ampamna a strip of newspaper and told her to go deliver it to Sopak to smoke. While the girl was away doing this, Wandi speedily picked up her basket and slipped out of the house. She was not quite quick enough, however, because as Ampamna skipped back to her house, she caught sight of Wandi disappearing down the path leading to her coffee garden. The little girl burst into tears and tried to run after her mother. She was prevented from doing this by her adolescent sister, Yengia, who, following Wandi's instructions, carried her into the house and blocked her way so she couldn't leave again. A battle between these two sisters then raged for well over half an hour, with Ampamna screaming and crying and throwing herself on the floor and Yengia telling her that she would be disembowled by *sangguma* witches the minute she left the house. All of Yengia's talk to the little girl was in Tok Pisin. At one point though, a young man walked past Wandi's house and, hearing Ampamna's tantrum, asked Yengia in Tok Pisin, "What is she crying about?" (*Em krai long wanem?*) Yengia, lowering her voice, answered in Taiap: "She wants to go with her mother" (*ɔkinana maya-rɛki*). Yengia's code-switch in this instance is particularly illustrative of the status that Taiap comes to assume as a secret code in dealings with young children, because the man who asked about her sister's crying was a man who had married into Gapun from the village of Pankin. Although this man had acquired a good understanding of Taiap, he did not speak it and was normally not addressed in it.

The vernacular also increasingly comes to be associated with reprimand and scolding.[15] Between the ages of about 1;6 and 2;4, children in the village come to learn that they can ignore their parents' warnings and threats until the parent begins to purposely speak to them in the vernacular. Once, 4-year-old Bapong and his playmate were trying to climb up a betel nut tree near the outskirts of the village. Bapong's father, Marame, happened to see the children from his veranda, and he called out to them in Tok Pisin, "Don't climb up [the tree] for betel nut" (*I no ken go antap long buai*). Marame repeated this prohibitive at intervals of several minutes, but the two boys ignored him completely and continued trying to wrap their arms around the base of the tree and scoot themselves up. After about a quarter of an hour, when Marame noticed that the boys were still trying to climb the tree and had actually progressed about a meter off the ground, he shouted, this time in Taiap, "Are you listening to my talk?!" (*Yu nam tarkwankutkɛ ŋayi namakut?!*) Immediately, Bapong and his playmate slid down from the tree and padded away slowly, looking abashed.

By the time children have reached Bapong's age, they have begun to participate actively in the gender-based peer groups that form in the village. Between the ages of 3 and 5, boys begin to spend less and less time in the company of their mothers and older sisters and more time with their older preschool brothers or cousins, whose play takes the boys out into the jungle for much of the day. Girls of this age also form play groups, but burdened by the toddlers that have been left in their care by mothers who are off leaching sago pith or hunting with their husbands, these girls usually remain closer to the village. In these peer groups, children of both sexes practice and develop their language skills as they play, explore their environment, recount stories, and argue with one another. But because these children are now speaking Tok Pisin, and because their older preschool siblings and friends are not active bilinguals, the language skills that are developed during this period continue to be language skills in Tok Pisin.

Children's competence in the vernacular

Although no village child under 10 actively commands the vernacular language, most children between 5 and 10 possess a good passive understanding of Taiap. As David's 7-year-old brother, Yaman, demonstrated by his active participation in his parents' conversation about the bird of paradise (Text 6.14), most children in this age group have no trouble following conversation in the vernacular, even though their own contributions to Taiap interactions are always in Tok Pisin. Passive knowledge of the vernacular is heavily facilitated in Gapun by the frequency with which caregivers translate their speech for children, and by the general prevalence of repetition and rhetorical code-switching in village speech patterns.

But in addition to this passive knowledge, a few of the little girls in the village under 10 also sometimes use elements of the vernacular even in their speech. These girls represent the tail end of the gender-based linguistic lag that characterized Tok Pisin's acquisition by the villagers. Women in Gapun began learning and using Tok Pisin later than their menfolk, and this historical pattern of acquisition is reflected finally by the fact that the only children under 10 who still use Taiap in any context at all are girls. No boy under 10 ever speaks the vernacular.[16]

Like adults, little girls use switches into the vernacular to achieve rhetorical effects. But unlike adults, the effects that these girls can achieve are limited to marking an utterance as bossy and funny.[17] Those girls who do occasionally use elements of the vernacular in their speech clearly consider such use to be a very marked choice, and they signal this by consistently drawing attention to this choice by marking vernacular utterances with exaggerated intonation and with laughter, as in the following examples:

Text 6.19

Yapa (7 years) > Esta (2;10):

Esta tu, ɛnɛ aŋgi bai mi paitim <u>mun-jisik</u> bilong yu.	Esta too, <u>right now</u> I'm gonna slap your <u>boil</u>.

[General laughter among Yapa's playmates.]

Text 6.20

Kama (6 years) > Masito (1;6)

Kama:	*Masi kam olsem kam olsem.*	K: Masi come this way come this way.
Yapa:	*Go go go*	Y: Go go go
Kama:	*<u>Yu wɛtak</u>!* [laughs]	K: <u>You come</u>! [laughs]

Text 6.21

Bup (7 years) > Yapa (7 years):

Yapa bai mi paitim maus bilong yu.	Yapa I'm gonna slap your mouth.
[pause, starts to laugh]	
<u>*Apɨr anakapɛ*</u>?!	<u>Where's</u> the <u>tongs</u>?!¹⁸

Girls also mark their vernacular utterances in this way on those relatively rare occasions when they use Taiap to answer an adult, as Kama
and Bup did when responding to Kapiru and Sopak (Texts 6.17–6.18).
Marking the use of Taiap as funny in these contexts may be a strategy
on the part of the children to deflect adult criticism of their language.
Most of the time, a child's speech in Taiap will go unnoticed and un-
commented on by adults. Children are never praised for their use of
the vernacular or encouraged to use it more often. The only time an
adult will draw attention to a child's use of the vernacular is when the
adult wishes to point out an error. This occurred when 6-year-old Kama
heard her father, Mone, offer his brother-in-law a leaf of tobacco to
smoke. Leaping to her feet, Kama snatched the proferred leaf from her
father's hand and ran over to the hearth to dry it, saying in an exaggerated authoritative voice:

Text 6.22

Kama:	*MI bai <u>aranjin</u>.*	K:	I'M gonna *aranjin* [dry the tobacco leaf].
Sopak:	*Tsk. <u>Kamama Taiap mɛr ɛŋgɔn wakarɛ</u>.*	S:	Tsk. Kama's Taiap isn't <u>good</u>.
Gom [Kama's 11-year-old brother, laughing]:			
	"*Aranjin!*"		"*Aranjin!*"
Mone:	*Aranjinkun* [the correct Taiap form] *I no* "*aranjin.*"	M:	*Aranjinkun* [the correct Taiap form]. It's not "*aranjin.*"
Gom:	"*Aranjin.*" [laughs]	G:	"*Aranjin.*" [laughs]

[Kama smiles shyly and sits down by the hearth to dry the leaf on a coal.]

Gom:	*Sɔkɔi* "*aranjin*" *nau.* [laughs]	G:	"<u>*Aranjin*</u>" the <u>tobacco</u> now. [laughs]

The adult tendency to draw disapproving attention to the mistakes
children make when they say something in the vernacular, while by no
means as common and consistently applied in Gapun as it is in other

language-shifting communities,[19] nevertheless appears to have an inhibiting effect on children's production of the vernacular. Several boys between the ages of 10 and 15 (among them Kama's brother Gom, who laughs at her here), for example, only rarely speak the vernacular in the presence of their parents and other adults, even though their command of the language is good.[20] When I asked these boys why they avoided speaking Taiap around their parents, they replied that they "felt shame" because they "fouled up" (*save paulim*) the vernacular.

Adults never draw attention to or correct any errors in Tok Pisin that children may make. In fact, here roles are reversed, and children take great pleasure in discovering, repeating, and mocking any parental errors in that language. Overt phonetic interference from Taiap to Tok Pisin, such as when older speakers, who do not distinguish between /r/ and /l/, pronounce a word like *bilak* (black/dirty) as [*birak*], is often seized upon and laughed at. And usage of obsolescent Tok Pisin words is also ridiculed by children. Old Raia was once severely reprimanded by his 15-year-old daughter because he used the outdated expression *harim smel* (perceive [lit. hear] a scent) instead of the more modern *smelim* (to smell). "What, you smelled it with your ears, ah?" his daughter taunted him, laughing.

A few of the little girls in the village who use formulaic phrases and commands in their speech to mark it as bossy and funny can, under very special circumstances, activate their passive competence in Taiap and produce longer stretches of speech. These circumstances never exist in the village, for there everybody understands Tok Pisin, and nobody ever demands that a child express her- or himself in the vernacular before her or his needs or desires are attended to.

Toward the end of my stay in the village, however, I began to record stories in Taiap by adolescents in order to be able to evaluate their competence in the vernacular. This task proved to be extremely popular, and large groups of young people and children gathered in my house on several occasions in order to tell a story and have it played back to them. In the general excitement and enthusiasm generated during these recording sessions, I was able to coax several girls, aged 6 to 8, to overcome their shyness and "shame" and try to tell a story using only the vernacular. Here is the narrative produced, in a timid whisper and after much nervous laughing, swallowing, and hesitation, by Paso's 6-year-old daughter, Kiring:

Text 6.23[21]

1 *Arɔ nɔn yim Pasɔ uh Awpa yim war-ki-nana   bɔk-a   uh*
day one we Paso uh Awpa we net-IRR-INTENT go:1PL-CONJ uh

2 [11-second pause] *gɔmar suman tan-ku-n-a*
                    fish   big   get-U:3SGfem-A:1SG-CONJ

3 *Samɛk-ŋi   pɔ-ku-n.   Pɔkun-api*
  Samek-ERG shoot-U:3SGfem-A:3SG shot it-CONSEC

4 *wasɔ-nɛt-a   uh tatu-k-ɔ-a*   (*da*)
  die-A:3SGmasc-CONJ uh fetch-U:3SGfem-A:3PL-CONJ now

5 *mum   nitu-k-rɔ.*
  sago pudding make-U:3SGfem-A:3PL

6 *Nitukrɔ-api,   ɔ-k-rɔ-api,*
  they made it-CONSEC eat-U:3SGfem-A:3PL-CONSEC

7 *da   gɔk.   Gɔk   uh* [twelve-second pause] *gɔk-a*
  now go:3PL go:3PL uh   go:3PL-CONJ

8 (unintelligible)-*a   mɔti gwɛk*
               -CONJ again come:3PL

Translation:

One day we Paso, uh, Awpa, we went to net [fish] and uh [11-second pause] he (or I) got a big fish and Samek speared it. After he speared it, he died and, uh, they took it and (now) they made sago pudding. After they made it, after they ate it, they went now. They went [12-second pause], they went and (unintelligible) and came back.

Without doubt, this was the first time in Kiring's life that she had to strain to say more than isolated, formulaic phrases in Taiap, and with that in mind, her narrative is impressive. She makes only two overt morphological errors: in line 1 when she omits the conjunctive suffix *-rɛ* on the end of *yim* (we) and on the end of the names Paso and Awpa;[22] and in line 4, when she incorrectly inflects the the verb "to die" to agree with Samek and not with the fish that he speared (the correct form is *wasɔtak*). Kiring uses a total of at least ten verbs in her short narrative (not counting the unintelligible verb in line 8), and, with the exception of "to die," each of these is conjugated flawlessly.

But despite the lack of overt morphological errors, Kiring's narrative is very different from anything that a fluent Taiap speaker would produce. She overextends the conjunctive morpheme *-a* (lines 1, 2, 4, 7, 8) and the morpheme of consecutivity *-api* (lines 3, 6) in a manner patterned on Tok Pisin *na* (and) and *pinis* (completed action), and she does this in a more thorough and systematic way than even the youngest fluent speakers – who also overextend in this way – ever do.[23] Moreover, Kiring's story is told disfluently, with long hesitations and pauses. While it generally conforms to village narrative conventions, the story's structure is very bare-boned and basic. It contains none of the details about participants, places, and actions that Gapun narratives demand. Referents are consistently oblique. Kiring begins speaking of "we," but then, from line 4 onward, changes to "they." It is also unclear who caught the fish in line 2. Because she omits the pronoun, the verb may refer to Samek or to herself. In addition to deviating starkly from the Taiap narratives told by fluent speakers, Kiring's story also differs greatly from the stories that she herself tells in Tok Pisin. In that language, Kiring's narrative competence is highly developed, and she regularly recounts stories of almost epic proportions in which the minutae of her adventures in the jungle are carefully described and detailed.

Nevertheless, that Kiring is able to activate her passive knowledge of the vernacular to even this extent is striking, and it shows that the passive bilingualism of some of these young Tok Pisin-speaking girls is very highly developed.[24] If they had to, children like Kiring might at this age increasingly begin to activate their knowledge of the vernacular and start using it in speech. As it is, however, there is no demand on children to speak Taiap, nor is there any reward for speaking it. The language capabilities of those children who do occasionally answer adults in the vernacular are either unnoticed or criticized and corrected.

Perhaps if some significant aspect of the traditional social system, such as initiation rites and seclusion, had remained intact in the village, then girls around Kiring's age would have been provided with a collective forum, grounded in the local culture and traditions, in which they could have begun to develop their skills in the vernacular. But at this crucial stage at which they could begin activating their knowledge of the language, village children are instead led away from local concerns. They go to school, where they become involved in friendships and networks with children from other villages with whom they must communicate through Tok Pisin, and where the vernacular is expressly forbidden. By the time they finish school, six years later, these girls have not only not been speaking the vernacular, they have also been exposed to a system of values that has nothing to do with village life and the ways of the ancestors, and where no vernacular language has any place at all. As it happens, this system of values is in many ways identical to the one held by the villagers themselves. The associations that exist in Gapun between a devalued traditional lifestyle and Taiap get strengthened through the school. The message conveyed to children in both the village and the school is that there is absolutely no reason for them to ever begin speaking their vernacular.

7. Contextualizing the self

At times, Gapun villagers display an awareness that something is happening to their vernacular. Sopak's critical aside that her daughter Kama's Taiap "isn't good," Kruni's occasional shouts that his grandchildren "are stupid in the vernacular," and Tambong's happy agreement that the vernacular of children nowadays is Tok Pisin are instances when villagers explicitly reflect upon aspects of the phenomenon of language shift that their community is experiencing.

Reflections of this nature are never frequent and always brief. And even though villagers sometimes voice opinions ranging from irritation to fatalistic acceptance of their children's lack of production in Taiap, nobody can really understand why children's verncular competence "isn't good." "We haven't done anything," Sopak's husband, Mone, once explained with a resigned shrug of his shoulders when I asked him why he thought none of the village children spoke Taiap:

We, all the mothers and fathers, we want our children to learn the vernacular. We try to get them to speak it, we want them to. But they won't. They're all Tok Pisin people (*ol man meri bilong Tok Pisin*). They're *bikhed*. I don't know why. Before, kids, they heard their mother speak the vernacular, their father, and they just followed them (*bihainim ol tasol*) and spoke it. Now no. Just Tok Pisin.

As far as villagers like Mone are concerned, children like Kiring who do not actively command Taiap have rejected it. They ought to be able to speak it, they should speak it, but they don't. They're all "Tok Pisin people." In the villagers' experience, this is a difference between the present generation of children growing up in Gapun and the children from "before," all of whom "followed" their parents and spoke Taiap. Nobody in Gapun, however, pays much attention to this difference. With this one exception regarding their decision about language, boys and girls in the village are seen to be much the same as children always have been. They still start out as irritable, aggressive *hed*-strong little babies, and they still gradually come to display *save* and take their place in the everyday life of the village.

The fact that children nowadays display their developing *save* through Tok Pisin and not Taiap is not unsettling for anybody. There are two main reasons for this. First, the connotations of social solidarity, generosity, maturity, Christianity, and modernity that Tok Pisin has come to acquire in village discourse make that language a supremely appropriate one for the expression of *save*. But, second, *save* in Gapun is not only expressed through language choice. In order to be considered a competent member of Gapun society, children must learn, among other things, how to listen, how to structure their talk so that it makes sense to other people, how to present themselves in talk, how to respond to the talk of others, and how to evaluate other people. This knowledge, too, is *save*. This kind of very basic knowledge, although it is bound up with and communicated through language, is not, however, conceptually tied to any one language in particular.

Because talk – with the exceptions of language used during a *kros* and a child's first words – is most readily interpreted by villagers as expressive not of individual opinions but of social sensitivity, a fundamental understanding that children must acquire in order to be able to participate in village life is that people often do not mean what they say. This understanding must be apprehended and applied to interpretation of all speech, regardless of whether the talk is in Tok Pisin, Taiap, or in a combination of those (or any other) languages. The separation of message and meaning is another dimension of the *hed/save* dichotomy, in the sense that villagers do not look to a person's words in order to gain insight into her or his *hed,* her or his autonomous self. Words, what one uses to express *save,* are regarded most often as show. Children must come to perceive the gap that is felt to exist between what a person says and what he or she really thinks, and they must learn how to structure their presentation of self and their understanding of others in the context of that gap.

The groundwork for doing this begins to be laid from the earliest interactions between mother and child in the maternity hut. Here language directed at the infant is minimal, and a mother's intentions to feed her baby, or wash it, or pierce its boils are most often revealed not through verbalization of those intentions, but through the action of performing them. When verbalizations with the child do begin with simple *em ia* routines, the separation that villagers perceive between message and meaning is immediately foregrounded through the common practice of getting children to stop crying by drawing their attention to animals and objects that are not really present.

Two other early verbal routines serve similar functions. The early *em ia* routines, in addition to becoming more complex as children mature, also evolve into and interweave with calling-out and naming routines, which mothers begin initiating with their children from about 18 months. Calling-out routines frequently start as part of a distraction routine, and if a child continues to fuss after an *em ia* sequence, the mother will direct the child's attention to the village plaza and tell her or him to "*singautim*" (call out to; Taiap <u>ga</u>-) a relative or playmate whom the mother has just thought of or caught sight of.

Until children have learned to respond to the prompt to "*singautim*" someone, caregivers follow the directive to call out to a particular person by saying the person's name in a high-pitched, breathy voice, with a vocative *-o* affixed to the end. Sometimes, particularly if the child being told to call out shows signs of responding, a caregiver will supplement the name being called out with directives, said as if by the child, in the same high, soft voice.

Text 7.1

Sopak > Masito (1;6)

Masi.	Masi.
Singautim Andu.	Call out to Andu.
Singautim em.	Call out to her.
"Andu! Andu-o!	"Andu! Andu-o!
Andu kam-o!"	Andu come-o!"
Uh.	Uh.
Singaut.	Call out.
"Andu kam pilai wantaim mi-o!"	"Andu come play with me-o!"

Naming routines begin at the same time as calling-out routines, and the two routines frequently flow in and out of one another. Naming routines differ from calling-out routines in that, instead of telling the child to call out to a named person in a high voice directed toward the village, the caregiver in this case expects the child simply to repeat the name of a person or object. Naming routines are initiated by either telling the child, "*Yu tok: X*" (You say: X) or, more frequently, by simply saying the name to be repeated in a flat, emphatic voice and waiting for the child to repeat it.

Text 7.2

Sopak > Masito (1;10)

Sopak: *Masi.*
Masito: *Ah?*
Sopak: *Gero.*

Masito: *Gero.*
Sopak: *Kak.* [Gero's brother]
Masito: *Kak.*
Sopak: *Mandidam.* [Gero's sister]
Masito: *Medida.*

As in all caregiver–child interactions, children are never pressed to respond; if they do not react to the prompt after two or three repetitions, caregivers drop it. If the child does respond to the prompt and repeat the name, the routine may be continued. It will end, usually after only several turns, when the caregiver gets distracted or bored and turns her or his attention to something else.

Like the *em ia* routines, in which words and their referents are linked only occasionally and incidentally, calling-out and naming routines often occur in the absence of any of the referents being spoken about. In Sopak's talk to Masito above (Text 7.2), for example, none of the children she names were present at the times of the exchanges.

Instead of linking names to their referents, caregivers, in their talk with young children, tend to link names to other names in metonymical clusters. This habit is especially evident in extended calling-out and naming routines, and is illustrated in Text 7.2, in which Sopak names several members of a sibling group for Masito. On another occasion, Masito (1;11) had been fingering a forty-centimeter-long carving that her father had recently completed in hope that a carving buyer would appear soon. The carving was very intricate, consisting of a large figure of a man encrusted with various geometric designs, highly stylized representations of crocodile heads, and the head of a flying fox. Noticing that Masito was holding the carving, Sopak spied the head of the flying fox, a tiny detail on the large figure, and initiated a naming routine with Masito:

Text 7.3

Sopak:	*Jakɛp.*	S:	Flying fox.
Masito:	*Ah?* [looks at S]	M:	Ah? [looks at S]
Sopak:	*Jakɛp.*	S:	Flying fox.
Masito:	*Kɛp.*	M:	*Kɛp.*
5 Sopak:	*Agrana ia. Agrana.*	S:	It's Agrana. Agrana.
Masito:	*Ah?*	M:	Ah?
Sopak:	*Agrana.*	S:	Agrana.
Masito:	*Agana.*	M:	Agana.

Sopak:	*Agur kusir. Agur*	S:	Lone flying fox. Lone
10	*kusir* [laughs].		flying fox [laughs].

Here Sopak juxtaposes names that can refer to her neighbor Agrana. When she begins this sequence, Sopak makes no attempt to direct Masito's attention to the relationship between the word *jakɛp* (flying fox) and its immediate referent, even though it is unlikely that Masito could have known that *jakɛp* in this case referred to the small stylized protrusion on the underside of the large carving. Naming flying foxes, Sopak associates to Agrana, who is the only representative of the flying fox clan living in the village. This in turn leads her to call the Adjora-language nickname that many villagers jokingly use to refer to Agrana (*Agur kusir*; lit. flying fox one [lone/alone]). By juxtaposing these words in this manner and getting her to repeat them, Sopak is drawing Masito's attention to the fact that they are in some way related to one another. Just how they are related is not, however, explicitly indicated. And how they are related to particular referents is not even hinted at.

Even though Sopak's talk to Masito can ultimately be traced to a specific object held by the child, the purpose of this naming routine is clearly not to draw Masito's attention to that object and get her to identify it by name. Instead, Sopak conveys socially relevant information about Agrana. But the talk only becomes meaningful once it is contextualized in village social relations and thereby understood as referring to different aspects of Agrana. So like the villagers' understanding of Kruni's harangue about the youth group (Text 4.9) or Kem's oratory about preparing for a conciliatory feast (Text 4.7), Masito's interpretation of Sopak's speech must be based on information that is not contained in that speech. In order for Masito to be able to make sense out of her mother's talk, she has to embed it in a social context. Drawing children's attention to this embedding process is one of the primary structuring principles of language socialization practices.

As Sopak's speech to Masito illustrates, caregivers tend to group together the names of people or objects that all share some socially salient tie – for example, kinship, clan membership, different names for the same person, or, for objects, use in hunting or preparing sago. Even though the exact basis for grouping names together is seldom made explicit, by clustering the words together and saying them one after another, a relational theme is presented to the child and stressed.

Furthermore, since the meaning of an utterance is frequently not to be found in the child's immediate environment (since the actual persons or objects being named are often not present during the routines), children must learn to interpret meaning in terms of a word's relational placing in a network of associations. It is not uncommon for children to become acquainted with these associative networks surrounding a referent before they can identify the referent in the real world. Even though Masito might not know that the word *jakɛp* refers to flying foxes or to a particular clan or to a detail on the carving, she is presented in this interaction with the idea that *jakɛp* somehow "goes with" Agrana and *Agur kusir*. When she later acquires the range of referential meanings attached to *jakɛp*, she will do this against the background of this metonymical framework in relation to Agrana.

Caregivers sometimes present their children with oblique clues as to what they are actually referring to when they engage the children in naming routines of this sort. Here, for example, Sopak cues Masito to her subtext through the use of the Tok Pisin particle "*ia*" (line 5). *Ia* in this case serves a focusing function, foregrounding Agrana as the topic of talk.

Explicit social information is also sometimes given to children in caregiver speech, albeit in an offhand and nondidactic manner. Once when Tambong was busy preparing tobacco leaves for drying above her hearth, for example, Bini (1;8), sitting behind Tambong on the floor, pointed out into the distance.

Text 7.4

Bini:	[pointing] *Myia, myia.*	B:	[pointing] There, there.
Tambong:	[not looking] *Wanem?*	T:	[not looking] What?
Bini:	*Pk*	B:	Pk
Tambong:	*Pik, ah? I go kilim em. Em i kamautim tripela kaukau bilong mi.*	T:	A pig, ah? Go beat it. He's dug up three of my sweet potatoes.

In her response to Bini's prompt, Tambong typically does not answer by reinforcing the child's identification of the pig (with her back to Bini, she doesn't in fact even know if a pig is actually present) or by focusing his attention on the essential characteristics of that referent (by, for example, asking him "What color is the pig?" or "What does the pig say?"). Instead, Tambong's response immediately contextualizes Bini's words in the social world: Pigs dig up things belonging to people and deserve to be beaten for doing so. Tambong's brief remark contains a great deal of socially salient information about pigs, and provides Bini with a basis for relating them to other aspects of his social world, such as gardening practices and the consequences of violating other people's personal possessions.

Another way caregiver speech appears to alert children to the importance of observing social context is through its variation and inexplicitness. Adults make little attempt to be consistent or true in the information they give their children, and they may answer a child's question in a number of ways without explicitly indicating which answer the child should accept. On a day when Sopak was in a bad mood because she was hungry and had a headache, Masito (1;11) tried to engage her in a naming routine by calling the name of her favorite sister and playmate:

Text 7.5

Masito:	*Ma. Kama?*	M:	Ma. Kama?
Sopak:	*Kama i go mipela i no save long em.*	S:	Kama went we don't know where.
Masito:	*Ah?* [pause] *Ma, Kama?*	M:	Ah? [pause] Ma, Kama?
Sopak:	*Ah?*	S:	Ah?
Masito:	*Kama?*	M:	Kama?
Sopak:	*Kama i go Wongan.*	S:	Kama went to Wongan.
Masito:	*Ah?*	M:	Ah?
Sopak:	*Kama i go long bus. Em i go kisim ɔikɛ.*	S:	Kama went into the forest. She went to get <u>mangoes</u>.
Masito:	*Ma, Kama?*	M:	Ma, Kama?
Sopak:	*Sia aiata. Kama indai pinis. Snek i kaikaim em na em indai.*	S:	*Sia* <u>enough</u>. Kama died. A snake bit her and she died.

In order to evaluate these answers and judge which one, if any, is true, Masito would have had to have noticed and remembered when Kama left the house; who she was with; what, if anything, was said before she left; and what she had with her when she left. From very early on, children in the village are directed to attend to these kinds of details through the questions they are asked and through the kind of talk about others that they hear around them constantly.

With little to turn their attention away from themselves, the overwhelming bulk of the villagers' talk is devoted to one another. Men and women in Gapun spend a tremendous amount of time and energy observing and gathering information about the activities of others. Most homes are built so that villagers can survey large sections of the village from their verandas or through small peepholes poked through the thatch of their walls. Acoustics in the village are good, and Gapuners have sharp ears, so most conversations inside a house are readily audible to one's nearest neighbors and to anyone happening to stroll by. In addition to more surreptitious means of getting news, villagers constantly ask each other questions about their destinations and purposes. People walking through the village are often showered with questions, even if the answers to the questions are apparent. Striding across the village in the direction of the small mountain that lies directly outside Gapun, with a spear on his shoulder and dogs at his feet, a man will get asked by several different people as he passes their houses, "Are you going hunting? Up the mountain? Alone?" Apprehension about theft and adultery, never far below the surface in Gapun, is one of the reasons villagers like to keep themselves informed about the (supposed) whereabouts of others. Married women, in particular, keep relentless checks on the whereabouts of their husbands in relation to any sexually active adolescent girls.

In their untiring efforts to know about one another, Gapuners frequently depend on children. Unlike adults, children up to about age 15 are free to come and go in a large number of village houses. In addition, in their contact with other children and in their travels through the forest, adults know that children are likely to pick up interesting bits of news. Children are thus valued as information givers, and from very early on they are trained to attend to detail so that they can adequately answer any questions about a particular happening that an adult may have.

This training to be able to observe and report detail begins very early and is evident in the questions that caregivers ask their children. The types of questions most frequently directed at children under 6 are requests for information about the child's own feelings and desires. Before about 16 months, the constant guesses that caregivers make about their child's wants, based on the child's sounds and movements, are frequently verbalized, and mothers respond to a whining infant by saying, "She's hungry," before pressing a breast in the baby's mouth, or they will shout at a sibling who wants to play with a moaning baby, "Leave him! He's *kros*! He doesn't want to!" thus providing a verbalization for the child's behavior. As children get older, caregivers begin recasting these interpretations of the child's behavior as questions directed at the child. Such questions are not open-ended, but are typically cast as propositions suffixed with the Tok Pisin interrogative marker "*ah?*" (-*kɛ* in Taiap). So from about age 2, mothers begin to ask crying children "*Yu hangre, ah?*" (You're hungry, ah?) or "*Yu laik godaun, ah?*" (You wanna go down, ah?) before they take some course of action to quiet the child. The caregiver is thus still making guesses about what the child's behavior indicates, but he or she is now asking the child to confirm these guesses. In other words, children from age 2 onward begin to be confronted with the idea that it is proper to make assumptions about people's thoughts, desires, and intentions on the basis of that person's actions and that certain types of behavior in certain situations can be interpreted in specific ways. By asking the child to confirm the caregiver's interpretation of her or his behavior and vocalizations, caregivers draw the child's attention to this process.[1]

At the same time that caregivers begin asking children questions about themselves, they also start asking them about other people and things. Caregivers often ask children questions to which they themselves do not know the answers, such as "*Kinda ana?*" (Where's the tongs?) when these have been misplaced and cannot be found. This type of information question becomes increasingly prominent in adult speech to children as the children get older and begin to travel around the village with their siblings and relatives. Questions of this type typically focus on encouraging the children to remember and report socially significant details about their experiences that adults can use as a basis for evaluating and commenting on the behavior of others.

Sopak and Mone's 11-year-old son, Gom, had returned to Gapun after having spent several days in the nearby village of Wongan visiting friends. While in Wongan, Gom had been fed and looked after by Sopak's younger sister Angara and her husband, Sair. Returning from Wongan, Gom sat down on the floor of his parent's house and began eating an old sago pancake that he found on the *bed* above the hearth. At the time, Sopak and Mone were chewing betel nut and socializing with Sopak's younger brother Ambuli and two of Mone's sister's adolescent sons, Bowdi and Simbira. About half an hour after Gom's arrival, his father began to question him:

Text 7.6

Mone:	*Gom yupela sutim wanpela pik, ah?*	M:	Gom you [PL] speared a pig, ah?
Gom:	*Sair sutim asde.*	G:	Sair shot [one] yesterday.
Bowdi:	⌈ *Bikpela?*	B:	⌈ A big one?
Sopak:	⌊ *Nambar?*	S:	⌊ One?
Mone:	*Wanpela ah?*	M:	One ah?
Gom:	*Mm.*	G:	Mm.
Ambuli:	*Ambinɨnɨ pɔkunn?*	A:	How did he shoot it?
Bowdi:	[guessing] *Saksak.*	B:	[guessing] Sago.
Gom:	*Saksak napɔ.*	G:	Sago trap.
Ambuli:	*Anɨma napɔ?*	A:	Whose trap?
Gom:	*Mi no save.*	G:	I don't know.
Simbira:	*ŋaŋan napɔnɨ pɔkun.* [laughs]	Si:	He shot it in my trap. [laughs]

Gom:	[*Sia*! [laughs]	G:	[*Sia*! [laughs]
Sopak:	[*Sia*! [laughs]	S:	[*Sia*! [laughs]
Mone:	*Lusim Ambanamɛk . . .*	M:	Go past Ambanamek . . . [the name of an area of land]
Gom:	*Mm. Bilong Steven, bilong ol na bilong mipela.*	G:	Mm. Steven's, theirs, and ours.
Mone:	*Long rot yumi go kukim kunai ia?*	M:	On the road where we burned the field?
Gom:	*Mm.*	G:	Mm.
Mone:	*Long desela hap, ah?*	M:	There, ah?
Sopak:	*Ambin?*	S:	What?
Gom:	*I go na katim i go insait long bus.*	G:	[You] go there, leave the path and go inside the forest.

[three-utterance distraction]

Mone:	*Na . . . miŋankɛ?*	M:	And . . . a male?
Gom:	*Mi no save.*	G:	I don't know.
Sopak:	*Bɔr* [*miŋankɛ?*	S:	[A male pig?
Mone:	[*Bɔr miŋankɛ nɔŋɔr?*	M:	[A male or female pig?
Gom:	*Man.*	G:	Male.
Mone:	*Man, ah?*	M:	Male, ah?
Sopak:	*Ah?*	S:	Ah?
Gom:	*Yea!*	G:	Yes!
Bowdi:	*Bɔr iapirŋan? Iapirŋan? Pakas? Pakas, ah?*	B:	A fat pig? Was it fat? Scrawny? Scrawny, ah?
Gom:	*Iapir.*	G:	Fat.

In these kinds of contexts and through these kinds of questions, children are coached into acquiring the specific conventions of reporting their experiences and knowledge about others that villagers use in their talk to one another. Several of these conventions stand out in this interaction with Gom. The first is the way the interaction is structured in terms of the kind of participation engaged in by speakers. Gom here is cast in the role of information giver, and his part in this talk is to supply his listeners with the specific information that they request. Like those questions directed at young children to find out whether they are hungry or want to go down from the house to the ground below, the questions asked of Gom are all direct information questions that allow him to respond with minimal verbalization (compare David's responses to his mother's questions when he wants her to cut his string in Text 6.10). The participation structure of this interaction is consistent with the villagers' understanding that successful communication is the responsibility of the recipients of talk. Gom's audience here must do all the work; it is up to them to attempt to draw out of Gom the information they desire.

The information they desire is certain kinds of detail. All the questions asked in this interaction concern details about the spearing of the pig: How many were speared, how it was speared, where (i.e., inside whose land), was it male, was it fat. Details such as these are important to villagers because they enable them to assess the intentions of other people. Because language and expression through speech are usually considered to be expressive of *save* and social sensitivity, but not individual intention, the surest way for villagers to gain access to the thoughts of others is through the detailed observation of their behavior. Children are exposed to this idea throughout their childhood, as they listen to their own behavior being interpreted by others and assigned specific intent or emotion. Now, as they mature and begin to be questioned about their observations of the actions of other people, children observe this interpretive process being applied to others. They come to understand that in order to be acceptable to their listeners, their reporting must be focused on what they have observed in the social world. This observing is stressed from the very first *em ia* routines, in which children are distracted from their own worries and directed outside themselves to that social world. They are told to look, to see, to listen, and to observe what is going on around them. As they grow older, they discover that they must rely on their own observations of the action and talk going on around them in order to make sense of and determine the truth of the kind of information presented to them by their caregivers.

So in addition to providing children with a framework around which they learn to structure the reporting of their experiences, questions about detail also serve an important social function. By getting people to describe in as great detail as possible a person's behavior and the context surrounding the behavior, listeners prompt speakers to provide them with vital clues that they can discuss in order to interpret and evaluate that person's thoughts and intentions.

Here, for example, the details of the pig hunt are not just of passing interest to Mone and the others; they are important in evaluating the behavior of Gom's uncle Sair and his aunt Angara. The unstated question running throughout this entire interaction is: Why didn't Sair and Angara send some pig meat back to Gapun with Gom? Gom is old enough to realize this, and it is perhaps in order to try to defuse the bout of complaining about the couple's stinginess that inevitably will follow these questions that he at several points denies knowledge of certain key and, in this case, socially damaging details (such as the fact that the pig was speared in a sago trap on land to which Sopak and Mone have rights and the fact that it was male, that is, big) before finally divulging the truth.

Telling a *stori*

The observational skills and verbal means of expressing those skills that children in Gapun acquire while growing up all feature prominently in the most common speech genre in the village. This genre occurs at any time, but most often whenever villagers sit together and socialize in the morning before it gets too hot, or in the evenings after they have washed at their waterholes and eaten. At these times, small groups of siblings and their spouses often congregate on the veranda of someone's house or in someone's *haus win:* a small, roofed structure without walls that several men have constructed in front of their houses so they can sit with others and catch whatever slight breeze might waft through the village. If there are not too many conflicts brewing in the village, men sometimes drift over to Kruni's men's house in the evening and socialize with one another. In these relaxed, informal settings, the villagers of Gapun sit, chew betel nut, sweat, spit, swat at mosquitoes, and engage in a specific speech genre they call *stori* (*tik*).

A *stori* in Gapun is a narrative account, in Paso's words, of "where you went and what you saw." *Stori*s offer accounts of events the teller has either experienced himself or has heard about in a *stori* from someone else. The content of *stori*s ranges from telling about that morning's hunting trip, to retelling what Paso said that Sopak did with the sago grubs that Bit had announced were for herself, to explaining what one of the young men in Wongan claimed to have heard on the radio about the imminent Second Coming of Christ. *Stori*ing occurs in any size group, from between two to several dozen people. Gapuners feel uncomfortable with silence between people, which they interpret as a sign of conflict or hostility. So whenever members of a gathering suddenly run out of things to say, it is not long before somebody launches into a new *stori*, or anxiously begins urging others to *stori*.

Favorite topics of *stori* for both men and women are adventures in the jungle while hunting pigs or cassowary or while fishing in the shallow jungle streams, scandalous or outlandish gossip about fellow villagers or neighboring villagers not present during the telling, news of mysterious and possibly apocalyptic events such as a face appearing in the sago pancake of a woman in a Sepik village, past fights between Gapun and Sanae, and anecdotes about how the teller or someone else tricked another person into making a fool of her- or himself. Villagers laugh uproariously at their own mishaps and at those of others, and incidents in which either the narrator or some other protagonist flees strange sounds in the jungle or slips and falls in the mud while carrying a heavy burden are greatly enjoyed by everyone. Any incident that causes a person to completely lose control and *bagarap* (bugger up/make a mess of themselves) from fear or panic qualifies as an appreciated topic of *stori*. In an egalitarian society like Gapun, misfortune is an important idiom through which equality can be expressed. Not everybody is able to sell ten bags of coffee like Kem, but everyone has, at one time or another, fallen through a rotten bridge or been frightened by an ancestor's ghost. Men and women in the village all share these kinds of experiences; in laughing about one another's misadventures, they draw attention to this sharing and reinforce their appreciation and knowledge of the dangers and hardships of the rainforest. Villagers like to exaggerate these dangers when *stori*ing about them, and in order to make a mishap seem especially sensational, *stori*-tellers sometimes claim outrageously that the person being talked about became so frightened by a spirit, a snake, or a menacing noise that he or she fell to the ground and *pispis pekpek wantaim* (urinated and defecated on him- or herself). *Stori*s like this are absolute favorites with the villagers. They are always greeted with gales of hysterical laughter no matter how many times they are told. One such *stori,* about an old Sanae woman who became so frightened during an earthquake that she collapsed, began shaking, and *pispis pekpek wantaim,* was told countless times during 1986–7. Each time it was told, the listeners screamed laughing so hard that they had to hold their sides.

Villagers in Gapun *stori* to inform, entertain, and pass the time. *Stori*ing is the way in which Gapuners keep track of one another's doings, and it is the way news is spread throughout the village. *Stori*s are highly participatory events in which listeners are invited to draw on their past experiences and their knowledge of particular people and settings to contribute to both the telling of the *stori* and the subsequent evaluation of the action described in the *stori*. Listeners are expected to freely interrupt the *stori*-teller, questioning facts or challenging detail. They are also expected to decenter and imagine themselves as part of the *stori,* facing the same situation or predicament as the characters in the *stori*. Listeners pepper the telling of a *stori* with short evaluatory comments such as "*Mi les/ŋa mnda*" (How awful; lit. I'm sick of that) whenever the protagonist of the *stori* finds her- or himself in a sticky situation such as meeting up with a spirit in the rainforest or being clawed at by an irate cassowary, or "*Em nau/Gumɛ aŋgi*" (That's right) when the protagonist acts in a way the listeners agree with and approve of. Participation of listeners is necessary for a speech event to even be defined as *stori* by the villagers. One of the most characteristic features of *stori*s in Gapun is that they sometimes are told back at the original teller by one or more of the listeners, in an embellished form, immediately after their first telling.

One evening, Sake and her husband, Allan, sat on their veranda with Sake's younger sister Jari (19 years), Jari's good friend, Kem's daughter Yengia (20 years), Sake's older sister Erapo's son Aper (23 years), and a few other villagers and their children. It was later than the villagers normally stayed up socializing, but this night there was a clear sky and a *gutpela mun* (good moon, i.e., a full moon), so the village was bathed in a milky blue light, a cool breeze had come up, driving away some of the mosquitoes, and everyone was in a good mood. After several other people had *stori*ed about their adventures in the jungle that day, Sake announced that she had a *stori* to tell:

Text 7.7

	Sake:	Have you all heard? This man from Sanae, what's his name, Beni =
	Jari:	= Egwabia's husband.
	Sake:	Tsk. Not him. The husband of Egumamba's child. By his first wife.
	Jari:	Oh. ⌈ I thought Egwabia's husband.
5	Sake:	⌊ This man, Beni, he went into the jungle with his dogs. He we:::nt, killed a pig. Killed it, cut up dry leaves, burned the hair off it, cut it up. OK, he tied it to the thing here, <u>the carrying stick</u> =
	Aper:	= <u>Where did he spear the pig?</u>
10	Sake:	Tsk. Listen to the story. He came and got to the big path here, close to Songor's garden =
	Allan:	= coffee garden
	Sake:	Songor's coffee garden. Alright, he came and he saw one of his lovers standing there.
15	Jari:	Which woman?
	Sake:	I don't know/oh, what's her name, Mbgat's child.
	Jari:	Ampamna.
	Sake:	Not her.
	Jari:	Pataniya.
20	Sake:	Her. He saw her standing near the path. He went, came up to her and said: "My throat is dry. I want to drink your breast milk" [loud cries of surprise from audience]. That's it, there was no more talk, the man threw all his stuff on the ground and he stood there and drank at her breast [hysterical general laughter]. Alright, finished
25		drinking now, he got all his things and went back to the village. [Sake bursts out laughing. Everyone else is screaming with laughter.]

Aper:	*Sia!* This huge man with a beard here stands up drinking breast milk =	
Jari:	= He's got no shame.	

Yengia: He just stands in the middle of the path and drinks a big breast—
30   Mother's child! [an exclamation]

Aper: He went, killed a pig, carried it and came came came came came
       came, his throat is really dry: "Oh, I haven't got any water, what am
       I gonna drink now?" Goes and comes across the woman there picking
35   coffee, that's it, he tells her: "Oh please, my throat is really dry. I
       want to drink your breast milk." [new explosions of loud laughter
       from everyone]

Sake: [laughing hard] Ah, "I want to drink your breast milk."

Aper: [still laughing] Alright, he stands and drinks it, goes goes goes, finishes
       his wants now, tells the woman: "That's enough," gets his things and
40   goes back to the village. [everyone is still laughing]

Yengia: I wouldn't let him drink at my breast. I'd run way into the jungle.

Jari: Are you my child that you should drink my breast milk?! <u>Mother</u>. I'd
       grab a stick and break his big head.

Sake: He'll finish your milk, you won't have any now. Your baby will cry
45   in hunger: [you'll say] "Oh, I don't have any milk now. The man
       finished it all on the road." [general uproarious laughter]

This *stori* and the listeners' reactions to it are characteristic of the way in which informal talk is structured and elaborated on in the village. Sake begins by announcing that she has something to say in a lowered, urgent voice that promises scandal. She begins her *stori* in the usual way by identifying the protagonist. When *stori*s are about people who may not be known by everyone present, they are usually identified by their name, village, and relationship to someone else, such as a spouse or parent. When Sake leaves out this final bit of identification, her sister Jari elicits it by wrongly identifying the man in the *stori* as the husband of a Sanae woman named Egwabia. It is in the contexts of *stori*s like these that villagers like Jari test their knowledge of the kin ties of people in other villages. Gapuners like to know who is related to whom, and even young women like Jari can, with a fair amount of certainty, keep track of the extended kin relations of everyone in Wongan, of many people in Sanae, Singrin, and Watam, and even of some of the people in the Murik villages and Bien: a total of over 1,000 people.

Once Sake identifies the main character, Beni, by name, village, and kin relation to somebody known to most of the listeners, she begins her *stori*. In the course of her narrative, Sake adheres to the major requirements of a good *stori*: It must be a chronological, step-by-step tale, and it must be detailed. Villagers pay a great deal of attention to these points, and any departure from these norms evokes either immediate protest and correction from the listeners or the subsequent evaluation that the *stori*-teller "didn't *stori* good" (*ino stori gut/tik tandiu gurkru wakarɛ*").

*Stori*s are characterized by a fluid sense of moving toward something – an action, an encounter, or a difficulty – and then of moving back again, coming away and returning to the point of departure. This movement creates a certain amount of dramatic tension, and it is expressed by *stori*-tellers both in what they choose to tell about an incident and in the way they tell it. *Stori*s told by the villagers inevitably start by establishing the protagonist in a familiar setting (the town of Angoram or a bush house in the jungle, for example). This is the point from which the protagonist departs on her or his adventure, and the return to this place or a similar one signals the end of the *stori*. It is important not to let the *stori* "just finish in the jungle" (*pinis nating long bus*), as the *stori* told by 6-year-old Kiring did (Text 6.23). The starting point for most of the *stori*s told in Gapun is the village, and narration always begins by having the protagonist leave the village or her or his house to go do something – to fetch water, chop firewood, or work sago. Sake adheres to this convention when she begins her narration of events by explaining that Beni went into the jungle "with his dogs," meaning that he left the village to hunt. Movement occurs in the narrative itself in the transition from the orientation phase of the narrative, in which characters and starting point are identified, to the portion of the narrative that constitutes the reason for telling the *stori* in the first place. In Sake's *stori*, this transition from orientation to event sequence is marked on two levels. Syntactically, the transition is conveyed quite literally with a verb of motion (he went – "*em igo*" in the Tok Pisin original – line 6). It is also heavily marked by intonation. Sake sings the words "*em igo*:::" in an extended rising tone held over three beats, and in doing so she establishes a neat bridge between the *stori*'s content and its form. Her choice of verb and her extended intonation subtly and skillfully indicate two things: that Beni's walk through the jungle was long and that a transition is occuring in the narrative.

Once Beni kills a pig, Sake takes care to detail the actions that follow: He first cuts dry leaves off the surrounding trees in the jungle, then he places these over the carcass of the pig and lights them, thereby singeing off the hair. After this, Beni butchers the pig, ties the meat to a stick, and returns home. This is a very detailed description of an extremely commonplace action, and it is difficult for an outsider to understand why such detail is necessary. The details about the pig kill have nothing to do with the ultimate point of Sake's *stori*, and each person present at the telling of this *stori* has seen and participated in this procedure for preparing the carcass of a pig hundreds of times. They do not need the procedure described for them to know exactly what Beni would do with a pig he killed. An outsider wonders why Sake does not condense her description and simply tell her audience that Beni killed a pig and started back with the meat.

In concentrating so carefully on this type of detail, however, Sake is reaffirming the value that villagers place on the careful observation and description of detail. Whenever villagers evaluate the *stori*s of others, they do so primarily in terms of how detailed the *stori*s are. The reporting of detail is carefully monitored by listeners, and incorrect information such as saying that Kem sold two bags of coffee when he really sold three will immediately evoke sharp cries of "*Giaman!/Takwat!*" (Lie!) from any of the listeners who happen to know better.[2] All of the talk directed at Sake during her telling of the *stori* are questions and comments about detail: Aper wants to know where the pig was killed (line 9), Sake's husband, Allan, corrects her to be more precise, prompting her to specify the garden where Beni and his lover meet as a coffee garden (line 12), Jari wants to know the name of Beni's wife (line 2) and lover (line 15).

But when Sake describes the butchering of the pig's carcass, she is doing more than just supplying her listeners with detail; she is also demonstrating her mastery of the narrative genre. Sake carefully chooses her words to convey intense visual imagery and vividness to her narrative. Good *stori*s in Gapun are vivid stories, and skilled narrators describe people's actions with such fine attention to detail that the listeners can place themselves in the role of the people in the *stori* and imagine the event happening to themselves. The best *stori*-tellers in the village, like Kem, add sounds, expressive facial expressions and meaningful gestures to their narratives, crying out in mock terror in imitation of Wandi treading on a snake or miming a piece of firewood being thrown and striking a bone when *stori*ing about the time Sake broke her mother's brother's arm in a fight. For the villagers, the important thing is that even when accounts told in a *stori* were not experienced first-hand, the frame of "where you went and what you saw" still applies. This means that even if the teller has no connection at all with the events being narrated, as is the case in Sake's *stori*, the narrative must still be told as though the teller were present at the time, watching it all happen. The way narrators create the impression of first-hand experience is to concentrate, as Sake does here, on detail. The amount of detail worked into *stori*s in Gapun often makes it impossible to know for sure whether or not the narrator actually was present during the events that he or she describes. By focusing on detail, narrators direct the attention of their listeners to the actions being described in the *stori*. In doing so, they compel their listeners to pause, much as an onlooker or a voyeur would do, and "see" the actions being performed by the people in the *stori.* Sake's step-by-step description of Beni's preparation of the pig carcass is a rhetorically powerful means of evoking a vivid visual image of the event, as is her careful narration of the scene in which the protagonist of the *stori* sees the woman on the path, approaches her, speaks to her, throws down "all his stuff," and finally stands and drinks at her breast.

That the images in Sake's *stori* should be selected to convey a sense of seeing is no mere coincidence. The narrative stress laid on "where you went and what you *saw*" both reflects and reinforces the privileged position that villagers of Gapun have accorded sight as an instrument of knowledge. Although everyone in Gapun is aware that appearances can be misleading or deceptive, villagers rely heavily on the observation of people's actions when they evaluate their thoughts and intentions. Whereas language – what people say – is considered to "hide" things, seeing – the observation of what people do – reveals. The importance of seeing is a recurring theme in the villagers' practices of knowledge. The now defunct initiation rituals that all boys used to undergo, for example, were very much centered on "seeing." At each point in the initiatory sequence, something new was "revealed" (*kamap/mamanj-*) to the initiates: bullroarers, the sacred flutes, the *tumbuan* (masked, animated representations of the cult deities), the ancestoral carvings (*kandibwan*), cult sacra. And at each point, having seen these sacred objects, the initiates were informed that what they had previously heard (e.g., that the sounds whistling through the village from the men's house during funerary feasts were the voice of the *tambaran*) were lies. Seeing the sacred objects allowed at least part of their nature to be known.

In a similar way, the single most important source of knowledge about Christianity for the villagers is the seeing of illustrations that portray the various aspects of that religion. Villagers in Gapun never substantiate any of their claims about Christianity by referring to a specific liturgical text, partly because they do not read and command these texts, and partly because they feel that texts, like the spoken word, are inherently ambiguous.[3] On the other hand, villagers frequently find proof for their suspicions about the true nature of Christianity in the illustrations found in religious material like *Bel Bilong Man* or the booklet *Jisas i Karim Hevi Bilong Yumi* that Agrana approvingly produces during the course of his long tale of Genesis and the death of Jesus (Chapter 5). Unlike texts, the visual images in publications like these appear to be regarded by the villagers as more or less inherently true. To some extent, this depends on the fact that Gapuners, like other groups unfamiliar with certain types of two-dimensional representational techniques, are unable to differentiate between photographs and other means of graphic representation.[4] But the willingness of villagers to accept such pictures as "true" also arises from their understanding that in "seeing" something a great deal about it becomes accessible to knowledge and evaluation.[5]

Causing something to be known allows it also to be talked about, and *stori*s provide villagers with a context in which the actions of others can be discussed and evaluated. This is what happens next in the interaction around Sake's narrative. In her telling of the *stori*, Sake presents her listeners with a series of events, but she makes no overt attempt to judge or evaluate those events in her telling. As Gom is prompted to do in his telling of the details surrounding his uncle Sair's pig kill (Text 7.6), Sake simply describes a series of actions, leaving the evaluation of those actions to be collectively constructed by the listeners. Once Sake reaches the point of her *stori* and signals its closure by having Beni return to the village, her listeners assume the floor and do just this. They repeat that Beni drank at his lover's breast, at the same time that they now voice their opinions on Beni's behavior (lines 27–30). And after these initial evaluatory comments, Sake's *stori* gets retold and embellished by the listeners. This retelling and embellishment is one of the most characteristic aspects of Gapun *stori*s, and it underscores the essentially interactive nature of village narratives. In ways very similar to the public construction of consensus in men's house talk, villagers retell and modify *stori*s, collectively reworking them into a version to which many speakers have contributed.

Here it is Aper who assumes the role of reteller, and he begins to tell Sake's *stori* back at her and the others, as though they were hearing it for the first time. Aper concentrates his retelling of the *stori* on the drinking of the breast milk. He minimalizes the killing of the pig and instead elaborates on Sake's description of the breast-milk drinking incident, supplying the protagonist with thoughts ("Oh, I haven't got any water, what am I gonna drink?" [lines 32–3]) and the woman with a specific reason for being in the garden (picking coffee [lines 33–4]). When Aper once again reiterates the punchline of the *stori*, in a slightly embellished form (compare line 21 to lines 34–5), everyone listening to him explodes into as much laughter as they did the first time they heard the line from Sake. Indeed, Sake herself laughs as though she had never before heard the *stori*, and she repeats Aper's quote in a voice choked with laughter.

Aper finishes the *stori*, maintaining the structure presented by Sake, but once again contributing small flourishes of his own. His repetition of the verb "goes" ("*igo*" in the Tok Pisin original) for example, introduces the notion of duration (line 38), i.e., that Beni stood drinking the breast for a long time. He also invents a new line for Beni: "That's enough" (line 39).

Once the *stori* is retold by Aper, the listeners, still laughing, take the floor once again and evaluate the actions of the protagonists, decentering and telling each other what they would have done had they found themselves in that situation. Yengia and Jari both take the perspective of the young woman in the *stori* and voice their disapproval of the woman's passive response to the breast-milk drinking incident by announcing in scandalized language what their own reactions would have been. Yengia declares that she would run away in such a situation. Jari uses the common conversational ploy of addressing Beni directly (lines 42–3), as though he were present and she were talking to him. Placing herself in the context of the woman in the *stori,* Jari shouts at Beni: "Are you my child that you should drink my breast milk?!" She then informs her listeners that she would have bashed Beni's "big head" if he had asked to drink at her breast. Sake continues this type of decentered role playing by extending Jari's image further and imagining what would happen if a woman did let Beni drink at her breast.

Although the events described in Sake's *stori* are humorous and told primarily for fun, the same narrative structure and patterns of interaction are employed by the villagers whenever they discuss more serious matters in informal settings. Whenever anyone in Gapun or the surrounding villages becomes seriously ill, for example, the skills displayed here of adhering to narrative structures that demand chronology and detail, of observing and reporting, and of collaborating to produce a collective interpretation and evaluation of an event all serve important social functions.

Once when Jari's baby was so sick that everybody was convinced that the child was about to die, Sake and her husband took Jari and the baby to the Sepik village of Singrin (about a five-hour journey from Gapun by paddle canoe), where they paid a renowned old diviner to reveal the cause of the baby's illness. Before Sake or any of the others came back to the village, Agrana arrived at Sopak's house one day, returning from a short trip to Wongan. With him, Agrana brought the *stori* of what the diviner had said. Agrana *stori*ed (in a way that made it impossible to know whether or not he had actually been present at the divining session – it later turned out that he had been in another village at the time and had heard this *stori* – none of which turned out to be true – from someone else) that the diviner had disclosed that Jari had had sex with some man from the far-off Ramu village of Tarengi several months previous to her baby's illness and that she had laid her baby at the base of a tree while engaged in intercourse. During the time the baby was on the ground, Agrana recounted, a tree spirit (*devil belong diwai/kandap*) had stolen the child's spirit, and the illness was a result of this loss.

Upon hearing this explanation, Agrana, Sopak, Mone, and several of the couple's children who were sitting in the house at the time began to discuss the details of Jari's indiscretion. Everyone present began to think back and retrace all the happenings they had seen during the past few months that might shed light on this event. When had Jari left her baby alone long enough for her to rendezvous with a visitor from Tarengi? Sopak's daughter Basama remembered that one evening she heard Sake having a *kros* at Jari because she wasn't around to feed her baby. Basama recalled that Sake had shouted at Jari through the village: "Is it my baby that I should be carrying him around?!" Where could the couple have had sex? Sopak thought that they must have done it "in the cemetery by the trunk of the tree there," but then suddenly realized that the diviner "was speaking in riddles" (*tok bokis/kaikunumŋa nam*) and that the two must have had intercourse not at the base of a tree, as he had said, but near a patch of a particular kind of grass that Sopak had long maintained was the source of an evil magic used by sorcerers to kill people. A collaborative reconstruction of this event continued as all those present dredged their memories and contributed observations that gradually became connected and crystallized into an account of Jari's encounter with the Tarengi man and the theft of her child's spirit. Of course, it was agreed, Sake's *kros* at Jari occurred when she was away having sex.[6] And, yes, wasn't that when John, that man from Tarengi, was in Gapun, and, no, "He never sat down a little bit in the men's house," recalled Mone meaningfully at this point: "He was always going and coming, going and coming. Going and coming for what?"

Learning to *stori*

Like other verbal skills in the village, *stori*ing is something that village children are expected to simply acquire as they mature and their *save* breaks open. Most children seem to learn these skills in their play with older siblings and their peers so that, by the age of 7, the majority of village children have mastered the *stori*-telling pattern.

If young children are especially talkative, however, some mothers begin to explicitly prompt them from about age 4 to begin framing their accounts of their adventures and their observations in the *stori* format. Prompts to *stori* build on the information questions, like those directed at Gom (Text 7.6), that children have been receiving from 2 years of age. The prompts differ only in that children are now encouraged to expand their answers to information questions and frame them as narratives in accordance with adult norms. Sake's sister-in-law Tambong is one of the women in Gapun who sometimes tries to reframe her children's talk as *stori*. On one occasion when Tambong and her adolescent half-brother Mukar were sitting on her veranda chewing betel nut and smoking, Tambong's son Bapong (4;3) kept annoying his mother by running around the house with a long, pointed stick, whacking at imaginary spirits, singing, and talking loudly to himself. Tambong repeatedly told him to stop, and finally, in exasperation and making an effort to calm him down, she invited Bapong to *stori*.

Text 7.8

Tambong:	*Na . . . na yu toktok long nait mipela/ankel Jim ol kisim mipela i go antap long skul ia. Na yu stori gen. Na yu pundaun long haus ia tokim Mukar. [laughs] Long liklik haus yu pundaun ia.*	T:	And . . . and you talked last night: We/uncle Jim and the others went with us to the school. And you *stori* again. And you fell off the house, tell Mukar. [laughs] The little house you fell off.
Bapong:	*Yea, mi pundaun long haus ia.*	B:	Yeah, I fell off that house.
Mukar:	*Wanem haus?*	M:	What house?
Bapong:	*Em ia long Jim kisim mipela i go ia. Long Wongan ia. Long skul. Mipela/ren i kam *mipela wasim. Ren i wasim*	B:	That one, the one Jim took us to. In Wongan. At the school. We/ rain came and *we wet. Rain got
Tambong:	⌊ *singris bilong Bini. Yu tok: gaden haus bilong Yuki. Yuki=*	T:	Bini's ⌈ shirt all wet. ⌊ You talk: Yuki's garden house. Yuki=
Bapong:	*=Gaden haus bilong Yuki. Na mi pundaun ia.*	B:	=Yuki's garden house. And I fell.
Tambong:	*Yu tok: Yu sindaun i stap na yu pundaun.*	T:	You talk: You were sitting down and you fell.
Bapong:	*Mi tok mi pundaun.*	B:	I say/said I fell.
Tambong:	*Na yu krai.*	T:	And you cried.
Bapong:	(unintelligible)	B:	(unintelligible)
Tambong:	*Na yu tok: Yu krai.*	T:	And you talk: You cried.
Bapong:	*Mm?*	B:	Mm?
Tambong:	*Yu krai.*	T:	You cried.
Bapong:	*Yea.*	B:	Yeah.
Mukar:	*Na yu mekim wanem na yu pundaun?*	M:	And what were you doing when you fell?

[4-second pause]

Tambong:	⌈ *Yu sindaun tasol i stap* ⌊ *na pundaun.*	T:	⌈ You were just sitting and you ⌊ fell.
35	Bapong:	*Mi sindaun mi sindaun ia. Mi sindaun long paia. Ai bilong mi raun. Mi laik slip ia. Mi laik slip ia.*	B:	I was sitting. I was sitting. I was sitting by the fire. I was tired. I was falling asleep. I was falling asleep.
40	Tambong:	*Mi ting yu pundaun nating ia. Yu laik slip na yu pundaun.*	T:	I thought you just fell down. You were falling asleep and you fell down.
	Bapong:	*Em na yupela i no lukim mi tu.*	B:	Yeah, and you all weren't watching me.
		[6-second pause]		
45	Tambong:	*Na yu tok: Ren i pinis nau mipela i go long skul.*	T:	And you talk: The rain finished, we went to the school.
	Bapong:	*Ren pinis nau mipela i go long skul.*	B:	The rain finished, we went to the school.

Throughout this exchange, Tambong intervenes to get Bapong to focus his talk about his fall from the "little house" on detail and chronology. Through her interruptions and her prompts, Tambong guides her son to structure his telling in accordance with central characteristics of the *stori* genre. Tambong begins the exchange by inviting Bapong to retell an adventure that he had talked about the previous evening. She immediately frames this retelling as *stori,* partly by her use of that word (line 4) and partly by her direction to Bapong to focus on a particular detail of his adventure in the "little house" (i.e., his falling). As Bapong assumes the floor and begins to talk, Tambong interrupts him to tell him how he should have answered Mukar's question about the house (line 18). She also repeatedly prompts her son to detail the action of his falling (lines 22–34). Just saying "I fell" is not acceptable as a *stori* because such a description is not detailed or visual enough. Instead, Bapong is directed to break down the action of falling into a chronological event sequence with a beginning (sitting down), middle (falling), and end (crying). Bapong's description of what he was doing before he fell (lines 35–9) elicits a positive response from Tambong, because in relating that he was falling asleep, Bapong tells his mother something that she herself had not observed and that was important to know in order to be able to evaluate Bapong's sudden fall from the house. Tambong's final prompt occurs when Bapong neglects to signal the closure of his narrative in the required manner by moving away from the event sequence back to a normal state. After waiting six seconds for Bapong to close his *stori,* Tambong tells him what to say, and Bapong repeats his mother's prompt.

At only 4 years of age, Bapong is clearly already familiar with a number of narrative conventions. He responds to Mukar's question about the house by first identifying it, then by immediately contextualizing it within a narrative framework. Bapong seems to have already mastered the understanding that *stori*s must express spatial and dramatic movement, and he signals this understanding in his reply to Mukar by setting the scene ("In Wongan. At the school" [lines 13–14]) and by establishing the reason why he and the others were in the house in the first place ("rain came" [line 14]) before he goes on to talk about his falling. Bapong also seems to be aware of the importance of detail in his telling. Although he may not have known that the house that provided him with shelter from the rain and from which he fell belonged to Yuki, an old Gapun man living in Wongan, he did know that the shirt that he was wearing at the time of this incident belonged to his little brother Bini, and he works this detail of possession into his narrative account. Finally, Bapong appears already to have acquired a sense of the importance that villagers place on the observation of the actions of others, and he explicitly criticizes his mother for not "watching" him directly prior to his fall.

When adults like Tambong, or Sake, or Aper, tell each other *stori*s and respond to the *stori*s of others in appropriate ways, they do many things simultaneously. They demonstrate their knowledge of people and places, they display their skills of observation and of narration, they work together to evaluate the actions of others and to relate them to their own understanding of contexts, and, in doing so, they draw one another into a sense of shared knowledge, experience, and community. In telling *stori*s, villagers clarify for one another how events occur and how they should be understood. The structure and interactive patterns of each narrative told in the village is a subtle reminder to every villager of the importance of observation and remembering of detail, the privileged place of action in the evaluation of other people, and that personal evaluation should be avoided. The judgment of other people's actions should be collaboratively worked out in groups of people.

As children like Bapong learn to *stori*, they learn the conventions for doing all these things. They come to understand how and what to observe, how and what to talk about with others and how and what to evaluate in the actions and speech of others. In learning to *stori*, children acquire the understandings that villagers share for presenting the self and for comprehending and evaluating others. In learning to *stori*, children acquire fundamental knowledge about what it means to be a villager.

The fact that children in Gapun, as they mature, continue to acquire and display this kind of knowledge through their *stori*s is one of the main reasons villagers are not concerned that children do not speak the vernacular. The salient and crucial characteristic of *stori*s that determines their acceptability to listeners is not the particular language used to tell the *stori* so much as it is the particular and precise *use* of language. From the perspective of the villagers, as long as children learn to structure their talk in the proper way, providing detail and chronological framing, embedding their narratives in social life, collaborating with others to reach interpretations of their observations, and, in doing so, foregrounding a shared sense of experience and knowledge, then those children are considered to be Gapuners, regardless of the language they speak.[7]

Conclusion: The process of language shift

People know what they do; frequently they know why they do what they do; but what they don't know is what what they do does. Michel Foucault

When parents in Gapun blame their children for language shift, they are not being disingenuous. From the moment they are born, children in Gapun are thought to be in possession of intentionality and wills quite "strong" enough to be able to make early decisions about matters as basic as language choice. What adults who think about the language shift in the village do not consider, however, is that children would undoubtedly learn to speak the vernacular as they always have in the past if there were sufficient input and need to communicate in it. The fact that the children are no longer learning Taiap indicates that this kind of input and need are now lacking. In other words, what has changed in the village is not babies' and young children's evaluations and uses of language, but rather the evaluations and uses of language made by the caregivers of these small children.

In this respect, Gapun is similar to all other language-shifting communities that have been described by scholars. Always, the shift away from the vernacular language begins generations before the first monolingual speaker of the new language is produced by the community. The interval between the incipient stages of shift and its completion has been shown to be extremely variable, extending from as little as three generations in the case of immigrant groups (Boyd 1985; Clyne 1982; Fishman 1966) to nearly half a millenium, as in the case of languages like Scottish Gaelic (Dorian 1981) and Nahuatl in Mexico (Hill and Hill 1986).

In order to account for how the process of language shift begins and gains momentum, it is necessary to understand the reasons that adults have for incorporating the new language into their communicative repertoires in the first place. In the literature on language shift, people are said to begin learning dominant languages of greater currency than their vernacular because they are forced to do so through occupation, large-

248

scale in-migration of dominant-group members, or incorporation into a political entity in which that language is widely used, and/or because they choose to in order to be able to advance in a socioeconomic hierarchy that is controlled by members of the majority group.

There are elements of both coercion and striving for socioeconomic advancement in the villagers' incorporation of Tok Pisin into their linguistic repertoire. A focus on these concepts as such, however, would obscure the perspective from which the people of Gapun have acted. Certainly Gapun men away on the plantations were forced to learn Tok Pisin in order to be able to communicate with their fellow laborers and to follow the orders given by their overseers. And certainly these men understood this language to be linked to the white world that they believed had so much to give them. But the "meaning" and the implications of Tok Pisin were far deeper and much more profound than simple communication or social mobility.

The reasons for the enthusiasm toward and the spread of Tok Pisin throughout the verbal repertoires of all villagers, eventually even those who rarely if ever left Gapun, were not so much "pragmatic" or "socioeconomic," as those terms are commonly used in the sociolinguistic literature, as they were "cosmological," in the broadest anthropological sense of that word. The sudden appearance of white men in New Guinea and the new conditions of existence to which this fact gave rise were not, for the villagers, merely "social" or "economic" facts. They were, as Sahlins has stressed in his analysis of the Hawaiian reaction to European contact (e.g., 1985: 38), Maussian "total" facts: "social" and "economic" at the same time that they were "political," "historical," and, above all, "religious." Villagers believed, as they continue to believe, that the arrival of the white men was the harbinger of a new way of life. Their presence in New Guinea came to be understood in terms of an impending metamorphosis that would transform every aspect of the villagers' lives, including their physical beings. Although villagers could not achieve this transformation by themselves, they could attempt to hurry it along by heeding the admonitions of missionaries and colonial officials to change their lives and by scrutinizing white actions, words, and lifestyles for clues about how to change that the missionaries and others might want to remain hidden from them.

In their eagerness for the metamorphosis to occur, villagers immediately seized upon language as a "road," a way of making it happen. They considered that learning and speaking Tok Pisin, the language of the white men, would facilitate access to the secret underpinnings of white power and wealth. This attitude was grounded in traditional understandings of language and esoteric knowledge, and it is strongly evident even today in, for example, the villagers' opinions surrounding the Adjora language spoken in Sanae. That language carries extremely salient connections with magic and sorcery, and villagers feel that anyone speaking it has potential access to the secrets contained "inside" the language. This idea that knowledge of a language opens a channel to power is also apparent in the ways villagers conceive of and use their literacy skills. Having worked to acquire the technology of writing, villagers believe that they have learned a secret that they can apply to bring forth the cargo. Also, the original enthusiasm for Tok Pisin is currently paralleled by the interest of old villagers like Kruni in learning English, which they have recently understood to be the white man's true *tok ples* (vernacular).

Brought back to the village by young men returning from the plantations, Tok Pisin was incorporated into the villagers' communicative repertoire first through the speech of men. Many studies of other groups in Papua New Guinea (e.g., Laycock 1977, Mead 1931, Mühlhäusler 1979, Reed 1943, Sankoff 1976, Thurwald 1931) have observed that men returning to their villages after being away as plantation laborers immediately put the plantation Pidgin to work in their interactions with fellow villagers in order to bolster their reputation and display their knowledge of the outside world. Because of these ties to maleness, and because of the cosmological significance of Tok Pisin, it is likely that the language quickly began to be incorporated into that most male of village speech genres, oratorical speeches. In Gapun, the foundations of the current pattern of using Tok Pisin in oratories as a means of claiming authority in domains associated with white men and processes beyond the village were undoubtedly laid at a very early stage in the language's history in the village.

The use of Tok Pisin in oratorical speeches was the crucial point at which culture and language intersected in ways that changed them both. It was at this juncture that the village conception of *save* became available for linguistic marking in a way it had not been before.

The link between *save* and Tok Pisin had been available to be made by the villagers from the very beginning of their contact with white men, because the difference between Europeans and villagers was interpreted by Gapuners through their idiom of difference: their concept of "knowledge." Essentially, whites were understood (and are still understood) to be different from black-skinned people like the villagers and as having access to superior material wealth because they have more *save*.

The application of the concept of *save* to make sense of the white man's presence in their land was a "structure of the conjuncture" in Marshall Sahlins's sense: It was the point at which an indigenous cultural category was called upon to give meaning to a novel historical happening. But the moment villagers applied their concept of *save* to understand and interpret the presence and actions of white people, they changed the way in which *save* could be conceived. As soon as it became linked to the white man, the meaning of *save* came to be increasingly wrested away from the traditional contexts in which it previously had been articulated and understood, and eventually *save* came to be defined in opposition to those traditional contexts. Senior men and women, once considered to be exceptionally knowledgeable and accorded the most *save* in the village, now came gradually to be seen as *longlong/babasak* (stupid) and as purveyors of a useless and ultimately damaging way of thinking: The villagers, for example, destroyed all that remained of their traditional sacra after World War II because they heard that the cult leader "Yaring" had said that these things were "blocking" the return of the ancestors, who wanted to come back laden with cargo (Chapter 5). As young men returned from the plantations with small boxes of cargo (axes, steel tools, cloth, tinned foods, money), a new language comprehended in esoteric terms, and first-hand knowledge of a profoundly different, and infinitely more attractive lifestyle (that of the whites), their *save* came to be seen as superseding that of the old people, precisely because the *save* of these young men was seen to be of the same nature (or at least seen as having the potential to be of the same nature) as that of the white men, i.e., Christian, outward-oriented, and nontraditional. This compatibility between the *save* of young men and that of whites was underscored and strengthened each time white men had contact with the villagers. Priests spoke Tok Pisin to those who knew it best, and the positions of village authority instituted by the colonial powers (*luluai* and *tultul*) were available only to Tok Pisin speakers. The first *luluai* of Gapun, for example, was Waiki, one of the two men who first went away as plantation laborers.

As the village concept of *save* was undergoing a radical revaluation as a result of its being used to comprehend the presence of white people, the language of the white men was being meaningfully absorbed into the village context that most openly embodied and displayed *save* – i.e., oratories in the men's house. This absorption not only strengthened and reinforced the changes that were occurring in the meaning of *save;* by injecting Tok Pisin into oratorical speech, villagers also began to alter the means through which *save* could be expressed most effectively. From having been linked to warfare, initiation, the organization of funerary feasts – and verbal expression foremost through oratorical speech in Taiap – *save* now (while maintaining its associations to maleness and collectivism) became tied to Christianity, cash cropping, trying to become white – and verbal expression foremost through oratorical speech in increasing amounts of Tok Pisin.

As the expression of *save* became increasingly bound to Tok Pisin, the possibility arose of linguistically marking, in a similar manner, those aspects of the villagers' behavior that were considered *not* to be displays of *save*.

Like the original associations between *save* and Tok Pisin, the link between *hed* and Taiap had been available to be foregrounded by the villagers from the very beginning of their encounter with white men and Tok Pisin. For the first two or three decades after the first village men returned from the plantations, Tok Pisin was the exclusive property of males. Females did not begin actively using the language until after World War II. This meant that the linguistic behavior of males and females differed markedly for many years. This difference gave rise to a situation in which gender-based linguistic difference could be focused upon and exploited as a symbol of, or metaphor for, the gender difference itself.[1] Thus, as Tok Pisin increasingly came to be regarded as a symbol of maleness and *save,* a sociolinguistic space was created and eventually filled through an association of non-Tok Pisin speech with women and the numerous connotations that already surrounded them. In other words, the associations between women and *hed*, already salient in the traditional culture, were now strengthened and expressed by the fact that women did not know Tok Pisin and had *kros*es in Taiap.

Having marked both dimensions of the self linguistically, it now became possible for villagers to use Tok Pisin and Taiap as symbols of *save* and *hed* even in contexts other than those in which the links had originally developed. Thus, because *save* had come to be symbolized in important and salient ways by Tok Pisin, the use of that language even outside the context of oratory carried with it connotations of *save*. The vernacular, in turn, now carried its associations with *hed* to contexts that extended beyond talk by women. This process through which the two dimensions of self came to be differentiated linguistically has had far-reaching consequences for three major aspects of the villagers' verbal behavior: the rapidity with which and the manner in which Tok Pisin was allowed to invade the villagers' verbal repertoire, the villagers' code-switching patterns, and the ways language has come to be used and interpreted in child socialization patterns.

Incorporating Tok Pisin

The relative swiftness with which Tok Pisin was acquired by all villagers – including women, who never went off to plantations and who, before the advent of Tok Pisin, appear to have communicated with their neighbors by becoming multilingual in vernacular languages – is a function of the language's power to foreground the positive and socially valued dimension of the self. The connections that came to be sedimented out in Gapun between Tok Pisin and *save* resulted in that language crystallizing into a valuable possession to be acquired and displayed. The more Tok Pisin one was able to use, the less of a *bikhed* (big-headed, willful, stubborn, antisocial, and anti-Christian individual) and of a *bus kanaka* (country bumpkin, with all the attendant connotations of stupidity and laziness) one was able to present oneself as being.

In this light, it is noteworthy that the incorporation of Tok Pisin into the villagers' speech patterns did not develop into a rigid diglossic relationship in which Tok Pisin became a High language and Taiap a Low language, each being used in discrete and functionally separate domains. Instead, Tok Pisin became absorbed into the villagers' talk in such a way that there are constant mixes and switches between that language and the village vernacular. This form of incorporation is clearly linked to the symbolic associations ascribed to the two languages, in particular their links to self.

Although they are seen as conflicting, the two dimensions of self in Gapun are not ordered hierachically or perceived as being strictly separated. *Kros*es, for example, are inflammatory, socially disruptive, and considered to be the epitomy of *hed* in village opinion. But *kros*es are also, in some senses, displays of *save* as well, because after the protagonists have satisfied their desire to publicly abuse and accuse, the matter that provoked the *kros* is generally considered to be settled, or will result in some sort of settlement being arranged. It is considered to be far more dangerous when a person who feels wronged or offended does not air her or his grievance, because then the grievance will "remain in the stomach" (*stap long bel*) – the seat of one's emotions – and "give bad, i.e., antisocial thoughts" (*givim tingting nogut*), to the offended person. Unaired grievances frequently result in fights and/or, villagers believe, visits to sorcerers to have the offending person killed, sooner or later (cf. Besnier 1990, Boggs and Chun 1990, Watson-Gegeo and Gegeo 1990, White 1990).

Similarly, overt displays of *save* can sometimes be interpreted as containing dimensions of *hed*. Oratories that develop into harangues are occasionally perceived in this way, especially if the haranguer is not a big man of status or a skilled speaker. Another example of this is sometimes evident in food exchanges. In the food exchanges following a death or the settlement of a conflict, the kin groups involved are supposed to exchange roughly the same amount of food (both cooked and uncooked). An imbalance should, however, always be maintained in any single instance of exchange. In the case of a funerary exchange, the immediate kin (parents, children) and the matrilineal kin of the deceased

are expected to "settle" (*stretim*/*simb-*) the mourning of the joking kin
(the matrilineal line of the father; *wanpilai*/*jakum*) of the dead person
by presenting them with more food than they receive in return. In the
case of a conciliatory exchange, the close kin and matrilineal relatives
of the person(s), who are seen as bearing the most responsibility for
settling the conflict are expected to present the offended group with
more food than they receive in return. The receiving group always
immediately reciprocates such exchanges with food prestations of their
own, but these should not be on the same scale as the food they receive.
In this way, a debt remains pending, the exchange relationship is kept
open, and the receivers are expected to fully reciprocate and perhaps
even inflate the exchange relation later, when they are givers, i.e., next
time they find themselves on the side of the offenders or on the side of
a dead person. Occasionally, though, the receivers of food will "outdo"
(*antapim*) the givers by presenting them with what the givers agree is
simply too much food. This causes consternation and bad feelings, since
it is interpreted as a message that the givers have not been generous
and that the receivers are being willful and showing off. Such messages
are starkly out of place in food exchanges, which are seen as contexts
in which social bonding and group spirit – and, consequently, *save* – are
being embodied and displayed. Consequently, whenever this kind of
"outdoing" occurs, it results in many dissatisfied mumbles and disgruntled asides about the *hed* of the receiving group members.

The point here about language is that just as *hed* and *save* are not
absolute antimonies but rather two sides of the same coin or two dimensions of the same person, so are the languages that have come to
express those dimensions not kept separate. The more general point is
that cultural perceptions of the nature of language and the self may play
a more significant role than has generally been acknowledged in determining the course of language contact phenomena and the precise form
that these phenomena come to assume in a community.

Patterns of code-switching

As has been illustrated throughout this book, villagers' code-switching
patterns are extremely free-flowing and complex. One way of comprehending those patterns is to distinguish between two levels, or dimensions, of language usage and meaning. The first of these can be called
the "global," or "domain" (Fasold 1984: 183–6), level. This is the level
of usage and meaning on which villagers determine which of their languages should predominate across any given speech genre. On this level,
the salient associations that a speech genre per se has as a display of

hed or *save* constrain villagers' language choice (even as those associations are themselves reinforced and embodied in acting out those constraints). Thus the fact that oratory is strongly linked to *save* will ensure that Tok Pisin will predominate. Likewise, the fact that *kros*es are tied to and seen as expressive of a display of personal autonomy and *hed* will constrain speakers' use of Tok Pisin while they engage in this genre and will ensure that they mainly use the vernacular.

Co-occurring with these "global" considerations is another dimension of language usage and meaning that might be labeled the "interactional," or "rhetorical," level. This is the level of microanalysis, of the individual utterance. It is on this level that speakers exploit the possibilities of rhetorical effect available to them through their command of two languages. This exploitation may often be unconscious, as Gumperz (1982: 61) has pointed out. But it can also be influenced and triggered by cultural conventions such as concerns about internal harmony and balance (Chapter 3), or the desire to achieve rhetorical effects such as emphasis, drama, or gaining the floor.

A distinction between a "global" and an "interactional" dimension of language usage and meaning is useful when thinking about how Gapun villagers talk because it underscores the fact that the villagers can and do use language choice to express a variety of meanings on several levels simultaneously. These levels can intersect, as they do when Sake's sister Jari, in response to being shouted at by Sake and her parents, attempts to assert her autonomy by screaming in Taiap, "I'm gonna beat this baby and he's gonna die!" (Text 3.1; lines 76–7); or when Kruni switches to Tok Pisin to harangue the villagers that "This is your time now, Papua New Guinea, you're standing on your own feet – make your country" (Text 4.9; lines 50–1). Most frequently, however, these different meanings of usage and meaning do not neatly intersect, and the villagers' prime concern when code-switching is to convey rhetorical, not social, information.[2]

But although the "interactional," or "rhetorical," level is more important in accounting for the vast majority of particular instances of code-switching in the villagers' speech, the "global," or "domain," level is more significant in explaining language shift. Just as the initial incorporation of Tok Pisin into the villagers' speech was facilitated by the connotations that the language had acquired with *save*, so have those connotations come to influence how the villagers think about and use language. The more individuals wish to present themselves as having *save*, the more Tok Pisin they can choose to use. The combined effect of such decisions by individual speakers over countless interactions has resulted over time in more Tok Pisin being spoken in more contexts by more people. And the process is continuing. What may happen as less fluent Taiap speakers and increasing numbers of monolingual Tok Pisin speakers grow up and begin to take an active part in village life is that the "meanings" expressed by villagers through code-switching will become subject to a greater degree of negotiation and uncertainty. Because a growing number of speakers will not have enough control of Taiap to be able to code-switch rhetorically, this level of meaning may become increasingly less salient. The rhetorical dimensions of code-switching used by older speakers may come to be interpreted in "social" terms, and, as code-switching comes to be used more rarely, the majority of instances of such behavior may eventually be restricted to expressing information about social states and statuses.

Patterns of language socialization

The final major consequence that the linguistic marking of *hed* and *save* has had on the villagers is that it has affected language socialization practices. In their interactions with children, adults in Gapun act upon and reproduce their conceptions of what a person is, how a person should be treated, and how a person should express her- or himself. Parents project upon and re-create in their children the notions of *hed* and *save*. Babies are indulged and pampered so they won't get *kros,* and they are never forced to do anything, because people respect their personal autonomy, their *heds.* At the same time, because young children "have no *save,*" they are not spoken to or interacted with very much.

But the basic expectation of all parents is that their children will come to understand as they grow older that they must "suppress" their *hed* and show their *save.* Although there are many ways of showing *save,* the most common has come to be through the use of Tok Pisin in verbal interactions. And just as caregivers can choose to foreground their *save* by using Tok Pisin, so do parents unconsciously but deftly encourage children to show *save* – by speaking Tok Pisin. This encouragement takes its clearest form in parental interpretations of child vocalizations. The first three words a child is held to utter – long before children are, in fact, producing speech and at the stage in its development when the child is considered to embody *hed* – are in Taiap. Much later, when parents again begin attributing meaning to their children's vocalizations, this speech is now in Tok Pisin – and it occurs as parents begin to remark on the emergence or the "breaking open" of the child's *save.*

Like parents everywhere, adults in Gapun reproduce themselves and their ideas about themselves in their child-rearing practices. But because their concept of self has become split along linguistic lines, this reproduction is now generating change. As they have always done before, children in the village still come to understand that *hed* must be suppressed and that *save* should be displayed as they grow older. This much continues. What has changed is the fact that village parents now perceive the expression of *hed* to be linked to the village vernacular and the expression of *save* to be bound to Tok Pisin. So, what in actual practice comes to be "suppressed" in growing up is the Taiap language. And what is displayed is Tok Pisin. The continual reenactment of this process in village socialization patterns is the direct cause of language shift in Gapun.

The subtlety and complexity of this process is the reason why adult villagers do not understand it or are not really conscious of what is happening. Adults are doing nothing new, as far as they can see, when they raise their children. They accommodate the child's aggressive *hed* as they have always done, by anticipating its needs and desires so it doesn't have to get *kros*. And once the child's *save* starts to "break open," parents treat her or him much as their parents treated them. They gently structure their interactions with children in ways that foreground culturally valued ways of listening, extracting meaning from speech, reporting socially relevant information, and narrating detail. As far as linguistic input is concerned, parents do not appreciate that the bulk of their direct speech to children is not in the vernacular. Because they code-switch as much as they do in all their talk, adults are not aware that their code-switching patterns to children are systematically biased toward Tok Pisin. And even if they could somehow be made aware of this, their conception of knowledge as something generated from inside a child precludes adults from taking an active role in teaching their children language. As Sake's sister Erapo explained at one point, parents can teach their children to "call the names of things," but the children will only "start to learn" once their *save* breaks open inside them (Chapter 4). Children learn what they want to learn, regardless of what anyone else has to say about it. So adults are genuinely surprised when they notice that their children only speak Tok Pisin, and their own explanation that their children are strongly autonomous, stubborn, and simply unwilling to speak Taiap is logical and quite in line with their understandings of *hed*, of knowledge, and of the nature of children.

Culture change and language change

An overarching conclusion that can be drawn concerning the sociolinguistic situation in Gapun is that the intermeshing of cultural beliefs and the new social and linguistic realities that arose in the village upon the arrival in New Guinea of white colonialists has generated a dynamic

beyond the control or consciousness of anyone. The nature and complexity of such a dynamic has generally not been noted in the scholarly
literature on language shift. Therefore, one contribution that this case
study of a small group of people with a particular way of viewing themselves and the world can make to our understanding of language shift
is the documentation of the intricate ways in which people's interpretations of change affect how they talk to one another in mundane, day-
to-day interactions and how these patterns of interaction result over
time in language shift. This study of the process of language shift in
Gapun also raises a number of general points about the nature of shift,
and about the relationship between culture and linguistic change.

First, it is clear from the situation encountered in Gapun that the
macrosociological features (such as urbanization, industrialization, or
in- or out-migration) most often invoked to account for language shift
not only do not explain shift, as Gal (1979) has pointed out – these
features do not even have to be present for shift to occur. Although
present-day Gapun society is quite different from what it was at the
beginning of the century, the changes that have taken place there are
not primarily material transformations, and they are not the result of
drastic shifts in living standards, marriage patterns, or subsistence activities. The changes that have occurred in Gapun are in many ways a
result of the villagers' changing interpretations of their world.

Of course, like a great number of communities in late twentieth-
century Papua New Guinea, Gapun is rapidly changing, and it is not
improbable that macrosociological variables like industrialization or proletarianization would correlate significantly with language shift in a few
decade's time. For example, although men and women in the village
are as yet only very marginally involved in cash-generating enterprises,
they express a keen desire to shift away from subsistence agriculture to
cash cropping and, if they should ever get the chance, wage labor. From
friends and relatives in other villages, Gapuners have heard rumors of
Australian oil companies and Japanese timber corporations that pay
enormous sums of money for mining or logging rights on village lands.
These rumors are greeted with great enthusiasm in the village, because
it is believed that such companies constitute yet another newly uncovered
"road" to the cargo. "The companies" (*ol kampani*), the villagers tell
one another, are attempting to bypass the missions and the government,
and they are coming to "give" Papua New Guineans lots of money and
build "highways" for them. Every now and again someone wonders
aloud when these companies are going to get around to coming to Gapun
to present the villagers with their share of the money and with an impressive highway through their boggy land.

Another change that has been gaining momentum in Gapun since the 1970s is one affecting village residence and marriage patterns. Increasingly, young men in their late teens and early twenties who have been to school are showing impatience with village life and the demands placed on them by the big men that they use their "standard six education" to help make Gapun "come up." To escape the big men and to look for adventure, several of these young men habitually leave Gapun for extended periods of time, visiting friends or relatives in faraway villages nearer to urban centers like Madang or Wewak, returning to the village only briefly and occasionally before leaving again for somewhere else. When these young men marry, the chances are great that their wives will be women from outside Gapun. Young women also express a preference to marry men from outside the village. Everyone knows that most adolescent women are slyly on the lookout for suitable spouses from Wongan or some other "water" village, and this causes much consternation and dismay among the big men of several communities (Chapter 2). The preferences and actions of these villagers will continue to result in increasing numbers of exogamous marriages and, probably, in increasing out-migration by young villagers. Even if young men and women "pull" their spouses to Gapun to live, such mixed marriages will result in growing numbers of non-Taiap speaking adults living in the village.

Yet another change underway in Gapun is one that is affecting village social relationships. The general tenor of relations between villagers seems to be shifting away from a stress on village- and kin-based relations of solidarity toward a new emphasis on the autonomy of the nuclear family and on voluntary, monetarily oriented associations, such as the "youth group" discussed in Chapter 4. One sign of this shift of emphasis in village relationships has been the shift from communal maternity houses to small, private ones (Chapter 2). Another sign, which villagers note and occasionally comment upon, is the fact that most village men no longer regularly spend their evenings in the men's house socializing with one another. The majority of men under 30 prefer to stay at home after their evening meal, or to go with their wives to the house of a close relative, where they sit on the veranda and *stori*. None of these men show any interest at all in attaining the traditional big man status, which is hard work, and which involves devoting a great amount of energy and work to fostering a sense of community in the village, through skillful oratories and through dispays of generosity such as frequent distributions of cooked food to men who have congregated to socialize in the men's house. The only man in Gapun who still regularly sends food to the men's house is Kem. Older big men, like Kruni, no longer work sago and therefore cannot directly influence its distribution, and younger men never send anything to the men's house unless it is a payment for some type of work they want the men to help them perform.

In addition to a lack of interest in those traditional forms of status that in many ways symbolized the village as a collective, villagers are also increasingly downplaying certain behavioral patterns that used to reinforce collective identity.[3] The custom of meat distribution, for example, has become severely undermined in recent years. Traditionally, whenever a wild boar or a cassowary was killed, the hunter and his wife were obliged to send some part of a carcass (even if only a few pieces of skin) to each household in the village. By the mid- to late 1980s, however, it had become increasingly common for villagers to lie about their hunting success, "hiding" meat in the forest and distributing surreptitious chunks only to the households of their siblings. Some villagers frequently distributed nothing, claiming that they had to raise cash for some socially acceptable purpose such as their children's school fees and that they needed to sell the meat at a market in order to raise the money. (Such announced trips to the market were, in fact, rarely undertaken, and the meat withheld from distribution for this reason almost inevitably ended up being consumed by the family of the hunter). By 1987, villagers had even begun selling meat to one another for small sums of money. The introduction of money into village social relations in this way is a highly inflammatory issue in Gapun (mostly because not all villagers earn money; see Table 1.1 and Sake's *kros* about her house described in Chapter 4), but money and the ability to earn it has, not surprisingly, assumed connotations of *save* in the villagers' discourse. The incorporation into the villagers' relationships of the idea of money as yet another expression of *save* is clearly an antecedent to an increased monetization of those relationships.

Changes of this kind strongly suggest that had I arrived in Gapun in twenty years' time, I would in all probability have encountered a community with a significant percentage of exogamy, a weak sense of community, little kin-based solidarity, substantial differences in family incomes, and with a vernacular language spoken by no one under 30. In this context, correlations between language shift and in-migration, or proletarianization, or in-group socioeconomic differenciation would have been easy to make. What I would have missed in making such correlations, however, is that the groundwork for the changes that I observed had been prepared long before those changes actually occurred. In this sense, Gapun might be held up as a case in which the macrosociological changes that are occurring can be said not to have caused language shift, but rather, to have been *caused by* shift: in attitudes, perceptions of self, and ideas about language.

Finally, this study of language shift in Gapun suggests a number of specific cultural and linguistic characteristics that may render a community more or less "open" to shift. Those characteristics include:[4]

1) The type and predominance of code-switching practices in a community. In a community like Gapun, where villagers alternate between languages freely and continually in a single stretch of speech or discourse, language shift may occur more quickly than in communities with little code-switching. While the existence of extensive code-switching patterns in itself may not necessarily result in shift, this characteristic, combined with other ideas and patterns of language use (such as those discussed in the points below) may lead caregivers to provide their children with heavily imbalanced verbal input and not be aware of this. It may also give rise to a situation in which children do not need to learn the vernacular in order to follow and understand the oral performances of adults, since things said in the vernacular are frequently repeated in the majority language.

2) The degree to which the socialization of children is in the hands of other children. In Gapun, as in perhaps the majority of non-Western middle-class societies, children, from the age of 8 months, spend at least as much time with their preschool sisters as they do in the care of their mothers. In this village, the direct linguistic input that children receive from these older girls is much richer and more varied than what they hear from their mothers or from any other adult. But because these girls only actively command Tok Pisin, it is the only language they use to talk to their infant charges. As a result, infants rapidly become socialized into hearing and responding to that language in their play and their interactions with their caregivers. A general point here is that in communities like Gapun where children play a major role in the socialization of their siblings, once language shift begins and monolingual children appear in the community, the shift will continue at an accelerating rate.

3) The degree of multilingualism. In Gapun, speaking many languages is the norm, and multilingualism was traditionally something to be proud of. Like their founding ancestor, Kambedagam, villagers commanded an impressive array of languages. A consequence of this norm of multilingualism for language shift is that if people are used to having many languages spoken around them, then the phenomenon of a child talking to her parents in a language other than the one she was addressed in is unlikely to evoke notice or complaint. Also, in such communities, a sociolinguistic norm of accommodating others in terms of language choice will affect the rate of shift, because it will influence caregivers to accommodate their children by speaking to them in the majority language, if the children address them in that language.

4) The degree to which children are considered able to be taught.   In communities like Gapun, where the acquisition of knowledge is considered to be a personal process that occurs only when *save* breaks open, and where caregivers do not see themselves as teachers, it would be unthinkable for parents, even if they became sensitized to the shift and wanted to do something to prevent it, to suddenly decide to "make" their children start speaking the vernacular. This kind of understanding of knowledge, especially when it is coupled with interpersonal norms of noninterference in the affairs of others, will have decisive effects on the speed at which language shift, once begun, will progress.

5) The way in which the expression of positive and highly valued aspects of the self comes to be bound to expression through a particular language.   In the literature on language shift, this positive aspect of self is usually discussed in terms of ethnicity: Speakers of a minority language come to be characterized and come to see themselves as "fishers," or "peasants," or as some other category defined as inferior to those statuses represented by speakers of the majority language. To present themselves in a positive light, then, speakers of minority languages speak the majority language.

   This work suggests, however, that ethnicity is only one possible dimension of the process through which speakers of a minority language come to denigrate their own vernacular and assign a high value to the majority language. Furthermore, "ethnicity" may misrepresent the cultural underpinnings upon which local definitions of positive self-value rest. For example, if the changes taking place in the verbal behavior of Gapuners were analyzed in terms of ethnicity, it would be possible to claim that the villagers are shifting languages because they are shifting ethnic identity from what they see as *bus kanaka* (country bumpkin) villagers to modern citizens of Papua New Guinea. While this observation is in some sense accurate, it overlooks the crucial point that the "ethnic" statuses of both *bus kanaka* villagers and modern citizens of Papua New Guinea are themselves embedded in and articulated through the villagers' concepts of *hed* and *save*. *Bus kanaka*s, like the mysterious "upper Sepiks" whom the villagers occasionally discuss (Chapter 2), are *bus kanaka*s not because they are perceived to be ethnically different from Gapuners, but because they, like children, have not yet developed and fully taken advantage of their capacity of *save*. Gapuners perceive no intrinsic difference between themselves and *bus kanaka*s; they see the "upper Sepiks" in themselves and themselves – their capacity to change and be modern – in the "upper Sepiks." A focus on ethnicity, on the negotiation of boundaries between an "us" and a "them," would impose a dichotomy on a relationship between groups whom villagers view as similarly constituted and in possession of a common set of dispositions and capacities. A lesson to be gleaned from this example is that shift in ethnic identification as an explanatory device for language shift is not always illuminating. Instead of concentrating so intently on concepts like boundary maintenance and shift, future researchers of language shift may find it useful to decompose those concepts by devoting more time to exploring how locally grounded conceptualizations of self generate understandings of difference, and how those understandings of difference in turn influence a community's interpretation of its social world and of the type of verbal behavior that speakers feel presents them in the most positive light in that social world.[5]

6) The way change is conceptualized. During their fieldwork in Mexico, Hill and Hill (1986: 402–440) found that the Mexicano speakers with whom they worked do not view giving up Mexicano in favor of Spanish as especially dramatic or upsetting, partly because they see language change as little different from certain other types of change, such as changes in personal preferences, clothing styles, and types of houses. Hill and Hill argue that such an attitude has facilitated language shift because it has allowed Mexicano speakers to shift the basis of their ingroup solidarity relatively easily from expression through language (or clothing, or house type) to expression through some other medium, such as participation in the ritual kinship system (*compadrazgo*) that exists throughout the area.

Although the people documented in this study have ideas about change that are very different from those of Mexican peasants, the way the men and women of Gapun conceive of change has had similar repercussions for the way language shift is occurring in the village. The dominant conceptual framework in Gapun for interpreting and discussing change is one in which change is seen as something swift, meaningful, desirable, and dramatic. Expressions of this idea are evident in several domains of village life: from the contention that *save* "breaks open" in children, changing them in important ways from egocentric creatures to humans with the potential for social awareness; to the traditional initiation rites for boys and girls, which emphasized seclusion from everyday life followed by a sudden return to the village as men and women; to the belief that villagers change skin and become white when they die; to the hope that the millenium will soon arrive and transform everything in the villagers' world. In a context like this, where change is interpreted as meaningful and is accepted and even anticipated, language shift, once under way, can take root and spread in fertile cultural soil. The villagers' understanding of change in general shapes and constrains their understanding of linguistic change, making it difficult and incongruous for anyone in Gapun to view language change and the current shift to Tok Pisin in a predominantly negative light. In fact, such an opinion is never expressed in the village. Some villagers may occasionally find it annoying that their children or grandchildren don't speak the vernacular and perhaps can't even respond to a command in Taiap, but no one ever reifies language shift as an issue and talks about it as negative in itself.

Because change in the direction of white people is something that should happen and will happen, and inasmuch as language shift has become one element of the more profound metamorphosis that villagers believe to be on its way, Gapuners have gently but decisively shifted one important basis of their in-group solidarity away from *a language* as such to *the culturally correct use of language in interaction*. Until the 1970s, there was a direct and readily apparent isomorphism between being a Gapuner and speaking Taiap. Since that time, however, the appearance in the village of children who do not command the vernacular has meant that the idea of isomorphism between the village vernacular and identity as a villager is becoming increasingly diluted. Being a villager is no longer so much a matter of speaking Taiap as it is one of knowing how to use language appropriately in verbal interactions, especially in the verbal genre of *stori*.

Related to this shift is a change in another salient dimension of what it means to be a Gapuner: the relationship of an individual to the land. One of the defining features of a Gapun villager is land rights, and each person recognized as a Gapuner can claim access to and use of areas of land owned by one's matrilineal clan. Villagers continue to maintain a strong sense of identification with their land. What is changing, however, is their understanding of what their land is good for. From having been valued primarily for its links to the ancestors and for the richness of its wildlife and the fertility of its soil for sago palms and gardens, land in Gapun is rapidly being revalued in terms of its market potential. "Money is here with us, in our land" (*Moni i stap long yumi, long graun bilong yumi*) is a frequently recurring reminder in village oratories. What men who use this phrase mean is that land can be deployed to help Gapun "come up": It can be used to "pull" money into the village, to "fill up [the] village's bank" through cash cropping and perhaps through selling it to any interested "companies," should these ever get around to making an appearance in the village. Revaluing the land in this way will undoubtedly result in the weakening and eventual dissolution of the links that still exist in village thought between the land and the Taiap language. And when Taiap has lost the ability to symbolize the land, it will have lost the final affirmative value that it retains in the community. Seeing the land in a new light has already had one sociolinguistic consequence – it has resulted in the villagers' being abandoned by most of the Taiap-speaking *masalai* and other spirits of the forest who used to make their homes on Gapun land. Older men sometimes wonder quizzically where these spirits have gone: They no longer encounter them or their tracks when they travel through the rainforest to hunt or work sago. The spirits must be "hiding," the men conclude, clearing off the land in deference to the white man, who has come to Papua New Guinea to "change" it.

The end of Taiap?

What then is the future of the Taiap language? Is it on the final path to extinction, or can it possibly, somehow, be revived and maintained? Predictions about language shift are notoriously hazardous to make, and this is especially true when the shift is still in its initial phases, as is the case in Gapun. It was noted in Chapter 6 that it is not unthinkable that the present generation of nonvernacular speakers, especially those little girls who have a very highly developed passive competence in the vernacular, might increasingly learn to activate their knowledge of Taiap and perhaps even pass it on to their own children. Developments of this nature are known to occur in Papua New Guinea. Litteral (1990: 377), for example, cites the linguist Les Bruce as reporting to him that "many Alamblak [1,000 speakers, East Sepik Province] teenage boys were said to speak the vernacular poorly with much Tok Pisin influence because of attending school but when they became men and participated in male activities they moved toward more acceptable vernacular speech" (see also Hill and Hill 1986: 121–2).

We cannot know with certainty what will happen to Taiap in the years to come. We can, however, make educated guesses, and we can note that what, in fact, already has occurred in Gapun is a shift in language acquisition patterns: For the first time ever, children born and raised in Gapun are not acquiring Taiap as their first language. This shift in acquisition is being accepted, indeed, facilitated by adults, despite their firmly stated wishes that their children speak the vernacular. Given the dominant cultural associations documented throughout this book between *hed* and Taiap, and between *save* and Tok Pisin; given the ways these two languages were used in Gapun at the end of the 1980s; and given the ideas that the villagers hold about children, knowledge, personhood, language and change, it seems unlikely that children will ever be confronted with serious, consistent demands to speak the vernacular. As for the children themselves, they are now growing up in a context in which their relationships with their friends and relatives become established and elaborated through the use of Tok Pisin. One can doubt whether these children will ever have any significant reason in the future to alter the linguistic basis of those relationships.

Other factors that suggest a continuing demise of Taiap include the extremely small size of Gapun village, the only place where the vernacular is spoken; the increasing tendency toward exogamous marriages; the trends toward the atomization and monetization of village social relationships; and the villagers' active striving for further incorporation into the market economy. The coalescence of all these factors suggests a dark future for the Taiap language, and if the present patterns persist, it is likely that the vernacular will no longer exist as a language of everyday communication in thirty years' time.

Change, the villagers remind each other and hope, will come. But the changes that await them in the near future if present trends continue – proletarianization, a breakdown of traditional social bonds and a monetization of village relationships, frustration as what they perceive to be their material needs cannot be met by their cash incomes, the continuing demise of their language and traditions, and perhaps even the loss and destruction of large areas of their land by timber companies or multinational oil corporations – are not quite what anyone in Gapun has in mind or is prepared for.

At one point during our many conversations, Kruni's wizened old brother, Raia, surprised me by suddenly and uncharacteristically expressing great bitterness over the fact that the missionaries had caused the villagers to abandon their traditions and their cult deities (*tambaran*). Raia confided that in 1954, the year after his father, Aiarpa, died, he met a young *masta* from England in the town of Angoram. This *masta* told Raia that the missionaries lied to the people of Papua New Guinea. Villagers didn't have to devalue and abandon their traditional customs, this man said. Papua New Guineans, traditional religious rites and ways of thought, and even black skin were not inferior to or less valuable than Europeans, Christianity, and white skin.

"What do you think about that?" I asked Raia, taken aback by this insight, which I had never heard expressed by anyone in Gapun. "Do you think his talk was true?"

Old Raia chewed his betel nut slowly and was silent for a moment. I could follow his gaze as he looked away from me, out over the village where he had lived his life: over a small group of children near Sopak's house laughing and teasing one another in Tok Pisin, past the rickety village church where a picture of an ivory-skinned Jesus, donated by a missionary, hangs on the wall next to the altar, and finally toward his brother Kruni's men's house, where everyone knew that the village *komiti* would call a meeting later that day to talk of going to Wongan and cut grass at the school. When he did answer my question, Raia's voice was a tired, strained whisper. "I think this," he said softly, looking down: "I hope it's not true."

Appendix: On being a ghost

Since the early 1980s, there has been a dramatic increase in the concern with which anthropologists approach their representations of self, the Other, and the anthropological encounter in the writing of their ethnographies. The provocative work of scholars like James Clifford, George Marcus, and others, as well as the challenges posed since the 1970s by feminists in the field, have forced anthropologists to abandon any pretense of "objectivity" and to explore the implications of the understanding that they, in their work and in their writing, "construct" the Other.[1]

One important consequence of that exploration has been the injection of the ethnographer into the ethnography. Numerous writers have pointed out that throughout much of anthropology's history, acceptance of a positivist paradigm and the attempt to appear objective precluded the overt presence of the ethnographer in anthropological works. Because ethnographies attempted to be and were taken to be scientific treatises, explicitly subjective reflections of the author — if they were at all lengthy and if they occurred in any part of the book except the preface or the pastoral paragraphs at the beginning of Chapter 1 – have been long regarded as eccentric, unseemly, and unscientific. The current boom of ideas concerning the importance of reflexivity in anthropological work has ensured that this is no longer the case, and one of the most characteristic features of anthropological monographs published during the 1980s has been the (sometimes overpowering) presence of the ethnographer.

In this contemporary context, this book about Gapun may seem somewhat unfashionable. I have decided to present the material from the village with as little overt reference to myself as possible, and with no explicit textual tags pointing out how I arrived at the interpretations I present in the book. Instead, I have focused the text on examples of speech produced by the villagers and explained this speech by contextualizing it in the types of ideas I believe make it seem sensible to the villagers. The major motivation for writing the book in this way has been my conviction that, by presenting direct quotes and translations of what they villagers say, readers are placed in a better position to judge the soundness of the ethnographer's analysis and to imagine alternative interpretations. I have chosen this style of ethnographic writing in full awareness that it is a representational device, not a covert claim to stolid objectivity or noninvolvement in the village community.[2] At the same time, however, the central position that ideas about cargo and white people hold in the lives of the villagers makes it important that I clarify what my status as a ghost in the village involved and how it influenced my work and my relationships with the villagers.

My assignment as a ghost arose partly from a series of circumstances beyond my control that were connected to my arrival in the village. In order to find my way to Gapun from the provincial capital of Wewak, I sought out the Minister of Planning and Development, whose name had been given to me in Australia. This man, Mr. Tony Power, kindly agreed to help me get to the village, arranging for his brother-in-law to drive me as far as the Sepik-River village of Taway, where I would be able to hire an outboard-motor-driven canoe that would take me downriver to Gapun.

In Taway it turned out that the two men who knew the way to Gapun did so because they had a distant relative who was married to a Gapun woman, and they had once been to the village visiting him. So when we finally arrived in Gapun the next day after a hellish journey through log-clogged waterways, followed by a never-ending trek through waist-deep mud, the first thing these men did was install me in the men's house and send a child to go find their relative.

By that point, I was utterly exhausted and in a kind of stuporous daze from hunger and disorientation. My skills in Tok Pisin were minimal, so about all I could say to the curious villagers was that no, I was not a priest, which was the first question they all asked. I hung dully in the background while my guides (who had been informed by Tony Power's brother-in-law, who had spoken to me in English) presented the villagers with some sort of explanation of who I was, what I had come for, and that I would like to stay. This story was told first to the men and women who had begun to cluster in and around the men's house, and it was later carefully repeated to the relative of my guides when he arrived at the village from his garden. This relative of theirs, my guides from Taway had decided, would look after me during my stay in the village.

The distant relative into whose hands I had been passed turned out to be Allan Kasia, a man from the Sepik village of Mangan who was married to Kruni's formidable daughter Sake and who had been "pulled" from his village to come live with her. It so happened that Sake had had an older sister named Aioma, who had died a few years previous to my arrival in the village, shortly after giving birth to a boy. This child, whom Sake assumed mothering responsibilities for, died as well, several months after his mother. Apparently, villagers decided very quickly that I must be this dead child returned to life in new white skin. My sudden, unannounced appearance in the village, my interest in the language and kinship relations, my eating the same food as the villagers (something no white person in their experience had ever done, with the exception of Japanese soldiers during World War II), and my one unfortunate attempt to flee into solitude by finding a secluded spot in what I later discovered was the village graveyard, were all enough to confirm the suspicions of the villagers.[3]

Once it had been agreed that I was a ghost, the tale of my arrival in the village gradually became reconstituted in characteristic Gapun fashion to conform with this consensus. By the end of my stay in the village, people were telling one another, me, and anyone else they could get to listen that I had arrived in Gapun as a mere "baby" who "hadn't yet shaved," that I had promptly and pointedly asked to see my "mother," Sake, the moment I first entered the village (in village kinship terminology, children call all their mother's sisters "mother"), and that I spoke fluent Taiap from almost the first day of my arrival.

After they informed me of their understanding of the nature of my being, in the manner described in the prologue to this book, the fact that I was taken to be Sake's dead sister's dead child was not explicitly raised again by either myself or any of the villagers throughout most of my stay in Gapun. For a long time I was uncertain as to exactly what or who they thought I was. Then, in April 1987, during the spate of millenarian activity described in Chapter 5, I found out.

One evening as I was writing in my journal, a young woman in her twenties suddenly stumbled up into my house. This in itself was unusual, because women who came to my house almost never came alone, and especially not in the early evening, when most of them were busy preparing the evening meal for their families. What was even more unusual, however, was that my unexpected visitor wandered heavily around the house saying nothing except *"ples de Rod"* (praise the Lord), which she kept repeating in a catatonic monotone. After bumping into my mosquito net, my hearth, and my table, this woman then approached and bumped into me. She bent over at the waist and touched her forehead to my arm. She repeated this movement several times, while she intoned in solemn Tok Pisin:

I know about you. I know about you. Jesus is in my stomach (*bel*). I know about you. Jesus told me that when I die I'm going to go and be with you. Now

I'm revealing that talk. When I die I'm going to be with you. I'm going to go to Heaven. I'm going to go to that good place where you live. I know about your mother. I know about your mother. Aioma [Sake's dead sister] is your mother. Aioma is your mother.

By the time she got as far as "revealing" the name of my "mother," this woman was kneeling in front of me, rocking steadily back and forth.

A similar revelation occurred a few months later. Shortly before I was due to leave the village to return to Sweden, the villagers sponsored an all-night *singsing* (round of traditional singing and dancing) on my behalf. After the dancing had finished the following day, another young woman announced that she had seen "the spirit of Aioma" staring at me and crying from a darkened corner near the men's house at one point during the night. This vision was corroborated by several other villagers.

Despite my initial apprehensions about what the people of Gapun might expect or demand from a ghost, this status affected my relations with the villagers in much less dramatic ways than I had feared. If anything, their identification of me as one of their own (albeit in an altered state) seemed to predispose the men and women in Gapun to accept me into their community with a friendliness, graciousness, and ease that I found surprising and touching.

My white skin, however, starkly affected my general role in village interactions. I realized very early on in my conversations with the villagers that in order for me to understand their interpretation of the world, I would have to be ignorant. I would have to pretend not to know about many of the things that the villagers asked me about. Inanity is a difficult and uncomfortable role to consciously affect as a central dimension of one's identity, but in Gapun it was absolutely necessary that I be understood as unknowledgeable and inexperienced. There are two reasons why this is so, both of which are directly related to Gapuners' ideas about white people.

First, at the beginning of my stay in Gapun, villagers regarded me as an authority on the issues in which they were most interested, namely Christianity and the life and ways of white people. Like missionaries, patrol officers, carving buyers, and other whites whom they occasionally encountered, I was carefully scrutinized and gently pumped for the kinds of knowledge that the villagers believe is being hidden from them. In trying to answer the villagers' questions to the best of my ability, I quickly noticed two things: that the types of questions they asked seemed generated out of a number of assumptions about Christianity and the nature of white people that were very unfamiliar to me, and that some of what I told the villagers (such as a description of subways) was rapidly accepted and repeated on all sorts of occasions, whereas other facts (such as my insistence that white people had to work in order to earn money) received little response and were soon forgotten.

I found myself unable to get at the villagers' underlying assumptions about Christianity and white people. Asking someone, "How do you think white people live?" or requesting that that person "Tell me about Jesus" was impossible so long as I was considered to be the authority on such matters. Villagers either shrugged their shoulders and did not answer such questions, or, if they did answer them, they seemed to regard the questions as a kind of test and responded with recitations of what they remembered of Bible stories or priestly sermons heard long ago. Understanding this, I changed my interactive strategy and became vacuous. Instead of trying to answer the questions that villagers asked me, I now responded by explaining that I did not know. Happily, this was immediately accepted by the villagers, who explained my ignorance by bemoaning the fact that I was so young, much too young to have been informed of the answers to their questions by the "big men" in my "country." So abandoning hope that I would be able to inform them, the men and women of Gapun cheerfully took it upon themselves to enlighten me: about the world, about the Christian gods, and about the lives of white people. The information gathered in this type of inter-actional framework forms the basis of this book.

The second reason why it was essential that I adopt a pose of ignorance in my dealings with the villagers was because of their very strongly held belief that they are lied to and deceived at every turn by white people and by fellow "black-skinned" Papua New Guineans who have somehow acquired knowledge (*save*) about the ways of white people. This notion of being lied to is an extremely salient interpretive framework for every-one in Gapun, and villagers use it habitually to explain away any stories or ideas that too strongly contradict their own understanding of the way things are. To have attempted to answer the villagers' questions about Christianity and white people would have placed me in the position of continually undermining their already well-established ideas about the world, and this would inevitably have resulted in my being categorized, along with most other white people they have ever encountered, as someone who was "hiding talk" from them.

Gathering language data

My pattern of work in Gapun oscillated between socializing with and sometimes tape-recording village men and women in their homes, in the men's house, and as they traveled to other villages and to and from

the forest; eliciting and transcribing the vernacular language; and recording and transcribing caregiver–child interactions.

This latter type of work was by far the most time-consuming. Because
I was interested in understanding the interactional patterns that result
in monolingual children, my original research plan was patterned after
the work on language socialization done by Bambi Schieffelin among
the Kaluli of Papua New Guinea (Schieffelin 1979). Thus, soon after
arriving in Gapun, I chose five children from different families between
the ages of 18 and 31 months and set about recording them.

The goal was to obtain a monthly sample of three hours of speech
for each child. The recordings were planned to take place over a period
of three consecutive days for each child. A typical recording session
began as soon as it became light enough to see my notebook and the
counter on my tape-recorder (about 6:30 A.M.) and continued until about
5:30 P.M., by which time it had usually become too dark to see anything.
Having obtained the consent of the child's parents the day before I came
to record, I would arrive with tape recorder, microphone, and notebook
in hand, and I would settle myself into a corner near the hearth, which
was where most early morning interaction occurred. Throughout the
day I moved around with the child and her or his caregivers and recorded
any time the child I was interested in engaged in extended periods of
speech or when extensive verbal interactions involving the child occurred. While recording, I took continual notes specifying context, participants, spatial placement, and nonverbal behavior, matching these
notes to the counter on my tape recorder. Even while not recording, I
jotted down brief interactions between children and others, as well as
general observations about the behavior and speech of children and
those people who were around the children.

As soon as possible after the original recordings were made, I transcribed and translated the tapes into Tok Pisin with the help of the mother
or, on some occasions, the father of the child whom I had recorded. Transcription and translation work proved to be an enormously laborious and
tedious task both for myself and for the women and men with whom I
worked, and even though I paid them for this work, I am, like Bambi
Schieffelin (1990: 27), truly amazed that the villagers so patiently put up
with it. In some cases, such as in Sake's sister-in-law Tambong's family,
where several vernacular languages in addition to Tok Pisin were commonly used in interactions between adults and with children, transcription took up to twenty hours per hour of recorded speech. As time went
on and I gradually became more proficient in understanding the Taiap
vernacular, transcription time was reduced, but it never became less than
twelve hours per hour of recorded speech.

Despite the time it took and the tedium it involved, the process of transcription and translation was one of my most important sources of information for determining how the villagers viewed themselves, their children, and their language. It was during the recording and transcribing sessions that I first became aware of the *hed–save* dichotomy, for example. I thus thoroughly agree with Schieffelin (1990: 31), who, writing about her experiences of transcription among the Kaluli, remarks that:

> It should be emphasized that the preparation of an annotated transcript is not merely a mechanical data-collecting task but is itself a deeply ethnographic process. Annotation and translation require an ongoing discussion with native speakers about the significance of recorded events, culturally recognized types of speech interactions, and named discourse strategies, all of which contribute . . . to the interpretation of conduct and speech. [See also Merlan and Rumsey 1991: 243–4; Ochs 1979.]

Unfortunately, in spite of the value of recording and transcribing speech directed at and produced by children, my original plan of recording each of the five children that I had chosen once a month over a twelve-month period quickly proved to be impossible, not least because of the time it took to transcribe the tapes. It became clear that if I had pursued my original plan, I would be doing nothing else in the field except recording and transcribing. Because I was alone during most of my time in Gapun, however, and because I also needed to conduct a more general ethnographic study of the villagers in order to be able to contextualize and understand their language socialization patterns, it simply was not feasible to record as much as I had hoped to. In addition, a child's extended sickness or a family's sudden departure from Gapun as a result of conflicts or to visit relatives in Wongan made regular recording impossible anyway.

By the end of my stay in Gapun, I had recorded and transcribed 91 hours of speech, of which 37 hours are caregiver–child interactions; 12 hours are samples of natural speech between villagers in the men's house, in informal settings, and during *kros*es; and 42 hours are stories and myths told in both Tok Pisin and Taiap and interviews between villagers and myself in Tok Pisin. Some of my observations about children's speech are based on longitudinal data from four children: Sopak's daughter Masito (recorded in April, May, July, October, November 1986 and March 1987); Tambong's son Bapong and his little brother Bini (recorded in March, April, June, October 1986 and March 1987), and Paso's son David (recorded in April, July, October, November 1986 and January 1987). I also recorded in other households with small children, because after several months in Gapun, it seemed to me that caregivers varied in the amount and kinds of talk they directed at their children. Some mothers, like Sopak and Tambong, directed speech to their young children relatively often. Others, like Paso and a few of the other mothers, were less concerned with talking to their young children and could spend whole days saying very little to their toddlers. In order to understand how much of this variation was due to personality differences and how much it could be related to local ideas about children and language, I recorded during a three-day period at least once in virtually every household in the village that contained a child between the ages of 1 and 4 years. It is on the basis of these recordings and the notes made while observing caregiver–child interactions that I generalize about village language socialization patterns, even as I point out where these patterns vary.

Notes

Introduction

1   Through calculations based on more extensive data than were available to Sankoff, Laycock (1982: 37) revises this figure and estimates that 40 percent of the languages in Papua New Guinea are spoken by less than 500 speakers.

2   See Edwards 1985: 80 for a recent application of this line of argument in relation to Nigeria.

3   A similar conclusion concerning the relationship between language and boundary-marking has also been reached by linguists concerned with the extremely linguistically diverse situation among Australian Aborigines (Brandl and Walsh 1982; Sansom 1980: 38), and by those studying linguistic diversity in the Amazon basin (Jackson 1983, 1989).

4   The following entry in District Officer James Olifend's patrol report of the lower Sepik area, dated 8 March 1919, gives some idea of what Papua New Guineans had to face from the European and Australian colonial powers:

> Thursday, 13/2/19. Again visited ARAMOT [a village near the Murik Lakes. Olifend had passed through the village the previous day, but everyone fled into the jungle upon seeing him], and found village still deserted. Sent talk to bush by resident Missionary, Rev. Father SCHMIDT, that if the natives did not return to their village I would cook it [i.e., burn it down]. Waited 3 hours. Messages of both Tul Tul [a village official appointed by the Australians] and Father Schmidt received with sullenness and threats. Cooked village. Called at JANEMOT, and WOKEMOT and instructed the Tul Tuls to work on road to KAWP, and to clean up their respective villages. Proceeded on to DARPOAP....

[I am greatful to Hank Nelson for informing me of the existence of this report and to Michael Pigott for obtaining it for me.]

5   For a variety of opinions about this, see Chowning 1983; Goulden 1990; Keesing 1988; Mosel 1980; Mühlhäusler 1985c; Reesink 1990; Walsh 1978.

6   Even those who appreciated Tok Pisin's communicative power were usually patronizing in their assessments of the language. Margaret Mead, for example, explained for European readers that "Talk-Boy," as she calls it (referring to the fact that the language was spoken by Papua New Guinean men who worked for Australians and Europeans – all of whom were "boys" in the eyes of whites), was a "stark, unadorned language, without euphemism, without delicacy; racy, picturesque, exceedingly adequate, musical when well spoken, but withal graceless" (1931: 150). Mühlhäusler (1979:

276

103–140) provides a catalogue of the attitudes that have surrounded Tok Pisin over the years. See also Wurm 1985.

7 See Dimmendaal 1989 for comparative examples from Eastern Africa.

8 The figure of eighty-nine represents the total number of Taiap speakers – even those fluent in the language who do not reside in Gapun have been counted here.

9 See, for example, Dorian 1978; Dressler and Wodak-Leodolter 1977; Menn 1989; Romaine 1989; Schmidt 1985: 215–18; Trudgill 1978; Voegelin and Voegelin 1977.

10 For example, Fishman 1964, 1966; Lieberson 1980.

11 One study on language shift that explicitly confronts this issue is Gal's 1979 monograph on Hungarian–German language shift in Austria. Gal employs the concept of social network to account for speakers' language choices. Developing a line of argument similar to that known within sociolinguistics as "accommodation theory" (Giles, Bourhis, and Taylor 1977), Gal makes the point that "speakers' linguistic behaviors are constrained and shaped by the sorts of social contacts they maintain" (131–2). Using local criteria, Gal divided the people with whom she worked in the town of Oberwart into "peasants" and "nonpeasants," and she determined that "[f]or most informants the more peasants there were in their social networks, the more they used Hungarian, and the fewer peasants there were in their networks, the less they used Hungarian" (141). The concepts of "power code" (Spanish) and "solidarity code" (Mexicano) that Hill and Hill (1986) use to account for patterns of language choice among Mexicano speakers are also an attempt to explain how ethnic consciousness can come to affect intragroup communication.

12 The only partial exceptions to this of which I am aware is the work done on Australian Aboriginal languages by Schmidt (1985), who describes the language used by Dyirbal adults and adolescents, and by Bavin (1989), who writes about children's acquisition of Walpiri. Both these studies are by linguists, and they differ from the work presented in this book in that they concentrate on structural characteristics of language, not the sociocultural context of language learning.

13 A recent, exceptionally clear example of the way in which scholars will wave away the whole issue of how culture comes to bear on language shift is Edwards's 1985 exegesis on the subject. For this author, man is an economic animal, maximizing man, and culture is a list of specific traits that are separate from and dependent on economic conditions and considerations. "Most people at most times are committed to maximizing material well-being," he explains in his summary of why groups abandon their vernacular, "and it follows that a great deal of cultural 'stuff' [such as language] is expendable" (ibid.: 97). For a critique of the ways language change and culture change have been treated in literature concerned with the Pacific, see Kulick in press.

14 Of the others, two women came from Wongan, two women came from Sanae, one woman and one man were from Pankin, and two men were from Mangan (see Map 1).

15 The general thrust of these explanations is made explicit in Dorian's comparison between old-order Amish (who have retained their minority language) in the United States and the Scottish Gaelic fisher community that she studied (who have shifted to English). Formulating what she appears

to take as a general tendency, Dorian states that "so long as people lived, worked, and married among themselves, maintenance of their home language followed" (1981: 72). In Gapun, the maintenance of the home language has *not* followed from the variables listed by Dorian.

16   The vernacular equivalents of these two concepts are *kɔkir* (= *hed*/head) and *numbwan* (= *save*/knowledge). I use the Tok Pisin words throughout this book, in reflection of the villagers' own preference to name the concepts using those terms. It can also be noted here that the Tok Pisin term *save* is pronounced 'sáv-ei,' with stress on the first syllable. The word is a common one throughout Pacific Pidgins, and it probably derives from the Portuguese verb *saber* (to know). Another possibility, however, is mentioned by Mihalic (1971: 170), who suggests that *save* in Tok Pisin may instead derive from the New Ireland vernacular word *saavi* (to know, to grasp).

17   Exceptions to this are the extensive work done by L. Goldman on the language of settlement and dispute among the Huli (1980, 1983, 1987, 1988); B. Schieffelin's analyses of caregiver–child interactions and male and female speech patterns among the Kaluli (e.g., Schieffelin 1986, 1987, 1990); W. McKellin's (1984, 1990) work on allegorical speech among the Managalase; Voorhoeve's 1979 description of interpreted discourse in Papua New Guinea, and Merlan and Rumsey's recent monograph on language among Ku Waru speakers in the Western Highlands Province (Merlan & Rumsey 1991). Watson-Gegeo and Gegeo's work on the Kwara'ae of the Solomon Islands is also linguistically very detailed (e.g., Watson-Gegeo and Gegeo 1990, 1989, 1986; see also the articles in Watson-Gegeo and White 1990). Malinowski, of course, presented a great deal of language data in his work on the Trobriand islanders, but these data centered more on magical chants, songs, and myths than on everyday conversational patterns. A few recent anthropological works specifically address aspects of language use in Melanesian societies, but they are descriptive and nonlinguistic in nature, and they provide no transcribed examples of actual language use (e.g., Nash 1987; Brison 1989; Lederman 1984).

18   With the exception of several of the shorter text examples of three or four sentences, which were written down as soon as they were spoken, all speech extracts in this book are transcribed from audio recordings. See the Appendix for an account of the methods used for gathering data for this study.

Chapter 1

1   See Denoon 1989: 59.

2   I am not aware of any studies in the Sepik area that report on village income, so I have no material with which to compare the villagers' yearly income. It is my impression, however, that this is a very low income, and that neighboring villagers, especially those along the Sepik who have outboard motors, earn substantially more money than the people of Gapun.

3   The destruction of one's own possessions appears to be a widespread way of dealing with anger and shame in Melanesian communities. Burridge (1960: 95–7), for example, recounts how a Tangu man (Madang Province) had to be prevented from cutting down his own coconut palms after he had been involved in a shouting match with another man. Burridge analyzes the man's attempt to chop down his own palm trees as "an apparent attempt

to sever his connection with the village." Gell notes that Umeda (West Sepik Province) will sometimes cut down their own coconut palms, and explains that this act is "symbolically . . . almost equivalent to suicide" and a rejection of society (1975: 114–15). And Williams (1930: 332–3) reports that among the Orokaiva (Northern Province), "I have seen a dozen watermelons hacked into fragments and strewn upon the track. Their owner, finding them stolen, had demolished the whole crop and carried them to the path where the thief, whose identity he did not know, would pass and realize what he had done. Similarly, I have seen a young man return home at evening and find one of his spears taken from his verandah; when his enquiries failed to trace the spear he took an axe and razed his house to the ground before the eyes of the whole village." Other examples of this kind of behavior can be found in, e.g., Hallpike 1977: 236–7 and Hogbin 1963: 157.

4   Meeker, Barlow, and Lipset (1986: 47) present a Murik version of the two-brother myth. The major differences between the Murik version and the version known in Gapun are:

1)   The names of the two brothers are reversed – in Murik, Andena is the older brother and Arena the younger.

2)   In the Murik version, the older brother is "identified as nurturing, responsible . . . sexually moral . . . representative of communal projects and institutions" (ibid.: 46). In Gapun, such characteristics are not salient; there the older brother is portrayed as slow, vindictive, and stupid.

3)   The Murik version ends with the older brother remaining in a Murik village and the younger brother paddling off into the sea. In Gapun, both brothers are said to have "gone away" together.

5   The Pintupi people of Australia's Western Desert have similar ideas about the relationship between the world, white people, and their traditional mythological figures. "Gapun" could easily be substituted for the word "Pintupi" in the following quotation: "Pintupi mythology consists mainly of narratives of beings travelling from place to place. Consequently, all the places visited may be part of one larger story or myth. Each place is discrete and separate, but also is part of a continuous series of places linked by one story" (Myers 1986: 59–60).

6   Tamoane (1977) provides a lengthier and more detailed version of the Jari myth, as it was told to him by his grandmother in Darapap village, Murik Lakes. The Murik version is also discussed in Meeker, Barlow, and Lipset 1986 and Z'graggen in press.

7   Compare this understanding of geography and white society to the very similar one discussed by Kolig (1972) in his description of Australian Aboriginal groups in Western Australia.

Chapter 2

1   There is nothing to indicate that Taiap was ever any larger than it is now. As far back as anyone can remember, the language has been spoken by only one village.

2   For a comprehensive survey and description of Papuan languages, see Foley 1986 and Wurm 1982.

3   Laycock (1973; and Laycock and Z'graggen 1975) originally believed that

Taiap, which he calls "Gapun," was related to a geographically distant language called Bungain. This hypothesis was not based on very extensive data, however, and Bungain was later shown to belong not to the Sepik–Ramu phylum at all, but rather to the Toricelli language phylum (Sanders and Sanders 1980). Toricelli languages (discussed in Laycock 1975; Foley 1986; and Scorza 1985) are unrelated to the Sepik–Ramu phylum languages and are typologically very different.

A structural description of Taiap can be found in Kulick and Stroud (in press b). While there is little in our data to make us believe that Taiap, like Bungain, is a Torricelli language, and while our own work on the language confirms Laycock's observations about the basic similarities between Taiap and Sepik–Ramu languages, we remain uncertain as to what extent the language can actually be said to belong to the Sepik–Ramu phylum of Papuan languages (see also Stroud 1991: 17–27). The lexicon and morphology of Taiap are so unusual that it may be a true phylum-level isolate. The linguistic analysis of Taiap is continuing, and further analysis and comparative work will, hopefully, shed more light on Taiap's exact relationship to other Papuan languages.

4   A brief, general discussion of Ramu subphylum languages is found in Laycock and Z'graggen 1975: 757–60.

5   In the verb *nam-kru-ndak-ana* (they are going to tell her), for example, the subject or actor marker 'they' is actually signaled not by *-ndak-*, but rather by the combination of the morphemes *nd* and *k*. So a proper morphological breakdown of this verb would be:

Nam -kru   -nd-a-k -ana
tell   -U:IRR:3SGfem -S1-V-S2 -INTENT
                        | |
                        └3PL┘

A full discussion of the phenomenon of Taiap's discontinuous subject markers can be found in Kulick and Stroud in press b.

6   As can be seen in Table 2.1, Gapun also contains in-married speakers of Buna and Aion. The Buna speakers and one of the Aion speakers are men, and they almost never use their languages in Gapun, even when speaking to other native speakers of their vernacular. The other Aion speaker in Gapun is Ermina, a woman who, unlike Wandi (who after twenty years in Gapun still does not speak Taiap), has learned to speak the village vernacular. Ermina speaks Tok Pisin quite well, but she is one of the women in the village who prefers to use Taiap in her speech to others (an example of Ermina's speech can be seen in Text 6.2). She speaks Taiap so fluently and so consistently that villagers claim that she has "forgotten" her mother tongue.

7   The kind of reception that Aiarpa and Waiki may have received upon their return to Gapun is suggested in Thurnwald's (1931: 322) description of the return to his village of a Sepik male who had traveled with Thurnwald for several months as his guide, interpreter, and "boy":

Once I returned with . . . a recruit to the place where I wanted to stay and provided him with a box full of gifts – knives, axe blades, loincloths, belts, beads and sticks of Virginia tobacco. When our motorboat arrived his people were standing on the riverbank to greet us. He shouted across to them in his best newly acquired pidgin

English and even refused to talk his own language which he pretended to have forgotten. He allowed the box to be taken ashore and with a haughty gesture indicated that it was his. His relatives then opened it, and each one took out what he liked until it was empty, while my boy behaved all the time like a multimillionaire, knowing, of course, that the others would be obliged to reciprocate, giving him meals and perhaps even a feast in his honor. His uncle lifted him onto his shoulders, and with joyful shouts he was carried into his part of the village.

8   Mühlhäusler (1979, 1985d) provides accounts of the historical development of Tok Pisin from its inception as a jargon to its present-day status as a creole language.

9   Mühlhäusler (1979: 118) reports that Tok Pisin at this time in its history was commonly referred to by New Guineans as *tok waitman*.

10 Of the remaining six men, three apparently married local women and lived the rest of their lives near Rabaul; one returned briefly to the village but then left again, never to return; one man, who was accompanied by his wife, died during the period of his contract (the man's Gapun-born wife had accompanied him to Rabaul – she was the only village woman ever to leave Gapun in this way. She remained near Rabaul and married "plenty of men" before she died an old woman); and one man returned after the war to the village with his wife, who was from the Rabaul area, and their two children, who are now middle-aged adults living in Gapun.

11 Compare Reed's (1943: 286) observation that:

> The desire to emulate "finish time" boys [i.e., young men returned to the village after having worked as contracted laborers], who have traveled so far and seen so much is a motivating factor impelling youngsters to pick up a knowledge of pidgin. Groups of small boys among the [Sepik] Kwoma were frequently heard repeating pidgin words or phrases, or singing them as nonsense words to native rythms. This closely resembles similar child's play in our own culture, and achieves quite the same result. In this manner are learned the proper speech sounds and pronunciation; meanings can be acquired later.

Mead (1930: 40–1 and 1931: 147) has similar things to say about the acquisition of Tok Pisin in village contexts.

12 Multilingualism in Papua New Guinea is discussed in Sankoff 1977 and Laycock 1979.

13 The only senior woman still alive in Gapun in 1987 was Kruni's wife, Sombang. It is not clear why Sombang is not an active bi- or multilingual. Villagers explained it by saying that she was "*longlong*" (stupid), but her lack of production in other languages may also be related to her age or her sickness (which is described briefly in Chapter 1). Both these factors may have affected her memory and her language production capabilities (for a discussion of the effects of age and certain types of disability among bilinguals see Hyltenstam and Obler 1989). Whatever the reason for Sombang's lack of active bilingualism may have been, villagers regarded it as unusual enough to comment on, and they were agreed that senior women in the past actively commanded at least one other vernacular language.

14 See Herdt 1981: 334; Jolly 1987: 134; and Sankoff's general discussion 1977: 128.

15 Georg Höltker, the only researcher to ever visit Gapun before my own arrival in the village, trekked to the "old place" and spent a few hours

there in 1937. He stayed long enough to gather a short word list, which he published in 1938, prefaced by the weary prediction that "it will be awhile before any other researcher 'stumbles across' Gapun, partly because of the small chances of any profitable scientific exchange from this tiny village community, partly because of the arduous and difficult road to this linguistic island" (1938: 280).

16 Summarizing studies of the role of women in language change, Hill (1987: 121) recently made the observation that "women are more conservative than men in cases of stable variation, but are more innovative in cases of change in progress, particularly if the change is an assimilation toward an elite norm." This pattern is also clear in the case of language shift discussed by Gal (1978, 1979), and has been explained by showing that women in these communities have more to gain by using the elite language than they do from using the vernacular. This is an enormously complicated question, as Hill demonstrates in her discussion of women's speech in Mexicano, but at present it still appears that the men are leading the shift in Gapun through their own language behavior with other adults and with children (see Chapters 4 and 6).

17 Bentahila (1983), for example, reports that French–Arabic code-switching among bilingual Moroccans is viewed very unfavorably by the speakers themselves, even though it is in fact "a common feature of speech" (233). And within the British Punjabi-speaking community studied by Chana and Romaine (1984), code-switching, even though it was, again, extremely common, was negatively evaluated as "tuti futi," "broken up," or "not real" Punjabi.

18 The situation differs in this respect from that described by Sankoff (1976: 21) for the Buang of Madang Province, where use of Tok Pisin always apparently conveys a more authoritarian tone. For a more detailed account of code-switching in Gapun, see Kulick and Stroud 1990b and Stroud in press.

19 It is interesting to compare the villagers' negative characterizations of women and men from "water villages" with the way people from the Murik Lakes (a typical "water village" like Wongan in the eyes of the Gapuners) view inland "bush people" like Gapuners. Lipset (1984: 182–3) reports that the Murik "dismissed" bush people as "impoverished and isolated." "[A]s far as the Murik were concerned," he continues, "the bush people had no moral identity and [traditionally] their heads were fair game."

20 The two-brother myth about Arena and Andena, and the myth about Jari (both described in Chapter 1), including those names, may be of Sepik origin (see Chapter 1, notes 4 and 6), even though this is difficult to state categorically until more is known about the mythology of Adjora speakers. Villagers in Gapun and a learned man from Sanae once explained that Adjora speakers also have the two-brother myth, but the names in their version are Ndunara and Empinipi (see also Lawrence 1964 on the Rai Coast myth of the two brothers Kilibob and Manup, which is similar in several ways to Gapun's tale of Arena and Andena). In addition to the myths about Arena and Andena and Jari, Gapun also shared with Wongan, but not with Adjora-speakers, the female initiation rites described in Chapter 3, note 7.

21 The relationship that the villagers see between power, Tok Pisin, and Christianity is one of the main topics of Chapter 5. It can be noted here, however,

that such a link is extremely common throughout Papua New Guinea. Lawrence (1964: 68) reports that Tok Pisin was originally referred to by the Gari people of the Madang Province as the "language of deities." Reed (1943: 286), writing about the Sepik Kwoma, comments that "it was not ascertained that natives believe some of the white man's power to reside in [pidgin] words, but it is not unlikely that they do." And Meggitt observes that the main reason many Melanesians became literate was "so they could get a grip on the mission god and force from him his secrets" (1968: 302).

22 Many Sepik societies, although patrilineal, have strong matrilineal undercurrents. Bateson, for example, observed that "while the 'morphology' of the [Iatmul] social system is patrilineal, the 'sentiment' of the people is preponderantly matrilineal" (1958: 234). Recent monographs of the Murik, coastal neighbors of the Gapun villagers, describe the Murik descent system as "nonunilineal" and report that Murik culture is replete with what the ethnographers have chosen to call "the maternal presence" (Barlow 1984; Lipset 1984). Despite such matrilineal "sentiments," however, matrilineal descent is not widely found among groups in the Sepik region or on mainland Papua New Guinea. To the best of my knowledge, it has only been reported for the Bun (McDowell 1975), the Busama (Hogbin 1963), and some Tangu groups (Burridge 1960). Gapun thus appears fairly exceptional. My observations indicate, however, that the numerous Adjora-language-speaking groups to the east of Gapun are also matrilineal, as are the Kopar-speaking villages of Wongan and Singrin.

23 Most village parents with young children oppose the idea that anyone should "mark" a spouse for their children quite vocally. What upsets these parents is not so much the idea of an arranged marriage (some of their own quite satisfying marriages were arranged), but the risk that someone will die from sorcery if the child objects to the marriage and refuses to go through with it.

A problem with this changed attitude toward arranged marriages is that the big men in Gapun all want the young men and, especially, young women in the village to marry Sanae villagers, because they consider them to be hardworking "forest men/women" like themselves. It distresses and disgusts them to see that both young men and women prefer to marry people from Wongan. This problem is exacerbated by the fact that the only village with whom Gapuners intermarry that still insists on "marking" spouses for villagers is Sanae. But with the exception of Wandi's daughters, who have always maintained close contacts with Sanae because it is Wandi's native village, no village woman would ever dream of marrying a Sanae man, because they are afraid of them: "Men who kill us with sorcery" (*ol man bilong kilim mipela long poisen*), the women call them. The big men in Sanae, however, continue to seek to control at least some of the marriages in Gapun. If men and women who have been "marked" for Sanae villagers marry someone else, then veiled and sometimes not-so-veiled threats of sorcery periodically issue forth from that village.

In the two adult deaths that occurred in Gapun in 1986–7, the failure of young women to acquiesce to the marriage plans of the big men figured prominently as the cause of the deaths. In one case, an old woman's death was believed to have been brought on by sorcery in large part because her younger sister's four daughters adamantly refused to marry Sanae men. Three of these daughters were already married to men from other villages and had children; the single remaining daughter had a child out of wedlock and was known to have her eye on a particular Wongan man. Because of their responsibility for the old woman's death, both this daughter and her mother were beaten up with a large stick by the dead woman's daughter-in-law as they lay stretched out over the old woman's corpse, crying on her body.

The second death was that of Sake's sister Erapo's eldest daughter, a woman in her early twenties (this is the death on which Kruni comments on p. 89 in the text). She died a day after giving birth to a stillborn child, and the villagers concluded that sorcerers from Sanae had killed her because she ignored the big men's suggestions that she marry a Sanae man. When she did marry, it was to a man from Wongan who belonged to the parrot clan. During the early 1980's, two Wongan men of the parrot clan had married two Gapun women of the pig clan, and none of these men had *sens* (exchange "sisters") to give to men from the pig clan. When this pig-clan woman married yet another parrot-clan man from Wongan, and when the pig-clan men in Sanae realized that the parrot clan was making no preparations and had no real intention of providing a *sens* for any of these women, they killed the young woman through sorcery.

24   This is one of the most common patterns of warfare attested throughout New Guinea. Most monographs on Melanesian peoples contain information on warfare; examples are Godelier 1986; Hallpike 1977; Keesing 1982; Meeker, Barlow and Lipset 1986; E. Schieffelin 1976; and Tuzin 1976, 1980.

25   As will become clear in the text, the villagers' equation between femaleness and the 'wild' rainforest should not be taken to imply that they elaborate a simple woman:nature::man:culture dichotomy of the kind proposed in Ortner's much debated 1974 paper. As numerous studies of Melanesian cultures have shown, the distinction as Ortner originally stated it is not a useful means of viewing discourses on gender and male–female behavior in these societies (Errington and Gewertz 1987; Gillison 1980; Nash 1987; Strathern 1980, 1987; Williamson 1979).

26   Senior men also occasionally make such a judgment about the Taiap of other fluent male speakers, but never about themselves. Fluent female speakers in their thirties will, however, sometimes say that they themselves "foul up" the vernacular. What everyone who uses this expression means is that they sometimes cannot recall the word for a particular kind of tree or insect or some other object in the rainforest, or a verb for some rarely-spoken-about action. In village stereotypes, women can neither speak completely adequate Taiap or Tok Pisin. Since there were no coherent big women alive in Gapun during the period of my fieldwork, I was unable to investigate whether senior women considered that they had a full mastery of Taiap. A situation very similar to the one described for Gapun is discussed in Hill 1987.

27   Villagers recite the following utterance when exemplifying Kruni Maroka's original vernacular: *saŋnamarika ɔraŋnamarika apagai aguba kɛ kɛ kɛ kɔ kɔ kɔ.* This is all they know, but they claim to have heard that this Ur-language is still spoken in villages near Aiom in the Madang Province. Because of the difficulty in obtaining language data from this area, I have been unable to investigate the villagers' claims.

Chapter 3

1 To my knowledge, no custom like ɔndir has ever been described in the ethnographic literature on Melanesian societies, and it may be unique to Gapun and the Adjora-language groups to the east of the village (these groups have never been studied by anthropologists, with the exception of Thurnwald's early research on the Banaro; Thurnwald 1916). The only phenomenon of which I am aware that at all resembles the Taiap custom of ɔndir is the Australian Aboriginal custom of *mirriri*, in which a man attacks his sister (real or classificatory) if he hears her sworn at obscenely. Like ɔndir, which prescribed that an abandoned husband kill a matrilineal relative, *mirriri* strikes outsiders as difficult to comprehend because the victim of the aggression (for ɔndir, the matrilineal relative; for *mirriri*, the sister) is innocent of any provocation.

   Mirriri has been analyzed as a means of averting armed confrontation between the clans of the brother and his sister's husband (her most likely insulter) (Warner 1937), as a denial by the brother of any incestuous intentions toward his sister (Hiatt 1964), as an act of expiation for the foregrounding (through the insult, which is invariably sexual) of the sister's genitals and reproductive functions in the presence of her brother (Makarius 1966), as a "ritual expression of a social relation" between brothers and sisters (Maddock 1970), and as a specific manifestation of a more generalized pattern of ritualized agression in which people attack things as substitutes for people whom they for some reason cannot attack (Burbank 1985).

   Several of these interpretations, especially those proposed by Warner and Burbank, shed light on the Taiap custom of ɔndir, but a dimension missing in all of them is an account of how local ideas about provocation, blame assignment, and conflict settlement structure and lend meaning to the custom. All explanations of *mirriri* rely to varying degrees on structuralist or functionalist criteria to explain the custom. While these types of explanations are analytically neat, they do not account clearly for the feelings and motives that move people to act in the way they do. The important point to stress about ɔndir in this context is that killing an innocent maternal relative (who is also a fellow clan member) as a means of dealing with the anger and shame resulting from the loss of a wife is deeply grounded in the same cultural presuppositions that make it logical and meaningful for the villagers to destroy their own possessions when they feel insulted or put out by somebody else. In such a system, the major difference between chopping down one's betel palms, burning down one's house, and murdering a fellow clan member is one degree – killing a clan member ups the ante in accordance with the magnitude of the affront to the self, and it ensures that the loss of one's wife becomes an affair affecting the entire clan. The big men in Gapun were able to remember four cases of ɔndir in some detail, and a fuller analysis of the custom is in preparation for publication (Kulick n.d.).

2 Compare Abrahams (1962), who noted that the strict formal stucture of playing the dozens among black Americans is necessary because this type of verbal play is "perilously close to real life." See also Miller 1986: 210.

3 Compare Japanese mothers' calls to their children that *hito* (other people) are watching and evaluating their behavior (Clancy 1986).

4 For example, Scotton (1982), who argues from data on code-switching in Kenya that one of the reasons that groups maintain multilingualism is to have access to a variety of codes. She believes that code-switching can be explained as a speaker's desire to "negotiate the rights and obligations set that he or she wishes to be in effect for the exchange" (ibid.: 433). Her examples are very clear-cut cases of individuals code-switching for effect, for example, a local chief who pointedly switches into Swahili as an expression of authority in a context dominated by the vernacular language. While it is important not to ignore the existence of this kind of sociolinguistic dynamic in Gapun, it should be stressed that it does not account for the majority of the villagers' code-switches. I return to this point in the concluding chapter.

5 After completing this manuscript, Francesca Merlan and Alan Rumsey kindly allowed me to read the galley proofs of their (at that point, as yet unpublished) book *Ku Waru* (1991). Compare their discussion of the linguistic manifestation of what they call a Nebilyer "habitus of pairing" (1991: 241) to the points raised here about the sense of "linguistic balance" that villagers in Gapun try to achieve in their discourse.

6 Compare Sankoff's observations on the informational content of code-switched utterances among the Buang of Papua New Guinea (1971: 44).

7 Women in Gapun apparently also had initiation rites. Female initiation was called *murimuri*. The feature of *murimuri* that the old men who told me about this custom stressed most was that the young women were made to undergo a painful ritual in which they were made to squat on a long, thin stick covered in sharp spines (*dabɛ*). This *dabɛ* was placed on the ground. The young woman's mother's sister held her by her shoulders and made her repeatedly squat on the stick so that it entered the girl's vagina, ripping it and causing it to bleed profusely. After this, the girls were isolated in a large house for several months at a time. Here the girls would be decorated with special pointed hats (*kawaŋ*) that signified their status as taboo. The main characteristic of the stay in the house was that they would continually sing *sambak*, a song also sung by women at funerary feasts. This custom appears to have come from the coastal villages, because according to Kruni and Raia, all villages along the coast (Murik, Kopar, Singrin, and Wongan) practiced it. The "forest villages," i.e., Sanae and the villages inland toward the Ramu, did not practice *murimuri*. The custom was discontinued in Gapun at the end of the nineteenth century because, the big men say, having heard this from their own elders, there weren't enough big women in the village to perform it. (Compare Berndt's (1962: 106) description of a similar form of female initiation in the Eastern Highlands).

8 In male rhetoric women's genitals are considered to be a bewitching source of perilous danger and hypnotic pleasure. Dangerous, because the blood and "heat" of women saps men's strength and stunts (*daunim*) their growth. Raia once let it be understood that men these days are much shorter than they were only a generation ago because nowadays they have intercourse with women from an early age. He used an analogy of boiling water being poured into a plastic cup to convey to me a sense of what sex with women does to men.

Despite, or perhaps because of, this danger, female genitals have the power to obsess men and transform them into lowly, antisocial beasts. During a discussion in the men's house about women, several big men agreed that a man should not have sex with a woman during the day because the sight of female genitals would excite the man to such a pitch that he would not be able to think of anything else. "You wouldn't go anymore and sit down with the men in the men's house," Raia explained in a censorious tone, "you'd just think about this woman's *kan* all the time and worry about who was having intercourse with it."

9 This use of women by men to proclaim infringements, and the associations that Gapun villagers maintain between women and confrontational language, are remarkably similar to male and female linguistic roles in Madagascar. Keenan (1989: 137–8) reports that among the Malagasy with whom she lived, women "are associated with the direct and open expression of anger toward others," whereas men "tend not to express their sentiments openly. . . . They avoid creating unpleasant face-to-face encounters." Like the men in Gapun, Malagasy men "often use women to confront others with some unpleasant information. Women communicate sentiments that men share but dislike expressing." In Melanesia, Goldman (1986: 236), in his analysis of the presentational style of Huli (Southern Highlands Province) women, observes that "women evidence a greater proclivity to express their negative assessments of other people's talk as 'lies'. . . . This confrontational directness contrasts markedly with the metaphorical and circumlocutory nature of male speech assessments." And Nash (1987: 105), writing about the Nagovisi of West New Britain, writes that "men guard their talk and believe themselves to be discreet; women bring things out into the open."

10 Sake even inserts a brief code-switch into Kopar, the language spoken in Wongan (line 46).

Chapter 4

1 This point is made most elegantly and explicitly in Forge 1972. It is also an issue addressed by anthropologists working among Australian Aboriginal peoples, e.g., Myers 1986: 164–5 and Sansom 1980.

2 Men's houses (*haus boi/ambagai*) in Gapun, and in the Adjora language groups adjacent to Gapun, are built by and associated with specific clans. The houses are always built in anticipation of a major event, most usually a funerary feast to which the *tambaran* (in the form of sacred flutes) will be called, and they are built in the name of one man, who thereafter becomes the "owner" (*papa/ɔmɔ*) of the men's house.

In Gapun during 1986, there were two men's houses: a large, traditionally designed one built by Kem and his relatives and clan members (*Samaŋgi Maŋgam*), and a much smaller one built by Kruni and his relatives and clan members (*Nkɔp Arana*). Kruni's men's house, situated in the center of the village, was where the village men congregated to socialize with one another, and it was here that all of the village-wide meetings took place. Kem's men's house was usually referred to by men and women as the "big men's house" (*bikpela haus boi/ambagai suman*), and it was considered to have *powa* (power). This was where the sacred flutes were stored, and where the men congregated when they specifically addressed their ancestors on questions concerning illness. This men's house, built in the late 1970s for a major ceremony in which Kem's oldest daughter received the insignia (*kuskus/siman*) of her clan, rotted and fell apart in early 1987. Prior to this, in November 1986, another men's house was built at the opposite end of the village by Samek, a member of the parrot clan. This men's house was built in anticipation of the funerary feast to be held for Samek's mother, who had died on November 2. The house was larger and more impressive than Kruni's, but not as large as Kem's, and no sacred paraphernalia were kept there (the sacred flutes, after the collapse of Kem's men's house, had been moved into Agrana's house for safekeeping). After the funerary feast was completed in Samek's men's house (*Karatum*), the house became a meeting place for the men at the "up" end of Gapun. Consequently, many men stopped coming to Kruni's men's house to socialize, and the divisions in the village between the various sibling groups that live there became more emphasized.

3   Lederman (1984: 98) discusses a similar situation among the Mendi (Southern Highlands Province).
4   As there is, for example, among the Melpa in Hagen (A. Strathern 1975a: 187). Compare with the Kaluli, where, "when women are negotiating in the political arena or are involved in arguments, they make use of the same linguistic resources as men" (Schieffelin 1990: 10).
5   In fact, in July 1986, the village youth group received 400 Kina from the government. In getting the youth coordinator to fill out their application form for the money, the villagers had wanted to request enough money to buy an outboard motor. The youth coordinator didn't think the government would accept this request and, unknown to any of the villagers, he wrote down instead that the villagers wanted money for cement and corrugated iron to build a house to dry copra in. The 400 Kina they received was earmarked for this purpose, which no villager was interested in or knew how to go about building. The money was duly collected by the leader of the youth group and 100 Kina was deposited into the bank to "get big." The rest was taken back to the village and put in an old coffee jar. When I left Gapun in late June 1987, the money still had not been used, and people were unsure whether it still even existed.
6   At an early *yut* meeting, fees were decided on. These were:

clear a large area of forest for a garden	5 Kina
collect and carry coconuts to a central place so they can be shelled, cut, and smoked	5 Kina
pull a canoe from the forest to the water	4 Kina
cut, clean, and carry bark used for house floors	2 Kina
fence in a garden	2 Kina

Three things should be noted about these fees. First of all, they represent what the "employer" pays for the entire job; it is not the case that each worker receives, say, 5 Kina. Second, the fees changed for no obvious reason from time to time. Suddenly somebody would announce that they had heard that the fee for fencing in a garden, for example, was 3 Kina instead of 2 Kina. There was no written list of fees, and no one could ever confirm or deny such a sudden change. In actual practice, individuals paid whatever they thought the price of a service was at any one time. Finally, there is no relation at all between the amount of labor required to do a particular job and the amount of money that must be paid. Fencing in gardens, for example, typically is done in a few hours by a few village men. Clearing forest for a garden, on the other hand, is a mammoth task. On one occasion, the entire population of Gapun (with the exception of the very old men and women) rose at three o'clock in the morning to travel to Wongan to cut and clear a large area of primary rainforest for a Wongan man who had "bought" Gapun's youth group. Every man and woman worked all day long felling trees and clearing undergrowth, and they finished the job and returned to Gapun (a two-hour journey) at eight o'clock that evening. For this the Wongan man and his wife supplied the workers with food during the day and paid 5 Kina.

7   For large jobs requiring a full day's work, this was the praxis, although it was never agreed upon as such, and in fact many people insisted that it was wrong: If the form of payment was money, then that should be enough, was the most often voiced opinion on this issue. It appeared to be the case, however, that villagers felt deeply uncomfortable with this, and they felt a responsibility, anchored in the traditional system of payment with food, to feed the men and women who worked for them, even if they had paid them.

8   The original text is as follows:

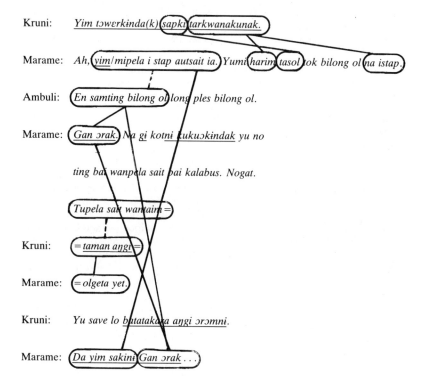

9   This kind of distancing seems to be a general characteristic of oratorical speech in many communities throughout the world. M. Rosaldo (1973: 218), for example, notes that among the Philippine Ilonogot, the structure of oratorical speech "creates a distance between the speaker as a private individual and the social self he presents to the debate." Myers 1986: 270–1 also describes a similar strategy of discursive "anonymization" in speeches held by the Pintupi of Australia. See also the various articles in Brenneis and Myers 1984, and Bloch 1975.

10 This contrasts starkly with the Anglo–American view that the responsibility for successful communication lies with the speaker, who is expected to strain to "get across" her or his viewpoints and thoughts to the listener. Reddy (1979) discusses in detail some of the implications of this notion of communication. Brett-Smith (1984) details the implications that a listener-centered view of communication has among the Bambara of Mali, and Clancy (1986) is a lucid analysis of this type of communication among the Japanese.

11 The ability to anticipate the needs and wants of others without having them verbalized is a highly salient and valued indication of *save*. Choked with tears of grief over the death of Kokom, her older half-brother's wife, Sopak expressed this understanding as she wailed loudly over the dead woman's body:

   ... Kɔkɔm, ginɔni raritakrɛ numbwanənni ɔrak ɔrak tarak iatitak ŋa rareŋgarrɛ kɔtareŋgar wakarɛ ...

   ... Kokom, you would always just look at me and think of me, you go get all sorts of things and bring them and give them to me
   whenever you would see me you would never ask [if I wanted anything; you would just give it] ...

   On another occasion, when Kruni was describing life in white society, he made the point that:

   If you want something [in the "countries"], you don't have to tell me with your mouth. I already know [and] I'll give it to you. Alright, me, too: If I want something of yours you'll understand my desire and you'll just give it to me. That's *save*. That's Belief. Now [in Gapun] this way doesn't exist. Now we [villagers] are like pigs.

12 This note was written by Allan (Sake herself is virtually illiterate). Allan crossed out his name at the end of the note, however, in what clearly is an attempt to emphasize that Sake is the one most affected by my decision whether or not to "help" the couple buy the rice. In order to fully understand this gesture, it is necessary to know that Sake and Allan were my adopted mother and father in Gapun, and they helped me and looked after me in numerous ways. By presenting Sake as the recipient of the rice (and as the one who will be shamed should she not produce any rice during the conciliatory feast), the couple is subtly reminding me of the responsibilities and feelings of helpfulness and sympathy that one should properly have toward one's mother.

13 Narration of historical or mythical events in the first person pronoun appears to be a common oratorical convention in both hierachically ordered societies (e.g., Sahlins 1981: 13–14 on Polynesian narrative conventions) and in egalitarian communities like Gapun or the Pintupi Aborigines of Australia (Myers 1986: 270). The rhetorical effects are the same: Speakers using this convention "*become* mythical heroes" (Sahlins 1981: 14, emphasis in orig-

inal), even as they "present [their] position as representing that of an external, authoritative source" (Myers 1986: 270), as Kruni does in his harangue. See also Merlan and Rumsey (1990: 96–8) for a discussion of additional significances this type of rhetorical usage may have.

14 This kind of use of Taiap by Kruni is similar to the way terminal Gaelic speakers in Nova Scotia have been reported to use their Gaelic. In both cases, the use of the vernacular languages is restricted to conveying affect. Such a restriction is probably a reflection, or indication, of language shift. Mertz (1989: 114) makes the point that in phases of shift, a community's vernacular language "ceases to serve as a regular medium for conveying semantico-referential information [and instead] gains pragmatic force for expressing affect and creatively molding the speech situation."

15 Sankoff makes a similar point about why Buang speakers switch to Tok Pisin during oratorical speech (1971: 44).

Chapter 5

1 Agrana here is referring to the much publicized visit of Pope John Paul II to Papua New Guinea in May 1984.

2 There are some striking similarities between Agrana's epic and what Lawrence (1964: 75–85) calls the "Third Cargo Belief," popular around Madang and the Rai Coast in the late 1910s–1930s.

3 This idea of changing skin appears to be a widespread one throughout much of New Guinea. Gell 1975: 320–1, for example, calls New Guinea "the classic area for myths about renewable skin" (see also Hallpike 1977: 26). The significance of the skin, which in Melanesian societies usually denotes both the body as well as the surface, has been explored by Read 1955; A. Strathern 1975b; and M. Strathern 1979.

4 Children receive lessons for several hours each week in "religious instruction," which in Wongan Community School means praying Catholic prayers and singing Catholic hymns. Although the school is government-run, the religious undertone is constantly present. The day begins and ends in "assembly" reciting the Lord's Prayer, and throughout the day, before each break, teachers lead the children in this prayer or in a shortened version, in which the children cross themselves, saying "In the name of the Father, Son, and the Spiritu Santu." Teachers or visitors entering the classroom are greeted in unison with "Good morning/afternoon, Mr. X. God Bless you."

5 This is common throughout Papua New Guinea. Swatridge (1985: 63) summarizes a comparative study of Melanesian millenarian movements by Strelan (1977), who identifies five major themes present in the vast majority of traditional Melanesian belief systems: the division of mankind, the conflict between the two brothers, the lost Paradise, the coming of the endtime, and the intervention of a savior-hero. Although traditional Taiap cosmology does not contain all these elements, Strelan's conclusion that "a religion containing these themes could digest the stories of the Tower of Babel, the murder of Abel, the expulsion of Adam and Eve from Eden, the Revelation of St. John, and the Incarnation without much difficulty" accurately captures something of what has happened in Gapun. For comparisons with other Melanesian groups, see E. Schieffelin 1981 for a similar conclusion as to why Christianity caught on as quickly as it did among the

Kaluli, and Lawrence's (1964) classic discussion of the genesis and elaboration of cargo beliefs in the Madang area. For comparisons with groups outside Melanesia, see Rivière 1981, who analyzes the consequences that the ideological "fit" between the Christian message and the traditional cosmology has had for the Trio Indians in Surinam.

6   The villagers' knowledge about Fr. Luttmer was supplemented by information kindly supplied by Fr. John Tshauder at the Divine Word Institute, Madang, Papua New Guinea.

7   Yali and his movement is one of the best known millenarian movements in Melanesia. It is described in detail in Lawrence 1964 and Morauta 1974.

8   Cahill, Angoram Patrol Report 9: 49/50, p. 4.

9   Literacy in Gapun is discussed in more detail in Kulick and Stroud 1990a and Kulick and Stroud in press a. For comparisons with other Melanesian societies, see Burridge 1960: 193–4; Meggitt 1968; Schieffelin and Cochran-Smith 1984; Swatridge 1985.

10 This belief is extremely widespread throughout Papua New Guinea, and it is explored in detail in Swatridge's 1985 book. See also R. Smith 1975, 1973, and McLaren 1975.

11 In fact, one Gapun child, Sopak and Mone's oldest son, Opi, did pass his standard six exams and was admitted to high school in the early 1980s. The expense of the tuition fees (250 Kina per year, including room and board) was extremely hard on Sopak and Mone, however, and after managing to pay them for 1½ years, they stopped paying, bitter that other villagers – despite the constant rhetoric that children should get education to "save" (*sebim*) the entire village – would contribute nothing toward the boy's tuition. Opi was dismissed from school, and has chosen not to return to the village. Rumors periodically fly through Gapun that he has joined one of the many criminal *raskol* gangs that exist in Wewak, Madang, Angoram, and other large settlements throughout the Sepik and Ramu regions. Partly because of Opi's marginal status in Gapun, partly because the villagers hesitate to give Sopak an opportunity to have a *kros* about the stinginess and hypocrisy of other villagers, and partly because Opi's successful passing of his exams weakens the men's arguments that village children are lazy and that teachers conspire against them, Opi is conveniently forgotten and never mentioned in the men's harangues and rhetoric about how no village child has ever gone on to high school.

12 The use of English as the language of instruction in all Papua New Guinean schools is the result of a complex number of social, historical, and political factors, but in large measure it can also be said to be an inheritance of colonial attitudes that denigrated all forms of Pidgin as "vile gibberish" (Murray 1924, quoted in Johnson 1977: 431) and that maintained that if Papua New Guineans were ever going to really "develop," they must necessarily do so in a "real" (read European) language (the Germans tried to teach New Guineans German, the Australians believed English was the answer). In the words of the government anthropologist F.E. Williams:

> In the first place the ability to speak, and better still to read, in the superior tongue [i.e., English] will open the gate to far wider fields of experience and knowledge: it will provide for the development – to what extent we cannot forsee – of the intellectual powers which, however hidden at present, we must assume the native to possess. (Williams 1935, quoted in Johnson 1977: 433)

Johnson 1977 is a detailed, concise report of language policies in Papua and New Guinea since the beginning of the twentieth century. See also

Barrington-Thomas 1976; Brammall and May 1975; Conroy 1973; G. Smith 1975; Stringer 1983.

13 This is another belief that is quite common throughout Papua New Guinea. Describing general trends in the country, Swatridge (1985: 96–7) comments:

> Parents sent their children to live with relatives in towns, rather than have them attend mission schools in the villages, and the reason was that government teachers taught in English, whilst mission teachers taught in Pidgin. Education [in those areas where it existed] had come close to being discredited in the late 1930s and 40s, because mission schooling was not delivering the goods. . . . Inasmuch as the missionaries taught in Pidgin, the people suspected that they were concealing the cargo secrets, and that they were doing this quite deliberately. . . . Pidgin was a half way house on a road that wound back to the village. An old man complained to the researcher, Wotten: "They did not show us the straight road that would lead us to your knowledge, you ideas, your language."

14 Giraure 1975: 101.

15 Information about what happens in the local community school in Wongan was gathered by listening to children's talk about school, by interviewing the teachers and those men and women in Gapun who had attended the school for any length of time, and by sitting in on classes for a period of two weeks in November 1986.

16 This process, repeated in hundreds of schools and with thousands of children throughout the country, has resulted in serious social problems in Papua New Guinea. Male students who leave school, taught for years about the desirability and superiority of white people's ways of living, unable or uninterested in participating in local village life, stream to Papua New Guinea's urban centers, where they often find themselves unemployed and homeless. A common end point of this process is membership in one of the many *raskol* (petty gangster) gangs that terrorize these centers (see e.g., Swatridge 1985: 126–53).

17 Similar attitudes of distrust and dislike toward Europeans formed the basis of the millenarian movement near Madang in the 1930s that was inspired by a Bogia man called Mambu. Burridge (1960: 184) reports that Mambu told his followers that white men were exploiting them:

> But a new order, a new way of life was at hand which was dependent on no longer submitting to white men, whether they were missionaries, administrative officers, planters or traders. The ancestors had the welfare of their offspring very much at heart. Even now some were in the interior of the volcano of Manam island, manufacturing all kinds of goods for their descendents. Other ancestors, adopting the guise and appearance of white men, were hard at work in the lands where white men lived. Indeed, said Mambu, the ancestors had already dispatched much cargo to Kanakas [i.e., to Papua New Guineans]. Cloth for laplaps, axes, khaki shorts, bush knives, torches, red pigment and ready-made houses had been on their way for some time. But white men, who had been entrusted with the transport, were removing the labels and substituting their own. In this way, Mambu said, Kanakas were being robbed of their inheritance. Therefore, Kanakas were entitled to get back the cargo from white men by the use of force.

18 This image of sealing people in cases and sending them in this way to European countries also appears in Raia's account of what Australians did to Germans in Papua New Guinea during World War I (Chapter 1).

19 This does not mean that all white people are dead Papua New Guineans. Villagers believe that many white people have no direct relation at all to

Papua New Guinea, just as they themselves have no direct relation to "the countries." And after death, even former Papua New Guineans live together undifferentiated from whites in "the countries." However, there is also the belief that some Papua New Guineans grieve so much for their relatives and friends after death that they leave "the countries" for short periods to return to their native villages, bringing with them gifts and money. Because they have died and "changed skin," these returned villagers are white. Any villager in Gapun can recite at least three or four stories of faraway villages where this has occurred, although after my own arrival in the village, the people there had a returned spirit of their own to talk about. It was decided very quickly after my initial arrival in the village that I was the son of Sake's dead sister Aioma, who had died at the age of only several months a few years before I appeared in Gapun. This belief was maintained throughout my stay in the village. I discuss it in more detail in the Appendix.

20   The terminology is Worsley's (1957).
21   This is Lawrence's (1964) conclusion. It has recently been echoed by Swatridge (1985: 149), who at the end of his study on millenarian thought in Papua New Guinea, asserts:

> It would be a bold spirit who would assert that cargoism is a spent force [in Papua New Guinean communities]. It is still manifest in traditional forms in the Western Highlands, among the Enga, and in villages and urban slums elsewhere. And cargoism is not dead, as an underpinning philosophy, even on the university campuses, and in the House of Assembly. Cargo activities may be muted, they may even be eradicated, or be laughed out of court. But the intractable, hard core epistomology of cargoism survives – and it deserves to be taken seriously.

Strelan (1977: 11; cited in Swatridge 1985: 67) also makes the important point that:

> the idea is often propounded that, with opposition from the government and the church, supported by planned educational drive and economic development, cargo cults and cargo thinking will gradually disappear. These, however, are oversimplified solutions based on a superficial analysis of a complex problem.

Chapter 6

1   This even holds true, in a slightly modified way, of private speech acts such as prayer and magic. In both cases the speaker considers her- or himself to be engaging in a discourse with God or the ancestors/*tambaran*. Although the speaker expects no verbal reaction from God or the ancestors/*tambaran,* he or she does expect these deities to respond to the talk by acting on it.
2   Sopak does not translate the word "chicken" into Tok Pisin (where the equivalent is *kakaruk*), but this word is one of the many Taiap nominals that are habitually used by the villagers even when they speak Tok Pisin. See Chapter 2 and Text 6.14.
3   One reaction to this argument would be that Tok Pisin, a creole language only about one hundred years old, really is easier than Taiap, and the villagers are correct in sensing this. This is an issue of enormous complexity, but one response to such a reaction would be to point out that linguists are overwhelmingly in agreement that whole languages cannot be ranked in relation to one another on the criterion of simplicity. Certain structural features, such as phonological inventory or morphology, are more complex

in some languages than they are in others, but complexity in one area is generally counterbalanced by relative simplicity in other areas. The Chinese dialects, for example, all have an extremely uncomplicated morphology and a complex suprasegemental system (tones). Likewise, Taiap has a complex morphology (relative to Tok Pisin), but in terms of syntactic constraints, it is less complex than Tok Pisin.

Even though whole languages cannot be ranked for simplicity, however, it is not unusual for individuals to judge languages as "easy" or "hard." Part of this judgment is known to be based on the extent to which salient structures in another language diverge from what one is used to in one's own language (that is, the extent to which phonological or grammatical elements in a language are perceived by hearers/learners of that language as being "marked"). This appears to be what has happened in the case of Taiap: Villagers speaking other languages and coming into contact with Taiap experienced the gender distinctions in the forms of the verb to which they paid most attention as unusual and "marked," and they therefore labeled the entire language as "hard." So what we are dealing with when other villagers and the Gapun people themselves evaluate their language as "hard" are not qualified linguistic judgments so much as impressionistic evaluations.

4 See Laycock 1977: 133–4; Nekitel 1985: 172–7; and Goldman 1987 for additional examples of baby-talk registers in Papua New Guinea societies.

5 Based on a sample of twenty-seven languages, Ferguson (1978) lists cluster reduction, liquid substitution, reduplication, and special sounds as universal features of baby-talk.

6 According to Malcom Ross (personal communication), the Taiap baby-talk form *sisi* (pig meat) may be derived from the Proto-Western Oceanic form *jiji* ("fat," i.e., the edible substance). The baby-talk form *sɔsɔ* is the same as the Proto-Western Oceanic form *soso* (urinate, urine).

   The Taiap baby-talk form *maka* (drink/consume) is similar to another Austronesian word, in this case, the Indonesian form for "eat," which is *makan*.

7 This is an interesting fact in light of Ferguson's (1978: 212) claims that "core items in a baby talk lexicon tend to persist for long periods of time (e.g., two thousand years for Latin-Spanish *pappa* 'food')" and his contention that "the special lexicon may be very conservative," remaining essentially the same for long periods of time" (215–16). Compare the Gapun situation to Bavin's (1989: 277) report that young Walpiri (Australia) mothers have recently been incorporating English words into their baby-talk lexicon. Unfortunately, Bavin does not mention whether the English incorporations are replacing their Walpiri eqivalents.

8 Pye documents a similar variation in the use of baby-talk in the Quiche Mayan community that he studied. He also noted that much of the word reductions and sound substitution occurring in speech to children in the community were not didactic so much as imitative (1986a: 89).

9 Women in Gapun will nurse other women's babies for short periods if the mother is very sick or for some reason not on hand when the baby continues to cry. The ideal, however, is that this situation never arise.

10 Words spoken by children in the vernacular are transcribed in the same phonetic-based script used for Taiap speech by adults. This is done solely for the sake of orthographic consistency, and it does not necessarily imply that children command the phonological system of Taiap.

11 Scollon and Scollon (1981: 133) describe a similar belief among the Chipewyan speakers they worked with in Canada. These people "assume that Athabaskan languages take a lifetime to learn well," and consequently do not consider that children begin to speak before they are around 5 years old.

12 This point, and the arguments in this chapter and in this book as a whole concerning why children in Gapun do not acquire the village vernacular, should be seen in marked contrast to the recent tendency in discussions of language shift in Papua New Guinea to invoke the "difficulty" of vernaculars in relation to Tok Pisin as a major factor influencing their decline. Writing about the Abu' language, for example, Nekitel (1984: 93) asserts that "[t]here are . . . certain general aspects of the vernacular that appear difficult to master and may subsequently discourage children from learning the language." Foley (1986: 28, 1988: 182) makes similar claims about why children are not learning Papuan vernaculars.

The results of this study, which is the only detailed analysis to date of language socialization patterns in a language-shifting community, indicates clearly, however, that the objective linguistic "difficulty" of Taiap (to the extent that this is at all possible to assess from the point of view of the child language-learner) *plays no role at all* in the nonacquisition of that language. While superficial observation of child–caregiver interactions would suggest that village children do indeed receive a great deal of input in Taiap from their adult caregivers, a close analysis of these interactions reveals that speech directed to children is, in fact, systematically biased toward Tok Pisin, in the ways outlined in this chapter. So the reason Gapun children are not acquiring the village vernacular is that they simply are not receiving enough input in it and encouragement to use it. If, after taking this study into account, linguists writing about language shift wish to persist in claiming that vernacular languages in themselves are factors directly contributing to their own decline, then it is incumbent upon them not only to demonstrate that children are in fact receiving enough input in those languages to be able to find them difficult and reject them, but also to specify the cognitive processes that might be involved in a child's assessments of one linguistic system as more "difficult" than another.

13 " . . . *my bird of paradise*" is a construction commonly used in both the villagers' Taiap and Tok Pisin (in which the corresponding phrase would be *kumul bilong mi*). The use of the possessive in this case is a kind of joking possessive claim that the speaker uses to emphasize that he or she was the first one to spot the object being discussed. An equivalent in colloquial American English would be "that bird of paradise that I've got dibs on."

14 Studies of childhood bilingualism have consistently shown that children go through a stage in which they freely mix elements from their languages before they eventually come to separate the languages into discrete linguistic systems (e.g., Arnberg 1981; Fantini 1985; Vihman 1985). How and when this language differentiation occurs is one of the major areas of contention among researchers studying bilingual children. Some researchers (Bergman 1976; Genesee 1989; Lindholm and Padilla 1978, 1979; Padilla and Liebman 1975; Pye 1986b) believe that the child's languages develop as separate systems from the very beginning and that mixing is the result of the child's lack of vocabulary items in her or his languages. A more widely held view, however, is that bilingual children begin with a single linguistic system that only gradually comes to be differentiated into separate languages. This process of differentiation has been summarized in a model of bilingual development first presented in Volterra and Taeschner 1978, and later expanded in Taeschner's 1983 monograph.

According to this model, children acquiring language in bilingual environments where parents consistently apply a one-person–one-language strategy in their interactions with the child begin with a single lexicon that contains elements from both languages. From as early as 1;8, the child begins to realize that there are two lexicons, and will use equivalents (corresponding words in the other language) to attract the listener's attention. At this stage, however, the same syntactic rules are applied to all the child's utterances, and this, in combination with the fact that the child lacks equivalents for all words in her or his vocabulary, results in the impression of "interference" and "mixing" in the child's speech. In the third stage, which begins near the third year, the child has successfully differentiated the two languages both in lexicon and syntax. Interference and overextensions from one language to the other continue to occur, but these decrease at an accelerating rate as the child grows older.

Volterra and Taeschner's model of bilingual language differentiation, as well as all debate on this subject, centers on the language of children who become active bilinguals in their early years. The same process of differentiation must, however, also occur even in children raised in bilingual environments who do not become active bilinguals, such as the present generation of children in Gapun.

In the case of these children, it would appear from their nonlinguistic behavior (such as Masito's whining when Sopak speaks in the vernacular in Text 6.1 at the beginning of this chapter) and from the language they initially produce (such as repeating Tok Pisin words in adult conversations but not Taiap words) that they have managed to separate the two linguistic codes even before they begin to talk. That Gapun children can do this prior to speech may hinge on the late stage at which they begin to talk. Bizzari (1977; summarized in Taeschner 1983: 13) cites evidence indicating that "the child who begins speaking at a late age realizes that he is dealing with two different linguistic codes from the moment he begins to use their first words." But Gapun children's prelinguistic language separation and absence of syntactic or morphological mixing may also be evidence against Volterra and Taeschner's three-stage theory, and it may support the arguments of those like Meisel, who contends that "an individual [i.e., a child] exposed to two languages from early on [is] capable of separating the two grammatical systems without going through a phase of temporary confusion [i.e., of syntactic and morphological mixing]" (1989: 35).

Exactly when the late-speaking children of Gapun come to understand that there are two separate codes and how they come to separate them, particularly in the absence of a strictly applied one-person–one-language strategy, remains an open question. But it is a question meriting attention in other bilingual communities, because the type of fluid and mixed linguistic input that Gapun children receive is much more characteristic of the input to children growing up in the world's numerous bi- and multilingual communities than is the consciously applied one-person–one-language strategy. In Gapun, a factor that clearly aids the children in separating the languages used in the village is the fact that the language in which they are most often directly addressed and to which they must attend is Tok Pisin (cf. Harrison and Piette's 1980 paper, in which they argue that "[bilingual] children are greatly influenced by the language addressed to them, and are far less affected by utterances heard but directed to others" [p. 221].

15 Metraux (1965) and Redlinger (1978) have also noted this tendency for the nondominant language to be a "scolding language."

16 This means that boys of this age never use any vernacular morphology or verb phrases in their speech. They do use Taiap nominals in their Tok Pisin, but neither I nor any villager considers this to be vernacular speech.

17 Here we may be seeing the genesis of the phenomenon that Weinreich (1964: 95), and Dorian (1981: 78) report – that languages frequently take on connotations of humor in their terminal stages.

18 This is an even more sophisticated use of language than the other two examples, because here Bup intentionally mixes Taiap (*anakapε* – where) with the Adjora word for tongs (*apir*). This unexpected mixing brought peals of laughter from Bup's playmates.

19 In her study of a Dyirbal-speaking community in Australia, for example, Schmidt (1985) found the tendency of elderly speakers to correct younger speakers' Dyirbal was directly contributing to the decline of the language, since apprehension about being corrected resulted in younger speakers hesitating to speak the vernacular to their elders. This same phenomenon was noted by Hill and Hill (1986) in several of the Mexicano-speaking communities in which they worked. Like Schmidt, Hill and Hill conclude that the "purist discourses" propounded by middle-aged men, which stigmatize modern Mexicano speech as being too heavily Hispanicized and degenerate, tend to "work against the survival of the language" (1986: 140, see also Hill 1990). For an example of this phenomenon in contemporary Papua New Guinea, see Nekitel 1985: 249.

20 Because the shift to Tok Pisin in Gapun has been extremely rapid, the vernacular does not appear to have gone through any of the processes of morphological simplification and decay that have been documented for languages for which the process of shift has been gradual (see Dorian 1981; Dressler 1981; Hill and Hill 1986; Schmidt 1985; articles in Dorian 1989). Although this aspect of Taiap has not yet been analyzed in any detail, there do not appear to be any major structural differences in the Taiap spoken by the oldest and the youngest villagers. The only obvious systematic difference between the Taiap spoken by older people and adolescents is that young speakers under about 16 years systematically overextend the Taiap bound verbal suffix -*api*. In the vernacular, this morpheme expresses consecutivity. It is affixed to the end of the verb in the subordinate clause, and it signifies that the performance of an action is dependent upon the completion of the verb phrase onto which -*api* is suffixed. For example:

Gi mum	*ɔkurɔ-api*	*pεmkɔ-a*	*gɔk*
3PL sago jelly	consumed-CONSEC	got up-CONJ	went

"After they ate [their] sago jelly, they got up and left."

In everyday speech by fluent adult speakers, the use of -*api* to express temporal relations in this way is relatively limited and somewhat marked: Most villagers prefer to express consecutivity through clause juxtaposition. In the vernacular speech of most youths under the age of 16 however, -*api* occurs frequently. For many of these young speakers, -*api* is used as an equivalent of the Tok Pisin morpherne of completedness – *pinis*. The major difference between *-api* and *pinis* is that, whereas the former is a morphological marker of subordination that functions to express temporal relations between clauses, *pinis* is an aspectual marker signifying that an action is completed.

21 I have simplified the morpheme glosses in this text, omitting aspects such as Taiap's double-subject marking, in order to make it more accessible to nonspecialists. Interested readers should consult Kulick and Stroud in press b for a detailed description of the morphological structure of Taiap verbs.

22 The correct use of this conjunction can be seen at the beginning of the narrative presented in note 7, Chapter 7.

23 In Taiap, the verbal conjunctive morpheme *-a* is a syntactic coordinator of verb phrases, not a conjoiner of clauses, as the Tok Pisin conjunction *na* is. The ways in which the vernacular bound suffix *-api* differs from Tok Pisin's *pinis* is discussed in note 20 above. Neither *-a* nor *-api* is used to chain verbs in the way Kiring uses them here.

24 It seems probable that this generation of girls will become what Dorian has called "semi-speakers" of the vernacular. Semi-speakers are members of a speech community who "have a very partial command of the productive skills required to speak the dying language," and whose contributions in vernacular speech are limited to "very short phrases made up of high-frequency vocabulary in the simplest structures." However, despite their limited productive capabilities, these speakers "have almost perfect command of the receptive skills required to command [the vernacular]" (1982: 32–3). This excellent passive competence permits them to successfully participate in vernacular interactions, although they use this competence more or less exclusively with fluent speakers, not with other semi-speakers.

Chapter 7

1 In this sense, Gapun contrasts starkly to other societies described in the ethnograpic literature, such as Samoan (Ochs 1988: 128–44), Kaluli (Schieffelin 1990), and Managalase (McKellin 1990: 336). In all of these cultures, men and women disprefer to publicly wonder about what another person is thinking, and other people's thoughts or intentions are not acceptable topics for discussion, as they are in Gapun.

2 Compare this to Bauman's 1986: 22 account of story-telling conventions between dog traders in the southern United States. Among members of this group, details – even farfetched ones – are never challenged, because "to call another man a liar in [the context of story-telling] . . . is to threaten his 'face' with some risk and no possible advantage to oneself." Heath (1983) also discusses cultural variations on the role of exaggeration and lying in story-telling.

3 This point is explored in greater detail in Kulick and Stroud in press a.

4 See, for example, Chagnon (1977: 155) on how the Yanomamö of the Amazon Basin perceive illustrations. Like the Yanomamö, the villagers of Gapun believe that the images they see in their religious booklets of Heaven, Hell, Satan, the Virgin, Jesus, and others are actual photographic images taken by priests and other white people in the same way that I took pictures of them with my camera. Just as the photographs they saw of themselves

were reproductions of reality, so are images of Biblical characters and scenes reproductions of real things. Graphic images are proof for the villagers not only that these things exist, but also that white people have access to these sacred places and personae.

5   It should probably be made clear that the material from Gapun supports M. Strathern's recent contention that there is a general "Melanesian view that appearance is deceptive" and that "the relation between external surface and inner substance is always a matter for speculation" (1988: 122, 361n24; cf. Barth 1987: 70; Merlan and Rumsey 1991: 224-44). It is important to keep this basic understanding in mind in order to avoid confusing the role of sight in Melanesian practices of knowledge with the role that sight has been accorded as an instrument of knowledge in Western culture (e.g., Foucault 1975 on the role of the "gaze" in Western discourses of knowledge). My contention here is simply that for Gapuners, seeing, of all the senses, is considered to provide people with the best basis for evaluation of a person's thoughts and intentions (see also Kulick and Stroud 1990a: n9, and White 1990: 62).

6   The contradiction here between the observation that Sake had a *kros* at Jari because she was burdened by Jari's baby and the contention that the spirit of the baby was stolen by a *kandap* when Jari lay the child at the base of a tree during sex was not considered by anyone present at this gathering.

7   The following *stori*, told by a 19-year-old fluent speaker of Taiap, illustrates the structural similarities between narratives told in Tok Pisin and those recounted in Taiap.

Yim ripim Maramɛ-rɛ   ɔmin-dɛ   Sakɛ-rɛ   ɔmin-dɛ,
we   before Marame-CONJ spouse-CONJ Sake-CONJ spouse-CONJ

yim Bɔjimar priɛk.   Priɛk-a   bɔk, arɔ nɔn yim Sakɛ-mat-
we Bojimar went up   went up-CONJ went day a   we Sake-POSS-

-ɔmin-rɛ   je-rɛ   wɔkɛ. Wɔkɛ, je-num-gi   bɔr nitaŋgrɔ
-spouse-CONJ dog-CONJ went   went dog-PL-ERG pig found him

kiŋgagɔk,   taman babasaktukɔ. Rɔbin-rɛ   Taiga-rɛ   gi   nekɛr
chased him all   got lost   Robin-CONJ Tiger-CONJ they alone

ɔŋganukɛ. Bɔr agraŋka   niŋ sindɛr. Ɔŋganguk, yim prikɛ
bit him   pig emaciated   bone just   bit him   we went down

Sakɛ-ma-ɔmin-rɛ   tataŋgrɛ. Tataŋgrɛ, pɔŋgrɛ,   Sakɛ-ma-
Sake-POSS-spouse-CONJ saw him saw him   speared him Sake-POSS-

-ɔmin-ŋi   dɛr   ninkun, nɔmir   karkun, grip, pɛrɔŋgrɛ
-spouse-ERG path made   carrying stick cut   vines tied him

kiŋgaɔrikɛ. Kiŋaɔrikɛ   Amjig ainimɛ ɔpɔŋgrɛ. Puŋgrɛ,
took him down took him down Amjig there   singed him butchered him

wɛkɛ num-ni.   Wɛkɛ num-ni,   ŋa kandaw-i   nitin,   ŋa
came village-ALL   came village-ALL I   hunger-ERG affected me I

tatakut . . .
slept

Translation:
Once, me, Marame and his wife, Sake and her husband, we went up to Bojimar [an area of jungle owned by the crocodile clan, where Sake and Allan have a hunting

house]. We went up [and] one day me and Sake's husband went [hunting] with the dogs. We went, the dogs found a pig and chased him [but] they all lost him. Only Robin and Tiger fought with him. [It was] an emaciated pig, just bones. They were fighting with him [when] we came up. Me and Sake's husband saw him [i.e., the pig]. We saw him, speared him, Sake's husband cut a path [through the jungle to get to the dead pig], cut a carrying stick [and] vines, we tied him up [and] took him down. Took him down, [at] Amjig [another area of jungle] we singed the hair off him. We butchered him, came [back] to the village. Came [back] to the village, I was hungry, I slept. . . . [This story continues as the narrator describes the hunt he participated in the following day].

Conclusion

1 See Dorian's 1980 discussion on the significance of "linguistic lag" as a marker of ethnicity, and Hill (1987) on gender and lag.
2 This observation should be seen in light of the contentions of linguists like Susan Gal, who maintains that code-switching (which she refers to as "conversational language switching") is always socially meaningful. In accounting for code-switching behavior among Oberwart peasants on the Austro-Hungarian border, for example, Gal (1979: 175) concludes that "speakers allude to the large-scale social changes occurring in Oberwart when they engage in conversational language switching." While such "allusions" can be said to occur at times in Gapun, the vast majority of individual code-switches are, in my view, not meaningful in this way. It is also interesting to note that this socially-motivated explanation of Gal's could only account for half (N = 20) of the code-switches she found in her own data.

   If code-switching behavior itself is seen as shifting and processual (rather than as an ephemeral and seemingly static "middle and variable step" [Gal 1979: 173] in the process of language shift), however, then Gal's contentions about code-switching coming to convey social meanings may have a more general validity in situations of shift. This is the point made in the paragraph that follows this note in the main text. See also Stroud in press; Hill 1987: 130.
3 Compare Tuzin's recent description of the shift that has occurred "from a collectivist to an individualist value orientation" (1988: 97) among the Ilahita Arapesh of the middle Sepik. This shift, which Tuzin attributes primarily to the definitive collapse of the *tambaran* cult in the 1970s and to the acceptance by large numbers of villagers of evangelical Christianity and Western-derived means of dispute arbitration (i.e., taking problems to court), is resulting in the dispersion of villagers and the "death" of Ilahita village.
4 These factors concentrate on cultural and social aspects of language use. Another level of "openness," not detailed in this book, concerns the ability of the vernacular linguistic system itself to adopt and incorporate new elements from other languages. This type of "openness" is one of the main topics of Hill and Hill's 1986 monograph; see also Woolard 1989: 356.
5 Several months after completing this manuscript, I came across a volume on ethnicity in the Pacific (Linnekin and Poyer 1990: 10) where very similar reservations about the concept of ethnicity are expressed. "A major prob-

lem with employing the rubric of ethnicity," the editors explain in their introductory chapter, "is precisely that it is Western ethnotheory and therefore may ignore significant distinctions – both internal and external – recognized by local people themselves. For this reason the goal of this volume is to investigate, rather than to assume, the formation of distinctions within and among Pacific societies."

Appendix

1 The literature on this topic has grown logarithmically in the past few years. The standard place to begin has become the articles in Clifford and Marcus (1986) and the review article by Marcus and Cushman (1982). Among other works that problematize ethnographic writing and the role of the anthropologist are Herzfeld (1983) and Dywer (1982). More recently, Clifford (1988) and R. Rosaldo (1989) have attempted to respond to criticisms about the apolitical, "navel-gazing" (e.g., Freidman 1987) nature of the concern about reflexivity in ethnographic texts, and Geertz (1988) is a thoroughly enjoyable book about how different anthropologists have managed to create a sense of ethnographic authority through the way they write.

2 Cf. Geertz's snippy remarks on what he refers to as "text positivism" ethnography (1988: 145).

3 Compare Hallpike (1977: 31–3), who had similar experiences and was assigned a similar ontological status among the Tauade of Papua New Guinea.

References

Abrahams, R. 1962. Playing the dozens. *Journal of American Folklore* 75: 209–20.

Allen, J. 1982. Pre-contact trade in Papua New Guinea. In R. May and H. Nelson (eds.).

Arnberg, L. 1981. *The effects of bilingualism on development during early childhood: a survey of the literature.* (Linköping Studies in Education Reports No. 5.) Linköping, Sweden: Linköping University.

Barlow, K. 1984. Learning cultural meanings through social relationships: an ethnography of childhood in Murik society, Papua New Guinea. Ph.D. dissertation, Department of Anthropology, University of California, San Diego.

Barrington-Thomas, E., ed. 1976. *Papua New Guinea education.* Melbourne: Oxford University Press.

Barth, F. 1987. *Cosmologies in the making.* Cambridge University Press.

Bateson, G. 1958 [1936]. *Naven.* Stanford, Calif.: Stanford University Press.

Bauman, R. 1986. *Story, performance, and event: contextual studies of oral narrative.* Cambridge University Press.

1983. *Let your words be few: symbolism of speaking and silence among seventeenth-century Quakers.* Cambridge University Press.

and Sherzer, J., eds. 1989 [1974]. *Explorations in the ethnography of speaking.* Cambridge University Press.

Bavin, E. 1989. Some lexical and morphological changes in Walpiri. In N. Dorian, (ed.)

Bentahila, A. 1983. Motivations for code-switching among Arab–French bilinguals in Morocco. *Language and Communication* 3: 233–43.

Bergman, C. 1976. Interference vs. independent development in infant bilingualism. In G. Keller (ed.), *Bilingualism in the bicentennial and beyond.* New York: Bilingual Press.

Berndt, R. 1962. *Excess and restraint.* Chicago: University of Chicago Press.

Besnier, N. 1990. Conflict management, gossip, and affective meaning on Nukulaelae. In K. A. Watson-Gegeo and G. M. White (eds.).

Bloch, M., ed. 1975. *Political language and oratory in traditional society.* New York: Academic Press.

Blom, J. P., and Gumperz, J. 1972. Social meaning in linguistic structure: code-switching in Norway. In J. Gumperz and D. Hymes (eds.), *Directions in sociolinguistics.* New York: Holt, Rinehart, & Winston.

Boggs, S., and Chun, M. N. 1990. Ho'oponopono: a Hawaiian method of solving interpersonal problems. In K. A. Watson-Gegeo and G. M. White (eds.).

Boon, J. 1982. *Other tribes, other scribes: symbolic anthropology in the comparative study of cultures, histories, religions and texts.* Cambridge University Press.

Bourdieu, P. 1977. *Outline of a theory of practice.* Cambridge University Press.

Boyd, S. 1985. *Language survival.* Göteborg: Department of Linguistics, University of Göteborg.

Bradshaw, J. 1978. Multilingualism and language mixture among the Numbami. *Kivung* 11(1): 26–49.

Brammall, J., and May, R., eds. 1975. *Education in Melanesia.* Canberra: RSPacS. Eighth Waigani Seminar.

Brandl, M. M., and Walsh, M. 1982. Speakers of many tongues: toward understanding multilingualism among Aboriginal Australians. *International Journal of the Sociology of Language* 36: 71–81.

Brenneis, D., and Myers, F., eds. 1984. *Dangerous words: language and politics in the Pacific.* New York: New York University Press.

Brett-Smith, S. C. 1984. Speech made visible: the irregular as a system of meaning. *Empirical Studies of the Arts* 2: 127–47.

Brison, K. J. 1989. All talk and no action? Saying and doing in Kwanga meetings. *Ethnology* 28(2): 97–115.

Burbank, V. 1985. The Mirriri as ritualized aggression. *Oceania* 56(1): 47–55.

Burridge, K. 1960. *Mambu: a Melanesian millenium.* London: Methuen.

Cahill, A. 1950. Angoram Patrol Report 9: 49/50. Port Moresby: National Archives.

Chagnon, N. 1977. *Yanomamö: the fierce people.* New York: Holt, Rinehart, & Winston.

Chana, U., and Romaine, S. 1984. Evaluative reactions to Punjabi/English code-switching. *Journal of Multilingual and Multicultural Development* 5(6): 447–73.

Chowning, A. 1983. Interaction between Pidgin and three West New Britain languages. Canberra: *Pacific Linguistics* A-65.

Clancy, P. 1986. The acquisition of communicative style in Japanese. In B. Schieffelin and E. Ochs (eds.).

Clifford, J. 1988. *The predicament of culture.* Cambridge, Mass.: Harvard University Press.

and Marcus, G., eds. 1986. *Writing culture: the poetics and politics of ethnography.* Berkeley: University of California Press.

Clyne, M. 1982. *Multilingual Australia.* Melbourne: Riverseine.

Colburn, M. 1985. The creolization of Tok Pisin in urban centers and its impact on Madang vernaculars. Unpublished manuscript.

Conroy, J. 1973. *National Education Strategy: Papua New Guinea education plan review and proposals.* Boroko, PNG: Institute of Applied Social and Economic Research. Monograph 9.

Cooley, R. 1979. Variation in Delaware: a dying language. Paper read at the conference on non-English language variation, University of Louisville, Louisville, Ky., October 12, 1979.

Denison, N. 1977. Language death or language suicide? *International Journal of the Sociology of Language* 12: 13–22.

Denoon, D., with Dugan, K., and Marshall, L. 1989. *Public health in Papua New Guinea: medical possibility and social constraint, 1884–1984.* Cambridge University Press.

Dimmmendaal, G. 1989. On language death in eastern Africa. In N. Dorian (ed.).

Döpke, S. 1986. Discourse structures in bilingual families. *Journal of Multilingual and Multicultural Development* 7(6): 493–507.

Dorian, N. 1978. The fate of morphological complexity in language death. *Language* 54: 590–609.

1980. Linguistic lag as an ethnic marker. *Language in Society* 9: 33–42.

1981. *Language Death: the life cycle of a Scottish Gaelic dialect.* Philadelphia: University of Pennsylvania Press.

1982. Linguistic models and language death evidence. In L. Obler and L. Menn (eds.), *Exceptional language and linguistics.* New York: Academic Press.

(ed.) 1989. *Investigating obsolescence: studies in language contraction and death.* Cambridge University Press.

Dressler, W. 1981. Language shift and language death – a protean challenge for the linguist. *Folia Linguistica* XV/1–2: 5–28.

1988. Language death. In F. Newmeyer (ed), *Linguistics: the Cambridge survey.* Cambridge University Press.

and Wodak-Leodolter, R. 1977. Language preservation and language death in Brittany. *International Journal of the Sociology of Language* 12: 33–44.

Dutton, T. 1978. The "Melanesian problem" and language change and disappearance in southeastern Papua New Guinea. Unpublished manuscript.

1985. *Police Motu: iena sivarai.* Port Moresby: University of Papua New Guinea Press.

and Mühlhäusler, P. 1989. Are our languages dying? Keynote address for the Annual Conference of the Linguistic Society of Papua New Guinea, Port Moresby, 28–30 June 1989.

Ross, M., and Tryon, D. eds., in press. *The language game: papers in memory of Donald C. Laycock.* Canberra: Pacific Linguistics.

Dwyer, K. 1982. *Moroccan Dialogues.* Baltimore: John Hopkins University Press.

Edwards, J. 1985. *Language, society and identity.* Oxford: Blackwell.

Elmendorf, W. 1981. Last speakers and language change: two California cases. *Anthropological Linguistics* 1: 36–49.

Errington, F., and Gewertz, D. 1987. *Cultural alternatives and a feminist anthropology.* Cambridge University Press.

Fantini, A. 1985. *Language acquisition of a bilingual child: a sociolinguistic perspective.* Clevedon, Avon, U.K.: Multilingual Matters.

Fasold, R. 1984. *The sociolinguistics of society.* Oxford: Blackwell.

Ferguson, C. 1978. Talking to children: a search for universals. In J. Greenberg (ed.), *Universals of human language. Vol 1. Method and theory.* Stanford, Calif.: Stanford University Press.

Fishman, J. 1964. Language maintenance and language shift as a field of inquiry. *Linguistics* 9: 32–70.

1966. *Language loyalty in the United States.* The Hague: Mouton.

Foley, W. 1986. *The Papuan languages of New Guinea.* Cambridge University Press.

1988. Language birth: the processes of pidginization and creolization. In F. Newmeyer (ed.), *Linguistics: the Cambridge survey. Vol. IV, Language: the socio-cultural context.* Cambridge University Press.

Forge, A. 1972. The Golden Fleece. *Man* 7: 527–40.

Foucault, M. 1975. *The birth of the clinic: an archeology of medical perception.* New York: Random House.

Friedman. J. 1987. Crick's Cracks. *Social Analysis* 21: 80–2.

Gal, S. 1978. Peasant man can't get wives: language change and sex roles in a bilingual community. *Language in Society* 7: 1–16.

    1979. *Language shift: social determinants of linguistic change in bilingual Austria.* New York: Academic Press.

Geertz, C. 1988. *Works and lives.* Stanford, Calif.: Stanford University Press.

Gell, A. 1975. *Metamorphosis of the cassowaries.* London: Athlone Press.

Genesee, F. 1989. Early bilingual development: one language or two? *Journal of Child Language* 16: 161–79.

Giddens, A. 1979. *Central problems in social theory.* London: MacMillian.

Giles, H., ed. 1977. *Language, ethnicity and intergroup relations.* London: Academic Press.

    Bourhis, R., and Taylor, D. 1977. Towards a theory of language in ethnic group relations. In H. Giles (ed.).

Gillison, G. 1980. Images of nature in Gimi thought. In C. MacCormack and M. Strathern (eds.).

Giraure, N. 1975. The need for a cultural programme: personal reflections. In J. Bramhall and R. May (eds.).

Godelier, M. 1986. *The making of great men.* Cambridge University Press.

Goldman, L. 1980. Speech categories and the study of disputes: a New Guinea example. *Oceania* 50(3): 209–27.

    1983. *Talk never dies.* London: Tavistock Publications.

    1986. The presentational style of women in Huli disputes. Canberra: *Pacific Linguistics* 24: 213–89.

    1987. Ethnographic interpretations of parent child discourse in Huli. *Journal of Child Language* 14: 447–66.

    1988. *Premarital sex cases among the Huli.* Oceania Monograph 34.

Goodwin, M., and Goodwin, C. 1987. Children's arguing. In S. Philips, S. Steele, and C. Tanz (eds.).

Goulden, R. 1990. *The Melanesian content in Tok Pisin.* Canberra: Pacific Linguistics B-24.

Griffin, J., Nelson, H., and Firth, S. 1979. *Papua New Guinea: a political history.* Victoria: Heinemann Educational Australia.

Gumperz, J. 1982. *Discourse strategies.* Cambridge University Press.

Haiman, J. 1979. Hua: a Papuan language of New Guinea. In T. Shopen (ed.), *Languages and their status.* Cambridge University Press.

Halliday, M. 1975. *Learning how to mean: explorations in the development of language.* New York: Academic Press.

Hallpike, C. R. 1977. *Bloodshed and vengance in the Papuan Mountains.* Oxford: Clarendon Press.

Harrison, G. J., and Piette, A. B. 1980. Young bilingual children's language selection. *Journal of Multilingual and Multicultural Development* 1(3): 217–30.

Heath, S. B. 1983. *Ways with words: language, life and work in communities and classrooms.* Cambridge University Press.

Herdt, G. 1981. *Guardians of the flutes.* New York: McGraw–Hill.

Herzfeld, M., ed. 1983. Signs in the field: semiotic perspectives on ethnography. Special issue of *Semiotica* 46(2/4).

Hiatt, L. 1964. Incest in Arnhem Land. *Oceania* 35: 124–8.

Hill, J. 1987. Women's speech in modern Mexicano. In S. Philips, S. Steele, and C. Tanz (eds.).

    1990. Structure and practice in language shift. Paper read at Conference on Progression and Regression in Language, Botkyrka, Sweden, 13–16 August 1990.

Hill, J., and Hill, K. 1977. Language death and relexification in Tlaxcalan Nahuatl. *International Journal of the Sociology of Language* 12: 55–67.

    1986. *Speaking Mexicano: dynamics of syncretic language in Central Mexico.* Tucson: University of Arizona Press.

Hogbin, I. 1963. *Kinship and marriage in a New Guinea village.* London: Athlone Press.

Hollyman, J. 1962. The lizard and the axe: a study of the effects of European contact on the indigenous languages of Polynesia and Island Melanesia. *Journal of the Polynesian Society* 71(3): 310–29.

Höltker, G. 1938. Eine fragmentarische wörterliste der Gapun-sprache Neuguineas. *Anthropos* 33: 279–82.

Hooley, B. 1987. Death or life: the prognosis for central Buang. In D. Laycock and W. Winter (eds.).

Hughes, I. 1977. *New Guinea stone age trade.* Canberra: Australian National University.

Hyltenstam, K., and Obler, L., eds. 1989. *Bilingualism across the lifespan.* Cambridge University Press.

Jackson, J. 1983. *The fish people: linguistic exogamy and Tukanoan identity in northwest Amazonia.* Cambridge University Press.

    1989 [1974]. Language identity of the Columbian Vaupes Indians. In R. Bauman and J. Sherzer (eds.).

Johnson, R. 1977. Administration and language policy in Papua New Guinea. In S. Wurm (ed.).

Jolly, M. 1987. The forgotten women: a history of migrant labour and gender relations in Vanuatu. *Oceania* 58(1): 119–39.

Keenan, E. 1989 [1974]. Norm makers, norm breakers: uses of speech by men and women in a Malagasy community. In R. Bauman and J. Sherzer (eds.).

Keesing, R. 1982. Introduction. In G. Herdt (ed.), *Rituals of manhood.* Berkeley: University of California Press.

    1988. *Melanesian pidgin and the Oceanic substrate.* Stanford, Calif.: Stanford University Press.

Kolig, E. 1972. Bi:n and Gadeja: an Australian Aboriginal model of the European society as a guide in social change. *Oceania* 43(1): 1–18.

Kulick, D. in press. Language shift as cultural reproduction. In T. Dutton (ed.), *Language change, culture change: some case studies from the South Pacific.* Canberra: Pacific Linguistics.

    n.d. Killing your *kandere:* on the Taiap custom of murdering an innocent maternal relative as a means of dealing with anger and shame. Unpublished manuscript.

Kulick, D., and Stroud, C. 1990a. Christianity, cargo and ideas of self: patterns of literacy in a Papua New Guinean village. *Man* 25: 286–303.

    1990b. Code-switching in Gapun: social and linguistic aspects of language use in a language shifting community. In J. Verhaar (ed.).

    in press a. Conceptions and uses of literacy in a Papua New Guinean village.

In B. Street (ed.), *Cross-cultural approaches to literacy*. Cambridge University Press.

in press b. The structure of the Taiap (Gapun) language. In T. Dutton, M. Ross, and D. Tryon (eds.).

Lanza, E. 1988. Conversations with bilingual two year olds. Paper read at Eleventh Annual Meeting of the American Association for Applied Linguistics, New Orleans, December 17–29, 1988.

Lawrence, P. 1964. *Road belong cargo*. Melbourne: Melbourne University Press.

Laycock, D. 1973. *Sepik languages: checklist and preliminary classification*. Canberra: Pacific Linguistics B-25.

1975. The Torricelli Phylum. In S. Wurm (ed.).

1977. Special languages in parts of the New Guinea Area. In S. Wurm (ed.), *New Guinea area languages and language study, Vol. 3. Language, culture, society and the modern world*. Canberra: Pacific Linguistics C-40.

1979. Multilingualism: linguistic boundaries and unsolved problems in Papua New Guinea. In S. Wurm (ed.).

1982. Melanesian linguistic diversity: a Melanesian choice? In R. May and H. Nelson (eds.).

and Z'graggen, J. 1975. The Sepik-Ramu Phylum. In S. Wurm (ed.).

and Winter, W., eds. 1987. *A world of languages: papers presented to Professor S. A. Wurm on his 65th birthday*. Canberra: Pacific Linguistics C-100.

Lederman, R. 1984. Who speaks here? Formality and the politics of gender in Mendi, Highland Papua New Guinea. In D. Brenneis and F. Myers (eds.).

Lieberson, S. 1980. Procedures for improving sociolinguistic surveys of language maintenance and language shift. *International Journal of the Sociology of Language* 25: 11–27.

Lindholm, K., and Padilla, A. 1978. Language mixing in bilingual children. *Journal of Child Language* 5: 327–35.

1979. Child bilingualism: report on language mixing, switching, and translations. *Linguistics* 211: 23–44.

Linnekin, J., and Poyer, L., eds. 1990. *Cultural identity and ethnicity in the Pacific*. Honolulu: University of Hawaii Press.

Lipset, D. 1984. Authority and the maternal presence: an interpretive ethnography of Murik Lakes society. Ph.D. dissertation, Department of Anthropology, University of California, San Diego.

Lithgow, D. 1973. Language change on Woodlark island. *Oceania* 44(2): 101–8.

Litteral, R. 1990. Tok Pisin: the language of modernization. In J. Verhaar (ed.).

MacCormack, C., and Strathern, M., eds. 1980. *Nature, culture and gender*. Cambridge University Press.

Maddock, K. 1970. A structural interpretation of the Mirriri. *Oceania* 40: 165–76.

Makarius, R. 1966. Incest and redemption in Arnhem Land. *Oceania* 37: 148–52.

Marcus, G., and Cushman, D. 1982. Ethnographies as texts. *Annual Review of Anthropology* 11: 25–69.

May, R., and Nelson, H., eds. 1982. *Melanesia: beyond diversity*. Canberra: ANU Press.

McDowell, N. A. 1975. Kinship and the concept of shame in a New Guinea village. Ph.D. dissertation, Department of Anthropology, Cornell University, Ithaca, N.Y.

McKellin, W. 1984. Putting down roots: information in the language of Managalase exchange. In D. Brenneis and F. Myers (eds.).

1990. Allegory and inference: intentional ambiguity in Managalase negotiations. In K. A. Watson-Gegeo and G. M. White (eds.).

McLaren, P. 1975. Schools and knowledge in Astrolabe Bay. In J. Brammall and R. May (eds.).

Mead, M. 1930. *Growing up in New Guinea.* London: William Morrow and Co.

1931. Talk-Boy. *Asia* (31): 144–51.

Meeker, M., Barlow, K., and Lipset, D. 1986. Culture, exchange, and gender: lessons from the Murik. *Cultural Anthropology* 1(1): 6–73.

Meggitt, M. 1968. Uses of literacy in New Guinea and Melanesia. In J. Goody (ed.), *Literacy in traditional societies.* Cambridge University Press.

Meisel, J. 1989. Early differentiation of languages in bilingual children. In K. Hyltenstam and L. Obler (eds.).

Menn, L. 1989. Some people who don't talk right: universal and particular in child language, aphasia, and language obsolescence. In N. Dorian (ed.).

Merlan, F., and Rumsey, A. 1991. *Ku Waru: language and segmentary politics in the western Nebilyer valley, Papua New Guinea.* Cambridge University Press.

Mertz, E. 1989. Sociolinguistic creativity: Cape Breton Gaelic's linguistic "tip." In N. Dorian (ed.).

Metraux, R. 1965. A study of bilingualism among children of U.S.–French parents. *French Review* 38: 650–65.

Mihalic, F. 1971. *The Jacaranda dictionary and grammar of Melanesian Pidgin.* Brisbane: The Jacaranda Press.

Miller, P. 1986. Teasing as language socialization and verbal play in a white working-class community. In B. Schieffelin and E. Ochs (eds.).

Morauta, L. 1974. *Beyond the village: local politics in Madang, Papua New Guinea.* London: Athlone Press.

Mosel, U. 1980. *Tolai and Tok Pisin: the influence of the substratum on the development of New Guinea Pidgin.* Canberra: Pacific Linguistics B-73.

Mühlhäusler, P. 1979. *Growth and structure of the lexicon in New Guinea Pidgin.* Canberra: Pacific Linguistics C-52.

1985a. Syntax of Tok Pisin. In S. Wurm and P. Mühlhäusler (eds.).

1985b. Inflectional morphology of Tok Pisin. In S. Wurm and P. Mühlhäusler (eds.).

1985c. Tok Pisin and its relevance to theoretical issues in creolistics and general linguistics. In S. Wurm and P. Mühlhäusler (eds.).

1985d. Internal development of Tok Pisin. In S. Wurm and P. Mühlhäusler (eds.).

1989. On the causes of accelerated language change in the Pacific area. In L. E. Breivik and E. H. Jahr (eds.), *Language change: contributions to the study of its causes.* Berlin and New York: Mouton de Gruyter.

Myers, F. 1986. *Pintupi country, Pintupi self: sentiment, place and politics among Western Desert Aborigines.* Washington and London: Smithsonian Institution Press.

Nash, J. 1987. Gender attributes and equality: men's strength and women's talk among the Nagovisi. In M. Strathern (ed.).

Nekitel, O. 1984. What is happening to our vernaculars? *Bikmaus* 5(2): 89–97.
    1985. Sociolinguistic aspects of Abu'. Ph.D. dissertation. Department of
    Linguistics, Research School of Pacific Studies, Australian National Uni-
    versity.
Ochs, E. 1979. Transcription as theory. In E. Ochs and B. Schieffelin (eds.).
    1986a. Introduction. In B. Schieffelin and E. Ochs (eds.).
    1986b. From feelings to grammar: a Samoan case study. In B. Schieffelin and
    E. Ochs (eds.).
    1988. *Culture and language development: language acquisition and language
    socialization in a Samoan village.* Cambridge University Press.
    and Schieffelin, B. 1984. Language acquisition and socialization: three de-
    velopmental stories and their implications. In R. Shweder and R. Levine
    (eds.), *Culture theory: essays in mind, self and emotion.* Cambridge Uni-
    versity Press.
    and Schieffelin, B., eds. 1979. *Developmental pragmatics.* New York: Aca-
    demic Press.
Olifend, J. 1919. Patrol report. Victoria: Australian Archives, File No. 404–11–
    245,
Ortner, S. 1974. Is female to male as nature is to culture? In M. Rosaldo and
    L. Lamphere (eds.), *Women, culture and society.* Stanford, Calif.: Stanford
    University Press.
Padilla, A., and Liebman, E. 1975. Language acquisition in the bilingual child.
    Bilingual Review 2: 34–55.
Philips, S., Steele, S., and Tanz, C., eds. 1987. *Language, gender and sex in
    comparative perspective.* Cambridge University Press.
Platt, M. 1986. Social norms and lexical acquisition: a study of deictic verbs in
    Samoan child language. In B. Schieffelin and E. Ochs (eds.).
Pye, C. 1986a. Quiche Mayan speech to children. *Journal of Child Language*
    13: 85–100.
    1986b. One lexicon or two? An alternative interpretation of early bilingual
    speech. *Journal of Child Language* 13: 591–3.
Read, K. 1955. Morality and the concept of the person among the Gahuku-
    Gama. *Oceania* 25(4): 233–82.
Reddy, M. 1979. The conduit metaphor – a case of frame conflict in our language
    about language. In A. Ortony (ed.), *Metaphor and thought.* Cambridge
    University Press.
Redlinger, W. 1978. Mothers' speech to children in bilingual Mexican-American
    homes. *International Journal of the Sociology of Language* 17: 73–82.
Reed, S. 1943. *The making of modern New Guinea.* Memoirs of the American
    Philosophical Society, Vol. 18. Philadelphia, Pa.
Reesink, G. 1990. Mother tongue and Tok Pisin. In J. Verhaar (ed.).
Rivière, P. 1981. 'The wages of sin is death': some aspects of evangelisation
    among the Trio Indians. *Journal of the Anthropological Society of Oxford*
    12(1): 1–13.
Romaine, S. 1989. Pidgins, creoles, immigrant and dying languages. In N. Do-
    rian (ed.).
Rosaldo, M. 1973. I have nothing to hide: the language of Ilongot oratory.
    Language in Society 2: 193–223.
Rosaldo, R. 1989. *Culture and truth.* Boston: Beacon.
Sahlins, M. 1981. *Historical metaphors and mythical realities.* Ann Arbor: Uni-
    versity of Michigan Press.

1985. *Islands of history*. London and New York: Tavistock Publications.
Salisbury, R. 1972. Notes on bilingualism and linguistic change in New Guinea. In J. Pride and J. Holmes (eds.), *Sociolinguistics*. Middlesex: Penguin Books.
Sanders, A., and Sanders, J. 1980. Defining the centers of the Marienberg language family. *Pacific Linguistics* A-56: 171–96.
Sankoff, G. 1971. Language use in multilingual societies: some alternate approaches. In G. Sankoff 1980.
   1976. Political power and linguistic inequality in Papua New Guinea. In G. Sankoff 1980.
   1977. Multilingualism in Papua New Guinea. In G. Sankoff 1980.
   1980. *The social life of language*. Philadelphia: University of Pennsylvania Press.
Sansom, B. 1980. *The camp at Wallaby Cross*. Canberra: Australian Institute of Aboriginal Studies.
Schach, P., ed. 1980. *Languages in conflict*. Lincoln: University of Nebraska Press.
Schieffelin, B. 1979. Getting it together: an ethnographic approach to the study of the development of communicative competence. In E. Ochs and B. Schieffelin (eds.).
   1986. Teasing and shaming in Kaluli children's interactions. In B. Schieffelin and E. Ochs (eds.).
   1987. Do different worlds mean different words? An example from Papua New Guinea. In S. Philips, S. Steele, and C. Tanz (eds.).
   1990. *The give and take of everyday life: language socialization of Kaluli children*. Cambridge University Press.
   and Cochran-Smith, M. 1984. Learning to read culturally: literacy before schooling. In H. Goelman, A. Oberg, and F. Smith (eds.), *Awakening to literacy*. London: Heinemann
   and Ochs, E., eds. 1986a. *Language socialization across cultures*. Cambridge University Press.
   1986b. Language socialization. *Annual Review of Anthropology* 15: 163–191.
Schieffelin, E. 1976. *The sorrow of the lonely and the burning of the dancers*. New York: St. Martin's Press.
   1981. Evangelical rhetoric and the transformation of traditional culture in Papua New Guinea. *Comparative Studies in Society and History* 23: 150–6.
Schmidt, A. 1985. *Young people's Dyirbal: an example of language death from Australia*. Cambridge University Press.
Scollon, R., and Scollon, S. 1981. *Narrative, literacy and face in interethnic communication*. Norwood, N.J.: Ablex.
Scorza, D. 1985. A sketch of Au morphology and syntax. *Papers in New Guinea Linguistics No. 22*. Pacific Linguistics A-63.
Scotton, C. M. 1979. Code-switching as a "safe choice" in choosing a lingua franca. In W. McCormack and S. Wurm (eds.), *Language and society: anthropological issues*. The Hague: Mouton.
   1982. The possibility of code-switching: motivation for maintaining multilingualism. *Anthropological Linguistics* 24(4): 432–45.
Sherzer, J., and Woodbury, A., eds. 1987. *Native American discourse: poetics and rhetoric*. Cambridge University Press.
Siegal, J. 1986. *Language contact in a plantation environment: a sociolinguistic history*. Cambridge University Press.

Smith, G. 1975. *Education in Papua New Guinea*. Victoria: Melbourne University Press.

Smith, G. P. in press. Prospects for the survival of two minority Morobe languages. In T. Dutton (ed.), *Culture change, language change: some case studies from the South Pacific*. Canberra: Pacific Linguistics.

Smith, R. 1973. The School at Wankung: an anthropological study of Western education in rural *Papua New Guinea*. Ph.D. dissertation, University of Queensland, Brisbane, Australia.

1975. Discontinuities in education at Wankung. In J. Brammall and R. May (eds.).

Snow C., and Ferguson C., eds. 1977. *Talking to children: language input and acquisition*. Cambridge University Press.

Strathern, A. 1975a. Veiled speech in Mount Hagen. In M. Bloch, (ed.), 1975b. Why is shame on the skin? *Ethnology* 14: 347–56.

Strathern, M. 1979. The self in self-decoration. *Oceania* 49(4): 241–57.

1980. No nature, no culture: the Hagen case. In C. MacCormack and M. Strathern, (eds.).

ed. 1987. *Dealing with inequality: analysing gender relations in Melanesia and beyond*. Cambridge University Press.

1988. *The gender of the gift*. Berkeley: University of California Press.

Strelan, J. 1977. *Search for salvation: studies in the history and theology of cargo cults*. Adelaide: Lutheran Publishing House.

Stringer, M. 1983. Cognitive development and literacy in Papua New Guinea: a study of the appropriateness of the Gudschinsky method for teaching children to read. M.A. thesis, School of Education, Macquarie University, Australia.

Stroud, C. 1991. *Language, literacy and code-switching in a Papua New Guinean village*. Stockholm: Department of Linguistics, Stockholm University.

in press. The problem of intention and meaning in code-switching. *Text* 12.

Swadling, P. 1984. Sepik prehistory. Paper presented at the Wenner-gren foundation for anthropological research, International Symposium, Basel.

Swatridge, C. 1985. *Delivering the goods: education as cargo in Papua New Guinea*. Manchester: Manchester University Press.

Taeschner, T. 1983. *The sun is feminine: a study on language acquisition in bilingual children*. Berlin: Springer Verlag.

Tamoane, M, 1977. Kamoai of Darapap and the ledgend of Jari. In G. Trompf (ed.), *Prophets of Melanesia*. Port Moresby: Institute of Papua New Guinea Studies.

Taylor, A. 1968. A note on the study of sociolinguistics with particular refence to Papua New Guinea. *Kivung* 1(1): 43–52.

Thurnwald, R. 1916. *Banaro society*. Memoirs of the American Anthropological Association 3, no. 4: 251–391.

1931. Studying savages in Melanesia. *Yale Review* 26: 313–32.

Trudgill, P. 1978. Creolization in reverse: reduction and simplification in the Albanian dialects of Greece. *Transactions of the Philological Society* 1976–77: 32–50.

Tuzin, D. 1976. *The Ilahita Arapesh*. Berkeley: University of California Press.

1980. *Voice of the Tambaran*. Berkeley: University of California Press.

1988. Prospects of village death in Ilahita. *Oceania* 59(2): 81–104.

Verhaar, J., ed. 1990. *Melanesian pidgin and Tok Pisin*. Amsterdam: John Benjamins.

Vihman, M. 1985. Language differentiation in the bilingual infant. *Journal of Child Language* 12: 297–324.

Voegelin, C., and Voegelin, F. 1977. Is Tubatulabal de-acquisition relevant to theories of language acquisition? *International Journal of the Sociology of Language* 43: 333–6.

Volterra, V., and Taeschner, T. 1978. The acquisition and development of language by bilingual children. *Journal of Child Language* 5: 311–26.

Voorhoeve, C. 1979. Turning the talk: a case of chain-interpreting in Papua New Guinea. In S. Wurm (ed.)

Walsh, D. 1978. Tok Pisin syntax – the East Austronesian factor. Canberra: *Pacific Linguistics* A–54.

Warner, W. L. 1937. *A black civilization: a study of an Australian tribe.* New York: Harper & Row.

Watson-Gegeo, K. A., and Gegeo, D. 1986. Calling out and repeating routines in Kwara'ae children's language socialization. In B. Schieffelin and E. Ochs (eds.).

Watson-Gegeo, K. A., and Gegeo, D. 1989. The role of sibling interaction in child socialization. In Zukow, P. G. (ed.), *Sibling interaction across cultures: theoretical and methodological issues.* New York: Springer Verlag.

1990. Shaping the mind and straightening out conflicts: the discourse of Kwara'ae family counseling. In K. A. Watson-Gegeo and G. M. White (eds.) and White, G. M., eds. 1990. *Disentangling: conflict discourse in Pacific societies.* Stanford, Calif.: Stanford University Press.

Weinreich, U. 1964. *Languages in contact.* The Hague: Mouton.

Wentworth, W. 1980. *Context and understanding: an inquiry into socialization theory.* New York: Elsevier North-Holland.

White, G. M. 1990. Emotion talk and social inference: disentangling in Santa Isabel, Soloman Islands. In K. A. Watson-Gegeo and G. M. White (eds.).

Williams, F. E. 1930. *Orokaiva society.* Oxford: Clarendon Press.

Williamson, M. H. 1979. Who does what to the sago: A Kwoma variation of Sepik River sex-roles. *Oceania* 49(3): 210–20.

Woolard, K. 1989. Language convergence and language death as social processes. In N. Dorian (ed.).

Worsley, P. 1957. *The trumpet shall sound.* London: MacGibbon and Kee.

Wurm, S., ed. 1975. *New Guinea Area languages and language study.* Vol. 1: *Papuan languages and the New Guinea linguistic scene.* Canberra: *Pacific Linguistics* C–38.

ed. 1979. *New Guinea and neighboring areas: a sociolinguistic laboratory.* The Hague: Mouton.

1982. *Papuan languages of Oceania.* Tubingen: Gunter Narr.

1985. The status of Tok Pisin and attitudes towards it. In S. Wurm and P. Mühlhäusler (eds.).

1986. Grammatical decay in Papuan languages. Canberra: *Pacific Linguistics* A–70: 207–211.

Laycock, D., Voorhoeve, C., Dutton, T. 1975. Papuan linguistic prehistory, and past language migrations in the New Guinea Area. In S. Wurm (ed.).

and Mühlhäusler, P., eds. 1985. *Handbook of Tok Pisin (New Guinea Pidgin).* Canberra: Pacific Linguistics C-70.

Z'graggen, J. in press. The myth of Daria. In T. Dutton, M. Ross, and D. Tryon (eds.).

Index

Abu' language, 5–6
Adam and Eve, 157–9, 163
Adjora language, 61, 64, 66, 69, 74, 75–6, 82–3, 84, 86, 89, 188, 227, 250
Angoram (Bien) language, 69
Austronesian languages, 62
authority, in discourse, 143–4, 148, 250, 290–1n13 (*see also* harangues)
autonomy, 19, 48–51, 95, 101–4, 106, 109–11, 114–17, 119, 145, 209, 248, 255, 256, 259 (*see also* provocation, *kroses*)

babies: development affects mother, 97–8; early vocalizations, 191; language directed to, 97, 191
baby-talk registers, 15, 197–9, 295nn4–8
banks, 143, 148, 172, 174, 176, 264
"big men," 103, 139–40, 142, 259
bishops, 161, 176, 186, 187
blame assignment, 53, 54, 106, 110, 146, 176–8
Buang language, 6
Buin language, 2
bus kanaka (country bumpkin), 11, 196, 253, 262

calling-out routines, 225
cargo cults, 23, 186, 249, 263; inspired by Ninga, 166, 186; inspired by Raphael, 167, 188; inspired by "Yaring," 165–6, 167, 186, 251; in 1987, 31, 52, 167–8, 188, 270–1; scholarly discussions of, 185
cash cropping, 18, 39, 45–7, 81, 251, 258, 264
Chambri language, 2
change, cultural attitudes toward, 160, 186, 263–4, 266
changing skin, 60, 102, 160, 163, 166, 168, 171, 183–4, 185, 186, 189, 249, 263, 270, 291n3

children: first words, 101–2, 116, 122, 202; and *hed*, 17, 100–3, 114, 116, 202, 209, 223–4, 248, 256, 257; how they learn, 120–2, 257, 262; as information givers, 230–4; and *kroses*, 111; learn to *stori*, 243–7; and *save*, 120–2, 196–7, 202, 224, 256, 257
Christianity (*see also* cargo cults, literacy, schooling, Tok Pisin, white people): after WWII, 165; and development, 10–11, 60; as interpretive framework, 160–3, 175; intertwined with millenarianism, 165–7; and pictures, 240–1, 299–300n4; as secret knowledge, 161; villagers' first meeting with, 163–5
clans, 86–9, 98–9, 139, 142, 164
code-switching, 11, 21, 253–6, 286n4, 287n10; adults to children, 194–6, 199, 202–9, 214–17; attitudes toward, 75, 77; by children, 215–20, 289n18; and Christian worship, 188; consequences for language acquisition, 113, 210–18, 257, 261; to construct rythmically patterned discourse, 112–13, 132, 255; cultural determinants, 253–4; gender differences, 90–1; in *kroses*, 111–13, 117; and language shift, 255–6, 257, 261, 301n2; in men's house, 132, 134, 142–8; structure of, 75–9
contextualization, 106, 135, 138, 143, 190, 227–9, 246
contraception (*kip*), 35, 92
contracted labor, 4, 17, 31, 56, 66–8, 72, 165, 250–1, 281n10

detail, 221–2, 229, 233, 235, 237–9, 242, 246, 247
development (*kamap*), 55–60, 102, 143, 147, 189, 259, 264
diglossia, 253
diminutives, 134, 138, 145
directives, 202–4, 209

315

East Sutherland Gaelic, 9–11, 248
"egalitarian bilingualism," 3
em ia routines, 121–2, 191–4, 224–5, 226, 233
Enga language, 1
English, 5, 83, 178, 180, 187, 250
Erima Nambis language, 6
ethnicity, 10–11, 262–3, 301–2n5 (*see also* language shift)
ethnography of speaking, 22–3

face play, 100, 191
forms, 174, 180

games, 177; caregiver–child, 210
"giving back mouth," 54, 110–11

harangues, 139–44, 145, 146, 147, 176, 227, 253
"hidden" talk, 134–5, 138, 240
Hiri Motu, 5
Hua language, 7

"Innovative Finance," 172–4, 176
intention, 48–9, 100–1, 230–1, 233, 257, 299n1

Jari (mythological ancestress), 58, 158, 162, 279n6, 282n20
Jenkenga Ojenata (clan Ur-mother), 89
Jesus, 31, 158–60, 162, 163, 176, 182, 186, 234, 240, 267, 270, 272
Jews, 158

Kaluli, 15, 16, 273, 274
Kambedagam, 69, 85, 90, 157, 162, 261
Koiari language, 6
Kopar language, 61, 66, 69, 73, 74, 75–6, 80, 85, 86, 90
*kros*es, 35, 49–54, 104–17, 119, 126, 130, 144, 145–6, 147, 224, 252, 253, 260, 287n9
Kruni Maroka, 90, 142–3, 148
kumu karamap, 182

language: children begin speaking, 101, 209–14; expressive of social competence, 48–9, 122, 126–32, 135, 139, 144–5, 148, 223, 224 (*see also* oratorical speeches); and gender, 125, 252; interpretations of children's speech, 201–5, 256; and the land, 85–6, 89–90, 264–5; local conceptions of, 190–1, 233; and schooling, 222; spoken in Heaven, 188
language separation, by children, 213–14, 296–8n14

language shift: and baby-talk register, 198; and ethnicity, 9–11, 262–3; and ethnography, 8–9; and gender, 218–22, 282n16; initial phases, 248–52; in Papua New Guinea, 5–7; scholarly approaches to, 8–14, 258, 277–8nn11, 13, 15; villagers' awareness of, 73–4, 214–15, 223, 247, 257–8, 264; villagers' explanation of, 13, 16–17, 223–4, 248
language socialization: and contextualization, 224; in language shifting communities, 12–13; scholarly approaches to, 14–16, 248–9
"language suicide," 12–13
linguistic accommodation, 75, 91, 122, 135, 144–5, 195, 197, 214, 261–2
literacy, 32, 136–9, 143, 145, 168–75, 180, 186–8

marriage, 18, 81–2, 86–7, 113, 259, 266, 283–4n23
maternity houses, 93–6, 200, 259
men, stereotyped as sociable, 115–16, 122–3, 145–6
men's house, 33–4, 122–3, 147–8, 259–60, 287–8n2
methodology, 271–5
metonymy, 227–8
Michael Somare, 182, 190
modernity, 10–11, 21–2 (*see also* Tok Pisin); and men's speech, 146–9
money, 45–7, 129–31, 260, 266; and land, 264–5
multilingualism, 3, 69–73, 74, 90–1, 252, 261

Nahuatl (Mexicano) language, 248, 263
naming, 86, 98–9
naming routines, 225–6
narrative conventions, 142–3, 221–2, 246
Numbami language, 6

ɔndir, 103–4, 285n1
oratorical speeches, 49, 103, 122–44, 145–9, 227, 250–3; and dissociation, 127–31, 133–4, 143, 290n9
Original Sin, 157
ownership, 49, 98

Papua New Guinea: colonial history, 3–5; as the "last country," 59, 157, 163, 184; reasons for linguistic diversity, 1–3
Papuan languages, 62–3
past, villagers' attitudes toward, 188–9
peer groups, 217

"Place of Dead Souls," 157, 159, 162
Pope, 159–60, 182, 183–4, 190
possessions, 44–5, 47–51; villagers destroy
    their own, 35, 50–2, 103, 106, 114,
    278–9n3, 283–4n23
postal service, 174–5
post-partum taboos, 96–8
pregnancy, 92–3
provocation, 51, 98, 102–4, 134, 138–9,
    144–5

questions, 229–30; to children, 230–4, 243

reciprocity, 113, 253–4
referent identification, 121–2, 224, 226–8
repetition, xv, 77–8, 111–13, 121, 125,
    131, 132, 134, 142, 190, 218
rhetorical questions, 110–11

sacred flutes, 164–5
Samoa, 15, 16
sangguma, 31, 216
schooling, 175–80, 184–5, 186, 199, 222
Selepet language, 2–3
self, as duality, 19–21, 144, 253–4
"semi-speakers," 13, 24, 299n24
Sepik–Ramu languages, 63
siblings, role in language socialization,
    199–201, 217, 261
sight, as instrument of knowledge, 239–
    41, 245, 246, 300n5
skin color: consequences for fieldwork,
    ix, 271–2; and *save*, 185, 250
sorcery, 19, 30, 31, 32, 37, 38, 55, 60, 78,
    82, 89, 93, 97, 100, 106, 113, 119, 139,
    147, 175, 185, 243, 250, 253
stori, 234–47, 264
"structure of the conjuncture," 19, 250–1
subways, 59, 163, 271
"supress *hed*," 19, 102, 115, 117, 119–20,
    256, 257

Taiap: adults correct children, 219–20;
    associations to land, 85–6, 264–65;
    attitudes toward, 7, 13, 83, 84–5;
    children's competence in, 73, 217–22;
    future, 265–6; as "hard," 61, 66, 196;
    number of speakers, 7, 61; as phatic
    punctuation, 177; relationship to

neighboring languages, 62–6; as secret
    language, 85, 216–17; as scolding
    language, 217; structure of, 63–5;
    "two language" mystique, 64–6, 90;
    and women, 89–91, 116–17, 252
thoughts: not accessible through words,
    48–9, 126–7, 224
Tok Pisin: children begin speaking, 211–
    14; children correct adults, 220; early
    history in Papua New Guinea, 4–5;
    early patterns of acquisition, 68; entry
    into Gapun, 66–8, 249–52; and
    gender, 66–73, 218, 250–2; gets
    attributed to children, 116, 202–9,
    256; and modernity, 11, 147–9, 251; as
    powerful, 84, 249–50; previous names
    for, 4; reports that it is replacing
    vernaculars in PNG, 5–7; thought to
    be vernacular of whites, 67, 83–4, 249;
    ties to Christianity, 72, 187–8, 251
transcription, 273–4
two brother myth (Arena–Andena), 57–9,
    89, 115, 183, 279n4, 282n20

"upper Sepiks," 146–7, 262–3

village incomes, 45–7
village meetings, 123–4

warfare, 87, 103, 113, 115, 122, 164, 251
Watam language, 69, 74
white people: conceptions of, 180–5; early
    meetings with, 67–8; resentment
    toward, 182–3, 293n17; stories about,
    55–7; white children, 177, 181–2
women: evaluate one another as mothers,
    100–1; as foundation of clan strength,
    88–9; as "hot," 56, 94, 96, 97; and
    oratories, 125, 133, 145; stereotyped
    as divisive, 115–17, 119, 145–6; as
    traditional, 91
words, and power, 82, 84, 249–50, 282n21
World War I, 66–7
World War II, 38, 56, 59, 68–73, 81, 165,
    182, 183

Yabem language, 6
youth group, 129–31, 259, 288–9nn5–7